REGRESSIONS IN MENTAL DEVELOPMENT:
Basic Phenomena and Theories

REGRESSIONS IN MENTAL DEVELOPMENT:
Basic Phenomena and Theories

Edited by

THOMAS G. BEVER
Columbia University

LAWRENCE ERLBAUM ASSOCIATES, PUBLISHERS
1982   Hillsdale, New Jersey   London

Lawrence Erlbaum Associates, Inc., Publishers
365 Broadway
Hillsdale, New Jersey 07642

Library of Congress Cataloging in Publication Data

Main entry under title:

Regressions in mental development.

Includes bibliographies and indexes.
1. Developmental psychology. 2. Regression (Psychology) I. Bever, Thomas G. [DNLM: 1. Regression (Psychology)—In infancy and childhood. WS 350.8.D3 R343]
BF713.R44   155.4   82-2520
ISBN 0-89859-095-5   AACR2

Printed in the United States of America

10 9 8 7 6 5 4 3 2 1

Contents

PART II: EARLY CHILDHOOD

PART III: MIDDLE CHILDHOOD

PART IV: NEUROLOGICAL MODELS

REGRESSIONS IN MENTAL DEVELOPMENT:

Basic Phenomena
and Theories

1 Introduction

Thomas G. Bever

"Of that and all the progress more and less
Resolvedly more leisure shall express."
All's Well that Ends Well
Act V.iii

Science depends on noticing that things which seem identical are different, and conversely. In psychology, one cannot assume that apparently identical behaviors are due to identical mechanisms. The precocious 4-year-old who counts from 1 to 10, may not do so in the same way as a normal 8-year-old. Conversely, an adult crawling awkwardly under the dresser after a lost button may in fact be crawling in the same way as an infant.

The work reported in this book involves the problem of classifying the true nature of a behavior as it appears during child development. For example, parents often report that their newborn infant smiles at them. Is this smile psychologically the same smile as that of an adult?

The answer to such a question bears on the psychological theory what an adult human is. On one view, an adult is a quantitative accumulation of innate patterns, and acquired habits: The child's smile *is* the same as the adult's, in all theoretically crucial respects. The alternative view describes an

1

adult as an epigenetically unique creature, projected out of preceding stages but not caused by them; the child's smile differs from the adult's.

There is little direct evidence on which view is correct. However, certain early behaviors disappear during childhood and later reappear. This prima facie is evidence in favor of the epigenetic view of how adults build up their behavioral capacity. Clearly, if skills are additively accumulated they are not likely simply to disappear and reappear during development. The following articles explore the theoretical and empirical issues involved in the early appearance of a behavior, its "disappearance" and its later "reappearance." The varied research attests to the existence of many such behaviors. There is considerable disagreement about the descriptive and theoretical status of the phenomena. Nevertheless, the authors agree that such facts demonstrate that the additive view of adult behavior is incorrect: Mental growth must be the result of dynamic restructuring processes.

The study of developmental regressions has received sporadic attention during the past century. The resuscitation of interest reflected in this book in part started with a serendipitous discovery by two of the authors (JRM and TGB) in 1966. They had recently visited the laboratory of J. Piaget and—like many—were convinced that Piaget's experimental techniques underestimate the cognitive capacity of young children. Their focus was on the child's conservation of number when an array of balls is changed in shape, as in the change from (a) to (b).

$$o\ o\ o\ o \qquad\qquad\qquad o\ o\ o\ o$$
$$o\ o\ o\ o \qquad \rightarrow \qquad oooo$$
$$\text{(a)} \qquad\qquad\qquad\qquad \text{(b)}$$

A typical Piagetian result is that young children (ca. 4 years) systematically decide that the longer row in (b) has more, even though, they observe its genesis from (a) and originally agree that the two rows in (a) had the "same." Mehler and Bever thought that perhaps the child was simply giving a superficial answer because it didn't care about rows of clay balls: They designed a similar experiment, except that they used rows of actual candies, and a paradigm in which the child got to eat the candies in the row he chose. They also thought that the task of recognizing that two rows have the "same" number is confusing in English since "same" can also refer to the objects themselves: the notion that one row has "more" seemed easier to comprehend; so they used a paradigm as in (c) and (d), in which an original inequality is conserved under length transformation of one of the rows.

o o o o   →   o o o o

o o o o o o   oooooo

(c)   (d)

They set about the experiment in the usual way, making sure first that each child understood that sometimes it could keep the row it chose as having more, taking care that the child knew which row had more in (c) and observed the transformation to (d).

At first, the results were disappointing. Four year old children seemed to perform only slightly better on (c) → (d) with candies than with clay balls; the children still tended to choose to eat the longer row in (d), the one with fewer candies. The original subject paradigm, however, called for two-year-olds as well, and the research assistant continued to interview young subjects, while the project designers themselves had largely given up hope.

A curious and totally unexpected phenomenon appeared in the data—two-year-olds performed the (c) → (d) task almost *perfectly*, both with candies and with clay balls. At first the experimenters did not believe this. In fact, they feared there was some kind of experimenter bias. They refrained from informing the research assistant about the first results and had her run an entirely new experiment: The results were the same—two- and six-year-olds solved the (c) → (d) problem, four-year-olds systematically failed to solve it.

The researchers interpreted these results as due to three maturational factors—(1) an early basic cognitive capacity of young children (age two) to conserve those relationships that they can grasp at all, (2) a later development (age four) of a time-and-energy-saving strategy "if something looks bigger it has more," and (3) the ultimate mastery of integers (age six). They argued that while aspects of (2) and (3) may be learned, the skill manifest in (1) would seem to be innate.

This raised some concern in the field, as did other aspects of their claims, especially those concerning the use of the conservation of *in*equalities. Gradually, however, other researchers replicated the crucial aspects of the original results and the phenomenon became an accepted scientific fact, whatever it's interpretation might be.

The papers in this volume attempt to interpret, explain, or explain away such developmental regressions in a variety of different areas. In spring 1975, a group of scholars interested in such problems met for several days to discuss their individual findings and the underlying theoretical issues. The following articles reflect both the discussions at the original conference and succeeding years of thinking, reading, and writing.[1]

ACKNOWLEDGMENT

The original conference on which these papers are based was organized by T. Bever (Columbia University, New York), J. Mehler (CNRS, Paris), and H. Nathan (OECD, Paris). It was supported financially by the OECD and the CNRS.

---

[1]The original conference benefited from the active participation of several additional participants—M. Imbert, A. Jonkheere, H. Nathan, and L. Wolpert.

I INFANCY

2 Basic Patterns of Psychogenetic Change in Infancy

Colwyn Trevarthen
University of Edinburgh
Edinburgh, Scotland

INTRODUCTION

Theory of how human intelligence develops in infants and children has so far taken little from what we now understand about brain growth. It has not come to terms with the fact that the major cerebral structures are present in advanced stages of anatomical definition at birth (Trevarthen, 1979a, 1980a). There are also undeniable implications of evolutionary theory still poorly assimilated into developmental psychology. The capacity of children for remembering new experiences and for imitating the behaviors and opinions of adults evidently has blinded psychologists to inherent modes of mental function that regulate the growth of this conscious and voluntary life.

Like all other life functions, mind processes of humans must be regulated by innate structures that, in this case, will define adaptive limits and prescribe functional tendencies or goals in perception, motivation, and behavioral action. Mental structures, again like all other living structures, also will regulate the course of their own formation—they will guide mental growth. Darwin was well aware that the problem of how natural selection creates viable forms of life to anticipate ways of living is tied up with the equally difficult problem of how a fertilized egg divides to become a large multi-cellular adult with an integrated set of mutually adjusted organs and tissue

7

activities. The life systems in an organism confer a coherent power of action that defines what dependable features of the environment will become resources for life. At the same time, the organism forms itself. Evolution is thus a history of adaptations in life histories (De Beere, 1940).

Pure mentalism in psychology, with no comprehensible reference to a material substrate, and mechanistic reductionism in physiology and genetics, with too simple and too confined physical conceptions, conspire to make inadmissible the epigenetic approach to mental development that evolutionary theory requires. Developmental psychology is thus frequently in the position of having no possible theory of psychological development. The absurd extreme positions of nativism or empiricism explain away the crucial problem. The life history of the mind is left obscure.

Embryogenesis of the brain is, in fact, uniquely elaborate, especially in human beings. Cerebral systems conferring consciousness, intentional action, human feelings, and comprehension of meanings are certainly in a very rudimentary state at birth but just as surely are anticipated in the immensely complex neural systems that appear during the fetal period. Although the fetal brain is not entirely cut off from afference due to stimulation of peripheral receptors, it is mainly self-organized (Hamburger, 1973; Oppenheim, 1974; Trevarthen, 1973).

Psychological studies of infants are becoming sufficiently accurate and experimentally subtle to reveal that newborn brain systems do indeed confer complex mental processes from birth (Bower, 1978; Trevarthen, 1979). They show, as well, that the subsequent maturation of these mental systems is constrained by intrinsic relations in patterned nerve tissues and not just inserted in a compliant random nerve network by patterns of stimuli reinforced by simple homeostatic principles. Experimental neurobiological studies show that the vast increase in fine interneuronal contacts and the selection of new patterns of nerve cell action that go on throughout postnatal life are paced and directed by the antecedent brain systems even though they are simultaneously validated by patterns in stimuli (Trevarthen, 1979a, 1980a).

The following may be taken as cardinal principles of psychological development that follow from the way growth of brain and body have been determined in evolution by natural selection.

A developing child will be strongly disposed to certain forms of action. These patterns in attending, object prehension, locomotion, communicating, etc., shape experience from birth and thereby influence the course in which knowledge develops. Predispositions to perceive the world in ways that relate directly to innate forms of movement act like filters to select particular, developmentally useful forms of stimulus input. They transform information to answer intrinsic needs. Thus the experience of a child of a particular age is automatically a complement to spontaneous intentions or motives that, because they arise from brain embryogenesis, do not reflect events in the past experience of that child.

Spontaneous actions of young infants will be preparatory to consciously governed intentions of the adult. These psychological actions will undergo systematic changes that will resemble visible transformations of morphology in the growth of an embryo. In an embryo, organs appear in rudimentary form as interacting parts of a growth system. Even at this stage the organs are stamped with adaptive structure far in advance of any effective function in the task to which they are fitted. The organization of the eye as an optical instrument, months before birth, is a familiar example. We can expect infants to show, for example, elaborate prefunctional activities that foreshadow the use of gesture and speech in communication because communication is vital to psychological development after birth.

The primordial organs of embryos show mutual and competitive adjustment within the coherent framework of the body. In the process of interacting they increase the body's integrity. They undergo cycles of differentiation, multiplying their diversity of structure, and complementary reintegrations that involve selective loss of parts. The whole of this predictable set of processes is a consequence of selective retention in evolution of adaptive intercellular activities. These activities are transmitted from generation to generation by the gene mechanism, but come into existence epigenetically, through interaction of gene products.

Just as with the organs of an embryo body, psychological functions of the newborn may be expected to take their places in active and highly regulated processes of competition and cooperation as they begin postnatal growth. These events make both mental change and learning possible, determine the conditions in which learning may occur, and explain why a particular psychological function may fail for a time while other processes are emerging in the system. It is in this perspective that we shall view evidence for 'dips' in psychological growth.

Our own researchs with infants leads us to reject the notion that knowledge is acquired by compliant assimilation of perceptual information, in forms determined by reality outside the subject. We believe the evidence is clear that patterns of motivation, governing behavioral action from inside the infant, are fundamental in psychological change and that different modes of intention determine the strategy and the achievements of psychological growth in the early years. Indeed, our work might be described as the natural history of infant motives (Trevarthen, 1980b). It is from this viewpoint that I wish to discuss evidence for basic morphogenetic strategies in the emergence of some of the most important psychological abilities of infants. Included are several apparent deviations from a monotonic accretion of competence such as would result from the impress of experience and reinforcement of acquired habits.

Latent Attending Movements of the Eyes—Birth Arousal and Neonatal Avoidance of Stimulation

Infants 2 to 3 weeks of age, though usually sleepy and frequently discoordinated in activity, show bouts of finely organized conjugate, saccadic eye displacement (Fig. 2.1). These are coupled to less precise orientations of the head and of the trunk and limbs. From these eye movements, we may conclude that infants are born with the rudiments of an integrated neural space–time mechanism in which successive coordinated orientations to separate loci may be specified (Trevarthen, 1974a, 1978). Observations of two of my own children and one other subject within an hour after birth showed me the main oculomotor generator functions. My sons had normal full-term births with no complications, except that in one case the birth was artificially induced by hormone injection on the due date because he was slightly on the large side. The other child was born at home in California with no medical assistance and the birth was easy. I consider this an ideal opportunity to observe the activity of a newborn in optimal condition.

The three infants were active, with eyes open, in the first hour after birth. They made systematic orienting movements in which the two eyes were coupled in conjugate manner. The eyes moved in intricate association with the eyelids and with small lateral and vertical head rotations. Head and eye turns also were associated frequently with postural changes and limb orientations. From cinefilm I determined that there were bursts of saccades that traced out irregular elliptical cycles in the air, with displacements in the lateral direction being by far the most common and the most extensive. I obtained an electrooculographic (EOG) record during a favorable period of quiet–alert wakefulness from one of my sons, at 9 days after birth (Trevarthen1974a, 1974b). This record confirmed that neonatal saccades may be very close to adult saccades of intermediate size (5–15°) and that they are generated by some flexible oscillator with a fundamental period of about 300 msec (Fig. 2.1). This same time base is a feature of oculomotor scan when an adult is in a state of exploratory attention (Yarbus, 1967).

These findings show how an intrinsic neural eye-movement mechanism, which will become essential for maintaining the flow of visual consciousness, is present in the newborn brain. It is not difficult to observe the rhythmic eye movements in the period just after birth. Mothers, fathers, midwives, and pediatricians often say that babies may be very "alert" and active immediately after delivery. Noirot, who with Alegria (Alegria and Noirot, 1978) has shown that newborns will turn to look for the source of a human voice, reports that this active, alert period is much diminished by the first feeding (Noirot, 1979). If the mother has been given anesthetics or depressive drugs the baby is frequently less active, and eye movements are observed to be less well-coordinated (Richards, 1976). Birth trauma or shock also appears to

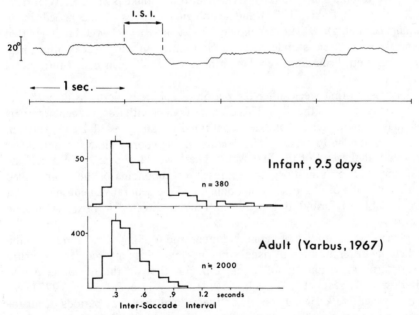

FIG. 2.1   Above: Electrooculogram of a 9-day-old infant. Conjugated saccades show dynamic characteristics close to adult saccades.

Below: The frequency histogram of saccades of the baby is similar to that of adults scanning a large painting. The principal intersaccade interval (I.S.I) is near .3 second.

cause irregularities in expression of this function, which is associated only with a particular favorable inner state of organized activity in the newborn brain. Somewhat less well-conjugated eye movements also are produced in irregular bursts under closed lids in neonatal Rapid Eye Movement (REM) sleep (Prechtl & Lenard, 1967).

Although there is evidence that newborns may fixate selectively, and object pursuit movements may be obtained from infants in the first minutes after birth, I would stress that the measured orienting of newborns may not be entirely dependent on perception of space in which objects are located or in which they are in motion. Well-formed and well-ordered eye movements may be produced without the benefit of patterned stimuli. They may be recorded in the dark with infrared video or with an EOG.

The infant visual receptor system is visibly immature at birth. Some authors believe the cone mechanism and fovea to be nonfunctional. The pupil and lens show little activity. Newborns are incapable of focal attention, (i.e., selective orientation to detail). Evidence from monkeys (Hubel, Wiesel, & LeVay, 1977; Rakic, 1977) and histological studies of the neocortex in infants (Conel, 1939–1963; Yakovlev & Lecours, 1967) would indicate that central visual circuits undergo great elaboration in early weeks after birth. (For detailed discussion, see Trevarthen, 1979a; Trevarthen, Murray and Hubley, 1981).

During the first week, after the period of apparent alertness at birth, the baby sleeps most of the time. This drop into sleep, with less frequent intervals of quiet–alert activity, has been confirmed by analyses of EEG developments in the early weeks. The feeding of newborns shows a correlated increase at the end of the first week. There would appear to be a delicate balance between inhibitory or suppressive components of the brain linked with metabolic or vegetative functioning, and the generative neuron nets that are capable of formulating active movement directed toward the outside world.

Physiological studies of neonatal kittens and monkeys lend support to the belief that differentiation of visual stimulus-analyzing units requires exposure to patterns of visual stimuli at a particular time in the postnatal period (Barlow, 1975; Hubel & Wiesel, 1970; Hubel, Wiesel & LeVay, 1977). We have no definite knowledge of when the critical period or periods occur for man. I suspect that the eye movements around birth, in which the infant appears to be absorbing visual experience somewhat inefficiently, may not be necessary for visual development. Exposure to pattern in the luminous environment with morphogenetic benefits really may begin sometime in the third or fourth week, when there is a marked increase in the amount of time the infant spends in the quiet–alert state, inspecting visual structure. However, even newborns modify the direction of their saccades and the dwelling of fixations to pick up visual patterns, and these eye movements may feed in patterned stimulations needed to aid differentiation of developing cortical circuits (Haith, 1976; Salapatek, 1975).

Well-Controlled Pickup of Visual Information by the Head–Eye System

Selective visual attention undergoes rapid growth after 4 weeks from birth, and apparently the process of focal visual analysis, with precise and selective fixation aimed to structural features in the environment and inside the boundary contours of objects, is mature to a first level of efficiency by the end of the fourth month. Measurements of dishabituation of visual orientation to repeated stimuli show that neonates under 8 weeks do not react to change of a stimulus figure inside a boundary contour that does not change (Milewski, 1976; Salapatek, 1975). A visual function that gives high salience to a perimeter that defines an object/surroundings or a figure/ground distinction is obviously of advantage to object detection.

Observations of scanning and tracking by infants also confirm the findings from dynamic retinoscopy that show a maturation of lens accommodation largely completed by the fourth month (Haynes, White, & Held, 1965). Accommodation produces a focused image for objects of different depth. The second important component of the visual orientation system, the head–neck system, develops heightened proficiency at the same time (Trevarthen, 1974b). That is, the head–neck system provides a stable base for visual focalization and participates in visual tracking efficiently at the time accommodation beings to function well.

Apparently, fine saccadic inspection, with conjugate saccades of less than 2 degrees, does not develop until at least the second 6 months of the first year. Corroborating this idea of a separate, later developing perception mechanism concerned with assimilation of detailed local information, Humphrey and I have found that fine saccadic inspection is the only component that is absent from the oculomotor activity of his monkey, Helen, who made the fullest recovery of vision on record after near total removal of her striate cortex (Humphrey, 1974). Held and others have found that the visual acuity of 2-month-olds is less than one-tenth that of adults, (Leehey, Moscowitz-Cook, Brill, & Held, 1975). This would not prevent detecting the general nature of nearby events in a 3-D space, but it certainly would rule out visual control of fine manipulation, seeing small things far away, and recognizing subtle texture differences. There seems to be a significant jump in visual resolution starting about 6 months after birth, when visually controlled manipulation is beginning (See Trevarthen, Murray and Hubley, 1981 for review).

Oculomotor activity is generated in the brainstem. It is adjusted to visual input in the midbrain roof, posterior diencephalon and cerebral cortex. Physiological research with monkeys shows that the visual regulation of eye movements is not primarily reflexive (Bizzi, Kalil, & Tagliasco, 1971). Foci for visual centration may be established independently of stimuli. Selective looking involves enhancement of response to visual input at the relevant cerebral locus ahead of the orienting movement of the eyes. The relevant changes in activity of nerve cells betweel the retinal input and the oculomotor system have been observed in the deeper layers of the superior colliculi and the posterior cortex of the monkey (Mohler & Wurtz, 1977).

Vision of form is not achieved just by assembly of samples of local feature information taken by the fovea. Spatiotemporal relations between discontinuities and contrasts in the stimulus array are established between parallel inputs from peripheral visual points. This is particularly clear for "ambient vision"—the field of visual processing in which posture, locomotion, and orienting are controlled. Transformations of the image of the whole field, or extensive parts of it, give kinetic information on which this vision depends. High acuity "focal vision", which resolves differences in the spectral composition and brightness of light for a central territory a few degrees in extent, depends on elaborate information sorting by the striate cortex, which has a greatly enlarged representation of the central field, especially the fovea.

Evidence from psychophysical tests and discrimination experiments with infants agrees with anatomical and physiological data indicating that foveo-striate vision undergoes considerable elaborations in infancy. Neonates perceive visual events and discriminate objects by their motion relative to the background, but they fail to detect features inside bounding contours (externality effect [Milewski, 1976]), much as does peripheral vision in the adult. The evidence does not suggest that the cortex is nonfunctional at birth or that the midbrain visual system is fully active then, but central vision is probably much less developed than a near peripheral band. Far peripheral vision may be relatively underdeveloped as well. Neonates do respond to an expanding peripheral contour, or rapid change of the overall light flux, as if it represents an object approaching collision with them (Bower, 1974). Evidence for perception of persons by infants, as different from perception of nonliving objects, is taken from preferential looking tests, from observations of the effects of change of visual stimuli on sucking and breathing and on facial expressions, and from movements of the hands. The studies of Papousek (1969), Papousek and Papousek (1975), Oster (1978), and Alegria and Noirot (1978), described later, are particularly important for the neonatal period.

We may conclude that both the mechanism of looking, which will regulate selection of particular visual experiences, and the perceptual categorization of stimuli in terms of useful kinds of events, located in nearby space and giving evidence of certain changes of location or form, are active at the time of birth. Looking is also integrated with hearing and with touch in the hands from the start (Bower, 1974; 1978). Subsequent developments transform the resolving power of vision and the selective strategies of looking. Presumably the function of seeing becomes increasingly distinct from other modalities of experience as the special characteristics of all the receptor systems become more sharply and richly defined. Periods of rapid change in visual information uptake during the first year (e.g., at 4 to 6 weeks and at 4 to 6 months) appear to coincide with developments in both communication and manual prehension. Probably anatomical changes in the brain's motivation systems are inherently regulated to occur in conjunction with changes in the visual information uptake system.

Later in infancy, and on into childhood, developments in visual awareness certainly will involve anatomical differentiations in extrastriate visual cortex. Areas of the temporal cortex and of the temporoparieto-occipital junction are probably most important for maturation of visuo–spatial or visuo–constructive sense, facial recognition, reading, and other forms of visual information pickup, all of importance to the skills of culture. However, we know little about the neuroembryological regulation of these developments (Trevarthen, 1979a).

As in all other systems of intelligence, no single level of motor process governs uptake of visual experience. The "looking" mechanism is an embedded set of control systems which involve almost all the muscles of the body. The different components attain maturity at different times. May we regard this as a model for "ups" and "downs" in performance? The general function, sampling the visual array, is there from the start; downs in performance would be related either to periods of increase of new, more refined levels of control or to increased activity in suppressive mechanisms that are an essential part of the central integrating circuitry of the brain.

Coordination of Reaching and Grasping: Parallel and Interacting Systems in a Hierarchy of Motor Structures

In the second form of behavior more detail can be given about development by progressive differentiation of motor components.

Film studies of the arm and hand movements of infants from the first week until 6 months after birth show that a coordinated reach-and-grasp pattern, which may be aimed toward objects that attract the visual fixation of the infant, is already established in the brain at birth (Trevarthen, 1974b; Trevarthen, Hubley & Sheeran, 1975; Trevarthen, Murray and Hubley, 1981). This pattern of movement is at first weak and stereotyped. A precursor movement pattern may be traced to the fifth month of gestation in the early fetus (Humphrey, 1969).

The neonatal reach-and-grasp movements are essentially nonfunctional. They are best described as prefunctional (i.e., an embryonic manifestation of a latent functional pattern). It is already clear from their shape that their ultimate usefulness is to obtain prehension of objects and to manipulate them. To achieve effective performance (i.e., actually to reach for and pick up objects of varied mass, rigidity, hardness, and form and with varied location relative to the body), a highly predictable and predicting sequence of events must take place in the brain. An integrated and proprioceptively guided arm displacement is required to transport the hand through space to the object's location, and then hand orienting and closure must adjust with prediction to grasp variously shaped and sized objects or their parts. Ultimately, tight ongoing visual control of hand movements is essential to their most refined use. The finest adult finger movements, as in drawing, writing, or watch-making, have a fantastically precise and intimate relation to visual perception of shape in small dimensions. Their precision is magnified when a microscope is used.

The movements of neonatal prereaching show that orientational equivalence of eye and hand is established and active in a rudimentary form at birth, but that it is very weakly and only partially controlled perceptually. The developmental changes during the first few months show that, although practice is essential to full development, the interlocking system of controls required for visual grasp and reach is produced by developments generated spontaneously, within the brain. Reach and grasp is limited by a sequence of brain developments and is simultaneously adapted to respond to environmental information and to information returned by reafference from inside the body itself. It is not created within an unorganized nerve matrix by a learning process that assembles reflex arcs.

For the present purpose, I wish to concentrate first on the changes that occur between the first and fourth months, when reaching is said to disappear; I then comment briefly on the maturation of effective reach and grasp after 5 months.

The view of many workers that newborns cannot reach to objects would appear to be due to the fact that most detailed observations have begun after 6 weeks, when the prereaching pattern is no longer clear. There is a bias toward omitting observations that would verify a developmental decline in function (see Bower, 1974; Mehler & Bever, 1968a, 1968b, who discuss erroneous conceptions arising from this bias.)

Film observations confirm easily that the prereaching pattern is a real and complex component of action in the first month and that it has some perceptual sensitivity to objects near the infant, within a "reaching space." (Fig. 2.2). The prereaching is a rudimentary form of mature reaching. There is no reason to suppose it is a different motor function, and it is always possible to see the reach-and-grasp pattern at 3 and 4 months, provided the infant is in an appropriate state of arousal and intensity of activity (Fig. 2.3). We see the pattern progressively complicated, however, evidently by an increase of "stickiness" or "inertia" in the participation of the proximal limb segments. Upper arm on shoulder and lower arm on elbow move more strongly, but disruptively, in correlation with the visible increase of muscle bulk in the second month (Fig. 2.3). Sudden, jerky, or "gummed up" changes in directions of arm displacement give evidence of inhibited central motor commands or of an increasingly powerful blockage in mechanoreceptive reaction to inertial forces generated by displacement of the increasingly heavy arm. There is anatomical and physiological evidence that in this period receptors in the muscles and tendons are undergoing extensive differentiation. Central interneuron networks and neuromuscular junctions undergo development as well. Reflex responses of infants submitted to stretching of the muscles show that mechanoreceptor input is more effective at this time (Twitchell, 1965). I think the introduction of proximal limb control systems,

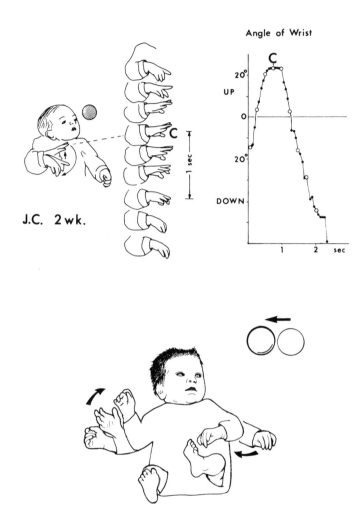

FIG. 2.2   Prereaching patterns combine opening and closing of the hand with wrist and arm movements that aim the hand in the direction of an object that has been located visually and oriented to. The two-week-old shown above makes a hand movement without arm extension.

The lower drawing shows the limb displacement of a four-week-old watching an approaching ball. The right hand makes a prereaching movement, opening with palm oriented to the ball at the mid-point of wrist displacement.

FIG. 2.3 Reaching attempts in the transition period. The full prereaching pattern may still appear when the infant is quiet (left), but frequently arm movements are more vigorous and hand movements are less (middle and right).

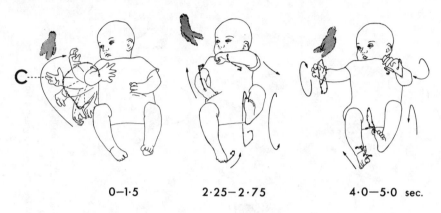

| 0–1·5 | 2·25–2·75 | 4·0—5·0 sec. |

J.C. 9 wk.

which will give the infant power to guide and regulate any arm transportation in space with much greater efficiency and variety, is responsibe for the apparent loss of reach and grasp, because the total pattern of action is temporarily disorganized. There is evidence that fetal sensorimotor circuits can be modified by addition of interstitial inhibitory components that mask previously generated motor patterns (Humphrey, 1969; Oppenheim & Reitzel, 1975).

As the arm movements become more vigorous but less fluent, the hand frequently fails to open and close; apparently the grasping component is temporarily blocked as well (Fig. 2.3). But in adult activity, vigorous, forceful arm movements are not coupled with delicate opening and closing of the fingers. It would be mechanically dangerous for this to occur because collision with hard surfaces would damage the open hand. As a rule, vigorous displacements are alternative to manipulation. They are used for speed, or to exert high levels of force. The two kinds of action, hitting or pushing versus delicate manipulation, are intercalated in adult behavior, so that the manipulatory performance is composed of rhythmical packets of hand transportation interspersed with periods of manipulation in which the wrist and fingers are

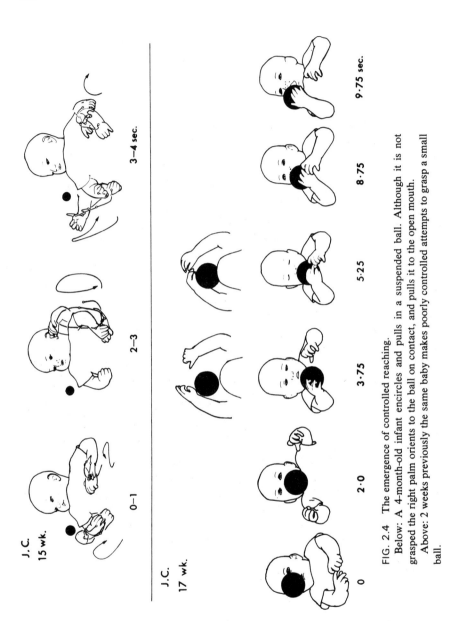

FIG. 2.4   The emergence of controlled reaching.

Below: A 4-month-old infant encircles and pulls in a suspended ball. Although it is not grasped the right palm orients to the ball on contact, and pulls it to the open mouth.

Above: 2 weeks previously the same baby makes poorly controlled attempts to grasp a small ball.

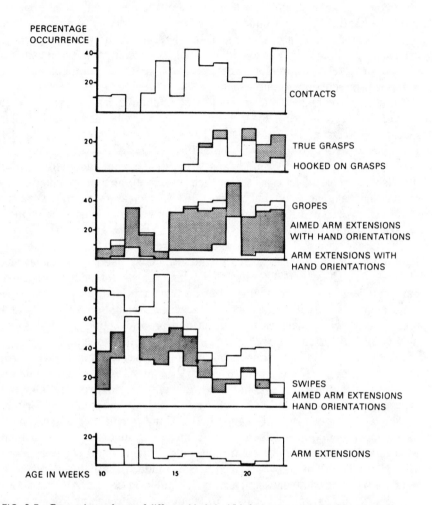

FIG. 2.5   Proportions of acts of different kinds in 15 infants observed with the aid of film over the period of development of true reaching. The different classes of action are defined to be mutually exclusive. Fast ballistic movements (swipes, aimed hand extensions, hand orientations) are replaced by well-controlled and effective movements coordinating distal and proximal segments. (True grasps, which support the object, hooked-on grasps, gropes, aimed arm extensions with hand orientations) "Contact" is an arbitrary and uninformative measure of success, dependent especially in early stages, on the placing of the object by the experimenter. Unaimed arm extensions may be gestures of communication.

undergoing complex local movement, generally under tight visual control, while the hand is kept in a smooth predetermined trajectory of displacement or is kept motionless in one place. In the determination of this patterning, central programing will be involved in spinal cord, brain stem, basal ganglia, and cerebrocerebellar circuits, to determine the spatiotemporal goal of each movement or sequence of movements.

All who have made detailed studies of infant reaching (Piaget, 1953; White, Castle & Held, 1964), particularly those who have studied film records (Halverson, 1943; McGraw, 1943), agree that effective reach and grasp begins about 16 to 18 weeks after birth (Fig. 2.4 and 2.5). The baby, having gained mastery over modulated arm displacement and adjustment to the displacements of an object, can then make well-aimed grasping movements that take hold of and support it. It is clear from psychological experiments that the baby at this age already has achieved visual perception of space relations outside the body and of object size and shape (Bower, 1978). Grasping rapidly becomes efficient thereafter, and from 6 months on, the normal infant is occupied with handling, manipulating, and displacing objects. Von Hofsten (1979) has found that adjustment of reaching after moving objects, to predict their rate of displacement and intercept them, is made as soon as infants make controlled reaches after stationary objects, at 4 to 5 months. He concludes that vision and proprioception constitute one unitary spatial system onto which the motor space is mapped.

In agreement with this conclusion, we have observed that hand regard, thought by Piaget (1953) and by White, et. al. (1964) to be primarily responsible for creating eye–hand coordination, is an expression of the process by which intimate eye–hand regulations are differentiated for fine manipulation (Trevarthen, 1974a, 1974b). Hand regard, like manipulation itself, depends upon an effective nerve–muscle system for proximal limb segments that is capable of controlling or stabilizing hand position in the visual field. Our films show that hand regard is indeed alternative to reaching out to or tracking an object seen, just as manipulation itself is. An infant does not need to look at his or her hand to locate it when reaching to an object. Hand regard hinders, rather than helps, reaching. Another functional interpretation, not automatically to be discounted, is that hand regard is an avoidant form of interpersonal expression. It is, indeed, one of the stereotyped acts of an infant disturbed by failure of face-to-face interaction with a person (Murray, 1980).

The above description of the development of control over the mechanism for reaching is in agreement with present understanding of the primate motor system, due principally to the anatomical researches of Kuypers and his school. Kuypers' definition of proximal and distal motor systems and his developmental studies with monkeys (Kuypers, 1962, 1973) confirm that throughout the brain and on both the motor and sensory side the mechanisms controlling proximal arm segments are distinct from those that are essential to the distal mechanism of the hand and that important changes take place separately in them after birth. Split-brain studies support the same distinction (Brinkman & Kuypers, 1972).

I believe that the ups and downs of reaching in infancy during the first year reflect differentiation, in alternation, of the proximal and distal motor components. The programed relationship of reaching and grasping never disappears. It shows different degrees of expression as the essential afferent and efferent conditions for its full expression are mastered, progressively and alternately.

A Note on the Theory of Brain Mechanisms of Voluntary Action and Their Development

It has become more obvious in recent years that, in the cerebral organization of structures for voluntary control of movement, a fundamental functional distinction is to be made between the mechanisms that orient body parts carrying specialized receptor and effector organs by displacing proximal structures and trunk segments, and those mechanisms that control distal segments to adjust to detailed elements of surroundings. In the distal faction of the movement mechanism, eyes, lips and tongue, hands, and feet may be associated by coordinated action of proximal components, and there is a very special relationship between eyes, mouth, and hands related to the psychological functions that perceive the identities or uses of objects (Trevarthen, 1978).

Separate organization in the brain of an axio–proximal motor system on the one hand and an array of distal motor systems on the other is, it would seem, the basis for development of conscious and voluntary control in terrestrial vertebrates. Fine focal functions are evolutionary and developmental differentiates of the orienting functions by which the whole body is moved. Developments in orientational control are vital to the production of integrations that bring focal functions together. Delicate processes of manipulation, for example, can occur only if the activities of the proximal segments of the arm and orientation of the head and eyes are stabilized to provide a foundation.

In the infant we see interlocking and perhaps competitive development of the different levels in this inherited hierarchy of motor function. When the individual is mastering for the first time the weighty mechanical system of the arm, trunk, and neck during the second, third, and fourth months, distal functions have to mark time, even temporarily receding in importance. Immediately afterwards they show a sudden burst of development. I think this description makes clear that the apparent loss of function on the perceptual or cognitive plane is constructive when the full range of functions involved, especially the motor activities and their direct afferent controls, are considered.

A parallel account can be given for the apparent disappearance of walking. Newborn infants make integrated stepping movements with alternation of the limbs, if they are appropriately supported and if they receive the right distribution of stimulation from contact of the feet with the surface (Peiper, 1963). Afterwards, they tend to respond to being stood on a surface with the rapidly strengthening thigh and calf muscles, so they push or jump. Their walking or stepping movements when they are held to stand are then infrequent and spasmodic. However, one cannot say *walking* has disappeared at this time, because walking consists of supporting the whole body on two legs and transporting it by alternate pacing. A great deal of muscular, skeletal, and neural development is required before the infant will achieve this. The systems of standing in balance, involving proprioception from vision and the vestibular organs and of the mechanical receptors beneath the surface of the skin in muscles and joints, has to mature before real walking can begin. Development of functional refinements in the cerebellar cortex and associated brainstem structures is parallel with the long postnatal maturation of both locomotion and prehension.

Physiological experiments with locomotion in quadrupeds and humans prove that coordination is based on formulation of central motor programs, and these are essential for the integration with locomotion of perception of the terrain and of targets or goals (Bernstein, 1967; Greene, 1972; Grillner, 1975). That centrally programed patterns of stepping are also present in humans at birth should not be surprising. A striking manifestation of locomotor coordination is the so-called "reflex swimming" of neonates discovered by McGraw (1943). It is certainly not just a reflex phenomenon.

I prefer to speak of the early reach-and-grasp coordination as *prereaching* because that seems to me a perfectly straightforward description of an embryonic state of a voluntary system that is, as yet, very incomplete in its necessary controls. For the same reason I should call the early walking pattern *prewalking*, because it is a rudimentary outline of an alternating and cyclic pattern of balancing and locomoting that will become functional for the first time about a year later, after the body and the perceptual and cognitive mechanisms have undergone considerable development.

This psychobiological analysis, which could be given in far greater detail, referring to the specific anatomical changes in the brain as well as changes in muscle and skeletal structures, shows how any given isolated adaptive function in behavior dependent on central neuronal circuits may, indeed must, remain coordinated and integrated with the whole of the body system of action. In like way, in the embryo, no individual differentiated organ may undergo separate development beyond the point at which it loses integration with the rest of the body.

Experimental studies of embryos involving surgical transplantation show that autonomous differentiation of parts is in dynamic equilibrium with reintegrative processes that create and sustain the whole. In the generation of the nervous system, integrative psychological functions, which ensure that all the specialized parts (hands, eyes, etc.), will work in conjunction with one space of action and synchronized in one frame of time, are determined by the general anatomy of the brain. A human newborn already has a unified cerebral mechanism and a number of specialized subsystems that will serve functions of selective attention and selective action. For this hierarchical structure to become fully active and coordinated in a discriminating awareness, a long process of development has to occur, but the integrity of the system is ensured by a mapping of the body into the brain, which throughout all its parts is organized along somatotopic lines (Trevarthen, 1973, 1977, 1978).

In thinking about more abstract psychological functions like those involved in conscious representation, and particularly those involved in human communicative intelligence, we are unable to give anatomical description of the mechanisms involved, but we must assume that these functions, too, are laid down by differentiation of components inside a general neuroanatomical field, and we must also expect that the various specialized partial functions will from time to time become subordinated to the requirements of integrated or total psychological function.

Intersubjectivity in Infancy

I wish now to describe developments in the communicative development of infants suggesting that the fundamental processes of perception and cognition, and also the deeper processes by which individual voluntary action grows, are in constant competitive interaction with mysterious but very powerful psychological mechanisms that ensure interpersonal and social cooperation in human intelligence. This last function, social cooperation, is of course the most special feature of human intelligence. It gives humans adaptive domination over all other forms of life, and unlimited power to acquire and transmit techniques for mastery of the environment.

When I first began to observe systematically the spontaneous activities of infants, I quickly became impressed with the astonishing precocity of their sensitivity to persons and, above all, their motor powers of expression, which influence attentive adults very strongly.

In Edinburgh, we have observed communicative interactions between mothers and infants when the babies are in the second or third month after birth. If allowed to communicate freely, the mother and infant engage in highly regular, conversation-like exchanges in which it is clear that the infant exercises the primary control of events (Trevarthen, 1976,1977; 1979c; Trevarthen, Hubley & Sheeran, 1975). The mother, by attending closely and responding in a friendly way, with specific forms of vocalization, face expression, head movement, touching, etc., provides an essential substrate for the baby to communicate with, but she is excited to do so by the very specialized actions of the infant and by the organization into expressive episodes of these actions addressed to her by her baby. She may be described as an optimal stimulus for conditioning (Papousek & Papousek, 1975) simply because the infant is adapted to communicate with her.

Within the cycles of infantile expression we find rudiments of the elaborate and culturally modified acts by which adults express their experiences, intentions, and interests to one another. Most remarkable are lip and tongue movments that we label *pre-speech,* because they have the outline form of speaking and because they occur in the "right place" in the exchange for the function of uterances (Fig. 2.6). Prespeech movements are expressive

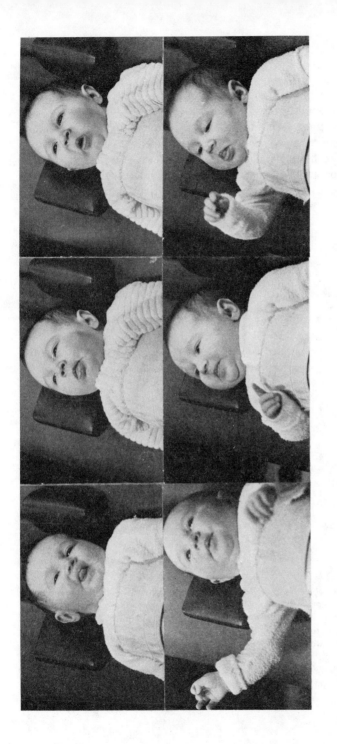

FIG. 2.6 Facial expressions and gestures common in early face-to-face communication. A 7-week-old girl.

Top: Lip and tongue movements of prespeech

Bottom: Hand raised above shoulder with finger movements synchronized with prespeech, index finger pointing.

movements of the mouth that frequently are not voiced, although vocalization is related to them from the start (Trevarthen, 1979b).

Associated with prespeech are systematic forms of hand movement, similar in form to stereotyped gesticulatory movements that adults make in communication. We have distinguished a "hand-wave" pattern (Fig. 2.7) and conclude from our films that index-finger pointing or "indicating" is present as a differentiated, potentially communicative signal as early as the

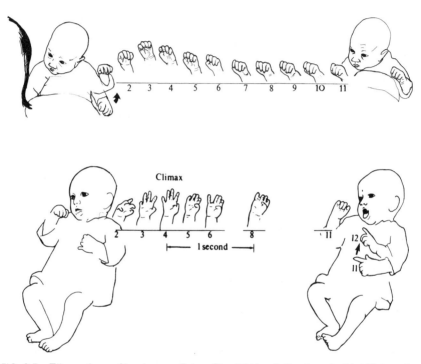

FIG. 2.7   Film analyses of hand waves. Below: The right hand of an 8-week-old girl interacting with her mother opens rapidly to expose the palm to the partner, with the hand held above shoulder level. Numbers indicate successive ¼-second intervals. Three seconds after the start of the right hand movement, the left index finger is raised in synchrony with mouth opening and tongue protrusion. These were not imitated movements.

Above: A 3-week-old girl does not raise her head completely, but seeks her mother's eyes and makes a movement with the left hand. The movement is much weaker, but of the same general form as that of the older infant. Note slight opening of hand at the climax (Step 4).

second month (Fig. 2.6) (Trevarthen, 1979b, 1979c). There appear to be many other rudimentary gestural forms.

We find it necessary to describe the social response of infants as taking place over a wide range of levels of animation. Sometimes expressive activity is restricted to the fingers and mouth and to the eyes, face, etc. At other times the whole body is moving in larger bursts, which are frequently accompanied by excited shouts or calls that are less finely articulated. The mothers immediately and unconsciously interpret these changes in level of animation as expressing different feelings and intentions of the infant, and express these interpretations in their speech.

Cutting across changes of excitement are changes of mood or emotion. In perturbation experiments, in which we systematically modify the mother's response with the aid of instructions to her, Lynne Murray has shown that the infant's expression of unhappiness or dejection on the one hand, and happiness or playfulness on the other, is tightly dependent on the success of communication. This leads us to an investigation of the structure of emotionality and its relationship to the reciprocal and predictive control of communicative action (Murray, 1980; Sylvester-Bradley & Trevarthen, 1978; Sylvester-Bradley, 1980).

It is significant that a very rich period of embryonic communication takes place in the period from 6 to 15 weeks, when reaching is described as disappearing. This period we refer to as that of *primary intersubjectivity* (Trevarthen, 1979b). It establishes the first form of communicative interaction for its own sake. Primary intersubjectivity may be regarded as the prototype of diadic communicative interaction in humans (Fig. 2.8). Adult and infant engage in mutually supportive and complementary acts that constitute a true interpersonal interaction.

When controlled reaching appears at the end of the fourth month, we note important changes in the attentional predispositions and in the curiosities and spontaneous intentions of infants (Sylvester-Bradley & Trevarthen, 1978; Trevarthen & Hubley, 1978). Apparently, a major organization of the whole mental system takes place at this time, leading to revolutions in cognitive ability, and also changing completely the rules of communication. This is the time when our subjects show a "cooling" of their interest in chatting with the mother except in "games of the person," where the mother offers her face or hands to the baby to touch and tease, or else herself does gentle teasing of the baby. In many instances, babies at this time quite rudely refuse direct smiling, eye-to-eye contact and "protoconversation" exchange. They may

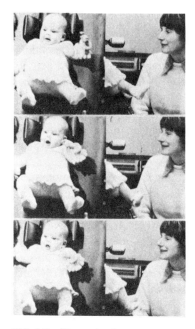 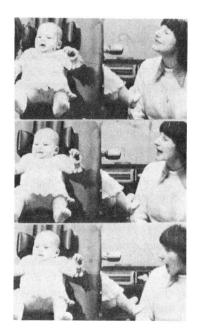

FIG. 2.8   The cycle of expression and reply in a communicative interaction between a 7-week-old and her mother. From film.

Left: The mother watches, smiling, while her daughter vocalizes and makes a geature with her left hand.

Right: When the infant has finished the mother makes a mocking reply.

even actively avoid the mother's gaze and turn their heads away as soon as she comes close to address them. They do this, it would appear, to establish a different balance between attention to the mother and attention to surroundings and to objects nearby. The consequence is that the mother's interest in the infant changes as she is strongly led by the baby to change her tactics, and to become much more interested in joining in with what the baby is doing to objects, and to create games that will amuse the baby. She also begins to communicate through various ways of profering objects to the baby. She develops new styles of presentation which cause her infant to laugh.

After this period of transition, in which teasing play is common, we observe the development of a new form of communication we term *secondary intersubjectivity* (Trevarthen & Hubley, 1978; Hubley & Trevarthen, 1979) This is triadic and friendly play with and about things and experiences shared. No longer is communication merely between the two partners; it now has an outward direction as well, to bring in topics. In the first part of this period of development the topics are established most often by the infant. Later the infant becomes delighted to receive hints about novel forms of activity from adults. In other words, toward the end of the first year the baby becomes a natural pupil to the teacher, which, in turn, the mother has become. While understanding better what others want and receiving their instructions more deliberately, the infant also shows greater power of initiating cooperative "turns" in play and in performing a shared task (Hubley & Trevarthen, 1979). There is a heightened awareness of "self," or of the circumstances and manner of what the baby does. This, too, is the time of the beginning of *protolanguage,* in which infants, using gestures as well as modulated vocalizations, exchange acts of meaning, sometimes instructing their partners or declaring interest in an indicated event to them (Bates, Camaioni, & Volterra,1975; Bruner, 1975; Halliday, 1975).

It should be emphasized that our detailed observations are quite inconsistent with the view that the child's learning ability and voluntary communications are fabricated from without by the mother. Indeed we think it more correct to say that the pupil role grows in the infant and that this causes the teacher role of the mother who is, no doubt, adapted to become a teacher in and of herself. She too is human, and it is the cooperative interaction of two humans that is developing through changes taking place in both of them. On biological grounds it seems quite reasonable to conclude that the initiative for change should rest primarily with the least developed of the two persons, though the more mature might be expected to take control over more refined aspects of the patterning.

A special relationship grows between mother and infant or other primary caretaker and infant as a result of learning, and it is interesting to observe that the transformation of intersubjectivity around the period of 6 months is much more pronounced for this most privileged person. For example, when the baby shows a new negativity with the principal partner, other persons who may be described as "friends" are, we note, still treated in a highly sociable way. In other words, it is the privileged relationship of the main "attachment" that undergoes most pronounced developmental change. Also, the games played with the mother are uniquely developed. They include formulae or habitual patterns that form a private language or cooperative routine between them.

These observations seem to prove that cognitive development in the first year is integrated within interpersonal development and that the whole field of the developing infant intelligence brings together a communicative competence and competence of the individual to perceive and operate upon the world of objects on his or her own. I think the dynamics of development, including periodic recessions in new components of performance, reflect mainly the developmental regulations in the *interpersonal* sphere, and this leads me to a theoretical prediction.

I would suggest that all major revolutions and steps up in human intelligence observed during the life of a person will be found to be associated with changes in intrinsic communicative psychology. I am suggesting that each cognitive revolution is, in fact, subordinated to a revolution in the mechanism by which intelligence is established between the young person and older people upon whom a child's growth of knowledge is dependent. Important developmental changes also may occur in the communicative relations of adolescents and of adults of different ages, and these revolutions of social motives are certainly not less significant in highly elaborate social systems. They are essential to all human societies. I think the changes in infancy are universal in this sense.

Fluctuations in Expression of Acts of Communication

We have observed a number of "dips" in components of inherent infant communication. First, face regard, gestural and prespeech activity, and cooing, which become common around 6 weeks, decline after about 10 weeks. There is a change in the quality of interest in persons and of expression at that time, with vocalization beginning to play a more significant part as manipulation of objects develops. We believe that when babbling develops after 6 months, it combines a range of elementary actions of the vocal apparatus with articulatory movements of lips and tongue seen already in prespeech. Once again, the apparent disappearance is a change in expression of a function due to introduction of complementary components in a larger system. We would expect that every separate detail of the innate patterns of expressive action will be found to show comparable ups and downs as they adjust to one another and in relation to a structured system of intention to communicate. As with developments in reaching and grasping, these developments can be understood only with reference to intrinsic adjustments in the child's cerebral mechanisms that have an integrity from the start.

We can confirm Maratos' experimental finding (Maratos, 1973), replicated with experimental refinements by Meltzoff and Moore (1977), that very young infants are able to imitate specific acts of the mouth and hands and also movements of the head made by the mother. This *imitation*, which proves the infant to have an integrated representation for movements of expression, has a particular character. Like prereaching, or the eye movements of looking, it is affected by "state" changes in the infant. Only brief intervals of optimal arousal or intentional readiness for imitation occur. These are characteristically periods of quiet alertness; that is, the baby is neither extremely active or somnolent. Because the response, though it follows watching of the partner, is not preceded by deliberate striving for the matching form of act, it gives the impression of simply popping out. It often has a short latency (less than 1 second). I would call this type of imitation *magnetic* to emphasize that it is a fairly automatic, though unpredictable, expression of a potentially complex recognitive and expressive machinery that is as yet not well controlled by reafferent-sensitive orienting systems. The kind of automatic synchrony of neonate movements with mother's speech accents reported by Condon and Sander (1974) also seems to occur when the infant is less focused, though we have no definite information yet on how often it is that infants allow themselves to be paced in this way by sight and sound of the expressive actions of persons near them. There are difficulties to be overcome before the implied mechanism of puppetlike synchronization can be accepted. In particular, the inherent rhythm of the infant's movements, with cadence close to one that is strong in adult movements even when the infant is alone, has not been taken into account. The ensemble of movements may involve a much more active control by the infant than that assumed by the synchronization theory.

The specificity of neonatal imitations, for example tongue protrusion for tongue protrusion, hand movement for hand movement, proves that the neonate possesses an anatomical template for recognition of persons, without benefit of learning by association the linking up of rudimentary reflexive sensori-motor schemata. Such imitation, we find, declines during primary intersubjectivity when the infant is very much more involved in oriented self-expression. As I have said, during the second and third months it is the rule that the mother imitates the infant. Then the baby is influenced by the support given from the mother and by the reinforcing effect of the mother's sympathetic movements, but is rare to see a baby imitate a particular movement of the mother at this stage, even when a model is thrust upon the infant.

Imitation appears with increased frequency again toward 6 months and develops considerably after that time. This behavior involves the infant in a very marked orientation; an apparently puzzled or curious fixing of attention on the repeatedly presented model. In other words, the infant is led to imitate by insistent demonstrative action of the partner and does so after much successive approximation through a series of tentative attempts or oblique evasions. I would call this *discretionary* imitation because an element of deliberation or choice is evident in it. Piaget (1962) describes this behavior as "imitation through training," and then he calls it "pseudoimitation" and says that it does not last unless continually reinforced, as smiling is. However, this type of imitation has benefit for the older infant in that new acts, already outlined in the repertoire of the infant, may be changed to a more elaborate form. I think such innovations may be permanent.

This is not to say that some degree of deliberation is not evident in the earliest magnetic imitation. It is clear from some of Maratos' records of sound production that the infant's imitative sound making is different from spontaneous sound making—it sounds more "strained" or "artificial." There must be a highly complex intersubjectivity machinery in rudimentary but integrated form in the neonate brain. However, the matching to a model is more precise and much better regulated in the older subjects. Around 9 months or so the infant frequently becomes involved in imitative games in which some pickup by the mother from the infant is utilized by her, returned to the infant as a model, and then reconstructed by the infant in some special new form (Trevarthen & Hubley, 1978).

Finally, we have evidence that a type of *aversion of gaze*, similar in appearance to the very definite avoidance of the 5-month-old for the mother's face, may have a precursor in the baby of 2 to 3 weeks of age. Neonates definitely are capable of actively avoiding interpersonal confrontation. They seem more prone to avoid face-to-face interaction than 2- or 3-month-olds, although the latter avoid eye contact and monitor the mother in peripheral vision when her behavior is unfriendly or unresponsive (Murray, 1980).

When all the above indications are taken together, there begins to emerge a picture that the neonate in certain brief, favorable states of attention and arousal may represent a weak outline of the 4- to 5-month-old in many different respects. Without doubt, the developments we have described show that a remarkably complete outline of psychological functions is present in newborns, and that postnatal developments are regulated in part by interactions between the innate components as they become more elaborate with the benefit of stimuli from a highly organized environment to which they are adapted.

DISCUSSION AND CONCLUSION

From the beginning of his thought about the development of intelligence, Piaget clearly had in mind a simultaneous existence of two forms of growth mechanism. A continuous organization, a basic design or plan of intelligence that is present at all times after birth, expresses itself with increasing strength as development proceeds. In this, new elements of form and process arise by mutual assimilation or equilibration between differentiating structures—the operational schemata. In *Biology and Knowledge* (Piaget, 1971) he elaborated a general embryological theory he had been using throughout his work. His notion of *decalage,* and the idea of spiral development that repeats stages of growth, clearly depend upon the embryological metaphors he employed for the growth of intelligence and consciousness. However, it seems to me that he is too unspecific about the nature of the cerebral system of intelligence, too vague in his appeal to embryological concepts of differentiation and reintegration. The theory is very abstract and so elastic that apparently quite contradictory positions may be justified by it. For him a structure is more an idea than a reality.

Obviously, the theory of decalage is incompatible with SR learning theory, which predicts accumulative, continuous growth. Regular recurrence of form or function in a complex growth process requires a real, coherent anatomico-functional structure. Yet in his account of the sensorimotor period Piaget appeared to believe that primary spatial integration of behavior, and perception of objects as goals for specific acts, both require exercise for coupling together of reflexes by an associative process. He, like the learning theorists, left the integrative structure outside the system in its circumstances.

The facts of cerebral anatomy, especially comparative studies, lead one to predict that a primary field of integrating of all parts of the body in a space of behavior is given at birth (Trevarthen, 1973, 1978, 1979a). Also, more recent observations on infant behavior and particularly the experiments on space and object perception by Bower (1974, 1978), make it clear that very young infants are capable of much more cognitive integration than Piaget assumed for his Stages I to III. The studies of imitation give the same conclusion (Metzoff & Moore, 1977).

Piaget took eye-hand coordination as the prime example of sensorimotor development and the genesis of a primary action schema. But his account of it as a learning process (Piaget, 1953) is not accurate. Eye-hand coordination is not created by mutual assimilation of initially separate sensorimotor schemate for moving the eye and the hand. Although it is clear that the various control systems of this complex motor function are progressively adjused to one another and that they benefit by practice over many years in the attainment of the mature skill, the first coordination between eye and hand appears as the action of a preformed mechanism. Mounoud (1970) has concluded that there is an initial given integrity of sensorimotor schemata in the movement system and Bower (1974) has proposed that in the realm of perception the initial form of the object concept is an amodal one in which the sensory modalities are united syncretically, presumably in relation to a latent field of action. This leads to the notion that development, which proceeds by stages to more refined discrimination, modality by modality, is a result of differentiation of modality-specific perceptual systems out of the initially undifferentiated or amodal space field (Werner, 1948). This has an interesting parallel in the view of the phylogenetic evolution of cortical mechanisms in mammals put forward by Dimond and Hall (1969). The specialized "primary" receptor fields for vision, audition, and touch evolve out of a multimodal (or amodal) "association" cortex.

Bruner has emphasized that there is something artificial about descriptions of disappearance of psychological function that depend on how the investigator classifies the performance of children on tests (Bruner, Olver, & Greenfield, 1966). Loss of ability to perform a given test commonly seems to be accompanied by an advance in intellectual strategy, loss being the result of the subject treating the task in an imaginative way that is incompatible with the formalized wishes of the experimenter. Bruner's term "growth errors" (errors in performance *due to* growth rather than errors *of* growth) expresses his belief in the constructive nature of all such disappearances.

In reviewing the problem of temporary loss of ability to perform tests of intelligence during the development of the child, Donaldson (1971) takes the similar view that the only way to understand what is in fact occurring is to describe longitudinally the changes of function in detail. Every instance of "loss" on record may be considered as due to an advance in development of the performance of a function, with a considerable change in the rules of operation by which the task is solved. Recent work by Margaret Donaldson with James McGarrigle has shown how the development of meaning in the mind of a child has a natural structure that changes as children grow older and that the changes are very much concerned with transformation of the *interpersonal situation* inherent in the test. What the child being tested thinks the experimenter is doing or intending has a great influence on the kind of answers that the child gives to questions of meaning (Donaldson, 1977, 1978; Donaldson & McGarrigle, 1974). It also effects the way the child appears to perceive relations between objects and classifications of their properties in relation to one another (McGarrigle & Donaldson, 1974). Younger nursery-school children avoid making judgements in the abstract, out of familiar human contexts where purposes and cooperative involvements are clear.

I believe the difficulty we have had in discussing dips in learning arises fundamentally because experimental analysis of intelligence or of cognitive achievement leads to narrowing of the description, with the behavior of the subject being categorized in a limited set of criteria. To explain the pattern of development some attempt has to be made to perceive a growing system more completely, as well as in more detail.

With regard to motor coordination of the individual, I believe we must return to the concept of an innate spatial field in which the primary properties of actions of objects may be anticipated and in which it is possible for the newborn to specify alternative directions to act involving various parts of a complex body in coordination (Trevarthen, 1974a, 1974b; 1978). The attainment of full consciousness and skill depends on the progressive mastery, over many years, of productive functions that increase the power of differentiation within the field already outlined at birth. I should say that all the changes in this process must be sanctioned by internal self-regulatory developmental processes in which predetermined neural components are caused to react to one another and become both more distinct and more intricately associated. The way they associate determines how the effects of experience will accumulate.

A very simple model of such developmental elaboration may be seen in the neural system that makes possible binocular stereopsis for perception of detail in young cats and monkeys. This system has been much studied in recent years since its plasticity was discovered by Wiesel and Hubel (1965). The important point is that binocular integration, involving matching of inputs from the two eyes, is outlined genetically but depends on postnatal exercise and selection of competing nerve connections for its refinement (Barlow, 1975; Hubel, Wiesel & Le Vay, 1977). The same interplay of intrinsic specification of layouts and selective retention of refined connections under the influence of stimulus patterns from the environment is found in experimental and theoretical studies of the formation of eye brain connections in fish and amphibia (Trevarthen, 1979a). To cite a further example of how structure is progressively refined in the nervous system through interaction of parts and their exercise, reference may be made to the selective process by which adaptive neuromuscular junctions are formed in lower vertebrates to make a system of complementary components (Mark, 1974). Gottlieb's study of the development of a specific response to the maternal mating call by birds that begin their education before they are born exemplifies the interplay of genetic and environmental factors in the construction of adaptive mechanisms of the fetus (Gottlieb, 1971).

The modern theory of genesis of structure in the nervous system thus puts heavy emphasis on the interplay between components that enter into active competition or conflict at various times along the way to attainment of the mature system. On the one extreme is a highly determined nerve net that lays down all the primary functions and coordinates perceptual fields with fields of motor action. Its pathways are formed by large Type I neurons, the form of which is relatively independent of environmental influences. Between these, in the spaces between the terminals of Type I cells, is a very large population of small neurons, many of which are added postnatally. Type I neurons are all of antenatal origin. The discovery of microneuron multiplication after birth by Altman (1970) has opened the way for the notion of a constant selection within a huge population of interstitial or Type II cells that are added between and over the primary integrative system of Type I neurons that is laid down before birth (Jacobsen, 1973). Another account of the mechanism that confers flexibility to environmental influence within contraints established epigenetically may be given in terms of the successive processes of nerve cell multiplication, cell migration and death, cell branching with multiplication of interneuronal support cells (glia), and, finally, selective reinforcement or elimination of synaptic contacts in a field of billions. Each phase of selection opens the way for more refined selective influence from the environment.

Having opened the possibility of regulated development, with selection operating at all stages to establish balanced integrations between alternative components that are present in latent form and mutually adjusted very early, we now may clearly see the need for much more psychological work. We must add to our very faint picture of the basic perceptor motor or cognitive intentional system. We must try to discover what the neural mechanism may be for the special epigenetic field of human intelligence.

As mentioned previously, the integrative field by which the human infant obtains a synthesis of perception and voluntary action is subordinated to a field of *cooperative interpersonal action* in which the joint experiences of the infant with other people have a controlling effect upon the development of consciousness and skill. It is as if the competition for places in the growing mechanism of the mind has been carried to arbitration not merely outside the brain of the individual, but into a field where the brains of many individuals in communication play essential roles. Even in the first year of life the infant's cognitive growth is by education, that is, by encouragement and example from older, more experienced individuals who may have a very big effect indeed upon how the potentialities seen so early in the infant may be combined into effective components of intelligence. Usually this stage of an infant's life is spent in an intimate dependency on affectionate care of the mother, who becomes the main companion and instructor.

In *Play, Dreams and Imitation* (1962), Piaget brilliantly attempts to explain imitation as originating from reproductive and recognitive assimilation that is inherent in the voluntary intelligence of a subject acting alone. I believe this theory of an autonomous experiencer to be incorrect and that intersubjective processes, of which imitation is but a special case, require a specific new cerebral mechanism that is evolved to a unique level of sophistication in humans. In fact, voluntary organisms all show ability for contagious or cooperative action. This would seem to support Piaget's theory. But the behavior of a school of fish swimming in formation is, I submit, different *in principle* from that of communicating agents who "read" one another's intentions from small indications implicit in preliminary attentive and intentional movements. This "reading" of the mind's work depends on activities of highly evolved new motor organs like the face and hands, which have special valence for communication of mental operations and "states of mind." There is much evidence, now, for antecedents of social cognition in animals, the case of chimpanzees being most remarkable (Menzel, 1973). But none of the attempts to teach human language to apes have been fully convincing. Human infants cooperate in ways apes cannot imitate. This cooperation appears to be innate.

We have found that infants manifest built-in sensitivity to specialized expressve movements that adults make to them. That is, infants show innate intersubjectivity directly. The birth arousal phenomenon, which exposes very clearly many latent prototypical forms of psychological action in the neonate, including the fundamental unity of the space of intentional action (behavior space), also exposes the outlines of specialized interest in the expressions of persons. A brief subsequent "loss," or rather "eclipse," of these powers of action undoubtedly reflects the complex changes in the nerve network needed to establish effective control over perturbations that stand in the way of performance. Control is elaborated into consciousness, and into language, by many intricate stages of growth in the years that follow birth. It is clear that our knowledge of this process is still very meager, notwithstanding its close importance to all of us and its great significance in human affairs.

APPENDIX: METAMORPHOSIS AND PSYCHOGENESIS

When looking for a concrete and simpler instance of how a developing biological mechanism might reveal itself with both gains and losses in degrees of completeness from tim to time in a life history, I recalled the extraordinary nonlinear life histories of insect metamorphosis.

A butterfly inhabits two different ecological niches in the course of its life,

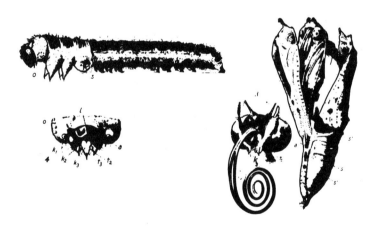

FIG. 2.9   Metamorphosis of a butterfly.
    A caterpillar, here seen moulting, has chewing mouth-parts. The butterfly, emerging from the pupal case on the left, has wings and mouth parts for sucking nectar. Two stages of the life cycle share a single body frame which is determined in the egg.

and there are radical changes of body structure and behavior to suit the changed conditions when a caterpillar changes to butterfly. This fantastic phenomenon has been subjected to detailed analysis. Experiments show that both the adult and the larval form are present, invisible but determined, in the embryo. Wigglesworth (1954) concludes that metamorphosis involves the same kind of process as that which determines the form changes of polymorphous insects. In the social ants or bees, different adaptive shapes of individuals, know as castes (worker,soldier, etc.), develop from essentially the same type of egg. Again, various components of different types of individuals must all be present in latent form in the embryo. Environmental factors, acting through a complex mechanism of regulatory devices, including hormone systems, determine what particular combination of characters will finally mature in a given individual just as closely similar factors determine the *order* of emergence of forms in metamorphosis through caterpillar and pupa to butterfly.

A further important point has been brought out by recent experiments using artificially created genetic mosaics. With this technique it is possible to tag lineages of cells from early embryo to adult, by inserting in them mutant genes that lead to distinctive color or morphology when the cells become mature. Then the fate of descrete patches of the body can be traced backward through development. "Fate maps" of the fruit fly embryo show that not only the morphological structures of the adult, but also behavioral elements related to separate parts of the nervous system are laid down in a single maplike or modulelike 3-D arrangement for both larva and adult in the embryo body (Benzer, 1973). In other words, the latent precursors of larva and adult body organs and brain share the same somatotopic or body-space scafold. So, in spite of the demonstration that two individuals are in one embryo, we have to acknowledge that the two individuals are really one individual, because they have the same single body form in common.

It is certain that biological development always proceeds in a somewhat twofold way, by generation of structures with "double meaning" in development. The overall outline of relations of symmetry, polarity, etc., between parts that will differentiate is physically determined within the egg at fertilization or immediately after. Products of gene action following egg fertilization become organized according to the fate map in an invisible, latent, but already highly specific material form during the embryo stage. What actually becomes functional is ultimately determined by regulation of gene and cell expression at different points in this map in the course of development.

It is quite clear that such a strategy of development would permit what Michael Halliday refers to as "previews" or "trailers" of psychological functions that will only really get into action at some later stage in development. In his detailed catalog of the growth of language of his son during the first 2 years he found several instances of this, confirming many earlier studies (Halliday, 1975).

The theory of metamorphosis offers a model system for transformations in development. When one adds to this the more general theory of development by cycles of differentiation and reintegration of parts within an overall body scheme, it then becomes possible to generate effects of spiral change, decalage, or repeated disappearance and reappearance of functions.

In an early stage of development, such as an insect larva or an infant, any fuction may be represented in a specialized morphological feature of that stage (abdominal legs of a caterpillar, sucking callous on the lips of a neonate), or the function (e.g., feeding) may exhibit metamorphosis, existing in different forms at different stages. Thirdly, the function may be a start in the formatin of an as yet partly integrated system, one that will attain full development only later, by progressive addition and combination of parts.

In infancy we find examples of all of these, and, in addition, there are many previews of adult functions that serve the process of development by establishing conditions for changes in *other* systems. One of the most extraordinarily precocious brain "organs" of humans is the asymmetric mechanism for regulation of speech and language, which, although it does not reach maturity until decades after birth, is already distinct as inequalities in the local anatomy of the two cerebral hemispheres in the fetus (Trevarthen, 1979a, 1980 a). No one doubts that the acquired skills of speaking and understanding speech are important in regulating mental growth in the child. It is important that their physical substrate is present, affecting the brain's activity, from before birth.

The growth of human intelligence is thus much more fantastic than insect metamorphosis because, while going through a wide variety of highly adaptive life stages progressively from infant through childhood to adult, it also permits the continual mutual adjustment of many complex alternative modes of mental action (thought, perceiving the world, acting on the world, communicating with persons) that gain expression with increasing differentiation throughout the whole course of individual life, and never "go away." Their emergence is different in each individual and changed in each generation. So a process of cultural evolution is kept in motion. The metamorphosis implicit in human psychogenesis is not only very much more elaborate and with more stages than the life history of a butterfly or housefly, but also has the special feature, which we claim is neglected by developmental psychologists, of setting up embryonic psychological relations between the infant and older partner from birth. This intersubjectivity becomes, we claim, the essential mechanism of development of intelligence in the mind, and the generator of human culture (Trevarthen, 1979c).

ACKNOWLEDGMENTS

Research on which this article is based began at Harvard University with support from the U.S. National Institute of Health to Professor J. S. Bruner and continued at Edinburgh under grants to the author from the Medical Research Council (No. 971/701/B) and the Social Science Research Council (HR 2263/1). This support is gratefully acknowledged. Thanks are also due to my colleagues Penelope Hubley, Lynne Murray, and Benjamin Sylvester-Bradley.

REFERENCES

Alegria J., & Noirot, E. Neonate orientation behaviour towards the human voice. *International Journal of Behavioural Development*, 1978, *1*, 291–312.

Altman, J. Postnatal neurogenesis and the problem of neural plasticity. In W. A. Himwich (Ed.), *Developmental neurobiology*. Springfield, Ill.: C. C. Thomas, 1970.

Barlow, H. B. Visual experience and cortical development. *Nature, 1975, 258* 199-204

Bates, E., Camaioni, L., & Volterra, V. The acquisition of performatives prior to speech. *Merrill-Palmer Quarterly,* 1975, *21* 205-226.

Bernstein, N. *The coordination and regulation of movements.* Oxford: Pergamon, 1967.

Bizzi, E., Kalil, R. E., & Tagliasco, V. Eye-head coordination in monkeys: Evidence for centrally patterned organization. *Science,* 1971, *173,* 452-454.

Bower, T. G. R. *Development in infancy.* San Francisco: W. H. Freeman & Co., 1974.

Bower, T. G. R. Perceptual development: Object and space. In E. C. Carterette & M. P. Friedman (Eds.), *Handbook of Perception* (Vol. VIII). New York: Academic Press, 1978.

Brinkman, J., & Kuypers, H. G. J. M. Cerebral control of contralateral and ipsilateral arm, hand and finger movements in split-brain rhesus monkeys. *Science,* 1972, *176,* 536-539.

Bruner, J. S. The ontogenesis of speech acts. *Journal of Child Language,* 1975, *2* 1-19.

Bruner, J. S., Olver, R. R., & Greenfield, P. M. *Studies in cognitive growth.* New York: Wiley, 1966.

Condon, W. S., & Sander, L. W. Neonate movement is synchronized with adult speech: Interactional participation and language acquisition. *Science* 1974, *183,* 99-101.

Conel, J. Le Roy. *The postnatal development of the human cerebral cortex.* (Vol. I-VI). Cambridge: Harvard University Press, 1939-1963.

De Beer, G. R. *Embryos and ancestors.* Oxford: Oxford University Press, 1940.

Dimond, I. T., & Hall, W. C. Evolution of the neocortex. *Science,* 1969, *164,* 257-261.

Donaldson, M. Preconditions of inference. *Nebraska Symposium on Motivation,* 1971, 81-106.

Donaldson, M. Development of conceptualization. In M. Vernon & V. Hamilton (Eds.), *Development of cognitive processes.* London: Academic Press, 1977.

Donaldson, M. *Children's minds.* London: Fontana, 1978.

Donaldson, M., & McGarrigle, J. Some clues to the nature of semantic development. *Journal of Child Language,* 1974, *1,* 185-194.

Gottleib, G. *Development of species identification in birds: An inquiry into prenatal determinants of perception.* Chicago, Ill.: University of Chicago Press, 1971.

Greene, P. H. Problems of organization of motor systems. In R. Rosen & F. M. Snell (Eds.), *Progress in theoretical biology* (Vol. II). New York: Academic Press, 1972.

Grillner, S. Locomotion in vertebrates: Central mechanisms and reflex interaction. *Physiological Reviews,* 1975, *55,* 247-304.

Haith, M. Visual competence in early infancy. In R. Held, H. Leibowitz, & H-L Teuber (Eds.), *Handbook of sensory physiology* (Vol. VIII). Berlin: Springer-Verlag, 1976.

Halliday, M. *Learning how to mean.* London: Edward Arnold, 1975.

Hamburger, V. Anatomical and physiological basis of embryonic motility in birds and mammals. In G. Gottlieb (Ed.), *Studies on the development of behavior and the nervous system* (Vol. I) *Behavioral embryology.* New York: Academic Press, 1973.

Haynes, H., White, B. L., & Held, R. Visual accommodation in human infants. *Science,* 1965, *148,* 528-530.

Hofsten, C. von. Development of visually directed reaching: The approach phase. *Journal of Human Movement Studies,* 1979, *5,* 160-178.

Hubel, D. H., & Wiesel, T. N. The period of susceptibility to the physiological effects of unilateral eye closure in kittens. *Journal of Physiology,* 1970, *206,* 419-436.

Hubel, D. H., Wiesel, T. N., & LeVay, S. Plasticity of ocular dominance columns in monkey striate cortex. *Philosophical Transactions of the Royal Society* (London) 1977, Series B *278,* 131-163.

Hubley, P., & Trevarthen, C. Sharing a task in infancy. In I. Usgiris (Ed.), *Social interaction and communication in infancy* (Vol. 4) *New directions for child development.* San Francisco: Jossey-Bass, 1979, pp. 57-80.

Humphrey, N. K. Vision in a monkey without a striate cortex: A case study. *Perception,* 1974, *3,* 241-255.

Humphrey, T. Postnatal repetition of human prenatal activity sequences with some suggestions of their neuroanatomical basis. In R. J. Robinson (Ed.), *Brain and early behavior: Development in the fetus and infant.* New York: Academic Press, 1969.

Jacobsen, M. A plenitude of neurons. In G. Gottlieb (Ed.), *Studies on the development of behaviour and the nervous system* Vol. 2 *Aspects of Neurogenesis,* New York: Academic Press, 1974.

Kuypers, H.G.J.M. Corticospinal connections: Postnatal development in the rhesus monkey. *Science,* 1962, *138,* 678-680.

Kuypers, H. G. J. M. The anatomical organisation of the descending pathways and their contributions of motor control, especially in primates. In T. E. Desmedt (Ed.), *New Developments in E.M.G. and clinical neurophysiology.* Basel: Karger, 1973.

Leehey, S. C., Moscowitz-Cook, A., Brill, S., & Held, R. Orientational anisotropy in infant vision. *Science,* 1975, *190,* (4217), 900-902.

Maratos, O. *The origin and development of imitation in the first six months of life.* Doctoral dissertation, University of Geneva, 1973.

Mark, R. F. *Memory and nerve-cell connections*. Oxford: Oxford University Press, 1974.

McGarrigle, J., & Donaldson, M. Conservation accidents. *Cognition*, 1974, *3*, 341–350.

McGraw, M. B. *The neuromuscular maturation of the human newborn*. New York: Columbia University Press, 1943.

Mehler, J., & Bever, T. G. The study of competence in cognitive psychology. *International Journal of Psychology*, 1968, *3*, 273–280. (a)

Mehler, J., & Bever, T. G. Reply to Jean Piaget. *Science*, 1968, *162*, 979–981. (b)

Meltzoff, A. N., & Moore, M. K. Imitation of facial and manual gestures by neonates. *Science*, 1977, *198*, 75–78.

Mounoud, P. *Structuration de l'instrument chez l'enfant: interiorisation et regulation de l'action*. Neuchatel: Delachaux et Niestle SA, 1970.

Murray, L. The Sensitivities and Expressive Capacities of Young Infants in Communication with their mothers. *Infants capacities for regulating interactions with their mothers, and the function of emotions*. Doctoral dissertation: University of Edinburgh, 1980.

Noirot, E. Personal communication, 1979.

Oppenheim, R. W. The ontogeny of behavior in the chick embryo. In D. H. Lehrman et al. (Eds.), *Advances in the study of behavior*. New York: Academic Press, 1974.

Oppenheim, R. W., & Reitzel, J. Ontogeny of behavioral sensitivity to strychnine in the chick embryo: Evidence for the early onset of CNS inhibition. *Brain Behavior and Evolution*, 1975, *11*, 130–159.

Oster, H. Facial expression and affect development. In M. Lewis & R. A. Rosenblum (Eds.), *The origins of behaviour: Affect development*. New York: Plenum, 1978.

Papousek, H. Individual variability in learned responses in human infants. In R. J. Robinson (Ed.), *Brain and early behaviour: Development in fetus and infant*. New York: Academic Press, 1969.

Papousek, H., & Papousek, M. Cognitive aspects of preverbal social interaction between human infants and adults. In M. O'Connor (Ed.), *Parent–Infant Interaction*. Amsterdam: Elsevier, 1975.

Peiper, J. *Cerebral function in infancy and childhood*. New York: Consultants Bureau, 1963.

Piaget, J. *The origins of intelligence in children*. London: Routledge and Kegan Paul, 1953.

Piaget, J. *Play, dreams and imitation in childhood*. New York: Norton, 1962.

Piaget, J. *Biologie et connaissance: Essai sur les relations entre les regulations organiques et les processus cognitifs*. Paris: Gallimard, 1967. Translated by B. Walsh, Edinburgh: Edinburgh University Press and Chicago: The University of Chicago Press, 1971.

Prechtl, H. F. R., & Lenard, H. G. A study of eye movements in sleeping newborn infants. *Brain Research*, 1967, *5*, 477–493.

Richards, M. P. M. *Effects on infant behaviour of analgesics and anaesthetics used in obstetrics*. Paper presented at the 5th Conference of the European Teratology Society, Gargano, Italy, September 1976.

Salapatek, P. Pattern perception in early infancy. In L. B. Cohen & P. Salapatek (Eds.), *Infant perception: From sensation to cognition*. New York: Academic Press, 1975.

Sylvester-Bradley, B., & Trevarthen, C. "Baby-talk" as an adaptation to the infant's communication. In N. Waterson and K. Snow (Eds.), *Development of communication: Social and pragmatic factors in language acquisition*. London: Wiley, 1978.

Trevarthen, C. Behavioral embryology. In E. C. Carterette & M. P. Friedman (Eds.), *Handbook of Perception* (Vol. III). New York: Academic Press, 1973.

Trevarthen, C. L'action dans l'espace et la perception de l'espace: Méchanismes cérébraux de base. In F. Bresson (Ed.), *De l'espace corporel á l'espace écologique*. Paris: Presses Universitaires de France, 1974. (a)

Trevarthen, C. The psychobiology of speech development. In E. H. Lenneberg (Ed.),

Language and brain: Developmental aspects. Neurosciences Research Program Bulletin,
1974, *12*, 570–585. Boston: Neurosciences Research Program. (b)

Trevarthen, C. Descriptive analyses of infant communication behaviour. In H. R. Schaffer
(Ed.), *Mother-infant interaction.* London: Academic Press, 1977.

Trevarthen, C. Modes of perceiving and modes of acting. In H. J. Pick (Ed.), *Psychological
modes of perceiving and processing information.* Hillsdale, N.J.: Lawrence Erlbaum
Associates, 1978.

Trevarthen, C. Neuroembryology and the development of perception. In F. Falkner & J. M.
Tanner (Eds.), *Human growth: A comprehensive treatise* (Vol. III). New York: Plenum,
1979. (a)

Trevarthen, C. Communication and cooperation in early infancy. A description of primary
intersubjectivity. In M. Bullowa (Ed.), *Before speech: The beginnings of human communication.* London: Cambridge University Press, (1979). (b)

Trevarthen, C. Instinct for human understanding and for cultural cooperation: Their development in infancy. In M von Crancach, K. Foppa, W. Lepenies, & D. Ploog (Eds.), *Human
ethology.* Cambridge: Cambridge University Press, (1979). (c)

Trevarthen, C. *Neurological development and the growth of psychological functions.* In J.
Sants (Ed.), *Developmental psychology and society.* London: Macmillans, (1980a).

Trevarthen, C. The foundations of intersubjectivity: development of interpersonal and cooperative understanding in infants. In D. Olsen (Ed.) *The social foundations of languages
and thought*: Essays in honor of J. S. Bruner. New York: W. W. Norton, 1980. (b)

Trevarthen, C., & Hubley, P. Secondary intersubjectivity: Confidence, confiding and acts of
meaning in the first year. In A. Lock (Ed.), *Action, gesture and symbol: The emergence
of language.* London: Academic Press, 1978.

Trevarthen, C., Hubley, P., & Sheeran, L. Les activites innee du nourrisson. *La Recherche,*
1975, *6*, 447–458.

Trevarthen, C., Murray, L. & Hubley, P. Psychology of infants. In J. Davis & J. Dobbing
(Eds.) *Scientific foundations of Clinical Pediatrics* London: Heinemann's Medical. In press.

Twitchell, T. E. The automatic grasping responses of infants. *Neuropsychologia,* 1965, *3*,
247–259.

Werner, H. *The comparative psychology of mental development.* Chicago, Ill.: Wilcox &
Follett, 1948.

White, B. L., Castle, P., & Held R. Observations on the development of visually-directed
reaching. *Child Development,* 1964, *35*, 349–364.

Wiesel, T. N., & Hubel, D. H. Comparison of the effects of unilateral and bilateral eye closure
on cortical unit response in kittens. *Journal of Neurophysiology,* 1965, *28*, 1029–1040.

Wigglesworth, V. B. The physiology of insect metamorphosis. *Cambridge monographs in
experimental biology,* 1954, *1*, Cambridge University Press.

Yakovlev, P. I., & Lecours, A. R. The myelogenetic cycles of regional maturation of the brain.
In A. Minkowski (Ed.), *Regional development of the brain in early life.* Oxford: Blackwell,
1967.

Yarbus, A. L. *Eye movements and vision.* New York: Plenum Press, 1967.

3 The Year-Old Infant: A Period of Major Cognitive Change

Philip R. Zelazo, Ph.D.
Tufts University School of Medicine
and
Tufts–New England Medical Center
Boston, Massachusetts

Bever and Mehler (Chapters 8 & 7, respectively) have called attention to an important recurring phenomenon in the cognitive development of the child. They have shown that declines in performance on a variety of seemingly unrelated responses may accompany the emergence of new or altered cognitive abilities. They have used a wealth of data, collected on numerous cognitive and linguistic tasks, to specify the behavioral characteristics of the emerging mechanisms allowing them to hypothesize about the nature of the mechanisms themselves. Moreover, their observation that "dips" in performance are often followed by altered cognitive abilities, although derived primarily from records on children between the ages of 2 and 5, appears generalizable to other cognitive levels.

Their observations are strengthened by a large set of independent data with infants showing comparable declines in some responses prior to the emergence of new cognitive abilities. Moreover, the behavioral changes in response to perceptual–cognitive tasks during infancy, like the data from the 2 to 5-year period, allow inferences about the nature of the changing cognitive abilities. The observation of similar response patterns during infancy and early childhood strengthens the validity of Bever and Mehler's observations and strongly implies that declines in some responses preceding emergent cognitive capacities may represent a recurring theme of cognitive development.

Not all "dips" in responding signify the onset of new or changed cognitive

47

capacities. Therefore, it is imperative to test directly for the hypothesized new capacities. Whereas some responses during infancy may change their meaning when they reappear, others (some of the documented behaviors occurring during the 2 to 5-year period, for example) may diminish and reappear as a result of different rules governing their production. In both instances, an altered cognitive capacity is hypothesized that bears new implication for additional behaviors that are themselves testable directly. The new cognitive capacity also may generate new responses showing an emerging rather than declining development. Thus, "dips" in development may function primarily as a clue to many other changes in behavior, not all of which form the same pattern. Moreover, the appearance of new mechanisms can and should be verified in a manner that is independent of the "dips" in particular responses.

The following series of experiments reveal declines and reappearances of fixation and vocalization in laboratory tests of information-processing capacities in infants. These data lend support to Kagan's (1971, 1972) suggestion that active thought may emerge toward the end of the first year of life. A host of new behaviors accompanying the postulated capacity for active thought strengthen the inferences drawn from the perceptual–cognitive tasks. The appearance of this important cognitive capacity at about 1 year may have been overlooked because gross motor performance has been used so heavily to infer cognitive ability.

THE RELIANCE ON SENSORIMOTOR PERFORMANCE
FOR THE ASSESSMENT OF COGNITIVE DEVELOPMENT

The assumption of sensorimotor intelligence in infancy, inherent in the maturational view expressed by Gesell (1925) and continued in the more recent tests of infant development (Bayley, 1969; Griffiths, 1954), has resulted in an emphasis on gross and fine motor actions either directly or indirectly (e.g., through imitation items) to assess infant cognitive growth (Brooks & Weinraub, 1976, pp. 19-58). Gesell regarded motor development as a maturational phenomenon that unfolded in a fixed and orderly sequence. Superior motor performance was assumed to reflect superior genetic structure and, therefore, superior cognitive ability. There is little evidence to substantiate the presumed direct relation between motor and cognitive development, although the assumptions still persist in the choice of items used in current tests of infant mental development (Zelazo, 1976a, pp. 87-104, 1976b, pp. 80-86, 1979, pp. 49-83).

Piaget (1952) assumes that the infant's intelligence is inherent in his actions and that the infant is not capable of symbolic thought until about 18 months of age. However, he acknowledges the role of subtle motor reactions such as eye movements and smiling in reflecting the infant's developing cognitive abilities. More importantly, he proposes an interactionist position that emphasizes the significance of both maturation and experience in the developing organism. Despite Piaget's interactionist view and his appreciation of the infant's more subtle responses, most past attempts to assess infant cognition from a Piagetian perspective have been restricted to gross and fine motor responses (Escalona & Corman, 1969; Uzgiris & Hunt, 1975). These scales of infant cognition rely heavily on measurements of object permanence, grasping, and reaching, for example.

Similar measures, along with many tasks in which the child is expected to imitate the actions of the examiner, frequently appear in traditional tests of infant development. The extensive emphasis on motor development, even in the mental portions of these scales, is illustrated by the moderately high correlation ($r = .55$) between the mental and motor components of the Bayley Scales of Infant Development (1969). Not only do many of the items on the Mental Scales require imitation that presumes a degree of motor facility of the upper extremities, but a willingness to comply with the examiner's requests is assumed also. Both the child's motor facility and compliance are confounded with attempts to assess the child's cognitive ability. Thus it appears that, in practice, the study of infant cognitive development has been yoked, to a large extent, to the study of infant motor development.

Over the past 20 years, there has been intense interest in perception, information processing, and attention in infancy, representing a marked departure from the assumption of sensorimotor intelligence, although this disparity is only beginning to come into focus (Zelazo, 1976a, pp. 87-104, 1976b, pp. 80-86, 1979, pp. 49-83). Subtle response measures such as visual fixation, searching to an auditory signal, and heart rate have been devised and refined for use with infants (Campos, 1976, pp. 1-31; Kagan, 1971; Kagan, Kearsley, & Zelazo, 1978; Lewis & Goldberg, 1969a; Zelazo, 1979, pp. 49-83). Moreover, the meanings of infant responses have been studied extensively with the intention of deciphering messages expressed through the infant's relatively limited behavioral repertoire (Kagan, 1971; Sroufe &

Waters, 1976; Watson, 1972; Zelazo, 1972). The explicit assumption that the infant has the capacity to process and store information with a central processing system that may use but does not require gross motor involvement, has emerged (Kagan, 1971; Lewis & Goldberg, 1969a, 1969b; Sokolov, 1963; Zelazo, 1972, 1979, pp. 49-83). For example, Kagan (1967), unlike Piaget, regards a schema as an abstract internal representation of an event with potential neural correlates in the brain. This view assumes that the infant has the capacity to process and store sensory information and can integrate information from several modalities at a central level (Zelazo, 1972, 1979, 49-83).

Along with the recent theoretical and methodological advances in the study of infant cognition, there is a beginning effort to assess systematically the development of attention and information processing during the first year of life. However, the initial attempts to assess processing ability (Eisenberg, Coursin & Rupp, 1966; Fagan, 1979; Fantz & Nevis, 1967; Lewis, 1970) were restricted in the age range studied and used relatively simple static stimuli. Thus, the examination of the processing of complex sequential visual and auditory events during infancy, approximating the stimuli that the infant engages in his daily world during the first year of life, has been undertaken only recently (Kagan, Kearsley & Zelazo, 1978; Zelazo, 1979, 49-83). We are left with assumptions that have not survived the test of research, on the one hand, and new hypotheses and procedures that offer great promise but have not been applied systematically to the development of cognition during the first few years of life, on the other. The research reported here, conducted with Jerome Kagan and Richard Kearsley, reflects an effort to redress this disparity, in part.

DIPS IN VOCALIZATION TO PERCEPTUAL–COGNITIVE EVENTS: EVIDENCE OF COGNITIVE CHANGE

Method

A series of sequential visual and auditory events were designed so that children could develop an expectancy for a particular event (called the standard) through repetition (Kagan, Kearsley, & Zelazo, 1978; Zelazo, 1979, pp. 49-83). After a fixed number of trials a discrepant variation of the standard (called the transformation) was presented and that, in turn, was followed by the reappearance and repetition of the standard. Thus, the child's reaction to the repeated event—his or her developing expectancy—and his or her capacity to assimilate the discrepant changes were assessed. In one event, the cube sequence (Zelazo, Kagan, & Hartmann, 1975), a 2-inch orange wooden cube was lifted out of a blue box and moved in a fixed "N" pattern for six trials. Without warning, either a moderately discrepant or a novel object was presented for three trials, followed by the reappearance of the standard for three additional trials. Thus, a 6–3–3 trial sequence was used. Each trial lasted 11 seconds and the interstimulus interval was 4 seconds. The moderately discrepant group viewed a 1½-inch cube identical to the standard except for size and the novel group watched a 1½-inch yellow rippled plastic cylinder bearing no relation to the standard. A control group continued to observe the repetition of the standard during trials seven through twelve.

In the light sequence, illustrated in Fig. 3.1, the children watched the presenter's hand lift a rod through a 240-degree arc and touch the first of three brightly colored bulbs. All bulbs lighted for 4 seconds before the presenter's hand returned the rod to the starting position and disappeared from view. The trial lasted 15 seconds and the interval between presentations was 4 seconds. During the transformation trials, children in the "no-rod" group watched the hand come out and the lights go on without the movement of the rod. During the "disordered" transformation, all the components of the light stimulus were retained, but in a markedly different sequence: The rod moved through the arc without the aid of the hand, touched the bulbs momentarily, but did not light them on contact. Instead, the bulbs were lighted upon the return of the rod to the starting position. The lights remained on for 4 seconds and went off with the appearance of the hand hovering over the bulbs. A control group observed the standard sequence repeated during the trials when the children in the experimental groups watched the "transformation" and "return" trials.

It should be pointed out that the light sequence is different from the cube sequence in several important ways. First, the light sequence is a more complex event that has a clear causal relation, requires time to unfold, and has more compelling stimulus properties. Second, the light sequence is more effective in sustaining attention and is useful through about 36 months of age, whereas the cube sequence ceases to be an effective elicitor of attention after about 12 months.

Two sets of experiments were conducted using approximately 250 child-

FIG. 3.1   Stimulus for rod–light sequence. (From Zelazo, P. R.   Reactivity to perceptual–cognitive events: Application for infant assessment. in R. B. Kearsley and I. Sigel (Eds.), *Infants at risk: Assessment of cognitive functioning.* Hillsdale, N.J.: Lawrence Erlbaum Associates. 1979.)

ren. In one set, patterns of responsiveness were examined cross-sectionally for boys and girls at 5½, 7½, 9½, and 11½ months of age. In a second series of experiments, the sample sizes were expanded, control groups were added, and the changes in responsiveness occurring between 9½ and 11½ months of age that were observed in the first sample were studied more closely. Duration of looking and of vocalization were coded on button boxes by observers concealed behind curtains on the sides of the stage resembling a puppet theater. The visual events were presented on top of the stage at eye level directly in front of the infant, who was seated on his or her mother's lap. Electrodes attached to the child's sternum and connected to EKG and cardiotachometer units were used to obtain beat-by-beat measures of heart rate. Increases and decreases in heart rate, like changes in muscle tension and respiration, have been shown to correlate reliably with cognitive activity (Kahneman, Tursky, Shapiro, & Crider, 1969). Stimulus sequences were coded, either automatically or by an observer, to provide an analogue of the event.

Stimulus and response signals were recorded on an eight-channel polygraph providing a time-locked printout of the entire event. Data were analyzed using four blocks of three trials each: the first and last three standards, the first three transformations, and the three return trials. The means of the three trials in a block served as the basic unit of analysis for fixation and heart rate. The total duration during a trial block served as the basic unit of analysis for vocalization, a less frequently occurring response.

Results For The Cube Sequence

Only a sample of the results will be presented—enough to address the primary theme of this chapter—namely, the identification of a major "dip" or discontinuity in performance accompanying the emergence of what appears to be a new cognitive competence. Examination of the responses to the perceptual–cognitive procedures during the first year reveals that the primary behaviors of interest—fixation and vocalization—generally show a reduction in incidence at 7½ and 9½ months, respectively, followed by increased reactivity at about 1 year.

Fixation. The mean fixation times for 5½-, 7½-, 9½-, and 11½-month-old children viewing the cube sequence ($p = .10$) are presented in Fig. 3.2a. On the average, looking was less at 7½ months than at the other three ages. A more detailed picture of the pattern of fixation over trial blocks is given in the Age X Blocks Interaction ($p < .001$) shown in Fig. 3.2b. Looking time on the first trial block actually increased with age. However, habituation to the standard stimulus on the second and fourth trial blocks was greatest at 7½ months, indicating that it was the reduction in sustained fixation that produced the dip in overall looking time shown in Fig. 3.2a. The 9½-month-old children showed the longest looking times to the discrepant stimuli (Block 3). The increase in looking time with age on the first trial block and the higher overall fixation accompanied by less rapid habituation among older infants contradicts the data summarized by Lewis (1970), who argued that looking times decreased more rapidly with increasing cognitive sophistication. This disparity in findings is probably a function of the relatively complex sequential stimuli used in this series of experiments. Thus, a paradoxical question to be asked about the results presented in Fig. 3.2a and 3.2b is why looking time to the same stimuli should increase with greater cognitive maturity. One possibility is that as children become more mature they bring more information to the stimulus situation; it may be that they look longer because they generate more associations to the stimuli.

Vocalizations.   The intertrial vocalization data, shown in Fig. 3.3, offer a partial clue to the fixation results. Mean duration of vocalization for 166 children over the four ages ($p < .005$) declined slightly at 9½ months before increasing sharply at 11½ months. This deflection in the pattern of increasing vocalization occurred precisely when looking time was at its highest level. A more detailed illustration of the vocalization pattern can be seen from the near significant Age × Sex × Block Interaction ($p < .10$) depicted in Fig. 3.4. The data in Fig. 3.4 are combined for both moderately discrepant and novel stimulus groups. Vocalization to the standard trial blocks began at a near zero level at 5½ months and increased at 7½ and 9½ months, especially for girls. The introduction of the discrepant stimuli on Block 3 and the reappearance of the standard 2-inch cube on Block 4 produced quieting among girls at these ages. By 11½ months, vocalization among girls occurred

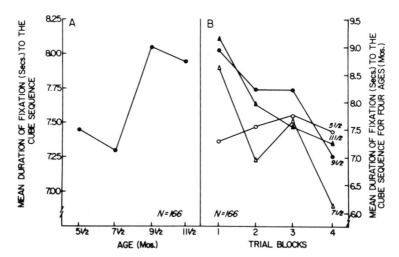

FIG. 3.2   Mean duration of fixation (secs) to the cube sequence over the four ages (a) and trial blocks (b).

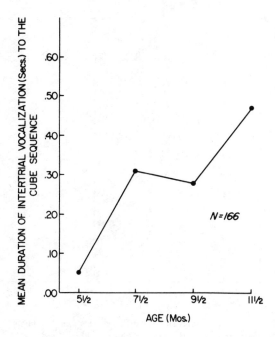

FIG. 3.3   Mean duration of intertrial vocalizations (secs) to the cube sequence over the four ages.

specifically to the introduction of the transformation and the reappearance of the standard, implying recognition or assimilation, whereas boys were only beginning to display quieting.

What is the basis for the increased vocalization among girls? How do we know that the renewed vocalization among girls does not reflect boredom, for example? Two factors imply that vocalization among girls occurred as a concomitant of stimulus-related excitement, rather than boredom. First, there was an overall increase in looking time, reflecting greater interest with age, especially at 9½ months. Second, and more importantly, it was determined in the second experiment with the introduction of a repetition control group that vocalization for girls occurred primarily to the appearance of the moderately discrepant cube and to the reappearance of the 2-inch cube following the moderate discrepancy .No increase in vocalization occurred to the novel or repetitive objects. The mean duration of vocalization during the interstimulus interval for 9½ and 11½-month-old boys and girls in the

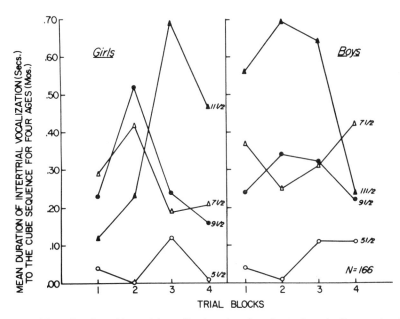

FIG. 3.4   Mean duration of intertrial vocalizations (secs) to the moderately discrepant cube and novel groups for boys and girls over the four trial blocks and ages.

moderately discrepant and novel groups is compared to the repetition control group in Fig. 3.5. There was a clear increase in vocalization for girls during the intertrial interval following the introduction of the small cube and the reappearance of the standard 2-inch cube. Thus, vocalization for girls occurred under conditions of moderate discrepancy. On the other hand, boys displayed vocal quieting and increased attention following the introduction of the small cube, implying increased interest, but not stimulus-related excitement.

Summary.   The two sets of data reveal a pattern of vocalization over the first year that implies a reorganization of responding, especially for girls. At 5½ months, vocalization was uniformly low. At 7½ and 9½ months, vocalization was high to the standard and was followed by quieting to the discrepant stimuli, implying that vocalization may reflect boredom under certain circumstances. The high level of vocalization among 11½-month-old boys in the repetition control group supports that interpretation. However, at

11½ months, vocalization among girls occurred specifically to the moderate discrepancy and not to the control or novel stimuli. These data imply that vocalization may bear new meaning toward the end of the first year, at least for infant girls.

Results for the Light Sequence.

Support for the argument that the dips in responses observed in the cube sequence are guided by changes in cognition can be found in the results of the light sequence, a more complex event that appears to be more difficult to assimilate.

Vocalizations.   Both the mean duration of vocalization and the percentage of children to vocalize during a trial block decreased at 9½ months of age. A total of 203 children were tested in the first experiment, using four variations of the light discrepancy. The percentage of children vocalizing at each of the four ages is shown in Fig. 3.6 ($F = 3.48$, df $= 3/171, p < .025$). The effect was similar to the decreased vocalization that occurred with the cube sequence, although the range of mean variation was modest. Examination of vocalization over trial blocks to the "no-rotor" light sequence also revealed a pattern that was similar to the cube sequence, especially for girls. Babbling was low at 5½ months and high but indiscriminate at 7½ months. Vocalization was generally lower and there was quieting to the discrepancy and return trial blocks at 9½ months, whereas vocalization to the discrepancy trial blocks increased at 11½ months. Ninety-two percent of the older girls vocalized to the reappearance of the standard following the "no-rotor" discrepancy, whereas only 33% of the 9½-month-old girls did so. Thus vocalization for girls, in particular, appeared as a diffuse and indiscriminate response at 7½ months, quieted at 9½ months (perhaps as a result of a maturing capacity for inhibition), and reappeared to the moderate discrepancy at 11½ months.

A more detailed examination of the changes occurring between 9½ and 11½ months was undertaken in a second experiment with the light sequence. A "no-change" control and an additional "disordered" discrepancy group were compared with the "no-rotor" discrepancy. Sample sizes were also increased to 12 infants of each sex at each age.

Analyses of the data collected with the additional groups and including trial blocks as a repeated measure are consistent with the results for the cube

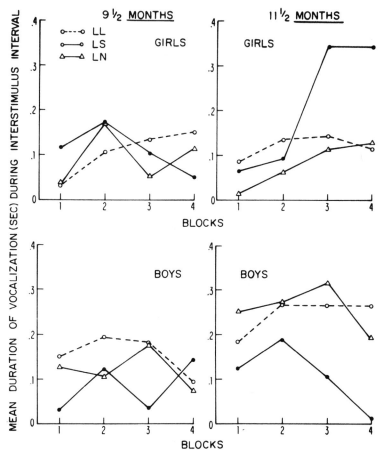

FIG. 3.5 Mean duration of intertrial vocalizations (secs) to the moderately discrepant cube, novel, and no-change control groups over the four trial blocks for boys and girls at 9½, and 11½ months. (From Zelazo, P. R., Kagan, J., & Hartmann, R. Excitement and boredom as determinants of vocalization in infants. *The Journal of Genetic Psychology,* 1975, *126,* 107–117.)

sequence also. The results for the mean duration of vocalization for the near significant Group X Sex X Block Interaction ($F = 1.77$, $df = 6/405$, $p = .10$) are displayed in Fig. 3.7. It can be seen that girls displayed increased vocalization to the reappearance of the standard following the moderate discrepancies, apparently as a concomitant of the excitement accompanying

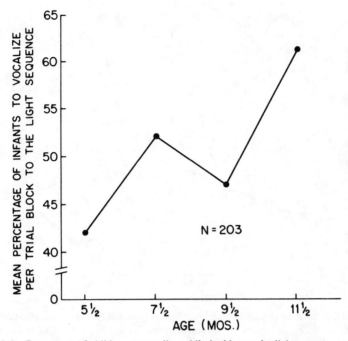

FIG. 3.6   Percentage of children to vocalize while looking at the light sequence at four ages during the first year. (From Zelazo, P. R. Reactivity to perceptual–cognitive events: Application for infant assessment. In R. B. Kearsley and I. Sigel (Eds.), *Infants at risk: Assessment of cognitive functioning.* Hillsdale, N. J.: Lawrence Erlbaum Associates, 1979.)

assimilation. Boys displayed increased vocalization to the repetition of the standard light sequence just as they did to the repetition to the 2-inch cube, presumably indicating boredom. An examination of the percentage of children to vocalize during a trial block parallels the results for the duration of vocalization and also indicates that older girls displayed increased vocalization to the reappearance of the standard following the moderate ("no-rotor") discrepancy and, to a lesser extent, following the "disordered" discrepancy. The percentage of girls to vocalize did not vary over trial blocks in the control group. Ninety-two percent of the older girls in the "no-rotor" group and 79% in the "disordered" group vocalized on the last trial block, in contrast to only 58% of the infants in the repetition control group.

Summary.   Vocalization to the light sequence, like the cube sequence, was high but indiscriminate at 7½ months, declined at 9½ months, and was

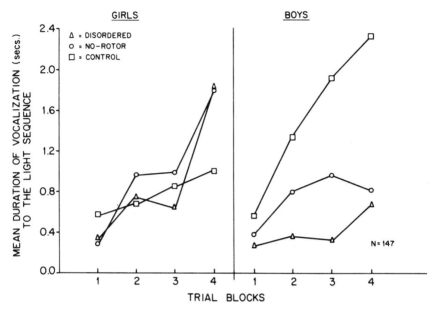

FIG. 3.7 Mean duration of vocalizations to the light sequence at four ages during the first year. (From Zelazo, P. R. Reactivity to perceptual–cognitive events: Application for infant assessment. In R. B. Kearsley and I. Sigel (Eds.), *Infants at risk: Assessment of cognitive functioning.* Hillsdale, N. J.: Lawrence Erlbaum Associates, 1979.)

followed by increased vocalization at 11½ months for infant girls. Moreover, the results from the second experiment with the light sequence, like the cube sequence, using additional discrepancy and control groups imply that vocalization among girls may accompany excitement associated with the assimilation of stimulus-related information. Thus, the vocalization data are consistent for both the light and cube sequences, indicating that the dip in responding at 9½ months is generalizable to a more complex, nonsocial stimulus.

Fixations.   Looking time to the light stimulus increased linearly with age, unlike the results of the cube sequence. The age main effect ($F = 6.29$, $df = 3/371$, $p < .001$) for mean duration of fixation reflects increased interest with maturity. Visual fixation rose from 7.8 to 8.1 to 8.6 to 9.0 seconds at 5½, 7½, 9½, and 11½ months of age, respectively, for a sample of 203 infants. Thus, the visual fixation data for the light sequence indicate increased interest with age and like the results for the cube sequence appear to contradict the finding of decreased interest with age to static visual stimuli reported by Lewis (1970).

Heart Rate Changes.   The results for heart rate help to explain the dips in reactivity that occur toward the end of the first year. The means of the two highest and two lowest values were obtained for four segments of the light sequence: base (a 3-second segment prior to the appearance of the hand), hand (a 3-second segment from the appearance of the hand to the lifting of the rod), rotor-light (an 8-second segment including the movement of the rod and lasting to the offset of the bulbs), and postlight (a 5-second segment lasting to the disappearance of the presenter's hand). Segments and trial blocks were treated as repeated measures in the analyses.

The results for the mean highest heart rate values during the base, hand, rotor-light, and postlight segments of the light sequence and for the four trial blocks in the "no-rotor" and control groups ($p < .005$) are presented in Fig. 3.8. The highest heart rate values—scored only if accompanied by visual fixation—show a distinct acceleration to the discrepancy (Block 3) during the rotor-light period in the "no-rotor" group, but not in the control group. A greater increase to the onset of the light without movement of the rotor (Block 3) is shown in the mean lowest values ($p < .005$) displayed in Fig. 3.9. Both the highest and lowest heart rate values accelerated to the discrepancy— in this case, to the deletion of the moving rotor—whereas no corresponding increase occurred in the "no-change" control group. The heart rate acceleration appears to be a correlate, although not necessarily a cause, of mental effort implying the onset of active thought in these infants.

Research with adults (Kahneman et al. 1969), which can be more carefully controlled, established an association between heart rate acceleration and mental effort. Kahneman et al. (1969) showed that heart rate increased as task difficulty in a digit problem situation increased. It is possible that the heart rate acceleration accompanying the discrepant perceptual–cognitive event in this experiment with infants also marks the occurrence of mental effort, perhaps due to tensing of the body during an attempt to understand the discrepancy. Individual records in this and subsequent experiments often show 5-to-10-beat accelerations during a single trial accompanied by uninterrupted quiet attention. Moreover, increased looking following the deletion of movement in the discrepant sequence implies that cognitive changes may be occurring within the infant.

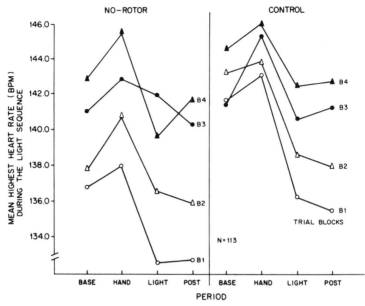

FIG. 3.8   Mean highest heart rate values (beats/minute) over trial blocks for the four periods of
the light sequence. (From Zelazo, P. R.   Reactivity to perceptual–cognitive events: Application for infant assessment. In R. B. Kearsley and I. Sigel (Eds.), *Infants at risk: Assessment
of cognitive functioning*. Hillsdale, N.J.: Lawrence Erlbaum Associates, 1979.)

The increased fixation with age to the same stimulus sequence and heart rate
acceleration to the discrepancy, especially when a compelling action component is deleted, implies that the 11½-month-old infant processes the
discrepant experience differently than the younger child. It appears that
whereas the 5½- and 7½-month-old has many responses to perceptual–
cognitive events at his disposal, they may be more automatic and less
intentional than for the 11½-month-old child.

The patterns for fixation (Fig. 3.2) and vocalization to the cube (Fig. 3.3,
3.4, and 3.5) and light (Fig. 3.6 and 3.7) sequences consistently illustrate a
progression from nonspecific responding at 7½ months, inhibition (for
vocalization) at 9½ months, and increased vocalization to the reappearance
of the standard following the moderate discrepancy at 11½ months. The
similarity of pattern for such different nonsocial stimulus sequences implies a
common determinant. One compelling possibility consistent with the overall
increase of looking time with age and heart rate acceleration to the modera-

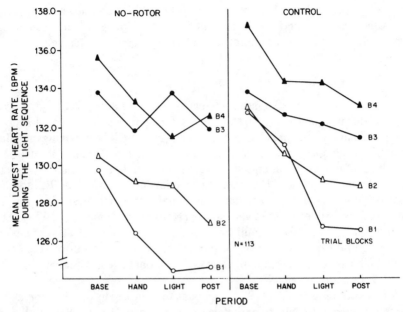

FIG. 3.9 Mean lowest heart rate values (beats/minute) over trial blocks for the four periods of the light sequence. (From Zelazo, P. R. Reactivity to perceptual–cognitive events: Application for infant assessment. In R. B. Kearsley and I. Sigel (Eds.), *Infants at risk: Assessment of cognitive functioning*. Hillsdale, N. J.: Lawrence Erlbaum Associates, Inc., 1979.)

tely discrepant light sequence at the older ages is that the infant's emergent capacity to generate his/her own thoughts may orchestrate the discharge of these responses. The dip in the infant data around 9½ months may announce the child's emerging capacity to inhibit his/her reactions to perceptual–cognitive stimuli and to choose among his/her responses. It is as though inhibition of reactivity (or wariness) allows other associations to occur. The stimuli remain the same over age; it is the infant who appears to bring a greater capacity for interest to the situation.

MANIFESTATIONS OF COGNITIVE CHANGE IN OTHER DOMAINS

The suggestion that a cognitive metamorphosis may set the stage for many of the behavioral changes observed at about 1 year gains support from a reexamination of these phenomena. A sample of research on the development of intentional vocalization, conservation of weight, stranger anxiety, separation distress, and the quality of the child's play reflects reasonable consistency with the argument of an underlying cognitive change.

Vocalization to Social Stimulation

By about 11½ months, the infant appears capable of activating associations readily and it appears that particularly infant girls use their vocalizations more exclusively to express their cognitive excitement. The changing meaning of vocalization does not appear to be simply a function of social interactional variables, although an "adequate" level of adult–child interaction appears to be a necessary condition. It appears that, following the trough at 9½ months, vocalizations begin to serve an intentional communicative function as suggested by Bruner (1975) and others (Harding & Golinkoff, 1979). The research with nonsocial stimuli implies that the excitement accompanying the recognition or assimilation of moderately discrepant information may form the basis for the communicative or intentional use of vocaliations after about 9½ months of age.

A recent finding by Roe (1975) indicates that the dip in vocalization at 9½ months is generalizable to infant boys in response to social stimulation. Mothers were asked to encourage babbling, cooing, and other neutral vocalizations during a 3-minute session of verbal interaction at 3, 5, 7, 9, 11, 13, and 15 months of age in two longitudinal samples of 28 firstborn boys. The percentages of time spent in neutral vocalization at each age for children with high and low Gesell developmental quotients are presented in Fig. 3.10 and indicate remarkable consistency with the results for nonsocial stimuli presented here. The language used by Roe to describe the pattern of results parallels the language used to describe reactivity to nonsocial sequences. Roe reported that "vocal responsiveness of the subjects to stimulation was high at 3 and 5 months, decreased appreciably around 9 months, and increased again around 11 months of age [p. 939]." The findings reported by Roe are also consistent with the suggestion made by Lewis (1959), who indicated that vocalization to spoken speech increases at around 10 months of age prior to the onset of the child's first spoken words.

It is tempting to suggest that reactivity, especially vocalization, at about a year becomes intentional. The female infant, in particular, appears to coordinate the expression of vocalization with her cognitive excitement. Vocalization in the service of assimilation may set the stage for preverbal

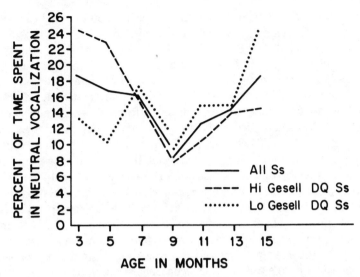

FIG. 3.10 Percentage of neutral vocalizations to verbal interactions during the first 15 months of age. (From Roe, K. V. Amount of infant vocalization as a function of age: Some cognitive implications. *Child Development,* 1975, *46,* 936–941.)

communication and the onset of the infant's first spoken words—an event placed by the Bayley norms at about 12 months. This suggestion is bolstered by Bruner's (1975) observations that it is not until after 10 months that gesturing, pointing, and intonation accompany vocalization in conversational situations. Cognitive prerequisites for speech are acknowledged (Bruner, 1975; Harding & Golinkoff, 1979), but it may be that the emerging capacity to generate specific associations represents a more precise and testable hypo-'hesis about the nature of the cognitive change that appears to occur to facilitate the onset of speech. The first spoken words not only demand a specific vocal utterance ("ball," for example), but require its association with a particular stimulus. Thus, the year-old child must have the capacity to activate specific thoughts and their auditory referents and to articulate the production of the remembered sound in order to label objects correctly.

Conservation of Weight

A description of the research on the conservation of weight among infants closely parallels the patterns of reactivity to the cube and light sequences described here. The development of the conservation of weight appears to culminate in the capacity to apply specific ideas to specific complex situations. Mounoud and Bower (1974) examined the infant's capacity to conserve weight by presenting babies small brass rods and measuring their arm drop and force of grasp. Six-to-seven-month-old infants did not display evidence of the capacity to conserve weights, despite short term practice. There was no correction for arm drop or force of grasp on successive presentations of small rods. Seven-month-old infants did not appear to understand the relation between weight and size, nor did they appear to understand that the same object would weigh the same on each presentation. In a description of this work, Bower (1974) reported that these infants appeared to "apply the same response to all objects regardless of their past experience with either the specific object or similar objects [p. 312]."

Nine-month-old children displayed some improvement. These infants began to display corrections in both arm movements and force of grasp on the second and third presentations of the same weight, implying an emergent comprehension of the relation between the stimulus and an appropriate response as a function of immediate prior experience. However, the same infants were not capable of predicting weight and size until about 12 months of age. Bower (1974) wrote that 12-month-old infants "know that the same object weighs the same on each presentation and that the longer an object is, the heavier it will be [p. 312]." This latter capacity—the prediction of the relation between size and weight—appears to be an example of the year-old infant's emergent cognitive capacity to activate a specific thought for a specific situation. The conservation of weight in infants appears to develop from indiscriminate reactivity at 7 months, to an emerging capacity for correct responding on the basis of prior experience at 9 months, to intentional reactivity in the service of specific ideas at 12 months. The 12-month-old infant has the capacity to generate the response (implying a specific thought) appropriate to a new situation; he or she knows precisely that the longer rod will weigh more.

Changes in Social Behavior

The regularity of reactivity to the complex sequential, nonsocial stimuli, implying the emergence of a new cognitive capacity, should bear implication for social behavior, as implied by the verbal interaction data reported by Roe (1975). If a new cognitive capacity develops around the end of the first year, abrupt changes in social behavior may occur also. A reexamination of a sample of the research on stranger anxiety not only reveals greater consistency among studies than usually acknowledged (Waters, Matas & Sroufe, 1975), but greater similarity to separation protest than previously supposed.

Stranger Anxiety. Waters et al. (1975) demonstrated that if degree of wariness is distinguished from more extreme measures of fear to strangers, agreement among existing studies is high. When the slightest indication of wariness (a wrinkled brow or a wary avoidant gaze) is combined with more extreme measures of distress (active withdrawal, resistance, a cry face, and audible crying), the reaction to strangers first becomes a statistically significant event at 8 months of age. The broad definition of wariness produced results in accord with Scarr and Salapatek (1970), Schaffer (1966), Schaffer and Emerson (1964), and Spitz (1965), who also suggested that the first signs of stranger anxiety appear at 8 months. However, if a more stringent definition of protest were used, such as audible crying in a majority of infants, stranger fear was not present even at 10 months in the Waters et al. (1975) sample, although a statistically significant increase in crying was shown. Using a scoring procedure that emphasized extreme measures of distress (crying, avoidance, and resistance) Morgan and Ricciuti (1965), pp. 253-295) found clear stranger fear at 12 months. If the age when a majority of infants display distress were used as the principal criterion and milder negative reactions were combined with extreme distress responses, Waters et al. (1975) and Scarr and Salapatek (1970) are in agreement in showing fear of strangers in 60% of their infants between 9 and 11 months of age. Thus, if milder reactions are used as the criteria, "stranger fear" first emerges at about 8 months and certainly occurs between 9 and 11 months, but if unambiguous distress, as indexed by audible crying and active avoidance, were used as the criteria, "stranger fear" did not occur until about 12 months.

The results obtained with nonsocial stimuli indicating inhibition of reactivity at 9½ months and reactivity to moderately discrepant information at 11½ months are in accord with the suggestion made by Waters et al. (1975) that wariness to strangers may represent something other than fear as inferred from audible crying. In fact, the nonsocial data imply that wariness and crying may be qualitatively different responses reflecting different processes. Wariness may index quiet, attentive inhibition occurring during information processing that may culminate in either uncertainty and protest or assimilation and a positive reaction, whereas crying and active avoidance may indicate clear protest reflecting apprehension or fear. Kagan (1972) suggested that the inability to understand a strange situation appears to result in apprehension and distress. The nonsocial data indicate that quiet attention and inhibition need not announce impending distress. The important point is that in these studies, an "active" reaction to strangers, as indicated by crying and avoidance, does not occur as a statistically significant phenomenon until about 12 months of age, when the child appears to have the capacity for active thought.

In most of the research on stranger fear, there is a crucial procedural step that is followed in order to elicit distress successfully. Morgan and Ricciuti (1965, pp. 253–295) explicitly demonstrated that stranger fear could not be elicited readily unless the child was physically separated from his mother—usually by a distance of at least 4 feet. This simple procedural manipulation reveals that operationally there is very little difference between the conditions necessary to elicit stranger fear and those used to demonstrate separation protest.

Separation Protest   In one of the more extensive and systematic investigations of separation distress, it was found that separation protest did not occur as a statistically significant event until about 12 months of age (Kotelchuck, 1972, 1976, pp. 329–344; Kotelchuck, Zelazo, Kagan, & Spelke, 1975). Kotelchuck observed 144 infants (12 boys and 12 girls at each age) in a series of carefully ordered sequences with mother, father, and stranger departures, occurring at 6, 9, 12, 15, 18, and 21 months of age. The child played with toys in the middle of the room equidistant from two seated adults. Unlike the stranger situation, the adults did not approach or pick up the infant, they simply departed according to a predetermined schedule after remaining in the room for 3 minutes. Crying, inhibition of play, following the adult upon departure, and touching the adult upon reunion served as the principal dependent measures.

The results for these four variables are displayed in Fig. 3.11. It can be noted that protest did not occur at 6 or 9 months of age, began at 12 months, intensified at 15 and 18 months, and declined at 21 months. An equally important finding from Kotelchuck's study is that protest was elicited when the infant was left alone with the stranger only and did not occur to mother or father separations per se. In other words, infants did not protest their mother's departure from the room, if their father remained behind. Similarly,

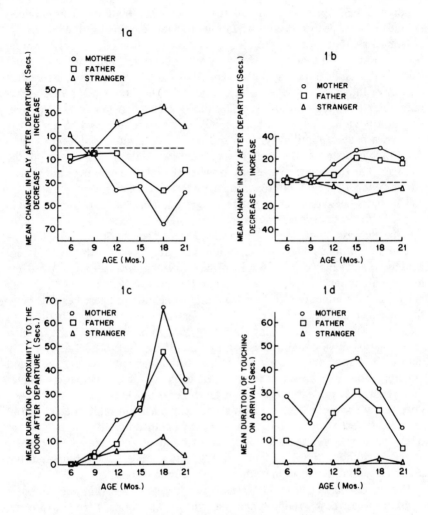

FIG. 3.11   Mean changes in duration of playing (a) and crying (b) and duration of proximity to the door following adult departure (c). Mean duration of touching occurs upon the return of the adult (d). (From Kotelchuck, M., Zelazo, P. R., Kagan, J., & Spelke, E.   Infant reactions to parental separations when left with familiar and unfamiliar adults. *Journal of Genetic Psychology*, 1975, *126*, 255-262.)

children did not protest their father's departure if their mother remained behind. Protest occurred only when the stranger remained in the room.

It may be that in both the stranger and separation sequences, a threat occurs to the child that he or she does not understand, resulting in distress. The child's understanding of the separation sequence is challenged when mother or father depart leaving him or her with the stranger in a reasonably unfamiliar situation. Similarly, the child's comprehension of the stranger situation is violated by the approaching stranger primarily when his or her mother, a base of familiarity, is at a distance. Both situations begin with a comfortable distance between the parent and child with respect to the stranger. The threat and distress occur when the relative distances are altered either by the stranger's approach or the parents' departure.

The widely held distinction between separation protest and stranger fear is blurred by the operational similarity between these situations, the results for the Kotelchuck et al. (1975) investigation of separation protest and the research on stranger fear. These similarities are at odds with the argument held by some (Ainsworth, 1969; Bowlby, 1969) that stranger anxiety reflects fear of unfamiliar people, whereas separation protest is a primary (although not exclusive) indication of infant–mother attachment. These results imply that stranger anxiety and separation protest may be closely related, if not identical, phenomena and that both may emerge as a result of the infant's changing cognitive capabilities. It may be that the year-old-infant not only detects a discrepant experience but has the capacity to question and anticipate the outcome of an event. If the capacity for thought is postulated, then separation protest and stranger fear may occur because conditions for uncertainty are created; the child may be able to ask himself or herself about the consequences of a stranger's approach or an unfamiliar situation that often includes a stranger. The capacity to activate an idea or hypothesis about a situation implies that several outcomes are possible, and the uncertainty may result in fear under these circumstances.

It may be that as a child learns through experience that separation is regularly followed by reunion and that with repeated or extended exposure, strange people become familiar (or do not produce harm), the distress diminishes. Indeed, mothers of 2-year-old children who explained both their departure and return and suggested a response during their absence, had children who protested less than mothers who did not follow these practices (Weinraub & Lewis, 1977). The explanation appears to prevent uncertainty. Moreover, in one study (Ross, Kotelchuck, Kagen, & Zelazo, 1975), 12-,

15-, and 18-month-old children protested three times as much when left alone with a stranger in an unfamiliar laboratory situation as children left with a stranger in their own homes. The results from this study imply that context plays an important role in the elicitation of separation distress and that the child assesses the consequences of the entire situation. It is reasonable to expect that an unfamiliar laboratory bears greater uncertainty than the child's home and therefore is more likely to elicit distress. Both stranger anxiety and separation protest are important social behaviors occurring toward the end of the first year that appear to be consistent with the hypothesis that the child acquires the capacity to generate ideas at this time.

Changes In The Quality Of Play

The nature of the cognitive change occurring toward the end of the first year of life is most clearly revealed through the quality of infant play. Zelazo and Kearsley (1977) showed that between 9½ months (when responding on the information-processing procedures is often constricted) and 11½ months (when reactivity often occurs specifically to the reappearance of the standard), infant play changes qualitatively. Simple stereotyped actions applied to most toys indiscriminately are replaced by the appearance of specifically appropriate functional uses. Functional play, operationally defined as the use of objects according to their appropriate adult-determined purposes, implies the emergence of specific hypotheses for specific situations.

A cross-sectional sample of 64 children, 8 infants of each sex, were examined during a 15-minute free play sequence at each of the four ages: 9½, 11½, 13½, and 15½ months. Six sets of toys lending themselves to 36 unambiguous appropriate uses were available to the children. In addition to the occurrence of functional play, relational play in which two or more objects were used in an inappropriate or idiosyncratic way and stereotypical play consisting of mouthing, waving, banging, and fingering of objects, were recorded.

The results for the three measures for each of the four ages are presented in Fig. 3.12. It can be seen that stereotypical play was highest at 9½ months and declined sharply over age. In contrast, functional play was lowest at 9½ months and increased steadily over age. It is particularly important that functional play did not become a statistically significant or reliably elicited phenomenon until 11½ months. Moreover, the mean number of different appropriate uses for the toys also emerged and increased linearly from .32 to

2.62 to 7.88 to 10.38 over the four ages from 9½ to 15½ months. Thus, there was a paradoxical increase in both the specificity and generality of object manipulations over this 6-month period. The older the child was, the more likely that he/she would know both the behaviors specific to a particular toy and the behaviors appropriate to different toys. It can also be seen in Fig. 3.12 that relational play appears to be a transitional behavior bridging the development from stereotypical to functional use of objects.

These data imply that the important change occurring over this age range is cognitive, not motoric. The neuromotor facility of the 9½-month-old infant is sufficient to perform many of the behaviors displayed by the older child; the primary change is a qualitative one that communicates the child's knowledge concerning the conventional uses for these objects. The 9½-month-old infant is very likely to bang the receiver of the toy phone, wave it, finger it, or mouth it; the 11½-month-old child is more likely to put the receiver to his or her ear, babble into it, or even attempt to dial the phone. The younger child will bang a toy spoon against a teacup or teapot, whereas the older child is more likely to stir imaginary tea, bring the spoon to his or her mouth, or even drink from the cup. What is clearly shown by the quality of the child's play is that the indiscriminate stereotypical actions of the 9½-month-old infant give way to stimulus-specific and appropriate responses by 11½ months, communicating the child's knowledge of these objects. However, the appearance of functional play is not only a vehicle of communication during this period, it is a compelling demonstration of the year-old-infant's capacity to generate specific associations readily.

SUMMARY AND CONCLUDING COMMENT

Each of the social and nonsocial situations discussed is remarkably con-sistent in revealing changes in behavior that imply a distinct change in infant cognition. Examination of the various measures presented here implies that infant responding develops from generally indiscriminate reactivity at 7½ months to inhibition at about 9½ months, followed by specific problem-related reactivity at 11½ and 13½ months. The data are in accord in showing vocalization to moderately discrepant information first occurring to the information-processing procedures at 11½ months. The research on the conservation of weight indicates that it is not until about 12 months that infants are able to predict the relation between size and weight. Moreover, a

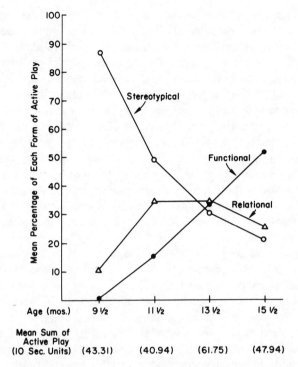

FIG. 3.12   Percentage of stereotypical, relational, and functional play at four ages between 9.5 and 15.5 months. (From Zelazo, P. R. & Kearsley, R. B. The emergence of functional play in infants: Evidence for a major cognitive transition. *Journal of Applied Developmental Psychology,* 1980,*1,* 95-117.)

reexamination of the research on separation protest and stranger anxiety implies that unambiguous "active responses" such as crying and avoidance do not reliably occur until about 12 months. The suggestion that reactions to each of these events is determined by the emergence of the capacity to generate thoughts specific to each situation is supported by the unambiguous display of appropriate uses for toys during play that first occurs for the majority of children at 11½ months and for all children in our sample by 13½ months. The data not only imply a major change in cognition around 12 months of age, but support Kagan's (1971) suggestion that the capacity for active thought—a phenomenon he called "hypothesis activation"—develops towards the end of the first year.

The many changes in behavior that occur toward the end of the first year are not likely to be coincidental. The infant is a rapidly developing, intricately coordinated and integrated organism. It is more likely that nature has provided for a common genesis for the newly displayed behaviors, including intentional vocalizations, the child's first spoken words, the functional use of objects, and "active" expressions of protest to unfamiliar and threatening persons in strange situations. It may be that the same cognitive change that permits the development of these behaviors also contributes to the child's development of independent walking (Zelazo, 1978), a view that challenges our traditional conception of sensorimotor development. These phenotypically different behaviors may be related by postulating a common cognitive prerequisite—the capacity to generate specific associations rapidly. The changes occurring in the quality of the child's play between 9½ and 13½ months illustrate that both specificity and diversity of behavior improve markedly.

It is parsimonious to postulate that the capacity to generate specific association quickly is a necessary, but not sufficient condition for the development of many of the new behaviors occurring toward the end of the first year of life. However, the fact that development of the various new behaviors is not uniform either among or within children implies that environmental factors may be essential for the expression of the basic cognitive capacity. In other words, although the basic cognitive capacity may be maturational in origin, it appears necessary for the child to have certain experiences by which he or she learns the expression of this basic ability in conventional ways. For example, it appears necessary to provide appropriate linguistic models and to reward the child's attempts to speak for productive language to occur. It appears necessary to provide experiences with other less familiar adults and with unfamiliar places for a child to resolve his or her uncertainty about strangers and strange places. It appears necessary to provide objects for a child and to demonstrate their appropriate uses, even incidentally, for functional play to occur. Each instance may be dependent upon the maturation of a common cognitive capacity, but the particular form of expression appears to be a learned phenomenon that is dependent upon a particular culture, family unit, and language. Postulating the maturation of the capacity for active thought is parsimonious because one construct appears sufficient to establish the underlying capacity for numerous changes in many domains of development and allows for the interaction of biological and environmental factors in their formation.

It might be asked why the construct "learning" is not sufficient to account for the many changes summarized here. Consider a specific instance. Why do children mouth, wave, bang, and finger objects indiscriminately at 9½ months, but use toys functionally only a few months later? To suggest that children require this time for learning to occur is not convincing because it does not account for the reasonably consistent time of onset at about 12 months. Why do children not begin to play functionally at about 5 months, for example? It must also be appreciated that the construct "learning" as used by behavioral psychologists implies a gradual process that strengthens with each trial and that is relatively specific to the object with which training occurs. The generalization of similar responses to similar objects would be expected from a learning point of view, but the occurrence of different responses to different objects as seen in the relatively rapid rise of functional play between 9½ and 15½ months is not easily accounted for. The data summarized here imply a cognitive readiness that occurs toward the end of the first year and accounts for the onset and acquisition of many new behaviors.

It is equally inadequate to postulate that neuromotor maturation alone permits the onset of these new behaviors. The 9½-month-old child displays many of the motor skills necessary to perform functional acts; it is the meaning communicated by the child's behavior, not so much the physical dexterity, that changes between 9½ and 13½ months. Bringing the receiver to the child's mouth requires much the same facility as bringing it to his or her ear. In the latter, but not the former instance, the child communicates his or her knowledge of the object's function or meaning. What neuromotor change permits the acquisition or display of this knowledge? What neuromotor change allows the child to communicate his or her thoughts through the quality of his or her play or through speech? It appears more likely that the child experiences a cognitive metamorphosis—akin to the acquisition of the capacity to generate ideas—that permits the expression, if not; the acquisition as well, of this knowledge. Contrary to the prevailing assumption of sensorimotor intelligence, it appears that the child's maturing cognitive faculties may aid the development of his/her gross and fine motor skills also (Zelazo, 1978).

The postulation of a cognitive metamorphosis during which the child acquires the capacity to generate associations readily requires some clarification. First, it should be made clear that the cognitive change occurs over a period of time; it is a range of time, not literally a point. Variation in age of onset is to be expected among children. Second, both the cognitive changes and the behavioral abilities that derive from this cognitive metamorphosis have precursors. It was suggested that the major dip in vocalization at 9½ months may be an indication of inhibition that may be a precursor of the capacity to generate specific ideas. Similarly, inhibition or wariness in social situations appears to be a precursor to active expressions of fear, including crying and withdrawal. Moreover, it was suggested that stereotypical play was a precursor to relational play, which, in turn, served as precursor to the functional use of objects. Third, the postulation of a cognitive metamorphosis does not attribute greater emphasis to maturational as opposed to environmental factors in development. It has been argued that although the hypothesized capacity to generate associations readily may be a maturational phenomenon to a large extent, the various expressions of this underlying ability appear to be heavily dependent upon environmental factors. The powerful role played by the environment is illustrated clearly in the acquisition of productive language by children with speech delays following the administration of appropriate procedures (Zelazo, Kearsley & Ungerer, 1979).

The development of procedures to detect this postulated underlying cognitive ability in the least intrusive manner, free from reliance on speech, gross and fine motor development, and the need for compliance with the examiner, has begun (Zelazo, 1979, pp. 49-83). This approach, based on reactivity to perceptual-cognitive events, carries clinical potential. Children with developmental delays who give evidence that they have passed through the postulated cognitive metamorphosis are more likely to overcome their delays with appropriate intervention. In other words, knowledge of this cognitive change and the capacity to detect the child's information-processing abilities, using procedures such as the light sequence, provide a sound basis for the application of procedures to overcome delays with speech, object manipulations, and motor development where the neurological status of the child is intact. Initial efforts at treatment with developmentally delayed children have been successful (Zelazo, 1979, pp. 49-83; Kearsley, 1979, pp. 153-180), implying that the postulation of the cognitive metamorphosis, although probably a maturational event, appears to be heavily dependent on environmental factors for its expression and possibly for its continuing development.

Finally, the infant data presented here support Bever and Mehler's observations with 2-to-5-year-old children that dips in some responses may signify changes in cognitive capacities. However, it should be cautioned that not all dips are important indicators of cognitive change. Therefore, it is necessary to derive new implications from the mechanisms hypothesized to be emerging and test for the predicted changes independently. For example, the dips in vocalization and the accompanied increased visual fixation and cardiac changes implying mental effort with the information-processing events led to the hypothesis that a major cognitive change occurs toward the end of the first year. Moreover, these and other data (Kagan, et al., 1978) implied that the capacity to generate ideas was an important aspect of this change, resulting in the operational definition of "hypothesis activation" as the functional use of objects in a free play situation. It is ironic that this hypothetico-deductive process, associated with strict behaviorism and animal research in the past, appears ideally suited for the study of major cognitive transitions in the developing child. The theme of "dips and drops in learning and developmental curves," encouraged by Bever and Mehler, promises to be a useful strategy for investigating important crests of information that are announced by troughs in development. At least for the year-old infant, these changes in behavioral indices appear to announce a cognitive metamorphosis. If the argument presented here is correct, the end of the first year of life may prove to be the dawn of active thought in the child.

REFERENCES

Ainsworth, M. D. Object relations, dependency, and attachment: A theoretical review of the infant–mother relationship. *Child Development,* 1969, *40,* 969–1025.

Bayley, N. *Bayley Scales of Infant Development,* New York: The Psychological Corporation, 1969

Bower, T. G. R.   Repetition in human development. *Merrill–Palmer Quarterly,* 1974, *20,* 303–318.

Bowlby, J.   *Attachment and Loss (Vol. 1),* New York: Basic Books, 1969.

Brooks, J., & Weinraub, M.   A history of infant intelligence testing. In M. Lewis (Ed.), *Origins of intelligence: Infancy and early childhood,* New York: Plenum Press, 1976

Bruner, J. S.   The ontogenesis of speech acts. *Journal of Child Language,* 1975, *2 ,* 1–19.

Campos, J   Heart rate: A sensitive tool for the study of emotional development. In L. Lipsitt (Ed.), *Developmental psychobiology: The significance of infancy.* Hillsdale, N.J.: Lawrence Erlbaum Associates, 1976.

Eisenberg, R. B., Coursin, D. B., & Rupp, N. R.   Habituation to an acoustic pattern as an index of difference among neonates. *Journal of Auditory Research,* 1966, *6,* 239–248.

Escalona, S. K., & Corman, H.   *Albert Einstein Scales of sensori-motor development.* Albert Einstein College of Medicine of Yeshiva University, New York, 1969.

Fagan, J. F. *Infant recognition memory and later intelligence.* Paper presented at the Biennial Meeting of the Society for Research in Child Development, San Francisco, California, March, 1979.

Fantz, R. L., & Nevis, S. *Fantz-Nevis Visual Preference Test.* Case Western Reserve, Cleveland, 1967.

Gesell, A. *The mental growth of the pre-school child,* New York: The MacMillan Co., 1925.

Griffiths, R. *The abilities of babies.* London: University of London Press, 1954.

Harding, G. G., & Golinkoff, R. M. The origins of intentional vocalizations in prelinguistic infants. *Child Development,* 1979, *50,* 33–40.

Kagan, J. On the need for relativism. *American Psychologist,* 1967, *22,* 131–142.

Kagan, J. *Change and Continuity in Infancy,* New York: Wiley, 1971.

Kagan, J., Do infants think? *Scientific American,* 1972, *226,* 74–82.

Kagan, J., Kearsley, R. B., & Zelazo, P. R. *Infancy: Its place in human development.* Cambridge, Mass.: Harvard University Press, 1978.

Kahneman, D., Tursky, B., Shapiro, D., & Crider, A. Pupillary heart rate and skin resistance changes during a mental task. *Journal of Experimental Psychology,* 1969, *79,* 164–167.

Kearsley, R. B. Iatrogenic retardation: A syndrome of learned incompetence. In R. B. Kearsley and I. Sigel (Eds.), *Infants at risk: Assessment of cognitive functioning.* Hillsdale, N. J.: Lawrence Erlbaum Associates, 1979.

Kotelchuck, M. *A child's tie to his father.* Unpublished doctoral dissertation, Harvard University, 1972.

Kotelchuck M. The infant's relationship to the father: Experimental evidence. In M. Lamb (Ed.), *The role of the father in child development.* New York: Wiley & Sons, Inc., 1976.

Kotelchuck, M., Zelazo, P. R., Kagan, J., & Spelke, E. Infant reactions to parental separations when left with familiar and unfamiliar adults. *Journal of Genetic Psychology,* 1975, *126,* 255–262.

Lewis, M. M. *How children learn to speak.* New York: Basic Books, 1959.

Lewis, M. Individual differences in the measurement of early cognitive growth. In J. Hellmuth (Ed.), *Exceptional Infant (Vol. 2),* Bainbridge Island, Washington: Brunner, Mazel, Inc., 1970.

Lewis, M., & Goldberg, S. The acquisition and violation of expectancy: An experimental paradigm. *Journal of Experimental Child Psychology,* 1969, *7,* 70–80. (a)

Lewis, M., & Goldberg, S. Perceptual–cognitive development in infancy. Generalized expectancy model as a function of the mother-infant interaction. *Merrill-Palmer Quarterly,* 1969, *15,* 81–100. (b)

Morgan, G. A., & Ricciuti, H. N. Infant's responses to strangers during the first year. In B. M. Foss (Ed.), *Determinants of Infant Behavior. (Vol. IV),* London: Meuthen & Co., 1965.

Mounoud, P., & Bower, T. G. R. Conservation of weight in infants. *Cognition,* 1974, *3,* 29–40.

Piaget, J. *The Origins of Intelligence in Children,* New York: International Universities Press, 1952. (French edition, 1936.)

Roe, K. V. Amount of infant vocalization as a function of age: Some cognitive implications. *Child Development,* 1975, *46,* 936–941.

Ross, G. Kotelchuch, M., Kagan, J., & Zelazo, P. Separation protest in infants in home and laboratory. *Developmental Psychology,* 1975, *11,* 256–257.

Scarr, S., & Salapatek, P. Patterns of fear development during infancy. *Merrill–Palmer Quarterly,* 1970, *16,* 53–87.

Schaffer, H. R. The onset of fear of strangers and the incongruity hypothesis. *Journal of Child Psychology and Psychiatry,* 1966, *7,* 95–106.

Schaffer, H. R., & Emerson, P. E. The development of social attachments in infancy. *Monographs of the Society for Research in Child Development,* 1964, *29,* (3, Whole No. 94).

Sokolov, E. N. *Perception and the Conditioned Reflex* (Translated by S. W. Wadenfeld) New York: MacMillan, 1963.

Spitz, R. *The First Year of Life,* New York: International Universities Press, 1965.

Sroufe, L. A., & Waters, E. The ontogenesis of smiling and laughter: A perspective on the organization of development in infancy. *Psychological Review,* 1976, *83,* 173–189.

Uzgiris, I., & Hunt, J. *Assessment in infancy: Ordinal scales of psychological development.* Urbana, Ill.: University of Illinois Press, 1975.

Waters, E., Matas, L., & Sroufe, L. A. Infants' reactions to an approaching stranger: Description, validation, and functional significance of wariness. *Child Development,* 1975, *46,* 348–356.

Watson, J. S. Smiling, cooing, and "the game." *Merrill–Palmer Quarterly,* 1972, *18,* 323–339.

Weinraub, M., & Lewis, M. The determinants of children's responses to separation. *Monographs of the Society for Research in Child Development,* 1977, *42,* (Serial No. 172).

Zelazo, P. R. Smiling and vocalizing: A cognitive emphasis. *Merrill–Palmer Quarterly,* 1972, *18,* 349–365.

Zelazo, P. R. From reflexive to instrumental behavior. In L. Lipsitt (Ed.), *Developmental psychobiology: The significance of infancy.* Hillsdale, N. J.: Lawrence Erlbaum Associates, 1976. (a)

Zelazo, P. R. Comments on "Genetic determinants of infant development: An overstated case." In L. Lipsitt. (Ed.), *Developmental psychobiology: The significance of infancy.* Hillsdale, N. J.: Lawrence Erlbaum Associates, 1976 (b)

Zelazo, P. R. Reactivity to perceptual–cognitive events: Application for infant asessment. In R. B. Kearsley and I. Sigel (Eds.), *Infants at risk: The assessment of cognitive functioning.* Hillsdale, N. J.: Lawrence Erlbaum Associates, 1979.

Zelazo, P. R. The development of walking during infancy: New findings and old assumptions. In J. R. Higgins, & A. Gentile (Chm.), *Movement organization in infancy and childhood.* Symposium presented at Columbia University, New York, Feb. 26, 1978.

Zelazo, P. R., Kagan, J., & Hartmann, R. Excitement and boredom as determinants of vocalization in infants. *The Journal of Genetic Psychology,* 1975, *126,* 107–117.

Zelazo, P. R., & Kearsley, R. B. *Functional play: Evidence for a cognitive metamorphosis in the year-old-infant.* Paper presented at the Biennial Meeting of the Society for Research in Child Development, New Orleans, March, 1977.

Zelazo, P. R., Kearsley, R. B., & Ungerer, J. *Learning to speak: A manual to aid the acquisition of productive language.* Boston: Center for Behavioral Pediatrics and Infant Development, 1979.

4 Trends in the Development of Imitation in Early Infancy

Olga Maratos, Ph.D.
Metera Babies' Centre
Aghioi Anargyroi Attikis
Athens, Greece

INTRODUCTION

Twelve firstborn female infants were visited bimonthly in their homes and tested for imitative responses to models perceived through three different sensory modalities; visual, auditory and kinesthetic. Results show that the imitative responses are given by some of the models as early as 1 month of age (e.g., tongue protrusion, mouth opening, and head shaking). Downward trends in the development of the imitative responses were observed between 1½ months and 3 months in some of the models and between 5 and 6 months in others. Such results show the precocity of the young infant in discriminating, processing, and reproducing models perceived through different sensory modalities. They also suggest that early cognitive development goes through a process involving early organizations, dissociations, and reorganizations of behavior during the first months of life. Imitation is viewed as a cognitive as well as a social phenomenon, functional in maintaining social communication. The trends in the early development of imitation are discussed.

Knowledge about the behavior of the newborn and the very young infant has undergone major changes during the last 15 years. The pioneering experiments of Lipsitt (1963), Siqueland and Lipsitt (1966), and Siqueland (1968), revealed the newborn's capacity to learn. The experiments of Engen,

81

Lipsitt, and Kaye (1963), showed that newborns possess a capacity for olfactory discrimination that is comparable to that of the adult, of Kobre and Lipsitt (1972) that their capacity for gustatory discrimination is also well developed, and finally the experiment of Eimas, Siqueland, Jusczyk, and Vigorito (1971) showed their capacity for subtle acoustic discrimination as early as 1 month of age. Regarding visual perception, Bower's (1966), Carpenter, (1973) and Carpenter, Tecce, Stechler and Freedman's (1970), experiments showed that it is also very well developed within the first month of life and that infants can discriminate a whole array of properties of visual stimuli. Intersensory coordination exists at birth (Wertheimer, 1961), and infants perceive within a common (homogeneous) auditory–visual space (Aronson & Rosenbloom, 1971).

In the early naturalistic observations of infant behavior, there are mentions of the imitative capacity of the newborn infant. However, such evidence was only anecdotal (Brazelton & Young, 1964; Gardner & Gardner, 1970; Valentine, 1930; Zazzo, 1957).

Animal studies during the early part of the century concluded that there is no imitation of purposive acts to be found, even among the primates (Watson, 1908). Later animal studies (Hinde, 1970; Thorpe, 1969) have stressed the importance of imitative ability in some birds, and among recent studies the term *imitation* is often used interchangeably with that of *observational learning*. No theoretical discussion has appeared so far regarding either the mechanisms involved in the occurrence of imitation or the evolutionary changes in the development of this capacity in animals.

Miller and Dollard (1941) were among the first to study imitation experimentally with children. Their account of imitative behavior was given in terms of behavior-contingency learning process, based on the paradigms of instrumental learning. There followed a series of experimental studies of imitation in children by Bandura, Ross and Ross (1966), Gewirtz and Stingle (1968), and others. Mowrer (1960) proposed that the systematic analysis of language learning provides the best paradigm for understanding imitative behavior. He labeled his theory the *Autism Theory*, because what is imitated early in life is one's own action, and habit formation is based on this process of repetition of one's own act.

According to Piaget's (1946) approach, imitation is a manifestation of the child's intelligence; the development of imitation is closely related to cognitive development during the sensorimotor period. Piaget claims that the limits of each stage in the development of imitation are set by the infant's cognitive capacity at the time. The origin of imitation, according to Piaget, is to be found in the repetition of the reflex, which becomes a circular reaction.

However, in view of the new data on the infant's precocity, it seemed timely to study experimentally the young infant's attempts at imitation, as well as the development of this capacity – if it existed.

The operational definition of imitation used in this study was the following: *imitation is a type of behavior that is descriptively similar to all or some of the characteristics of another person's behavior, or of one's own behavior, or of the movement of an object whether immediately perceived or remembered.*

The hypotheses set forward were the following:

1. Because some intersensory coordinations are present during the first month of life, imitation also will be present during that period.
2. The earliest manifestations of imitation will be limited to responses that include movements spontaneously performed by the infant.

The aims of the experimental study were: (1) to give a detailed description of imitative behavior as it develops during the first 6 months of life; (2) to make a comparison of imitative responses to three groups of models, each perceived through a different sensory modality, namely, visual, auditory, and kinesthetic; and (3) to describe and explain the regulating mechanisms and the processes present in the early development of imitation.

METHOD AND PROCEDURE

The sample consisted of 12 firstborn normal female infants selected from the population available at St. Mary's Hospital in London. All mothers belonged to the middle socioeconomic class and were the sole caretakers of their infants. Pregnancy, duration of labor, and perinatal factors were within the limits of normality (Prechtl, 1968).

Procedure

The infants were visited in their homes every 2 weeks from the age of 1 month to the age of 6 months. The visits took place immediately after a feeding. The infants were placed on a sofa in the supine position, with a pillow under the head throughout the control period and the testing session. The mother was in the same room but out of the infant's sight. The experimenter's face was within the infant's visual field and the infant could look at her at will. Before the testing session, each infant was observed for a control period of 12 minutes, during which spontaneous activities were recorded. This provided baseline data with which the infant's reactions to the tests were compared.

The Tests—Models for Imitation

The tests formed three groups that were described by the sensory modality through which they were perceived. There were visual (V) tests, kinesthetic (K) tests, and auditory (A) tests. The order of administration varied by group of tests; thus four infants were given the tests in the order VKA, four in the order AVK, and four in the order KAV. The assigned order for each child remained throughout the longitudinal study. Each test was administered three times, with an interval of 30 seconds between each administration.

Visual Tests

1. Four tongue protrusions without making any sound; this constituted one administration of the tongue-protrusion test.

2. Four tongue protrusions, accompanied by the sound "m."

3. Side-to-side rhythmical movements of the head. This test was a replication of Piaget's observations of his own children. The experimenter encouraged the infant to follow the movement of an object by moving it horizontally within the infant's visual field. In order to follow the movement of the object, the infant had to rotate her head from one side to the other at least three times. Once the head movement was thus obtained, the experimenter dropped the object and started to move her head the same way the baby was moving her own.

4. The same test as above accompanied by the sound "aa." The order of tests with or without sound was counterbalanced over infants and over ages.

5. Opening and closing of the mouth without emitting any sound; the opening and closing was repeated four times and this constituted one administration of the mouth-movements test.

Kinesthetic Test

6. The experimenter took hold of the infant's leg from the mid-calf and bent it and straightened it several times rhythmically. The test was given three times like all the others; the two legs alternated.

Auditory Tests

7.   When the baby was silent, the experimenter, while in face to face contact, emitted some vocal sounds selected from the spontaneous repertoire of infants under 1 year of age. They included single vowels and vowel groups, single consonants and consonant groups, and vowel-consonant or consonant–vowel groups. Examples: 'a', 'o', 'oa', etc., 'm', 'g', 'b', 'bvvv', 'pfff', etc., 'bu', 'ma', 'ag', etc.

8.   The recording of a baby's babbling consisting mainly of the sounds "m" and "aa" was played on a tape recorder; the duration of the recording was 15 seconds to make it comparable with the duration of the other tests. This was repeated three times with an interval of 30 seconds between the playbacks. The age of the baby in the recording was 4½ months.

9.   The recording of a baby's high-intensity crying was played on the tape recorder with a duration of 15 seconds repeated three times, allowing an interval of 30 seconds between playbacks. The age of the baby in the recording was 2 months.

During the administration of the recorded tests, there was no visual contact between the baby and the experimenter.

All auditory tests and the baby's vocal responses to them were recorded on a second tape recorder.[1]

---

[1]In the original study the group of tests included the following additional tests.

10. Sequential movements of the fingers of one hand performed by the experimenter. From 4½ months three additional tests were given.

11. The experimenter moved both hands within the infant's visual field by bringing them together and moving them apart.

12. The experimenter, positioned behind and above the infant's head, moved an object vertically within the infant's visual field. Once the infant followed three consecutive trajectories of the object, the latter was held behind and above the infant's head.

13. With the infant seated on her lap, the experimenter scratched her dress, then banged on her lap. The sequence was repeated three times.

14. The experimenter took hold of the infant's arm from the forearm and bent and straightened it several times rhythmically. The two arms alternated.

15. The experimenter took hold of the infant's both legs from the mid-calf, then bent and straightened them several times rhythmically with alternation of the movement in a "bicycle-like" movement.

The results to the above tests are not discussed, as no downward trend was observed in the development of the imitative response during the first 6 months of life. Imitative responses increased with age to all the foregoing tests, Nos. 10–15 (Maratos, 1973b).

THE BEHAVIOR CATEGORIES

The same behavior categories were coded during the control and experimental periods and across all tests. To say that a response is imitative, it is
essential to show that it is similar to the behavior of the model and that it occurs in response to it. It is also essential to show that it occurs (1) more frequently following the model than during the control period; and (2) in response
to a particular model (e.g., visual, auditory, or kinesthetic) and not equally to
each model.

The behavior categories that were observed and recorded during both the
control and the experimental conditions (with no stimulation, or during the
reaction time to each test) were the following:
— arousal (i.e. uncoordinated vigorous movements of all four limbs).
— head movements, side-to-side or vertical, rhythmical or not.
— arm movements, single or both hands.
— hand and finger movements, specifying if closed fist or open fingers.
— leg and foot movements, single or both legs, or feet.
— scanning the environment.
— eye fixation, specifying the object of fixation.
— looking away.
— mouth movements, specifying if sucking in the void, hand, finger, or any
  other object.
— tongue movements (i.e. licking or movements of the tongue inside the
  mouth).
— tongue protrusion as distinct from licking or tongue movements inside the
  mouth.
— smiling.
— whimpering and fussing.
— crying.
— vocalisation (i.e. any discrete voiced sound, excluding whimpering,
  crying, or indeterminate digestive sounds).

A second observer was present at ten of the 132 visits and recorded the
infants' behavior. Interobserver reliability reached .83.[2]

The different order in which the models were administered did not have

---

[2]Some sessions were recorded on videotapes and there are films available, illustrating the
typical imitative responses of infants of different ages to the tests administered for imitation.

TABLE 4.1.

Comparison of Means of Mean Responses Per Infant for Experimental Condition (Imitative)[a] With Control Condition (Occurring Spontaneously)[b]

Response	Age	Experimental Condition	Control Condition	t	Level of Sign
Tongue protrusion	1 month	5.67	.58	3.85	.005
Head movement	1 month	7.00	1.41	5.08	.005
Head movement	1.5 months	5.00	1.32	2.99	.01
Head movement	2 months	6.32	1.99	3.00	.01
Head movement	2.5 months	5.33	1.98	2.86	.01
Head movement	3 months	7.66	2.41	4.56	.005
Babbling	4.5 months	8.67	3.59	3.82	.005
Babbling	5 months	7.67	2.51	4.06	.005
Babbling	5.5 months	10.00	2.92	6.22	.005
Babbling	6 months	5.68	3.01	1.59	n.s.
Crying	1 month	4.66 (contagious)	0.00	3.00	0.1
Crying	1.5 months	2.00 (contagious)	0.17	1.50	n.s.
Crying	4 months	7.67 (imitative)	0.00	4.92	.005
Crying	4.5 months	7.67 (imitative)	0.00	4.92	.005
Crying	5 months	7.67 (imitative)	0.00	4.92	.005
Crying	5.5 months	7.01 (imitative)	0.00	5.80	.005
Crying	6 months	4.33 (imitative)	0.00	2.86	.01

[a]The mean responses to the tongue-protrusion and to the head-movement models during the experimental condition are responses to the silent models.
[b]Number of subjects = 12. Number of possible responses per subject at: experimental condition = 3, control condition = 12.

any effect on the frequency of the imitative response to the models for imitation.

RESULTS

The main results of this study show that: (1) as early as 1 month of age there is imitation, but it is limited to certain types of models, namely, at least two

TABLE 4.2.
Comparison of Frequency of the Same Response When Imitative and When
Given to Another Model During the Experimental Condition: Number of
Observations = 36 (3 responses × 12 infants at each age level)

Compared Models for Imitation	Response	Age	t	Level of Sign
TP—HM	Tongue protrusion	1 m.	4.70	.005
TP—HM	Tongue protrusion	1.5 m.	4.12	.005
TP—RB	Tongue protrusion	1 m.	3.90	.005
TP—RB	Tongue protrusion	1.5 m.	3.75	.005
HM—TP	Head movement	1 m.	3.87	.005
HM—TP	Head movement	1.5 m.	3.50	.005
HM—TP	Head movement	2 m.	5.79	.005
HM—TP	Head movement	2.5 m.	3.38	.005
HM—TP	Head movement	3 m.	5.33	.005
HM—VS	Head movement	1 m.	3.87	.005
HM—VS	Head movement	1.5 m.	3.50	.005
HM—VS	Head movement	2 m.	4.82	.005
HM—VS	Head movement	2.5 m.	3.38	.005
HM—VS	Head movement	3 m.	5.33	.005
RC—RB	Crying–"imitative"	4 m.	3.57	.005
RC—RB	Crying–"imitative"	4.5 m.	4.05	.005
RC—RB	Crying–"imitative"	5 m.	4.87	.005
RC—RB	Crying–"imitative"	5.5 m.	4.63	.005
RC—HM	Crying–"imitative"	4 m.	4.92	.005
RC—HM	Crying–"imitative"	4.5 m.	4.92	.005
RC—HM	Crying–"imitative"	5 m.	4.92	.005
RC—HM[a]	Crying–"imitative"	5.5 m.	5.80	.005

[a] Key to abbreviations: TP = Tongue-protrusion model (silent); HM = Head-movement model (silent); RB = Recorded babbling model; VS = vocal sounds performed by the experimenter; RC = recorded crying model.

facial grimaces, head movements, and some vocal models, and (2) there is a waning of these first imitative responses within the first 6 months of life.

Table 4.1 shows that imitative responses, although present in the spontaneous repertoire of the infant, as observed during the control period, were given significantly more often when the appropriate model was presented than when there was no stimulation.

Table 4.2 shows that imitative responses are given reliably to the relevant models and are not part of a state of general arousal or a non specific response of the infants to stimulation.

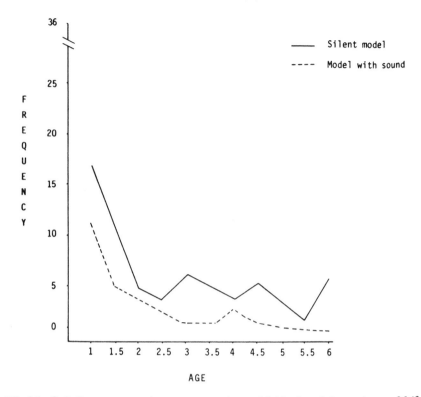

FIG. 4.1   Imitative response to the tongue protrusion model. Number of observations = 36 (3 responses x 12 infants at each age level).

For the statistical analysis of the trends in the development of the imitative responses through the first 6 months, the data were cast in age by frequency-of-response contingency tables. Trends within these tables were analyzed using Kendall's tau (τ), which gives the magnitude and direction of the trend, and z, which would indicate the statistical significance of the trend.

Trend tests were thus computed for the development of imitative responses to each test. Graphs were visually inspected and trend analyses were carried out for selected age levels. Similar analyses were done to test for trends in the development of spontaneous behavior categories.[3]

---

[3]The author is deeply indebted to Dr. Patrick Humphreys for his advice and help in the statistical analysis of this work.

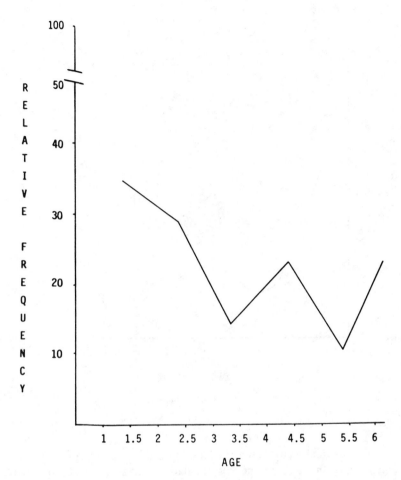

FIG. 4.2   Imitative response to the mouth opening model. Number of observations varies with age.

Fig. 4.1 shows the frequency at which the tongue-protrusion response was given to the tongue-protrusion model. The trend is quite clear and reaches signficance between 1 and 2 months. At 1 month all infants, except one, gave at least one imitative response to the tongue-protrusion model; by 2 months most infants stopped imitating the model, except one infant who kept

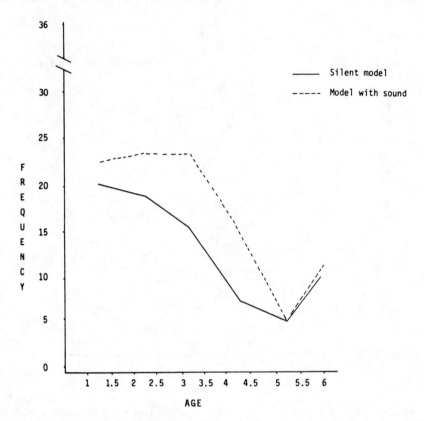

FIG. 4.3 Imitative response to the head movement model. Number of observations = 36 (3 responses x 12 infants at each age level).

imitating the model of tongue protrusion; it was discovered later that this infant was reinforced by her father for sticking the tongue out, as this became a privileged means of connumication between them. This finding suggests that learning takes place with respect to the response, and further research is needed to clarify the role of adult reinforcing of the imitative response of the infant. The author agrees with Meltzoff and Moore (1977) that reinforcing does not explain the imitative responses within the first 2 months of life but may be important for maintaining the response after it tends to disappear.

Fig. 4.2 shows the frequency of mouth movements given as a response to

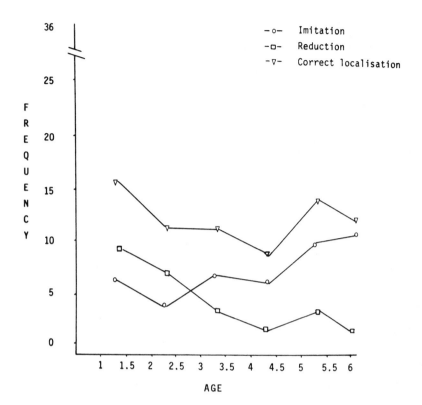

FIG. 4.4   Response to the one-leg movement model. Number of observations = 36 (3 responses x 12 infants at each age level).

the mouth-opening model. The general downward trend is the same for tongue protrusion, reaching significance between 1 and 3 ½ months.

It is worth noting that the downward trend of imitative response follows the downward trend of the spontaneous occurrence of mouth and tongue movements. In fact, the downward trend of the development of the spontaneous mouth movements also reached significance between 1 and 6 months. However, it is to be noted that the imitative responses to the mouth-opening model disappeared earlier than spontaneous similar behavior.

Fig. 4.3 shows the frequency of the imitative response to the head

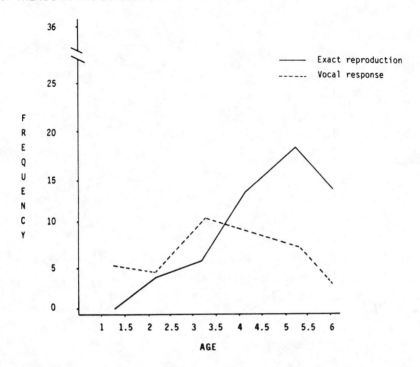

FIG. 4.5 Response to the recorded babbling model. Number of observations = 36 (3 responses x 12 infants at each age level).

movement model.[4] The downward trend reached significance between the ages of 2½ and 4 months.

Figure 4.4 shows the frequency of: (1) the imitative response to the one-leg movement model (this response involves only the correct leg, to the exclusion of any other behavior); (2) the response that was called "reduction," that is, the correct leg exclusively, but instead of the leg it is the foot that moved rhythmically up and down; and (3) the "correct localization" curve, which

---

[4]A *t* test was carried out to test for differences in the vocal response given to the tongue-protrusion and the head-movement models, depending on the presence of sound in the model. It showed that differences were significant for both models ($p < .001$).

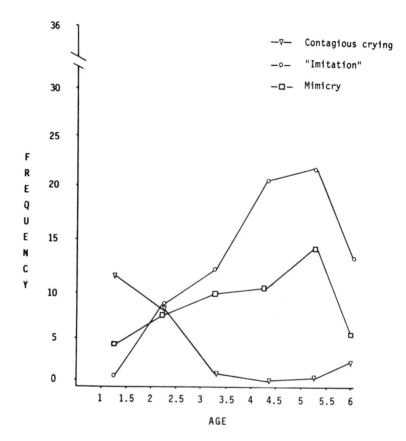

FIG. 4.6   Response to the recorded crying model. Number of observations = 36 (3 responses x 12 infants at each age level).

represents the imitative response and the "reduction" response put together. It is worth noting that a slight downward trend is obtained between 1 and 2½ months if one looks at the "correct localization" curve only, which does not reach statistical significance.

Finally, the responses to the auditory tests show similar developmental trends.

Fig. 4.5 shows the frequency of: (1) the exact reproduction of the recorded babbling model, that is, the vocal response including the sounds 'm' and/or 'a' exclusively; and (2) any other vocal response. Frequency increased with age at the beginning of its development but also started decreasing after 5½ months. The downward trend reaches statistical significance. The infants were followed up to 6 months only, so it is not known whether this downward trend would have continued.

Fig. 4.6 shows the frequency of the response given to the recorded crying model. The first type of response obtained for this model was "contagious crying," that is, the infant started crying upon hearing the model and did not stop unless picked up and comforted. This was the most common reaction until 2½ months and then disappeared. From 2½ months onward, the response called "imitation" started to occur and its frequency increased with age. It is interesting to note that this response decreased sharply between 5 and 6 months, this downward trend reaching statistical significance. This "imitative" response does not result in crying; it involves whimpering and vocal responses containing the vowel 'a' in an attempt of the infant to imitate the crying she heard. A third type of response to the recorded crying model was noted, namely mimicry, or the crying face the infant showed upon hearing the recorded model. This type of response increased between 2 and 5 months, then decreased sharply. Both trends reached statistical significance.

TABLE 4.3.
Imitative Response Trends[a]

Model for Imitation	Age Levels (in Months)	τ	z	Level of Sign
Tongue protrusion (silent)	1–2	−0.404	2.711	.01
Tongue protrusion (with sound)	1–2	−0.283	1.850	.05
Head movement (silent)	2.5–4	−0.258	2.073	.05
Head movement (with sound)	3–4.5	−0.204	1.631	n.s.
Mouth opening	1–3.5	−0.783	1.941	.05
Recorded babbling	5–6	−0.282	1.848	.05
Recorded crying	1–3	−0.485	3.172	.001
Recorded crying	5–6	−0.248	1.694	.05
One-leg movement	1–3	−0.205	1.532	n.s.

[a]The following imitative responses showed a positive trend, (i.e. their frequency increased with age): babbling, between 2–5.5 months, p < .001; finger movements, between 1–3 months, p < .001; scratching and banging, between 4.5–6 months, p < .001; and response to the vertical object movement, between 4.5–6 months, p < .01.

TABLE 4.4.
Spontaneous Behavior Trends

Behavior Category	Age Levels (in Months)	τ	z	Level of Sign
Mouth and tongue movements	1–6	−0.406	3.668	.001
Finger movements	1–4.5	0.322	2.114	.05
Vocalizations	1–3.5	0.401	2.510	.001

Finally, it is worth mentioning that although the infant's vocal responses to the experimenter's vocal sounds have not been included in this experimental study because of the unstructured way in which they were presented and because of the technical inadequacies of the recording equipment, the results can be considered as pilot. They indicate once more a manifestation of the phenomenon of a dip in the developmental curves.

From pilot work and the tentative analyses of data,[5] it is suggested that very young infants tend to imitate the pitch and the duration of a sound that they hear rather than the phonetic characteristics of a sound, as early as 1½ months of age, and that this capacity is later lost or taken over by the imitation of the phonetic characteristics of a sound around 4 months of age (Maratos, 1974).

Tables 4.3 and 4.4 summarize the trends of the development of the imitative responses and their statistical signifance at the different age levels, as well as the trends in the development of spontaneous behavior as observed during the control period.

DISCUSSION

From the point of view of cognitive development, these findings indicate that the infant at 1 month of age: (1) possesses a good discriminative capacity to perceive incoming information; and (2) also possesses intersensory

[5]The author is grateful to Dr. Anthony Costello of the Medical Research Council Unit for Environmental Factors, in London, who helped with this analysis, and to Dr. Anthony Hoare. who designed the apparatus for the technical analysis of these data.

coordination, as is shown by the successful imitation of models perceived through a different modality than the one that is used for the reproduction of the perceived model.

The unexpected finding of this experiment was the imitation of models that involve parts of the body that are not known visually (e.g. tongue and mouth movements). In such cases the interpretation of simultaneous matching of the model and imitative responses is inadequate. Such findings would lead to the hypothesis that the 1-month-old possesses a certain notion of his body schema; further evidence of such a hypothesis would be illustrated by the imitation of even more differentiated movements, such as lip protrusion, sucking movements, etc. This capacity of the newborn and older infant is by now well documented by the work of Meltzoff and Moore (1977), and Kaye and Marcus (1978). Meltzoff and Moore have confirmed our own finding of the imitation of the tongue-protrusion and the mouth-opening movements, and they have shown that as early as 2 weeks of age, infants imitate differentially three different facial grimaces and one manual gesture.

Some help in understanding such findings might come from the description of embryological development, and more specifically of the successive appearance of spontaneous movements and reflexes during embryological development. Humphrey's research data (1964, 1971) show in fact that the first movements to be observed in the fetus are in response to stimulation around the mouth. Spontaneous performance of the same movements is observed very early; at 14 weeks of embryonic life, tongue movements can already be observed. The fact that the prenatal history of the infant is relevant for understanding the course of development of early postnatal behavior has also been stressed by Prechtl (1969).

Another relevant fact is the coordination of reflexes that exists at birth, to be observed in the rooting reflex, which is also found in the fetus; Humphrey has called it prerooting (1964). Other examples of such coordination are the palmomental and the Babkin reflexes.

Mounoud (1971, 1974) has pointed out the coordination of postural reflexes that exists at birth and maintains that the organized totality of the reflexes becomes dissociated to allow for new differentiations to appear in the course of sensorimotor development.

The questions to be asked in this particular case of early imitation are mainly three: (1) why is the behavior lost in the course of early development? (2) in what way is the initial imitative behavior similar, or does it form the basis for the reconstruction of the behavior that will reappear later in the development? (3) does this early imitation, especially of the movements of the body that are invisible to one's self, necessarily imply a capacity for differentiation of the self in relation to the nonself?

One fact that must be stressed as far as the development of imitative behavior is concerned is that the downward trends are observed at different age levels to the different models (by 2 months for the tongue protrusion and for the mouth opening, by 2½ months for the contagious crying, and probably by around 4 months for the imitation of the pitch of vocal sounds). One could argue that the infant either loses his or her ability to discriminate incoming information or that he or she loses the motor ability to reproduce the model. However, it is well established that both the discriminative capacity and motor ability of infants increase with age. The author believes that it is more likely that the capacity for processing incoming information is momentarily lost. The state of organization of the reflexes that is present during the first few months of life permits the infant to assimilate external information into reflex schemes that are known to him or her and practiced through circular reactions. The dissociation process, and in this case the dissociation of the reflex coordination, would have to be present for a relatively long time, at least during the first 6 months of life, if it were to account for the loss of imitative capacity. As there is evidence that reflex coordination is in fact dissociated gradually and that the different reflexes disappear at different times during postnatal development, it seems plausible that the dissociation process may account for the dissociation of the imitative response as well.

Furthermore, it is the author's belief that imitation is functional in eliciting and maintaining social interaction of the infant with the human beings in his environment. Mutual imitation is a privileged form of communication before smiling and vocal responses develop. It is suggested, therefore, that the downward trend in the imitative response of facial grimaces coincides with the appearance of smiling and vocalizations that become more powerful means and forms of communication between mother and infant.

To answer the second question, namely, whether the initial response is similar to the later one, more research is needed, but some information is available from the pilot work (Maratos 1973a and 1973b) that preceded this experimental study, which indicates that although the end response (i.e., tongue protrusion) is similar in the two age levels at which it has been observed, namely 1 month and 9 months, the accompanying responses and the latency of the response differ. The 1-month old eventually sticks her tongue out, but goes through a long period of trial and error with accompanying tongue and mouth movements, and, once there is tongue protrusion, the behavior is repeated several times, in the manner of circular reactions as described by Baldwin (1925) and Piaget (1946). The 9-month old who imitates tongue protrusion behaves in a different way; that is, observes for a longer time and, after a long latency, imitates by using the appropriate behavior exclusively without having to try related responses first. Thus, although we believe that the first occurrence of the behavior forms the basis for its later reoccurrence we also believe that as cognition develops, the later stages are characterized by more differentiated and integrated behaviors and do not simply repeat an earlier form of the same behavior.

The author agrees entirely with Piaget's (1946) account of imitation as being the attempt of the infant to accommodate his schemes to the models offered by the external world. This is shown precisely by the attempts of the infant to use known schemes—patterns of behavior—in his first attempts of approximation of his behavior to the model, schemes that are then differentiated further until a perfect match is obtained. It is also worth noting that the first models that are imitated are the ones that resemble the infant's spontaneous and most frequent movements, in other words, movements that are assimilated to the infant's schemes at the particular stage of development, even if these are known to the infant only proprioceptively.

Finally, the third question, namely, of the necessity of differentiation of self from nonself for imitation to occur, is the most difficult one to answer, as one can only speculate; there is not sufficient evidence at this stage of knowledge to argue one way or the other. However, as there is evidence that imitative behavior at 1 month differs from the behavior at 9 months, and, as in other sections of cognitive development (e.g., object permanence, visual—motor coordination, stranger reaction, etc.), the differentiation of self from the nonself develops from a nondifferentiation state toward a perfect differentiation of self in relation to the environment, one could argue that the notion of differentiation of self from the nonself is not necessary to account for the early imitative responses that were observed in this study. Even though the infant seems to have a certain notion of his body schema, this does not necessarily mean that the self is fully differentiated from the nonself nor that all actions are controlled and identified as intentional acts. Further research is needed in the area of differentiation between self and others in the first months of life, possibly with experiments using mirror responses, in order to answer this question more reliably.

ACKNOWLEDGMENTS

This is a summary of results based on data collected between 1971 and 1973 for the author's doctoral dissertation entitled "The origin and development of imitation in the first six months of life", University of Geneva, July 1973. The supervisors of this thesis were Prof. Bärbel Inhelder and Prof. Pierre Mounoud, to whom the author is grateful for their guidance and fruitful discussions. The writer also wishes to express her gratitude to Dr. J.A. Ambrose for his support and help through all stages of this work, which was carried out at the Behaviour Development Research Unit, St. Mary's Hospital Medical School, University of London.

REFERENCES

Aronson, E., & Rosenbloom, S. Space perception in early infancy: perception within a common auditory–visual space. *Science,* 1971, *172,* 1161.

Baldwin, J.M. *Mental development in the child and the race.* London: Macmillan, 1925.

Bandura, A., Ross, D., & Ross, S.A. Some social antecedents of imitative behavior. In Y. Brackbill & G. G. Thompson (Eds.), *Behavior in infancy and early childhood.* New York: Free Press, 1966.

Bower, T. G. R. The visual world of infants. *Scientific American,* 1966, 215, 80–92.

Brazelton, T. B. & Young, G. C. An example of imitative behavior in a nine-week-old infant. *Journal of American Academy of Child Psychiatry,* 1964, *3,* 53–67.

Carpenter, G. C. *Mother–stranger discrimination in the early weeks of life.* Paper presented at the biennial meeting of the Society for Research in Child Development, Philadelphia, 1973.

Carpenter, G. C., Tecce, J. J., Stechler, G. & Freedman, S. Differential visual behavior to human and humanoid faces in early infancy. *Merrill–Palmer Quarterly,* 1970, *16,* 1.

Eimas, P. D., Siqueland, E. R., Jusczyk, P. & Vigorito, J. Speech perception in infants. *Science,* 1971, *171,* 303–306.

Engen, T., Lipsitt, L. P. & Kaye, H. Olfactory responses and adaptation in the human neonate. *Journal of Comparative and Physiological Psychology,* 1963, *56,* 1, 73–77.

Gardner, J. & Gardner, H. A note on selective imitation by a six-week old infant. *Child Development,* 1970, *41,* 1209–1213.

Gewirtz, J. L. & Stingle, K. G. Generalized imitation learning as the basis for identification. *Psychological Review,* 1968, *75,* 5, 374–397.

Hinde, R. A. The development of bird song. In K. Connolly (Ed.), *Mechanisms of motor skill development.* London: Academic Press, 1970.

Humphrey, T. Embryology of the central nervous system: with some correlation with functional development. *The Alabama Journal of Medical Sciences,* 1964, *1,* 1, 60–64.

Humphrey, T. Development of oral and facial motor mechanisms in human fetuses and their relation to cranio–facial growth. *Journal of Dental Research,* 1971, *50* (6, Pt. 1), 1428–1441.

Kaye, K. and Marcus, J. Imitation over a series of trials without feedback. *Infant Behavior and Development,* 1978, *1,* 141.

Kobre, K. R. & Lipsitt, L. P. A negative contrast effect in newborns. *Journal of Experimental Child Psychology*, 1972, *14*, 1, 81–91.

Lipsitt, L. P. Learning in the first year of life. In L. P. Lipsitt & C. C. Spiker (Eds.), *Advances in child development and behavior*. New York: Academic Press, 1963.

Maratos, O. *The origin and development of limitation in the first six months of life*. Paper presented to the British Psychological Society, Liverpool, 1973(a).

Maratos, O. The origin and development of imitation in the first six months of life. Doctoral dissertation, University of Geneva, 1973(b).

Maratos, O. Trends in the development of vocal imitation in the first six months of life. Presented to the British Psychological Society, Bangor, England, 1974.

Meltzoff, A. N. & Moore, M. K. Imitation of facial and manual gestures by human neonates. *Science*, 1977, *198*, 75–78.

Miller, N. E. & Dollard, J. *Social learning and imitation*. New Haven: Yale University Press, 1941.

Mounoud, P. Développement des systémes de représentation et de traitement chez l'enfant. *Bulletin de psychologie*, 1971, *25*, 5–7, 261–272.

Mounoud, P. La construction de l'objet par le bébé. *Bulletin d'Audiophonologie*, 1974, *4*, 419–438.

Mowrer, O. H. Learning theory and the symbolic processes. London: Wiley, 1960.

Piaget, J. *La formation du symbole chez l'enfant. Image, jeu et rêve. Image et représentation*. Neuchâtel et Paris: Delachaux et Niestlé, 1946.

Prechtl, H. F. R. Neurological findings in newborn infants after pre- and paranatal complications. In J. H. P. Jonxis, H. K. A. Visser & J. A. Toelstra (Eds.), *Aspects of praematurity and dysmaturity*. Leiden: Stenferd Kreose, 1968.

Prechtl, H. F. R. Brain and behavioural mechanisms in the human newborn infant. In R. J. Robinson (Ed.), *Brain and early behaviour*. London: Academic Press, 1969.

Siqueland, E. R. & Lipsitt, L. P. Conditioned head turning in human newborns. *Journal of Experimental Child Psychology*, 1966, *3*, 356–376.

Siqueland, E. R. Reinforcement patterns and extinction in human newborns. *Journal of experimental Child Psychology*, 1968, *6*, 431–442.

Thorpe, W. H. The significance of vocal imitation in animals with special reference to birds. *Acta biologica exp.*, 1969, *29*, 251–269.

Valentine, C. The psychology of imitation with special references to early childhood. *British Journal of Psychology*, 1930, *21*, 105.

Watson, J. B. Imitation in monkeys. *Psychological Bulletin*, 1908, *5*, 169.

Wertheimer, M. Psychomotor coordination of auditory and visual space at birth. *Science*, 1961. *134*, 1692.

Zazzo, R. Le problème de l' imitation chez le nouveau-né. *Enfance*, 1957, *10*, 135–142.

5 Regressions and Transformations during Neurological Development

Heinz F.R. Prechtl
Department of Developmental Neurology
University Hospital
Groningen, The Netherlands

INTRODUCTION

Development of neural structure and function has been viewed as a continuous and linear process in which an immature nervous system is transformed into its final adult form by the addition here and there of bits and pieces in a progressive way. Such a concept is insufficient in that it neglects a series of phenomena occurring during human and animal development, such as the disappearance of ontogenetic adaptations specific for early stages, and other discontinuities such as temporary relapses or regressions during the developmental process. This becomes especially apparent once the neurobehavioral repertory of the young infant is no longer accepted as being simply an insufficient and imperfect antecedent of adult traits.

The appreciation of the competence of early neurobehavioral mechanisms opened a new and fresh approach into the study of developmental processes of brain and behavior. Although far from being understood at present, mechanisms controlling progress as well as regress of neural structures and functions have been recognized. It is of great importance to realize that both these processes are essential in normal ontogenetic development.

Although not intended as a complete list of known signs of regression in ontogeny, a number of examples may illustrate the large variety of such phenomena. They include discontinuities in the development of neural structures such as neuronal cell death and the regression of specific neuronal elements of a transient nature. In the domain of neural functions, transient behavior patterns will be described that have a specific adaptive significance during a certain period of development. Another example of regressions are inconsistencies in the sequence of transformations of certain functions during their developmental course, as in the case of locomotion and grasping. They indicate not only how new forms of motor patterns take over from previous ones, but also which type of mechanisms may be involved in these transitions. Finally, regressions of neural functions will be mentioned that may be due to shifts of an equilibrium in the contribution of sensory systems or motor patterns. Originally dominant functions may become temporarily or permanently subordinate to other functions, which then become dominant. All these examples indicate that developmental progress includes steps of regression and resolution. Although reptiles, birds, and mammals do not show metamorphosis of their physical appearance, the changes in the neurobehavioral repertory resemble such a process even in the higher vertebrates. Changes in the complexity during development may entail loss of previously acquired properties. If looked at in terms of their mechanisms, these functions are not necessarily mere simple precursors for the later and more complex functions.

Discontinuities, relapses, and regressions may appear as *dips* in the developmental course of neural functions. The term "dips" is no more than a metaphor to describe a wide range of analogous phenomena whose underlying mechanisms may differ completely.

TRANSIENT BRAIN MORPHOLOGY

Even in nonmetamorphic vertebrates the developing brain undergoes transformations that consist not only of the addition of newly formed elements, but also of the disappearance of elements that seem to be functional at certain early stages. Neuronal cell death has been recognized as a fundamental mechanism of neurogenesis. Neurons are formed abundantly in various parts of the nervous system. Considerable numbers undergo degeneration during embryonic life despite having made functional connections. Although all the mechanisms regulating neuronal cell death are not yet understood, it is clear that an excess of neurons is eliminated (for review see Jacobson, 1978), and that a similar fate befalls many axons. There seems to be a relationship between the size of the target area of innervation (Sohal & Weidmann, 1978) and the number of surviving axons as well as neurons. Experimental manipulation of the target such as an increase in size can lessen the reduction in cell number (Hollyday & Hamburger, 1976). The reduction in the number of axons is related not only to neuronal cell death, but also, and even more importantly, to the elimination of collateral axon sprouts. Polyneuronal innervation has been found not only in fetal and infant muscles (Changeux, 1979; Redfern, 1970), but also in central neurons in the spinal cord (Conradi & Ronnevi, 1975), in the cerebellar Purkinje cells (Puro & Woodward, 1978), and in cortical neurons (Huttenlocher, 1979). All these studies indicate clearly that the synaptic contacts of developing muscle cells and central neurons are innervated by more neurons than there are in later stages and adulthood. Hence, the developing neural structure undergoes a true discontinuity and regression. Such a remodeling, affecting differentiated and functional elements, is a significant mechanism in normal development of the nervous system.

Besides these examples where quantitative reductions in existing classes of elements occur, there are other examples of elements that are transient in the sense that, following a limited period of existence, all members of the class disappear. They may serve particular tasks during development and are afterwards removed. A good example are the radial glial cells, which appear in early embryonic stages. They span the distance between the ventricular and pial surface in the developing telencephalon and cerebellum and are believed to act as a scaffolding and guide for migrating neurons. They disappear after the migration phase and may reappear as astroglial cells (Choi & Lapham, 1978; Rakic, 1978; Schmechel & Rakic, 1979).

The socalled Cajal–Retzius cells in the cerebral cortex also belong to the category of transient cells. These disappear in the human during the last part of gestation. Their function and exact fate is not yet clear, but they may be involved in a neurogenetic function (Persinger & Robb, 1976).

As a final example of transient structures, the dorsal horn cells in the fetal spinal cord of monkeys deserve mention. Although they receive afferent fibers from the spinal ganglia, they degenerate later and are replaced by another population of neurons (Knyihar, Csillik, & Rakic, 1978). While they are present (31st and 55th day of gestation), the first spinal reflexes appear (Bodian, 1968).

The aforementioned processes of remodeling in the developing nervous system seem to be strongly related to activity. Spinal cell death and disappearance of polyneuronal innervation of muscles can be delayed when activity of the neuromotor system is pharmacologically blocked (Pittmann & Oppenheim, 1978) or mechanically altered (Benoit & Changeux, 1975).

TRANSIENT NEURAL FUNCTIONS

The neurobehavioral repertory of young infants consists of a series of motor patterns that adapt the infant to the organismic requirements in his specific environment. Some of these patterns, such as those for feeding, are of a transient nature.

Let us take as a first example the rooting response of the human newborn (Prechtl, 1958). Prematures and some full-term newly born infants show rhythmical side-to-side movements of the head when a gentle stroke is given to the cheek or to a corner of the mouth. After some days, these rhythmic movements are replaced by directed and graded head turning movements toward the stimulating source, which results in its being reached with the mouth and grasped with the lips. Even when this pattern has been established for some time, a hungry baby may show again the ontogenetically earlier form of rhythmic rooting. Both neural patterns coexist for a period of time, until the earlier form disappears completely. The directed rooting to tactile stimulation is in its turn later replaced by visually directed head and mouth movements. It seems likely that the earlier motor patterns are merged in the later forms, but relapses into the earlier form are still possible for a certain time. (For a comparative study of other mammalian species see Prechtl & Schleidt, 1950, 1951).

The motor pattern for food intake is even more complexly organized than rooting but is likewise present for only a relatively short time in early development. What has wrongly been called the sucking "reflex" consists not only of rhythmical mouth, tongue, and jaw movements, but also requires an intricate coordination with swallowing and breathing. There exists a concomitant posture that occurs during sucking—a flexor synergism in the arms and fingers and an extension of the legs (Casaer, 1979, Prechtl & Lenard, 1968). The degree of expression of this posture depends on the vigor of the ongoing sucking. The rhythmical sucking movements themselves seem to be a centrally generated pattern similar to the chewing movements in the adult (Dellow & Lund, 1971). Complex neural mechanisms such as rooting and sucking are specific adaptations of young mammals to feeding with milk. When no longer needed after early life, they obviously disappear. They are not necessarily indispensable as precursors of other later developing mechanisms for intake of solid food. At the developmental transition of these two mechanisms there is sometimes a labile period during which feeding is less than optimal.

Other transient neural functions, restricted to early infancy, include the palmar and plantar reflexes, consisting of a flexion of fingers and toes after tactile stimulation of the inner side of hand and foot, and the Moro response, a rapid extension and abduction of the arms, followed by an adduction and flexion as a response to a brief vibration to the head. This vestibular response can be converted into a pure adduction and flexion pattern when a stretch is exerted on the arms previous to and during the eliciting stimulus (Prechtl, 1965). A further spectacular example is the stepping movements of neonates (Peiper, 1963). They consist of alternating leg movements, which occur when the awake infant is supported by an examiner in vertical suspension in such a way that the feet are touching the ground. When properly held, most infants can perform several steps, but often the feet become entangled because of the dominating adductor tonus, which causes the O-shaped legs to cross each other (Prechtl, 1953a). These stepping movements are transient and disappear 4 to 6 weeks after birth. The significance of these transient functions is not always so obvious as in the case of rooting and sucking. Palmar and plantar grasp response and the Moro response have outlived their adaptive significance in human evolution but have retained their purpose in the case of other primates. They are adjustments to the close contact with the fur on the mother, on whose body the young live. In the human infant they became vestigial functions. This explanation does not seem applicable to the stepping movements. Their nature still remains obscure. To what degree they are precursors of the later walking is not clear.

There may be anticipations of later functions, as is known from other examples. Neural circuits may develop and even become functional at a time when they are not yet needed. A striking example is provided by the episodic breathing movements of the fetus in the uterus, which have been rediscovered by Dawes (1973). Although described originally by Ahlfeld in 1888, they were neglected until their recent demonstration with ultrasound scanning technique. Breathing movements appear in development before they fulfill their ultimate role (i.e., gas exchange after birth). Their presence in the human fetus already 4 months before birth may not be without significance in another respect. At least in the rabbit fetus, fetal breathing movements have been shown to be important for an adequate differentiation of the fetal lung tissue (Wigglesworth & Desai, 1979). Moreover, in the rat fetus the innervation of the intercostal muscles may be related to the fetal breathing movements. Aberrant connections of intercostal nerves with "wrong" intercostal muscles are eliminated during fetal life after 18 days (Dennis & Harris, 1979).

Fetal motor patterns anticipating their ultimate function are therefore by no means only an early excercise of later patterns, though this may not always be obvious. In the case of the "smiling" in premature or full-term infants, which occurs during REM sleep or quiet wakefulness and involves one or both sides of the face, they appear spontaneously long before they become linked with a releasing visual stimulus—the face of the caretaker. This anticipatory motor pattern is so strikingly similar to the mature social smiling that it can be easily recognized by an observer. However, for a long time the dominating rule of the stimulus–response and of the reflex paradigms led people to call them grimaces elicited by gas pains, or "gastric smiles" (Gesell & Amatruda, 1945), while their real nature was overlooked.

In contrast to such precociously occurring motor patterns, which become linked to a later developing sensory apparatus—in the last case the visual system—Hamburger (1973, p. 59) has given an example of a complex motor pattern (i.e., hatching), that suddenly breaks through without trials if the trigger condition arises. These motor patterns do not occur earlier, although the neural machinery has developed "under the surface," without overt sign in the behavior. It must be assumed that they are temporarily inhibited.

THE PROCESS OF DEVELOPMENTAL TRANSFORMATION

There are two detailed longitudinal studies on the development of sensorimotor function available in the literature. The first is McGraw's (1943) classical investigation of the developmental course of several motor patterns in infancy. The second study is by Touwen (1976), who carried out the most detailed and comprehensive longitudinal investigation of healthy infants so far published. Fifty low-risk infants were examined in four weekly intervals from birth to the development of independent walking, employing an extensive and quantitative neurological examination. For our problem of the fate of transient sensorimotor mechanisms, two important aspects emerge.

Both studies document the overlapping coexistence of previous and successive motor patterns during the sequential developmental course. Moreover, Touwen (1976) describes in detail relapses in the development of patterns, a phenomenon he called inconsistencies. Although their expression varies according to the item and infant, responses such as the foot-sole response, the Moro response, the parachute reaction of the arms, the asymmetric tonic neck response, the rooting, and the locomotion in prone are especially inclined to such fluctuations in their maturation.

These observations have important consequences for our understanding of how these developmental transitions come about. They exclude the possibility of a structural remodeling of one neural mechanism into a new entity, indicating rather a coexistence of both mechanisms, at least for some while. There is, however, as an exception, one structure that is shared by all various motor patterns as their "common final pathway"—the motor units. Except for this rather trivial fact the neuronal machinery of developing motor patterns seems to involve different sets of elements. The following findings plead for such an interpretation. If the emergence of the voluntary palmar grasping were based on a remodeling of the machinery of the neonatal grasp response, a close time relation between the disappearance of the older response and the onset of the younger pattern should be imperative. Touwen (1971, 1976) found that no such close time relation exists, as expressed by a correlation coefficient between those two events of .12. Furthermore, there was no relationship between the disappearance of the radial palmar grasping and appearance of the pincer grasp. In the developmental sequence of the various types of voluntary grasping during infancy the wide range of overlap is striking. Hence, it can not be that later patterns simply incorporate the neural machinery of the earlier forms. Moreover, the regression into an earlier form also would not fit with such a process. An identical small red ball offered as stimulus elicits at various ages different types of voluntary grasping, but at a certain age an infant may grasp in different ways during one examination. Another example of a similar stimulus that elicits different types of responses is the following: When a newborn infant is vertically suspended and his feet touch the floor he will make alternating stepping movements. Four to 8 weeks later most of the infants no longer show this motor pattern (Touwen, 1976). The legs become engaged in other patterns such as flexion of the legs or in an extensor-supporting response. The same kind of stimulus condition elicits a different motor pattern, suggesting that the afferent system has changed its gating, recruiting other motor programs. The dominance of new patterns over older patterns, which disappear during development, can have its origin in an alteration of the sensory system.

A similar shift in dominance has been described between two different sensory systems. The maintenance of the upright posture is controlled by vestibular and visual system. Experimental tilting of the visual cues for spatial orientation indicates the contribution of vision at various ages. Brandt, Wenzel, & Dichgans (1976) found that 6- to 12-month-old children rely mainly on vestibular input and hardly respond to the visual tilt. At the age of 2 to 5 years, visual control dominates over vestibular orientation, and the children are swept off their feet when their visual field is tilted. At the age of 5 to 15 years, the effect is much less dramatic, because the vestibulum in part corrects the conflicting input from the visual system, and the posture is a result of the two messages.

Rivalry also can be observed between motor patterns. At an age when walking with support appears, the alternating steps often are hampered by simultaneous synchronous bipedal jumping movements. This rivalry for dominance became clear from slow-motion film analysis (Prechtl, 1953a). The apparent awkwardness of early walking is explained partly by this lack in separation of different motor programs, which is achieved only later with further differentiation of the neural mechanisms.

Another beautiful example of the process of transformation during development is the transition from a dorsiflexion to a plantar flexion type foot–sole response. With the development of supraspinal influences, which converge on the spinal segmental loops of the foot–sole response, a shift in the balance between the motor pools occurs (Touwen, 1976). The remodeling of the synaptic influences is a protracted process leading to a long period of instability of this neural mechanism in infancy. As a consequence, the responses are inconsistent from about 5 to 20 months of age, according to Touwen's results. The dorsiflexion does not disappear but is counterbalanced by a plantar flexion. Often these two systems neutralize each other perfectly and no movement of the big toe can be observed at all.

As a last example I want to mention complex neural mechanisms that evolve as an assemblage of independently developed modules. The voluntary grasp of a small object is such a complex function, dependent on a whole series of independent mechanisms such as visual depth perception with binocular vision and eye movements, a fine-graded control of body posture, the ability to execute an anticipatory shift of the center of gravity before the arm reaches out, the servo loops for smoothly directed arm movements, and fine finger movements, for which the function of the neuronal connections from the motor cortex to the cervical motoneurons are essential. A failure in the development of one single component impairs the total final complex mechanism. But this is not the whole story. There is evidence from monkeys that for voluntary grasping the animal must know his hands visually (Held & Bauer, 1967). The human infant goes through a phase of closely watching his playful hand and finger movements. This may be an essential prerequisite for the development of normal voluntary grasping. Because many of the afore-mentioned events or processes are seemingly remote from grasping, their importance as prerequisites may easily be overlooked.

THE MECHANISMS OF DEVELOPMENTAL REGRESSION AND TRANSFORMATION

In an attempt to formulate more systematically a list of theoretically possible mechanisms underlying the developmental processes of regression and transformation, the following statements may be made.

1. The Sensorimotor Machinery Disappears Totally.

Such a possibility exists in fact in species with metamorphosis. For example, the neural structure innervating the tail of a tadpole disappears during metamorphsis into the adult frog. Thyroxin regulates this process of regression. Although the functional relation with different larval and adult life conditions is evident in this example, this is less so in the case of the disappearance of a population of neurons in the dorsal horn of the monkey embryo. Knyihar et al. (1978) conclude: "The synaptic remodeling in the posterior quadrant of the embryonic spinal cord appears to be brought about by the death of an entire population of neurons, the borderline cells. These transient synapses may provide an essential step in the formation of the permanent and more complex nociceptive neuronal system in the primate spinal cord [p. 202]." Such a provisional neuronal system is not unique. Remodeling is also found in the synaptic network of the developing cerebellum and the visual system (Rakic, 1979).

2. The Sensorimotor Machinery Remains Intact but Comes Under Specific and Permanent Inhibition From Higher Centers.

This is a widely held view in classical neurology and neurophysiology, mainly based on the observation that lesions of the cortex in the adult may release the reappearance of infantile motor patterns (Pilleri & Poeck, 1964; Paulson & Gottlieb, 1968). Although it can not be denied that such pathological reflexes superficially resemble infantile motor patterns, their character is nonetheless substantially dissimilar. This is after all not too surprising because, except for the lack of the lesioned elements, the rest of the nervous system has all the properties of an adult nervous system, being strikingly different from the brain of a young infant. The highly imperative and invariant nature of these pathological reflexes is never seen in the normal infant. This converts these reflexes into caricatures of the graceful, flexible, and elegant motor behavior of babies.

Direct experimental evidence on the suppression of transient motor patterns by specific inhibition is meager. In her classical study on the effects of early hemidecortication in monkeys, Margret Kennard (1936) reports that the infantile palmar grasp reflex disappears in the hand contralateral to the lesioned side simultaneously with the one on the intact side. In a recent study on the regression of the sucking response in rat pups (Thexton & Griffiths, 1979), it was demonstrated that the decline of this response was also present in decerebrated animals, thus excluding the possibility of a tonic inhibition by an encephalic structure. They conclude that "some maturation process within the brainstem and/or peripheral nerves" was responsible for the change in the motor pattern.

3. The Sensorimotor Machinery Changes in the Composition of Elements as Well as Their Interconnections.

It could be imagined that a certain set of neuronal elements form a network and perform a certain function. This function would disappear during development if that particular structure is built in into a new structure, containing additional elements with new patterns of connections but including the original set. The newly emerging neural mechanism may be clearly different but may serve the same ends. Although this seems a highly economical and probable mechanism, it is difficult to find examples that would fit this model. On the contrary, coexistence of consecutively developing functions and easy reappearance of the "older" functions under various conditions make this possibility unlikely.

4. Sensory Channels Become Ineffective and Are Replaced by Other Sensory Channels Eliciting the Same Response.

Young songbirds such as chaffinches show as a feeding response a gaping movement. These movements can be elicited by acoustic stimuli and by vibration of the nest from the first to about the eighth day. After this, visual stimuli replace these other modalities. If the eyes are blindfolded 2 days after vibration becomes ineffective, a regression occurs, and vibration stimuli again elicit gaping (Prechtl, 1953b). Similarly, kittens root to tactile stimuli. Later, rooting is guided by visual stimuli, and tactile stimuli lose their effectiveness. After blindfolding, the tactile rooting reappears (Prechtl, 1952). The disappearance of these responses is due to a switch in the sensory channels. The original response pattern is replaced by new mechanisms that become dominant. However, the old pattern remains intact, at least for some time, but remains latent in the absence of experimental manipulation. A similar explanation, namely a shift in the dominance, may account for the previously quoted findings on the control of balance by vestibulum and vision.

5. The Same Sensory Mechanism Becomes Connected With a Different Motor System.

Motor patterns may disappear because the afferent channels become connected with a different motor program, such as in the developmental sequence of voluntary grasping and in the disappearance of neonatal stepping movements, mentioned previously.

6. Two Neural Machineries Develop Rivalry With Each Other.

Two newly developing motor patterns may interfere with each other, as in the case of bipedal jumping and alternating walking. They finally become separated and remain independent from each other. In the example of response to stimulation of the foot sole, the dorsiflexion pattern and the plantar flexion pattern come into an equilibrium at a certain period in development and neutralize each other (i.e., they both disappear). (For full discussion, see Touwen, 1976, p. 80.)

CONCLUSIONS

The examples mentioned in this chapter indicate clearly that normal development consists not merely of adding new neural components and functions to the existing repertory. Regression and disappearance of transient structures and functions are similarly important and essential characteristics of the developmental process. The existing age-specific transient functions can be explained partly as specific adaptations to the particular life conditions at a certain age range, partly as phylogenetic vestiges that have lost their significance in the functional repertory. The property of the developing neural machinery and function to increase in general complexity is counterbalanced by aspects of reduction of existing complexity, including regressions, relapses, and eliminations of components, and increasing organization in the particular instance may very well entail also a reduction in elements or in interactions. Only a full appreciation of these widely neglected aspects in the neurologic development will lead to a more balanced understanding of the intricate developmental processes of brain and behavior.

REFERENCES

Ahlfeld, F., *Über bisher noch nicht beschriebene intrauterine Bewegungen des Kindes.* Verhandlungen der Deutschen Gesellschaft für Gynäkologie, *2,* 1888, 203–210.

Benoit, P., & Changeux, J. P. Consequences of tenotomy on the evolution of multi-innervation in developing rat soleus muscle. *Brain Research,* 1975, *99,* 354–358.

Bodian, D. Development of fine structure of spinal cord in monkey fetuses. II. Prereflex period to period of long intersegmental reflexes. *Journal of Comparative Neurology,* 1968, *133,* 113–166.

Brandt, T., Wenzel, D., & Dichgans, J. Die Entwicklung der visuellen Stabilisation des aufrechten Standes beim Kind: Ein Reifezeichen in der Kinderneurologie, *Archiv für Psychiatrie und Nervenkrankheiten.,* 1976, *223,* 1–13.

Casaer, P. Postural behaviour in newborn infants. *Clinics in Developmental Medicine,* (No. 72). London; Heinemann, 1979.

Changeux, P. Molecular interactions in adult and developing neuromuscular junctions. In F. O. Schmitt & F. Worden (Eds.), *The neurosciences Fourth Study Program.* Cambridge; MIT Press, 1979.

Choi, B. H., & Lapham, L. W. Radial glia in the human fetal cerebrum: a combined Golgi, immunofluorescent and electron microscopic study. *Brain Research*, 1978, *148*, 295–311.

Conradi, S., & Ronnevi, L. O. Spontaneous elimination of synapses on cat spinal motoneurons after birth: do half of the synapses on the cell bodies disappear? *Brain Research*, 1975, *92*, 505–510.

Dawes, G. S. Revolutions and cyclical rhythms in prenatal life: Fetal respiratory movements rediscovered. *Pediatrics*, 1973, *51*, 965–971.

Dellow, P. G., & Lund, J. P. Evidence for central timing of rhythmical mastication. *Journal of Physiology*, 1971, *215*, 1–13.

Dennis, M. J., & Harris, A. J. Elimination of inappropriate nerve–muscle connections during development of rat emrbyos. Progress in Brain Research, *49:* The cholinergic synapse. S. Tucek (ed.). Elsevier, Amsterdam, 1979, 359–364.

Gesell, A., & Amatruda, C. S. *The embryology of behavior. The beginnings of the human mind.* New York; Harper & Brothers Publ., 1945.

Hamburger, V. Anatomical and physiological basis of embryonic motility in birds and mammals. In G. Gottlieb (Ed.), Behavioural embryology: Studies on the development of behaviour and the nervous system, (Vol. 1). New York; Academic Press, 1973.

Held, R., & Bauer, J. A. Visually guided reaching in infant monkeys after restricted rearing. *Science*, 1967, *155*, 718–719.

Hollyday, M., & Hamburger, V. Reduction of the naturally occurring motor neuron loss by enlargement of the periphery. *Journal of Comparative Neurology*, 1976, *170*, 311–320.

Huttenlocher, P. R. Synaptic density in human frontal cortex—developmental changes and effects of aging. *Brain Research*, 1979, *163*, 195–205.

Jacobson, M. *Developmental neurobiology* (2nd ed.). New York;Plenum Press, 1978.

Kennard, M. A. Age and other factors in motor recovery from precentral lesions in monkeys. *American Journal of Physiology*, 1936, *115*, 136–146.

Knyihar, E., Csillik, B., & Rakic, P. Transient synapses in the embryonic primate spinal cord. *Science*, 1978, *202*, 1206–1209.

McGraw, M. B. *The neuromuscular maturation of the human infant.* New York; Columbia Univ. Press, 1943.

Paulson, G., & Gottlieb, G. Developmental reflexes: the reappearance of fetal and neonatal reflexes in aged patients. *Brain*, 1968, *91*, 37–52.

Peiper, A. *Cerebral function of infancy and childhood.* New York; Consultant Bureau, 1963.

Persinger, M. A., & Robb, N. I. Cajal–Retzius cells as electrostatic guides for migrating neurons. *Psychological Reports*, 1976, *39*, 651–655.

Pilleri, G., & Poeck, K. Arterhaltende und soziale Instinktbewegungen als neurologische Symptome beim Menschen. *Psychiatria et Neurologia*, 1964, *147*, 193–238.

Pittman, R., & Oppenheim, R. W. Neuromuscular blockade increases motoneurone survival during normal cell death in the chick embryo. Nature, 1978, *271*, 364–366.

Prechtl, H. F. R. Angeborene Bewegungsweisen junger Katzen. *Experientia*, 1952, *8*, 220–223.

Prechtl, H. F. R. *Die Entwicklung der frühkindlichen Motorik* (part I, II, III). Göttingen; Institute for the scientific film, 1953. (Film) (a).

Prechtl, H. F. R. Zur Physiologie der angeborenen auslösenden Mechanismen. I. Quantitative Untersuchungen über die Sperrbewegung junger Singvögel. *Behaviour*, 1953, *5*, 32–50. (b)

Prechtl, H. F. R. The directed head turning response and allied movements of the human baby. *Behaviour*, 1958, *13*, 212–242.

Prechtl, H. F. R. Problems of behavioural studies in the newborn infant. In D. S. Lehrman, R. A. Hinde, & E. Shaw (Eds.), *Advances in the study of behavior*. New York: Academic Press, 1965.

Prechtl, H. F. R., & Lenard, H. G. Verhaltensphysiologie des Neugeborenen. In F. Linneweh (Ed.), *Fortschritte der Pädologie (Band II)*. Berlin: Springer Verlag, 1968.

Prechtl, H. F. R., & Schleidt, W. M. Auslösende und steuernde Mechanismen des Saugaktes (Teil I). Zeitschrift für vergleichende Physiologie, 1950, *32*, 257–262.

Prechtl, H. F. R., & Schleidt, W. M. Auslösende und steuernde Mechanismen des Saugaktes (Teil II). Zeitschrift für vergleichende *Physiologie*, 1951, *33*, 53–62.

Puro, D. G., & Woodward, D. J. Physiological properties of afferents and synaptic reorganization in the rat cerebellum degranulated by postnatal X-irradiation. *Journal of Neurobiology*, 1978, *9*, 195–216.

Rakic, P. Neuronal migration and contact guidance in primate telencephalon. *Paediatrics & Growth* (Suppl. 1), 1978, *54*, 25–42.

Rakic, P. Genetic and epigenetic determinants of local neuronal circuits in the mammalian nervous system. In F. O. Schmitt & F. C. Worden (Eds.), *The neurosciences fourth study program*. Cambridge; MIT Press, 1979.

Redfern, P. A. Neuromuscular transmission in newborn rats. *Journal of Physiology*, 1970, *209*, 701–710.

Schmechel, D. E., & Rakic, P. Arrested proliferation of radial glial cells during midgestation in rhesus monkey. *Nature*, 1979, *277*, 303–305.

Sohal, G. S., & Weidman, T. A. Development of trochlear nerve: loss of axons during normal ontogeny. *Brain Research*, 1978, *142*, 455–466.

Thexton, A. J., & Griffiths, C. Reflex oral activity in decerebrate rats of differential age. *Brain Research*, 1979, *175*, 1–10.

Touwen, B. C. L. A study on the development of some motor phenomena in infancy. *Developmental Medicine and Child Neurology*, 1971, *13*, 436–446.

Touwen, B. C. L. Neurological development in infancy. *Clinics in developmental medicine* (No. 58). London: Heinemann, 1976.

Wigglesworth, J. S., & Desai, R. Effects on lung growth of cervical cord section in the rabbit fetus. *Early Human Development*, 1979, *3*, 51–66.

II EARLY CHILDHOOD

6 Revolutionary Periods in Early Development

Pierre Mounoud
Faculté de Psychologie et des Sciences de l'Education
Université de Genève

INTRODUCTION

To take up again a text 4 years after its writing would necessitate such a fundamental recomposition that we cannot do it. Some remarks nevertheless will be made in the guise of a preamble.

This text takes a position in favor of a certain conception of the psychological development of the child, a conception that we consider "paradoxical" in comparison with usual conceptions. The conception presents itself in Piagetian theory, from which it derives, but diverges considerably from his theory on numerous points that are not made explicit in the text and that we articulate here.

The text focuses on mechanisms of development, on the processes permitting the passage from one organization of behavior to another within each of the large stages of development (infancy—childhood—adolescence). In other words, it attempts to show how the infant comes to infer new significations to the objects (or people) with whom he or she interacts or how new determinants of behavior are defined.

However the text does not sufficiently define: (1) what the infant constructs in the course of his or her development; and (2) that which makes possible these constructions. We will try to articulate these points briefly in order to clarify our position.

With regard to knowing what is constructed by the child, in the last few years our position has become more radical, in that we have come to criticize the Piagetian position according to which the child constructs structures or new forms of action or of thought. By way of an alternative hypothesis we now contend that the child does not construct new structures (new ways for treating information) in the course of his or her development. Nor does he or she construct, as Piaget (1947, 1967) believes, either the general coordinations of his or her actions or the logico–mathematical operations of his or her thought. In our view, formal structures (of actions and of reasoning) are not constructed but are preformed. Instead of constructing structures, the child in the course of development elaborates on internal representations (models or memories) conceived of as structurations or organizations of contents. These representations are elaborated by means of the formal structures that the child possesses. It is by the application of these structures that new representations are constructed. The constructed representations reveal or manifest more or less completely the structural capacities of the organism.

This first point leads automatically to the second, not treated in this text: what makes possible the elaboration of new representation, what gives the child the possibility of redefining and redetermining his or her behaviors differently at the different stages in the course of development. In this regard we propose that new coding capacities appear successively in the course of development. The appearance of these new capacities is subjected to a genetic regulation; it thus shows very little dependence on particular interactions that the child engages in with the environment, unless this is in a large, nonspecific sense. It should be recalled that for Piaget (1947, 1967) the construction of new structures is explained by an interactive process between preexisting structures and different environments or different aspects of the environment. For Piaget, the passage from one stage to the following is due to the achievement (or closing) of new structures, these new structures then revealing new aspects of the environment, with new dimensions engendering new interactions; this process can be endlessly repeated.

We attempt to schematize our position with the following propositions or postulates:

1. The forms or general structures of our actions (coordinations) and of our reasoning (operations) are preformed.

2. There exists in the roots of (internal) representations (particularly of the body) what we call *sensory representations.* These representations (coupled with preformed structures) determine the initial forms of behavior, that is to say the initial exchanges with the environment.

3. Development consists of the construction of new representations (models or memories) of objects, of self, and of other.

4. New representations are constructed because *new coding capacities* appear successively in the course of development. We propose to call *perceptive* those that appear at birth, *conceptual* those that appear around 18 months, *formal* or *semiotic* those that appear around 10 years.

5. The appearance of these new coding capacities is generated by a maturational process that depends only very indirectly on the interactions of the child with the environment (the nonspecific role of the milieu).

6. The construction of these new representations occurs according to a succession of periods or of phases (described in this chapter in terms of revolutions), whose occurence is equally strongly determined by a genetic regulation (phases of dissociation, integration, decomposition, and syntheses).

7. The constructed representations are directly dependent on the experiences that the child is involved in; the environment plays a specific role in this construction.

8. These new representations intervene in the functional exchanges that the subject engages in with his or her environment and that permit their organization (patterns, programs, procedures, schemes). Preformed sensorimotor organization at birth, perceptivo–motor organization at about 18 months, conceptuo–motor organization at about 10 years, and semiotico–motor organization at about 16 to 18 years.

The principal consequences of these propositions are the following:

1. The existence of stages and of periods are strictly genetically determined.

2. The passage from one stage to another occurs independently of the degree of achievement of preexisting constructions (up to certain limits).

3. The constructed representations are directly dependent on the contents

of particular experiences in which the child engages and even on the nature of previous exchanges. This is why the representations constructed reveal more or less accurately the structural capacities of the organism.

In conclusion, it is possible to say that in the Piagetian conception the structure of the environment plays a nonspecific role despite the interactionist aspects of his model. We are taking the contrary position that although the environment plays a nonspecific role in the appearance of new coding capacities in steps more or less fixed in the course of development, the role of the environment becomes specific in the elaboration of new representations. We have progressively developed this point of view over the past three years in various articles (Mounoud 1977a,b,c, 1979 in press; Mounoud & Hauert in press a, in press b; Mounoud & Guyon-Vinter in press).

It is generally accepted that around the age of 18 months an important period in the baby's life is completed. Much research has centered on this sensorimotor period during the last 15 years and has provided many examples of the great complexity of infant behavior, even immediately after birth. Our own research (Hauert 1980; Hauert & Mounoud 1975; Hauert, Mounoud, Mayer & Erkohen 1980; Mounoud 1973, 1974; Mounoud & Bower 1974; Mounoud & Widmer 1975; Mounoud & Hauert 1976; Mounoud, Hauert & Quennoz 1976; Mounoud, Mayer & Hauert 1979; Widmer 1980) provides examples of complex behavior at the beginning of the period as well as at its culmination, and our main theoretical interest lies in the possibility of establishing a developmental link between the processes at work in the beginning and at the end of the period.

During the first 18 months the infant repeatedly, and in different ways, reorganizes his or her relationships with the immediate environment. The transitions from one type of organization to the next could be called *revolutions,* because they profoundly modify the baby's relations with the surrounding world. The various "revolutions" appear to have two aspects in common: First, dissociations appear in the organization of the internal apprehension of objects (in the broad sense, including persons), which puts the objects on a different plane as fragmentary representations or prerepresentations; secondly, the revolution terminates in a new composition of the behavioral organization and in a new status of the objects as whole representations. Because these modifications are very gradual and fairly slow and also because experimental data on this period are still rare, their revolutionary character has not been perceived.

The clear demarcation between the sensorimotor period and the next stage traditionally has been considered to constitute a Copernican revolution (in Piaget's terms, see Piaget & Inhelder 1966) in the relationship between the child and his environment. However, despite the fact that the idea of "revolution" constitutes a pivotal concept in Piaget's theory, he describes each new acquisition as starting from a state of absence of organization and culminating in a state of stable achievement. In fact, Piaget focuses his descriptions on the elaboration of certain behaviors without considering the role and possible development of preceding behaviors.

This concept of development as a series of revolutions stands in sharp contrast to the still prevailing view of development as a cumulation of itemized acquisitions. In this view, the neonate has no, or only minimal, capacities, and the description of development is reduced to that of a succession of acquisitions, each of them totally novel and to an increase of capacities of discrimination. This conception of development has led to statements such as: The 4-to 5-months-old infant can grasp objects he or she is looking at; between 7 and 10 months the infant recognizes familiar persons; sometime during the second year the baby can imitate movements involving parts of his or her own body that he or she cannot see etc. Both the further elaboration and the earlier forms of the behaviors are ignored in such descriptions.

By contrast, in theories of development as a series of revolutions, the same reality will be seen as apprehended and mastered in different ways by the growing child. The relation between different parts of the body (traditionally called *corporal schema*) may serve as an example; the organization of these relations exists in different forms, each corresponding to a particular level of representation. At birth, this organization is determined by the postural reflexes, which allow the infant to put his or her hand into the mouth during the very first days of life. However, the shift toward a new organization of these movements subsequently produces an incapacity to put the hand into the mouth in certain postural positions. Similarly, the 18-month-old toddler who can touch different parts of his or her body precisely has once again reorganized these movements into a new structural whole. Much later, another type of reorganization of the same complex of postures and movements can be observed in the child's drawings ("draw a man") or imitations of other peoples' postures.

Parallels also can be found in the successive ways a child organizes internally the ties between the members of his or her family. The Oedipus complex—viewed as a particular instance of these ties—does not appear only once, at one particular period, neither does it disappear for good and all at a particular moment; on the contrary, it appears at different developmental stages and in function of different family contexts.

From 1964 to 1968, I studied some of the revolutions that characterize the development of children from 4 to 9 years of age through problem situations concerning the construction and use of certain instruments (Mounoud, 1968, 1970). It became clear that an important change takes place when the child makes the transition from mastery of direct manipulatory actions (using parts of the body) to that of actions by means of instruments.

The 4-year-old child possesses an *initial complex organization* allowing a perceptual–motor control of his or her manipulations and of their results. This initial organization develops gradually, and between 4 and 5 years a decomposition into constituent elements (that is, action elements such as touch, take, reach, avoid, circumvent, etc.) takes place. These constituent elements are reconstructed on a different level as *elementary conceptual organizations* that allow a new type of control, conceptual control, which is active in conjunction with the first type but bears only on the results of actions and not on the actions themselves. This development continues between the ages of 5 and 6, during which period the elementary organizations are regrouped into a *new, total conceptual organization* that cannot be decomposed into elements. At this point, the possibilities of control disappear momentarily. In the next stage, the child succeeds once again in decomposing the totality into *new partial organizations*. These partial organizations do not function parallel to the total organization (as is the case during the first step in this development) but combine progressively. The control of manipulations and of the situation is operated as regards both the total and the partial organizations, thus favoring their coordination into a *final complex conceptual or conceptuo-motor organization*. This final organization is the starting point of the next revolutionary period. Simultaneously the tools used or constructed by the child acquire progressively a different conceptual status.

These successive disorganizations and reconstructions modify the child's relations with the environment as profoundly as the development of the capacity to grasp objects modifies the relations between the infant and the surrounding world. The study of children's use and construction of tools, which grows out of sensorimotor control of hand and arm movements, thus leads back to the study of grasping in babies, a type of behavior that has not been investigated in developmental detail. The aim of our research since 1971 (Mounoud, 1973; Mounoud et al., 1974, 1975, 1976) has been to study the different levels of organization and control of grasping behavior in function of different physical properties of objects, particularly the construction by the baby, between the ages of 8 and 18 months, of physical invariants.

This research takes on particular importance if it is placed inside a general conceptual framework suggesting a new view of the child's development during this period. In the next part of this chapter I synthesize a number of new data on early development and sketch an outline of the conceptualization to which they lead.

The Postrevolutionary State of the Neonate

Embryonic development, in a sense, provides us with the prehistory of postnatal development. The intrauterine activities of the fetus are the result of certain revolutions that resemble those we observe later in the baby. Some of the infant's reactions during the first weeks of life are clearly the result of intrauterine history; they are traditionally called "reflexes" and qualified by the term *archaic*. These reflexes disappear after some months; if they do persist they indicate some disturbance of the nervous system. Little importance has been given to these reflexes, regarded as neonatal curiosities, and they have been studied only in a neurological, not in a psychological context. Their disappearance has been considered an indication that the infant leaves his or her links with the animal and vegetal domain behind and enters the superior, human, and "mental" area. Since the beginning of this century, however, a few psychologists have stressed the importance of these first reflex programs as the source of further development. Indeed, these reflexes determine the infant's reactions to the environmental stimulations, and nowadays we are beginning to discover that they are far better organized, differentiated, and more numerous than was thought (Mounoud, 1971). It can be postulated that:

1. The reflexes are not isolated, heterogenous mechanisms, but show a homogenous, total organization (i.e., they are reciprocally coordinated).
2. This initial coordination is necessary for the infant as well as for the child and the adult-to-be, inasmuch as further coordinations depend on it. (No identity of self or of others could be constructed without this initial organization).
3. The initial coordination carries within it the program for later reorganization.

At birth the infant's world is much better organized than had been thought. Already during the first year of life clearly differentiated reactions can be elicited (Lipsitt, 1967). The infant's perceptions may very well be not vague and indistinct, as has been supposed, but rather without meaning for him or her (just as a series of Chinese characters remains without meaning for those who cannot read them). Perceptions take on meaning when representations and new organizations introduce a schematization of reality.

A number of recent experimental data confirm the plausibility of these postulates. Grasping behavior in 1-week-old babies (Bower, Broughton, and Moore, 1970) is a clear example of an already existing coordination, the coordination between seeing and hearing (Aronson & Rosenbloom, 1971; Wertheimer, 1961). The complexity of the infant's organizing links with environment is even more striking in imitative behavior (opening the mouth, sticking out the tongue are some clear examples discussed by O. Maratos [Maratos, 1973 a, 1973 b]).

These types of reactions belong traditionally to the field of psychology, and one hesitates to call them reflexes. However, these reactions disappear when they are not conserved through external incitation just as reflexes in the more narrow sense do, and they do not seem to have any finality or reason—a fact that runs counter to common sense and shocks psychologists. What, indeed, is the "intention" behind such behavior? Does the infant stick out his or her tongue "in order to" reelicit an interesting sight, perceived just before? Does he or she turn the head "in order to" get into his or her mouth an object felt against the face? Does he or she stretch out the hand "in order to" close it on an object? It calls for some courage to ask such questions and for even more to answer them. In my view, though, the answer is unequivocal (if one thinks of the infant and not of the observer) The baby does not behave in these ways intentionally to obtain a certain effect but is linked to the environment by a specific organization (i.e., the nervous system at a certain point of development) that directs his or her reactions. In this sense, baby and environment, during the first days after birth, form a single organized entity. This idea of an initial adualism was elaborated by Baldwin, but the highly organized character of the union has only recently become clear. It is the combination of a state of adualism with the existence of highly diversified activity that led us to a new interpretation of the psychological importance of the very first period of life (Mounoud, 1974).

The Postnatal Revolutionary Period

At birth the infant manifests highly organized and perfectly adapted behavior in contact with the environment. However, his or her reactions are not actively controlled since he or she is submitted to unforeseeable environmental changes. To survive, the infant has to become capable of intervening actively in relations with objects and people and of controling them to a certain extent. This active intervention is a complex process that cannot bear immediately on all behavior but only on certain activities. Progressive control will be reached through a shattering of the initial organized totality whereby certain behavior becomes individualized and certain properties of objects become isolated from the numerous stimulations the baby receives. In a certain sense, this focusing of certain properties is the result of new representations (the construction of points of reference, of configurations of perceptual indices, etc.). The first psychological revolution in the child's life is this shattering of the organization of the infant–environment totality.

In our view, a parallel can be found in learning situations, even with adults. All learning is based on the existence of already installed activities and automatisms. This existing complex of behavior has to be decomposed and recomposed in a different way so as to be adapted to the new situation. Take, for example, certain aspects of driving. Moving one's feet, one up, one down, and vice versa, is easy, but when the movement of one foot commands the accelerator and the opposite movement of the other, the clutch, these movements have to be dissociated and the effect of each has to be appreciated in order to constitute a new coordinated automatism.

To come back to the infant, the initial phase of the first revolution takes place during the second or third month after birth. At that age, the infant is no longer able to easily put his or her hand into the mouth, he or she can no longer perform two activities at the same time, such as looking at something and nursing, and he or she no longer shows signs of distress when, in an experiment, he or she sees mother's face and simultaneously hears her voice reproduced at a different location. Such behavior can be interpreted in the sense that objects such as mother's breast or baby's bottle give rise to distinct representations according to whether they are seen, heard, felt, etc. Mother herself becomes something different when she is heard or touched, and these isolated perceptual representations cannot yet be regrouped into the genuine representation of a totality (i.e., a whole person).

In other words, the momentary deficit in the coordination of actions and the unitary apprehension of objects is compensated for by an elaboration of isolated activities and the representation of certain aspects of reality. I surmise that, at this point, these activities of the infant and the properties of reality acquire meaning. The infant does fewer things but does them better and begins to control actively his or her actions, which is essential for adaptation. The errors and confusions inherent in this phase of the revolutionary process derive, in my opinion, on the one hand from the lack of differentiation between the representations of certain features of objects and these objects in their totality and, on the other hand, from the confusion between a global activity and one of its constituents.

By the end of the sixth month after birth the infant identifies mother as a total object. Simultaneously the dissociated, and then isolated, action patterns have become coordinated. Many typical behaviors of this age (6 to 8 months) are fairly well known; being separated from familiar persons, particularly from mother, provokes anxiety reactions (Spitz, 1952). This final phase of the first revolutionary period is characterized by a progressive integration of partial, juxtaposed representations of objects, persons, and parts of the infant's own body. This new integration is based on the programing of the succession of substages that is already incorporated in the initial coordination of reflex behavior. Obviously, this first revolution does not take place in this fashion if the infant's environment provides very little or no stimulation; equally obviously, the meanings that people and situations take on are directly linked to specific features of the infant's environment.

The Second Revolution

It could be thought that the 6- to 8-month-old baby has reached a satisfactory relation with the environment. However, if one thinks of his or her anxiety reactions when confronted with disappearances or changes in persons and objects that have become familiar, the infant is not in a very comfortable position. It is precisely because he or she has come to recognize people that many changes and disappearances begin to disconcert and disturb him or her. From this point of view his or her control of the situation encountered is not yet satisfactory. A new adaptation is necessary, and it will be brought about by a coordination of the relations between the different representations. Such a coordination will lead to the construction of equivalences (substitutions of one person or object by another) and of correspondences (links between the different particularities and characteristics of one and the same person or object).

Similarly, the 6- to 8-month-old infant has reached a certain point in the mastery of his or her motor activities and in the knowledge of his or her own body. But once again, this achievement has its limitations. As regards grasping behavior, for example, these limitations can be clearly shown. Infants of this age cannot yet relate their different representations one to the other, they cannot coordinate the different properties of objects such as size, weight, brilliance, etc. When, in an experiment, one of these properties disappears, the object loses its identity. Though the infant has constructed an internal organization of a total object, the various features of the object cannot yet be dissociated; his internal construction cannot be analyzed. Consequently the different properties of objects cannot be related to one another, nor can different objects be related to each other. It is only during a second revolutionary period that the baby will succeed in controling his or her activities as regards this aspect of reality. This second revolution starts at about the age of 6 to 7 months, and comes to an end between the ages of 16 and 18 months. It leads to the construction of relationships between representations of objects (and persons) and their parts, with different properties and variations being taken into account. In contrast to the first, this second revolution concerns a state of dualism, where subject and objects are no longer fused into one totality.

The important modification introduced into the relations between the baby and his or her environment through this second revolution can be exemplified by our study of the organization and control of grasping behavior in function of certain properties of objects and their variations (which cannot be discussed inside the scope of this chapter). The 6-month-old infant appears to live in a world that is very different from that of the 18-month-old toddler; the infant is surrounded by unique objects, each leading to a particular representation and possessing absolute properties; the toddler lives in a world where objects can be related to each other as well as to their different properties, leading to an internally organized system of representations.

To conclude, it appears that the 18-month-old child has not simply arrived at a first form of object identification, but at far more complex organizations of which this identification is a symptom. In their complexity these organizations resemble, although on a different plane, the complex reasoning of 9- to 12-year-olds. The first revolution leads from an initial adualism to the capacity to identify objects and persons through nonanalyzable representations; during the second revolution the baby constructs new internal organizations, leading to object representation and the structuration of personal interrelationships.

The discovery of early forms of behavior that are generally attributed to

MOUNOUD

older children (such as imitation during the first weeks after birth or conservation of physical properties at 18 months) does not invalidate the interpretation of these later acquisitions but gives them a new meaning. Infant, toddler, child, and adult construct a succession of different organizations and representations of social and physical realities. Each of these revolutions ensures a different type of mastery of the relations the subject has with his or her environment.

ACKNOWLEDGMENT

The research reported in this paper was in part supported by Grants No. 1.676.72 and 1.0960.74 of the Fonds Nahoual Snisse.

REFERENCES

Aronson, E., & Rosenbloom, S. Space perception in early infancy: perception within a common auditory-visual space. *Science,* 1971, *172,* 1161–1163.

Bower, I. G. R., Broughton, J. M., & Moore, M. K. The coordination of visual and tactual input in infants. *Perception and psychophysics,* 1970, *8,* 51–53.

Hauert, C. -A. Propirétés des objets et propriétés des actions chez l'efant de 2 à 5 ans. *Archives de Psychologie,* 1980, *48,* 185, (95–168).

Hauert, C. A., Mounoud, P. L'organisation de la préhension par rapport aux différentes propriétés des objets. *Revue Suisse de Psychologie,* 1975, *34,* 264–265.

Hauert, C. A., Mounoud, P., Mayer, E., & Erkohen, M. Programmation des activités et soulèvements d'objets chez l'enfant de 2 à 5 ans. In J. Requin (Ed.), *Anticipation et comportement.* Paris: Edition du CNRS, 1980.

Lipsitt, L. P. Learning in the human infant. In H. W. Stevenson (Ed.), *Early Behavior: Comparative and Developmental Approaches.* New York : Wiley, 225–247.

Maratos, O. The origin and development of imitation in the first six months of life. Paper presented at the B.P.S. Annual Meeting, Liverpool, England, 1973 a.

Maratos, O. The origin and development of imitation in the first six months of life. Ph.D. Thesis, University of Geneva, July 1973 b.

Mounoud, P. Construction et utilisation d'instruments chez l'efant de 4 - 8 ans. *Revue Suisse de Psychologie,* 1968, 27, 1, 200–208.

Mounoud, P. *Structuration de l'instrument chez l'enfant.* Neuchâtel et Paris : Delachaux et Niestlé, 1970.

Mounoud, P. Developpement des système de représentation et de traitement chez l'enfant. *Bulletin de Psychologie,* 1971, XXV, 296, 5–7, 261–272. Translation in B. Inhelder & H. Chipman (Eds.) *Piaget Reader.* New York, Springer Verlag, 1976, 166–185.

Mounoud, P. Les conservations physiques chez le bébé. *Bulletin de Psychologie,* 1973, 312, XXVII, 13–14, 722–728.

Mounoud, P. La construction de l'objet par le bébé. *Bulletin d'Audio-phonologie,* 1974, 4, 6 suppl., 419–438.

Mounoud P. Gedächtnis und Intelligenz, In : Die Psychologie des 20. Jahrhunderts (Band 7, 3. Teil), Zürich : Kindler Verlag, 1977. (a)

Mounoud P. Cognitive development : Construction of new structures or construction of internal organizations. Communication at the *"Jean Piaget's Society,"* Philadelphia, U.S.A., 1977. (b)

Mounoud, P. Relation entre les régulations biologiques et les processus biologiques. *Vers l'Education Nouvelle,* Cahiers du CEMEA, Paris, France, hors série, 1977. (c)

Mounoud, P. Développement cognitif : construction de structures nouvelles ou construction d'organisations internes. *Bulletin de Psychologie,* 1979, *343,* 107–118.

Mounoud, P. L'utilisation du milieu et du corps propre par le bébé. In J. Piaget, P. Mounoud & J. P. Bronckart (Eds.), *La Psychologie,* Encyclopédie de la Pléiade, Paris : Gallimard, (in press).

Mounoud, P., & Bower, T.G.R., Conservation of weight in infants. *Cognition,* 1974, *3,* 29–40.

Mounoud, P. & Widmer, C. Reconnaissance de personnes et de situations à partir de différentes catégories d'indices chez le bébé de 0 à 6 mois. *Revue Suisse de Psychologie,* 1975, *34,* 267–269.

Mounoud, P. & Hauert, C. A. Préparation et contrôle des actions de soulèvement d'objets. *Cahiers de Psychologie,* 1976, *19,* 226.

Mounoud, P., Hauert, C. A., & Quennoz, L. Contrôle des activités de préhension lors de variations de poids des objets. *Le Travail Humain,* 1976, *39,* 186–189.

Mounoud, P., Mayer, E., & Hauert, C. A. Préparation of actions to lift objects of varying weight and texture in the adult. *Journal of Human Movement Studies,* 1979, *5,* 209–215.

Mounoud, P., & Hauert, C. A. Sensorimotor and postural behavior: its relation to cognitive development. In W. W. Hartup (Ed.), *Review of Child Development Research,* Vol. 6, The University of Chicago Press, (in press a).

Mounoud, P., & Hauert, C. A. Development of sensorimotor organisation in children : grasping and lifting objects. In G. Forman (Ed.), *Action and thought : from sensorimotor schemes to symbolic operations.* New York : Academic Press, (in press b).

Mounoud, P., & Guyon-Vinter, A. Representation and sensorimotor development. In G. Butterworth (Ed.), *Infancy and Epistemology,* Hassocks England : Harvester Press, (in press).

Piaget, J. *La psychologie de l'intelligence.* Paris : Armand Colin, 1947.

Piaget, J. *Biologie et connaissance.* Paris : Gallimard, 1967.

Piaget, J., & Inhelder, B. *La Psychologie de l'enfant.* Paris : Presses Universitaires de France, Coll. "Que sais-je", no. 369, 1966.

Spitz, R. *La première année de la vie de l'enfant.* Paris : Presses Universitaires de France, 1952.

Wertheimer, M. Psychomotor coordination of auditory and visual space at birth. *Science,* 1961, *134,* 1692.

Widmer-Robert-Tissot, C. *Les modes de communication du bébé. Postures vocalises et mouvements.* Paris : Delachaux et Niestlé, 1980.

7 Unlearning: Dips and Drops— A Theory of Cognitive Development

Jacques Mehler
C.N.R.S.
Paris, France

Cognitive psychologists generally believe that it will one day be possible to construct a formal theory not only of the normal stable functioning of the adult's cognitive apparatus, but also of the ways in which such a stable system develops. At the present time, Piagetians are by far the most coherent believers in the possibility of founding a genetic psychology capable of explaining the establishment of new conceptual capacities in terms of developmental processes that entail learning. If we consider, however, the magnitude of the chemical, hormonal, and general physiological changes that take place during growth, it appears overoptimistic to count on the discovery of a counterpart to these organic processes at the level of cognitive development, for the time being, at any rate. Purely descriptive theories of development have failed in the past and there is no a priori reason to expect that they will succeed in the future. Even when descriptive theories reveal phenomena that occur in a well-ordered time sequence, they fail to explain the sequence in the stages of development, the relationship between successive stages, and the reasons behind the progress from one stage to the next.

In spite of such critical theoretical deficiencies (not unique in psychology), cognitive development remains one of the most advanced chapters in the discipline, largely attributable to the contributions of Piaget and the ex-pistemologically oriented genetical psychologists of the Geneva school. These scientists have shown that development in general proceeds through an

133

ordered sequence of stages and that simplistic learning assumptions concerning development are factually incorrect. They have demonstrated also that the changes that occur during the development process must be conceptualized into some sort of a dialectic relationship between nature and nurture and that any arbitrary separation of the two is misleading. In fact, the Piagetians offer constructivism as a solution to this age-old debate. In addition, and this may be the single most important innovation in their contribution, they have vehemently argued that one capacity cannot be accounted for independently of all the other capacities that develop simultaneously. The correct level of description is one that does not separate the child's mnemonic capacity, learning ability, perceptual world, and so forth.

Though the contribution made by Piaget and his collaborators cannot be minimized, important methodological and conceptual limitations subsist in their epistemological theory. Since the epistemologists are more interested in the child's knowledge about what he or she does than in what he or she actually accomplishes, the data they consider crucial concern not the correct attainment of an aim, but rather what the subject can tell about attaining that aim. If they have thus concentrated on verbal justifications it is because they do not regard behavior as the most important level of analysis, but rather are interested in "equilibrated" cognitive ability. This "equilibrated" state is inferred by the psychologist from the child's verbal justifications rather than from his or her behavior. It is the congruence of the inferences that indicate the child's beliefs rather than the congruence and consistency of his or her actions.

Although the aforementioned aspect of epistemological research methodology is both important and original, some problems arise over its rather special concept of justification. Psychologists have found time and again that actions may be entirely unrelated to the justifications offered for them. Although both levels of investigation are of interest, neglecting the former in favor of verbal justifications is tantamount to a divorce with psychology proper. Furthermore, strict adherence to epistemological methods for investigating development to the exclusion of all others makes for explanatory discontinuity in the research in the area. Observations such as this, however, have become widely accepted nowadays and there is no need to dwell further on this point.

Our aim in this chapter is to outline a view of cognitive functioning that, although partial, has the advantage of presenting some of the known material in an orderly fashion and in such a way as to allow for the prediction of some new facts. This will be achieved, I hope, without using terms that are themselves in need of explanation.

THE AIMS OF A COGNITIVE THEORY

In a paper entitled *The study of competence in cognitive psychology* (1968b), Mehler and Bever proposed that "cognitive theory must present an axiomatic formulation of the processes which are involved in creative behavior." Creative behavior should be understood here as implying reasoning along abstract lines and, in general, behavior that is more or less independent of immediate situational variables. In that paper we further argued that cognition in general may be studied by examining three components: a characterization of the minimum *initial state* that can be observed in infants' basic functioning, a description of the natural ways in which adults perform when they have reached a *stable state,* and a *dynamic theory of acquisition* that, when coupled with maturational and other processes, enumerates the stages, their order, and their transitions during the passage from one to the other. We have referred to the mapping of the initial state to the stable state as a *learning function.*

Whereas a number of investigators have put forth valid arguments against the notions involved in the empiricist assumption that the environment can determine all the acquisitions of which an organism is capable (Chomsky 1965; Katz 1966), it is also clear that the nativist approach proposed during the last decade, mainly by linguists, has been misunderstood by psychologists. Obviously, mental achievements are heavily influenced by the joint functioning of innate and learned capacities. However, there is a sense in which it is quite fair to say that there is no innate capacity that does not depend on the environment's providing the occasion for it to manifest itself. Thus the disagreement between nativists and empiricists is frequently reflected in their choice but rather a matter of research strategies.[1] The former consider

---

[1]Beyond the question of research strategy, however, there is a crucial underlying conceptual difference that should be stressed. The rationalist psychologist, like the linguist, may be looking for invariants of cognitive structure in humans. That is, invariants or, as the linguist would call them, universals that can be found in every organism, under any environmental conditions, and regardless of differing historical antecedents and do not result from learning. Although few

that some of the dispositions that are typical of the human species must be determined empirically in order to achieve the kind of descriptive adequacy that we argued earlier should be the proper aim of at least some innate structures, without devoting research time to the theoretical or experimental investigation of such structures and their interaction with experience. As nobody now denies some species-specific dispositions, disagreement arises concerning their importance in the formulation of a theory of cognition.,

Of course, nativists claim that it is the specificity of cognitive structures that should constitute the critical aim of our research efforts, whereas for the empiricists it is the generality of underlying learning. Yet it seems quite evident that the understanding of cognitive functioning requires our understanding of the processes and structures characteristic of the initial and stable states. A word of caution, however, about initial-state research needs to be given concerning the difficulty of making statements about capacities that are

---

psychologists nowadays believe that the mind is structureless at birth or that learning or adaptation are entirely free and undetermined by environmental conditions, the constraints imposed by cognitive universals nevertheless have received very little attention. Even so, rationalist psychologists believe that it is both necessary and possible to describe an *idealized human subject* based in part on cognitive universals and in part on the rules and structural constraints that emerge from the interaction of these universals with the environment. In describing an idealized subject under simplified and idealized conditions, rationalistic psychology is dealing with aspects of behavior that are common to all members of the species. Thus, before a theory of thinking can be established along these lines, it makes no sense to talk, strictly speaking, about the intelligence of one or another human being. Rather, it becomes necessary to state the rules, structures, and constraints that can account for the ways in which one human being is like any other human being. In other words, it is precisely the characteristics that differentiate one individual from other that are best ignored.

The nativist and empiricist positions are not lacking in ideological consequences. The former often have been accused of formulating psychological theories that lead to a rigid determinism in ignorance of the effects that society has on behavior. It is said that nativism leads to the kind of formulation that Jensen, Herrenstein, and others have proposed. Furthermore, some of the most rigid and pessimistic views of man have come from the contribution of ethologists such as Lorentz and others, based on animal behavior. It is not because of their nativistic leanings that such views have been favored, but rather because of their strong empiricist interpretation of nativism. Once it becomes clear that the aim of cognitive psychology is neither that of accounting for differences nor that of making catastrophic predictions, but rather that of describing a putative idealized performance, arguments for initial species-specific capacities cannot be construed as having detrimental results.

Another point that might well be raised here concerns the methodological consequences of the different positions. It would be highly incorrect to look initially for universals that could not even

initially absent. In general, asserting the absence of a given capacity poses many methodological problems that are not easily surmountable. Furthermore, the determination of what the organism is capable of doing is easier and yields secure knowledge. Of course, when epistemologists conclude that a given capacity is absent in the performance and in the competence of very young children, they argue not only in terms of the child's performance on one task, but also in terms of performance in a whole series of situations and more particularly in terms of the actual action patterns that indicate that behavior is mediated by operations different from those an older child might use. In general, the Genevans look for "basic incapacities" that will "disappear" in the course of growth, whereas our research, as will be seen later, was and still is concerned with "basic capacities" that may "disappear" and accordingly increase the structural constraints of the organism. Rather than a linear pattern of development, we have found in our studies

---

in principle be construed as such in the absence of some specific interaction with the environment. It is nevertheless possible that these are the expression of more basic tendencies or universals, which are the proper level of investigation.

In this connection, some alternative approaches seem relevant. Chomsky (1956) has differentiated between substantive and formal universals. Although this seems a valuable distinction. We wish to propose another distinction that might be more interesting for the psychologist, and this concerns universals that conceivably can be tested in the absence of the behavior for which they are responsible. We might test, as Eimas et al. (1971) have done, categoric perception in the phonological discriminations of the very young infant. He has shown that it is possible to find traces in very young babies of the same distinctive-feature system that is employed by the adult. We could therefore state that the distinctive feature-system is rooted in biological dispositions whose existence can be empirically demonstrated in children who have not yet mastered the activities that such a system renders possible. However, we have some kinds of systems or behaviors that might be impossible to test in very young babies. Take, as an example, any of the very abstract rules that may be necesssary from the point of view of syntactic theory, such as global constraints, cyclical rules, etc. Perhaps even in principle it would be impossible to show that they are present in some form or other in very young infants. Thus, although some capacities appear too unstable for us even to conceive of testing, we can imagine ways of testing other innate capacities. We might therefore make a distinction between the innate capacities that constrain the initial state so severely as to make the remaining developmental envelope quite predictable and the kinds of universals that are not in themselves innate, but may be a composite of primary capabilities. The question we are raising concerns the status of maturational processes. Unless we can imagine a maturational process that is so constrained at the beginning that the outcome is impermeable to the environment, the distinction is one worth pursuing.

that advances in age can be associated with a poorer overall range of performance.

Because it has already been of interest for many decades, there has been much more research devoted to the investigation of the stable state than to that of the initial state. Piaget (1936) in particular has described some ad hoc established "plateaus" in the course of development, namely, stages corresponding to intermediary stable states. Unfortunately it seems unlikely that this rather appealing formulation will hold inasmuch as the stages as they were described are currently being severely questioned. Furthermore, even if we grant that such stages exist, the theory of development we end up looks remarkably like a regression of explanatory power, because we have no functional view of transition from an initial to a stable state. In fact, the problem with using one aspect of cognitive development (say, number or logical thought) to account for overall cognitive competence is that the aspects that are least understood are those that are most likely to serve as the explanatory devices in the system.

THE AIMS OF A THEORY OF COGNITIVE DEVELOPMENT

Human beings show a great capacity for modifying their behavior. However, theories of behavioral modification have always been of marginal utility insofar as theories of acquisition are concerned. Take, for example, language development. Language has been shown to be sensitive to modulation by behavioral modification. On the one hand, it has been shown that language cannot be spontaneously learned by induction only and, on the other, that learning by induction, as Fodor (1975) argues, can only fixate beliefs that we can project. Hence, any attempt to describe language as the consequence of behavioral modification alone will always be incorrect. A paradigmatic case would be phonological competence. It can be shown that phonology depends to a very large extent on the existence of highly specialized putative neurophysiological structures (Eimas, Sigveland, Jusczyk, & Vigorito, 1971; Morse, 1976) that develop in a predictable way from birth and whose normal functioning can only be arrested. Coupling this fact with the evidence that all potential sounds are easily discriminable at birth (Eimas et al., 1971; Trehub, 1976), it would seem possible at least in this particular case to consider growth as the successive loss of initial potential.

This thesis—that much of development consists of the loss of capacities that were present at birth rather than in the acquisition of new capacities—needs elaboration, however. Loss might occur, as in phonology, by the sheer disappearance of potential capacities, the net result being an increasingly narrow repertoire. It may also be that loss comes about because behavior that has been triggered in an isolated fashion becomes incorporated into a more general action pattern in such a way that it can be observed only as part of the program leading to the suppression of its isolated existence. What is lost in this case is the functional autonomy of certain capacities.

Many other accounts of loss of initial capacities can be proposed. For instance, a certain form of behavior can be an undifferentiated whole that is triggered initially by some stimulating factor. In the course of development, the stimulus may cease to be active and the behavior disappears. Eventually, this particular form of behavior will reemerge in a more autonomous and differentiated fashion. A case in point may be imitation of facial gestures[2]. Even further, a capacity may go from global to specific or from concrete to abstract, etc., the process of reorganization leading to a drop in the production of the capacity. But be it as it may, the critical issue that should be stressed by any theory of cognitive development is the fact that selection of potential may come to account for the stable-state functioning. Under a model of adaptation through loss, the stress is on innate capacities, the environment acting as a mechanism for the selection and development of these capacities. Everyday experience reflects and is in some ways consistent with this view of development through loss or delimitation. For instance, our society tries to teach certain things to children while they are young even though they and their parents may consider play and undirected activities more interesting and rewarding. This practice conforms with the observation that at maturity we have the ability to learn certain things but are no longer proficient at acquiring totally new abilities or, at any rate, not with the zest and ease that characterize the young child. Furthermore, although we are not surprised that a child can master the meaning of many thousands of words in a very short period of time, we do not expect equal feats of adults in university language courses.[3]

Given this state of affairs, one of the major aims of cognitive theory must be the specification of universal dispositions and capacities that serve as the basic tissue upon which environmental selection will leave its trace. This

---

[2]See in this volume the chapter by Olga Maratsos, who has done some of the pioneer work on this subject and whose results have to a large extent been confirmed by Meltzoff (1977).

[3]Notice for instance, the inadequacies inherent in the old and new approaches to langauge acquisition that have been influenced by experimental psychology. Eve Clark (1973) presents some worthwhile considerations on the conceptual basis for first language acquisition. All the considerations, interesting as they may be, however, lose sight of the essential question in lexical acquisition; namely, the dictionary explosion, of which all psychologists of language have had some awareness for the past decades.

requires a sort of "abduction theory" in the sense of Peirce (1958)—a requirement of the sort that Chomsky (1968) has discussed in connection with linguistic theory. That is to say, we must determine what the domain of the possible is, given the dispositions that seem to be present. The definition of the initial state, together with the characterization of a stable performance state, might allow us to fulfill another aim of cognitive theory, that of accounting for the fact that humans have the greatest capacity for learning or for behavior that is almost ideally suited to adaptation.

In this context, the relevant question concerns how the observed enrichment of performance can be reconciled with the theory that development consists of the loss of initial structure or its dwindling until it is incorporated into a more complex one. Although no complete answer can yet be given to this problem, we can nonetheless explore some of the results that have been gathered in recent years and analyze them in this context.

RELATIONAL JUDGMENTS

Since 1967 we have studied, in collaboration with Bever, the very young child's capacity for making relational judgments in a number of situations. When we first started working on these studies, we were somewhat confused about the meaning of the term "conservation." Because we were using a paradigm that was close to the one employed by Piaget, we believed that it was fair to speak of "conservationlike behavior." This no longer seems to us warranted. For a more balanced evaluation and critique of the Piagetian paradigm, see the debate between Chomsky and Piaget in Piattelli–Palmarini *Théories du Langage, Théories de l'Apprentissage* (1979).[4]

The question that most worried us in the course of our initial research was how to interpret the child's capacity to choose the more numerous of two rows of candies if some elementary notions of equality and addition as well as subtraction were not present. We found that the young child shows more or less spontaneously that he knows very well which of two sets has more when he is in competition with his siblings. Experiments carried out in Geneva indicated, on the contrary, that it is not until about age 7 that the child can say confidently whether quantity remains unchanged under irrelevant trans-

---

[4]English language version: *On langauge and learning: A debate between Chomsky & Piaget*, M. Piattelli-Palmarini (Ed.), Cambridge, Harvard University Press (in press).

formations. Rather than showing that the child must acquire new operations with maturity in order to perform correctly, our own experiment indicated that performance depends on some understanding of the conditions under which invariance will hold.

In the first problem of relational judgement that Mehler and Bever (1968a) tested, children were presented with two rows of candy. After making sure by questioning the children that they were convinced that two identical rows had the same amount of candy, we added two extra candies to one row while at the same time shortening it by compressing all the candies in that row. The child was asked to select one and only one row to eat and told that the experimenter would keep the other one. Very little verbal transaction therefore, was, necessary in this experiment. The results demonstrated that the performance of the younger age group (2.4 to 2.7) was consistently superior to that of children at 3.4 to 3.7. Our findings have since been replicated partially or entirely, although some investigators have failed to do so. Failure, however, may be due to the experimenter's using a verbal means of communicating with the child. Beilin (1968) argued that the very young child is attracted by the manipulations of the experimenter and will therefore always select the correct row because it is the one that was touched last. In a further study, however, Bever, Mehler, and Epstein (1968) showed that their results were incompatible with this interpretation and that insofar as could be judged from the situation employed, the very young child seems to select the more numerous row, not because of the experimental artifact, but because he or she thinks it is indeed more numerous.

Mehler (1971) carried out an experiment comparable to the one just described, except that instead of asking children to select a row of candy, they were presented with a situation that resembles the classic volume conservation experiment of Piaget and Inhelder (1941). Pretraining consisted of presenting two candies. As soon as the child had chosen one, the experimenter removed the other. We continued this pretraining until we were convinced that the children understood that they were entitled to take either one or the other but not both. The experimenter then took a candy in each hand and put one each into two identical containers, asking the child to confirm whether both had the same amount. This was repeated until both containers had ten candies each. The content of one container was then poured into a beaker whereas that of the other was emptied into the dish. The child was told he or she could have the contents in either the beaker or the dish and was asked to make a choice. Verbal interaction was thus again reduced to a minimum. We were interested in whether the very young child (as well as older children) would choose the taller container. Our assumption was that the child would select the container that he or she thought contained more candy. We had, in fact, every reason to believe that he or she was seeking to obtain as many candies as possible and that his or her cognitive structuring, and not greediness, was the developmental variable.

We were concerned throughout this experiment with strictly controlling any variables that might be construed as artifacts. To this end we placed the beaker to the right of the children as often as to the left. We also tried to make sure that both containers were reasonably symmetrical to the medial planes of their bodies and at the same distance. An equal number of boys and girls were included in each of the groups to the extent possible. All the children were selected from and tested in French public schools so that very diversified social strata were represented. The only constraint we placed on individual selection was that the child have been in France for at least 1 full year.

The overall results of this experiment, which are presented in Table 7.1, indicate that very young children select the beaker about as often as the dish. The performance of the intermediate age group is slightly different from a random one with a tendency by the children to chose the beaker rather than the dish. Chi-square is 3.85 ($p < .05$). Insofar as the older children were concerned, there is a preference for the taller container. These results seem thus to indicate that the very young child is not yet acting in terms of perceptual preferences or confusions, but rather has some comprehension that he or she has no extra candies to gain by choosing either the beaker or the dish.

It must be granted, however, that this interpretation is not justified if the results could be accounted for by artifacts like lateralization or attention. In general, the position of the container seems to play a secondary role, as Table 7.2 indicates. Children seem to develop a systematic preference for the taller container with age. It should be noted, however, that this tendency to choose

TABLE 7.1

Age	Number of Subjects who Chose Taller Container/Total Number of Subjects	Percentage
2.0–2.7	23/40	57.5
2.8–3.3	31/44	40.5
3.4–3.11	32/42	76.2

TABLE 7.2

| Age | Number of Subjects who Chose Taller Container When Presented on: | |
	Right Side	Left Side
2.0–2.7	14/20 (70.0%)	9/20 (45.0%)
2.8–3.3	17/22 (77.3%)	14/22 (63.6%)
3.4–3.11	17/21 (81.0%)	15/21 (71.4%)

the taller container increases more with age when it is presented on the child's left.

These results could be interpreted as indicating a lack of attention on the part of the very young child. If this were true, he or she could be expected to perform on a random basis, and the performance we have noted for older children would indicate only that they are following the situation with increasing attention. To show that this is not the case, we planned three controls in which numeric inequalities were introduced into the experimental design. Under our interpretation the younger children would necessarily have to pay some attention to the initial identity of volume as well as to intervening changes. These changes should not, however, alter the behavior of the older children, whose performance is controlled by the emerging perceptual heuristic of measuring the importance of volume and its height.

In order to test our hypothesis, we first carried out an experiment similar to the one described above, except that once the contents of the identical containers were transferred to the dish and the beaker, an extra candy was added to one or the other. To control properly for possible artifacts, the beaker was placed to the right of one half of the children and to the left of the others. The extra candy was added as often to the dish as to the beaker. Finally, we tried to have an equal number of boys and girls in each age group. In the results, presented in Table 7.3, selection of the correct container represents the choice of the one to which the extra candy was added.

TABLE 7.3

Age	Number of Subjects who Chose Correct Container/Total Number of Subjects	Percentage
2.0–2.7	60/83	72.3
2.8–3.3	51/79	64.5
3.4–3.11	42/74	56.8

The populations involved in this experiment are large enough to make these results quite significant. The younger children almost always chose the container with the extra candy. We can thus rule out the supposition that the group is operating at chance $\chi^2 : 2.68$ ($p < .001$). The second age group performs in much the same manner, most often selecting the container with the extra candy. However, the distribution is not at this age significantly different from what could be expected on the assumption that children are equally likely to select either container. Chi-square here is 3.42 ($p. < .1$). Of the older age group almost as many children chose the container with the extra candy as the one with less.

A second control that we carried out was identical to the first, except that the extra candy was added before instead of after pouring. The results of these two experiments are compared in Table 7.4. Whether the extra candy is added before or after pouring, the results remain significantly the same. The younger children perform more efficiently than the older ones. The greatest difference in the children's performance in these two situations occurs in the two extreme age groups, the intermediate age group being more or less equally proficient in either situation. It appears therefore that both the younger and older groups have strategies for selecting the correct container. The younger children seem to choose the container that appears to have more. The intermediate age group is, then, in a transitional period going from one strategy to the other.

Finally, our third experimental control consisted of introducing inequality by subtraction rather than addition. As soon as the contents of the two identical containers were poured into the dish and the container, the experimenter removed one candy. The experimental plan did not otherwise vary from the one described above for addition after pouring. The results of this experiment, which are given in Table 7.5, are for the extraction of the candy with a spatula. We should note that our results were somewhat

TABLE 7.4

| Age | Percentage of Subjects Who Chose Correct Beaker When Extra Candy Added | | |
	AFTER Pouring	BEFORE Pouring	Difference
2.0–2.7	72.3	63.5	8.8
2.8–3.3	64.5	60.3	4.2
3.4–3.11	56.8	47.0	9.8

TABLE 7.5

% Ss Correct Choice When:	Age			
	2.0–2.7		3.3–3.8	
	NCC^a/T^b	%	NCC/T	%
Crist. has more	21/32	65.6	6/16	37.5
Test tube has more	23/32	71.9	13/16	81.3
Number of Ss percentage	44/64	68.8	19/32	59.3

$^a NCC$ = Number of Ss making correct choice; $^b T$ = Total number of Ss

different when a candy was removed by tilting the container until one fell out. The crucial behavior, that of choosing the dish when the candy had been subtracted from the beaker, is reliably better in the younger than in the older children. Chi square is 3.87 ($p < .05$).

These results show convincingly that the performance of very young children is based on perceptual strategies and is *not* due to some artifact (i.e., choosing the container last touched by the experimenter). In this situation, the container last touched is the one the child must avoid to obtain more candy. An interpretation such as Beilin's therefore, could not, be compatible with the results for both addition and subtraction. This explanation of correct choices in the first case would necessarily require incorrect choices in the first case would necessarily require incorrect choices in the second and, as we have seen, very young children perform equally well in both situations. Furthermore, the younger children perform proficiently in both tasks whether the correct container is the dish or the beaker, whereas the older children tend massively to choose the beaker when it is the correct choice and only slightly less often when it is not. This indicates a fair appreciation of numerosity on the part of the very young child, at least when quantities are small or in cases where they vary by a single operation. The crucial behavior, that of choosing the dish when the candy has been subtracted from the beaker, is reliably better in younger than in older children. Chi-square is 3.87 ($p < .05$).

All of these results show that in tasks entailing the selection of a quantity presented in a volumelike arrangement, younger children tend to choose the container with more candies in it. The appearance or shape is of some importance, but generally speaking it is the intervening operations that determine the behavior of the child at 2.6. Furthermore, performance that is geared by numerosity rather than by appearance is equally good under addition or subtraction. In cases where there is no change in quantity, the younger child seems to have no preference between the containers, although there is a slight tendency to select the one to the right more often. In such cases the child seems to find such a choice simpler. This observation was made also in an independent experiment in which two objects were presented, one to the right and one to the left of the child, under the understanding that he or she could take and keep only one.

The research we have reported thus far indicates the presence of an initial capacity to judge numerosity independently of appearance. This capacity seems to undergo restructuring at the age of 3.5 and does not reappear until much later. However, when some notion of relative numerosity again emerges, the child will possess some remarkably different strategies from those initially used in solving the kinds of problems we have presented.

An account that may be interesting to explore in this context concerns the ability of the small child to judge numerosity in small sets and be able to perform reasonably well within such sets. Nonetheless, in time, the child has to relinquish his subsetizing in order to generalize properties of the sets he can master to sets that are even larger. Such a change in his action program requires testing and exploration of many parameters. This will eventually result in a stronger theory of numerosity, in spite of the fact that at the start only the undifferentiated action pattern is available. Traces of subsetizing are, however, present in the adult.

TOWARD A THEORY OF DEVELOPMENT

A variety of cognitive abilities are highly developed in 2-year-olds and in 6-year-olds but appear to be lacking in children of intermediate ages. It would be difficult, however, to assert that the processes underlying performance are the same at 2 and at 6 years. Children do not count at 2, whereas they do at 6. Even the most precocious 2-year-olds who appear to use numbers do not actually count objects but rather repeat sounds referring to numbers by rote. They are as yet unable to use this ability to determine which of two sets has the greater number of objects.

Because we cannot adequately interpret the characteristically inferior performance of 4-year-olds that indicates the temporary suppression of some acquired ability, our results need some explanation in terms of modifications that do not depend upon pure, cognitive, problem-solving capacity, but go beyond to include behavior that has both mnemonic as well as perceptual components. To account for our findings, we must postulate several processes and try to relate these to the data gathered.

The very young child may obtain correct responses because the functional validity of appearance is not yet as elevated as it will be at about 3.5. Thus, if not guided by appearance, he or she will make a numerical choice according to some appropriate operation. Nonetheless, the operation per se sometimes has validity beyond the establishment of the initial situation and thus, in some specific cases, some rows or sets will be selected because something has been added, whereas others will be avoided when something has been subtracted. Hence it would seem that operations that are possible at a very young age may be difficult for the child to articulate into action programs. Thus some perceptual preferences generally resulting from the compounding of operations, amounts or judgments can be established in the very young child although the functional validity of these is as yet low. If there is an increasing validity of the perceptual preference it must be because the global heuristics that yield results compatible with appearance, are simple to state and relate to the test situation. This concern with appearance must nonetheless be evaluated in the light of the child's information about irrelevant transformations. Does he or she believe at 3.5 and not at 2.0 or 5.0 that a change of appearance is in fact a change in numerosity, even if faced with information to the contrary? The only possible answer is no.

We have certainly no intention of denying the validity of Piagetian empirical findings. Furthermore, there is no reason to lend credence to those who want to see the behavior of 4-year-olds as a consequence of a shift in word meanings, etc. Such accounts are circular and come back to an implicit recognition of Piaget's point; namely, that something like a cognitive operation must appear at about this age. An alternative is possible, however.

The performance of 2-year-olds may be based to a great extent on a phenomenal mnemonic capacity. Very young children seem to perform extremely well in rather unstructured situations by sheer reliance on their capacity to register events even in their most incidental aspects. It would seem that memory traces go from more global to more analytic,[5] requiring

---

[5]See paper forthcoming in *U-Shaped Behavioral Growth*, S. Strauss (Ed.), N.Y., Academic Press (in press).

at the same time a greater scanning for environmental regularities in order for storage to occur. The discovery of regularities is also related to a greater reliance on rules, and rules allow a certain freedom from sheer memory.

Therefore, from what we have thus far observed, the progressive independence of the child from the registration capacity frees him or her from constraints that inhibited evaluation of the stimulus as it was presented. It is at about 3.5 that the child manifests a decrease of reliance on the memory store. This may be connected with the increased differentiation of memory traces at this age. The only way in which internal reorganization might ensue is through a total change in performance procedures whereby the child relies more on what he or she sees than on what he or she believes. This may be seen from the fact that increasing motivation to obtain more produces less of a decrement in performance at 3.5.

The results we have obtained allow us to state with some confidence that the loss of initial identity of sets under irrelevant transformations is not only logically unlikely, but also unsupported by empirical evidence. Logically there is no way out of the dilemma. Either the 2-year-old already has the notion of identity or there could be no possible training procedure that would force him or her to acquire that notion. Therefore, there seems to be little utility in attempts to demonstrate that at a given age notions as basic as identity are absent. More to the point would be a research strategy that seeks to demonstrate capacities that are in fact present at ages as young as we are able to test and then show that the utilization of these capacities is subject to many ups and downs before their functional validity as well as their concatenation with other operations is properly established.

A further issue that should be raised concerns the general significance of temporary decrements in performance with increasing age for development. Such decrements are by now well established by many studies and for many aspects of cognitive development. Why is it that the child must make mistakes before structured forms of being correct are established when he or she starts out by being able to give correct responses? One possible reason is that initially, although the responses are correct, they are so only in narrow and constrained environments and constitute plans of action so inefficient that the child is forced to replace them by rules and heuristics that work and are broadly applicable though not, at first, foolproof.

Another possible reason for decrements in performance is that this may be a totally wrong way of looking at development. In the same graph, we may be comparing performances that actually reflect entirely unrelated behaviors, so that what the child does at 2 may have absolutely no relation to what he or she does at 4. In fact, some excellent argument can be advanced to show that the underlying processes are entirely different at the two ages in the case of children dealing successfully with numerosity judgments. The major issue remains the description of the exact way in which the underlying mechanisms differ. Only then will it be possible to study how children shift from one procedure to the next.

It should be noted that a major reason for which it seems impossible at this point to give more concrete answers concerning the significance of the decrements in performance is that no learning theory exists that is valid for interesting changes in behavior. Given all the failures at developing satisfactory theories of learning, it is not at all surprising that no general view of dips in learning exists.

DISCUSSION

The results reported in this chapter as well as its theoretical framework date back to 1972, when the "Dips and Drops" paper was initially circulated. Since then, many things have changed in the field and many new results have become available. What must have sounded like a naive nativistic and mentalistic approach several years ago is now, broadly speaking, one of the dominant paradigms of cognitive psychology. Thus, the view first expressed by Chomsky (1965), that the child has many initial capacities that are subsequently modulated by environmental regularities much as the theories of the scientist are modulated by his observations, seems likely nowadays. In fact, that infants have mental capacities, perceptual, and even linguistic dispositions has been demonstrated by, among others, Eimas et al. 1971, Bower et al. 1971, 1977 and Trevarthan (this volume). In the light of such developments it is hardly surprising to see that 2-year-olds have some success in coping with certain parts of the universe that give 4-year-olds trouble. Such a result was of capital importance at a time when the paradigm established by the Genevans, and Piaget in particular, was not only the dominant one but almost the sole one in the field.

Things have changed a great deal in recent years. Fodor (1975) has made a cogent statement challenging the view that learning can lead to the discovery or invention of logically stronger systems than those that were available before. If the argument is shifted from the area of cognition in general to development in particular it suggests that shifting from one stage to the next in the Piagetian context cannot be attributed to learning. Thus it must be due to some other process, and the failings of Piaget's theory become obvious. Consequently, the possibility of the young child having templates governing his or her commerce with the environment and insuring that he or she ends up with efficient cognitive subsystems becomes a plausible view, and the irregularities of development are no longer surprising, given that development per se is challenged in favor of some other view, such as maturation or selection of a pool of capacities.

Mehler (1974) has suggested that development be looked on as both the maturation of specific structures (largely in agreement with the view often expressed by Chomsky) and the selection of innate dispositions by the particular environmental pressures. At that time, we stated that there is a great need to understand the way in which interaction with the environment, maturation, and, in general, growth bring about the integrated behavior characteristic of different ages (so well described in the work of Piaget). We furthermore argued that to accomplish this, a shift in emphasis from the study of what the child lacks to what the child loses might be a more satisfactory line of research.

Without relinquishing any of the ideas then expressed, I now see some major theoretical issues that need to be tackled urgently before any further progress can be made. I outline some of these in the following paragraphs:

1. Initial-state research (namely the study of the capacities of the newborn infant) has largely taken the following form : A capacity already well understood in the adult is postulated as existing in the infant. Ways of testing the infants are imagined, but insofar as the capacity is sophisticated, no satisfactory method is found. However, if the capacity is sensorial or perceptual, tests are generally carried out and demonstrate the infant's abilities. This kind of study generally filters out the higher-order capacities from the testing and this, undeniably, represents a problem.

2. Hypotheses on initial states, insofar as they are hypotheses to be tested in real time, always amount to hypothese of fixed structures (in the form of detectors, analyzers, specialized receptors, etc.) that are either selected or tuned by the environment. Though there is nothing in-

trinsically wrong with postulating such fixed structures, some problems do ensue. Thus, we postulate feature detectors, although nobody could reasonably imagine that the adult could use these in speech perception. The same applies to detectors of phonemes or of syllables, etc. Generally, the difficulty comes from the very fact that such structures supposedly function when triggered by a physical configuration. However, the major problem remains that context determines the outcome of perceptual or psychological processing in general. Hence, how can fixed structures, which respond to physical invariance exclusively, account for the characteristically context-sensitive fashion in which perceptual systems function?

3. In conjunction with the preceding issue, we must in general raise problems relating to the growth of knowledge. We know, for instance, that mathematics has developed in a steady fashion through the centuries. What is means here is the fact that at time t_{+1}, all the theorems that could be demonstrated at time t can still be demonstrated, whereas the reverse is not the case. Frequently such an increase in power comes about through a real growth in conceptual instruments. How can we account for such historical growth? Will the conclusions enlighten us as to how learning in the child comes about? In the same way, if we concentrate on the growth of encyclopedic knowledge, we realize that such cumulation can, by itself, bring about change. But what is the psychological import of such change?

Future formulations and research hopefully, should, clarify most of these issues. In the meantime, the program described in this chapter may offer a constructive framework within which to work. Furthermore, such a program should allow us to evaluate whether U-shaped curves are, in fact, an interesting phenomena per se or whether they are merely an indication of internal readjustments of cognitive structures.

REFERENCES

Beilin, H. Cognitive capacities of young children: A replication. *Science,* 1968, *162,* 923–924.
Bever, T. G., Mehler, J., & Epstein, J. What children do in spite of what they know, *Science,* 1967, *158,* 141–142.

Bower, R. G. R. *A Primer of Infant Development,* San Francisco, W. H. Freeman, 1977.

Chomsky, N. *Syntactic structures.* The Hague; Mouton, 1956.

Chomsky, N. *Aspects of the theory of syntax,* Cambridge; MIT Press, 1965.

Chomsky, N. *Language and mind,* New York; Harcourt Brace, 1968.

Clark, E. Some aspects of the conceptual basis for first language acquisition. In R. L. Schiefelbusch & L. L. Lloyd (Eds.), *Language perspectives—acquisition, retardation and intervention.* Baltimore; University Park Press.

Eimas, P., Siqueland, E. R., Jusczyk, P., & Vigorito, J. Speech perception in infants, *Science,* 1971, 171, 303–306.

Fodor, J. *The language of thought.* New York: Crowell Press, 1975.

Herrnstein, R. J. IQ, *The Atlantic Monthly,* 228, 43–64, 1971.

Jensen, A. R. How Much Can We Boost IQ and Scholastic Acheivement? *Harvard Education Review,* 39, 1–123, 1969.

Katz, J. J. *Philosophy of Language.* New York, Harper and Row, 1966.

Mehler, J. La développement des heuristiques perceptives chez le très jeune enfant. *Neuropsychologie de la perception visuelle,* H. Hécaen (Ed.), Paris: Masson, 1971.

Mehler, J., & Bever, T. G. Quantification, conservation and nativism, *Science,* 1968, *162,* 921–924. (a)

Mehler, J., & Bever, T. G. The study of competence in cognitive psychology. *International Journal of Psychology,* 1968, *3,* 273–280. (b)

Mehler, J. Connaïtre par Désapprentissage, *L'Unité de l'Homme,* M. Piattelli and E. Morin (Eds.) Paris, Le Sueil, 1974.

Meltzoff, A. N. Imitation of facial and manual gestures by human neonates. *Science,* 1977, *198,* 75–78.

Piaget, J. *LaNaissance de l'Intelligence Chez l'Enfant,* Neuchätel, Delachaux et Niestlé, 1936.

Piaget, J., & Inhelder, B. *Le Développement des quantités physiques chez l'enfant.* Neuchätel; Delachaux et Niestlé, 1941.

Piatelli–Palmarini, M. (Ed.) *Théorie du langage, theories de l'apprentissage.* Paris; Le Seuil, 1979.

Piatelli–Palmarini, M. (Ed.), *On language and learning: A debate between* Chomsky & Piaget. Cambridge, Harvard University Press, (in press).

Peirce, C. S. *Selected Writings,* New York, Dover Publications, 1958.

Trehub, S. E. The discrimination of foreign speech contrasts by adults and infants. *Child Development,* 1976, *47,* 466–472.

8 Regression in the Service of Development

Thomas G. Bever
Columbia University
New York

Discontinuities in development highlight underlying developmental processes that are gradual. In this chapter I focus on such apparent discontinuities in the emergence of language and related skills. I demonstrate that a commonly proposed model of mental development is consistent with specific regressions in the child's manifest mastery of certain linguistic behaviors. I outline the application of this model to two primary language-specific capacities—the mastery of phonetics and the mastery of sentence processing. In each case there is an early emergence of a basic unit, followed by a behavioral differentiation of the component parts of that unit. In phonology this is reflected in the initial development of "syllables" and a subsequent differentiation of "phones" during the first year of life. In syntax it is the initial develoment of a "canonical clause" and subsequent differentiation of it into phrases and words between 2 and 8 years of age. In each case, the analytic phase of differentiation is accompanied by a temporary decrease, a "regression" in manifest language behaviors and capacities. Maturationally concomitant developments in nonlinguistic behaviors show that, in the normal course, linguistic development parallels other cognitive skills. The import of this is that language acquisition can be seen to be similar to the acquisition of all behavioral systems, rather than presenting a unique, modality-specific developmental pattern.

153

A General Property of Behavioral Development

Consider first a common taxonomic description of mental growth. In this model, the child starts at any given point with certain fundamental canonical capacities. These capacities are subsequently refined, in the course of which they become broken down into constituent capacities—ultimately the constituents are reintegrated into a deeper reconstitution of the original behavioral capacity.

Three kinds of superficially different models share this dialectical property; the *organic* Werner (1957), the *interactionist* Piaget (1950), and the *empiricist* Bruner (1977). Werner (1954) outlines a standard developmental sequence that pervades all aspects of mental development:

syncretic—analytic—synthetic

In the syncretic stage, a given skill (ranging from movement to thinking) is behaviorally expressed holistically—the child uses set global schemata for behavior and organization of his or her experiences. During the analytic phase the child focuses on the isolation of component processes of a skill, ultimately reaching a stage of resynthesis of them into an integrated capacity.

Piaget (1950) outlines a similar course for the emergence of each relatively stable mental system. He generally is concerned with the child's mastery of *a priori* conceptual categories, such as the notion of existence, number, space, and time. In each case the child starts with control over some canonical aspect of behavior, then differentiates separate components of that behavior via self-examination, and finally regulates the operation of the separate components by means of a conceptual schema that equilibrates the operation of the separate components.

The empiricist grants the child initial behavioral schemata (e.g., a global arm movement); these are supplemented with refined schemata based on experience (e.g., controlled finger–thumb opposition), which are ultimately arranged (albeit by wordly contingencies) into integrated behaviors.

The mechanism of conceptual and behavioral discovery differs in each of these cases from the relatively central to the peripheral; it is not important for the present discussion which of these views is correct, especially because they borrow from each other in critical ways. Rather, it serves the purpose of this chapter to note that each kind of developmental theory includes a typical tripartite description of development: The child initially utilizes a canonical behavioral form, analyzes it into constituents, and reintegrates them into a broader basis for the same class of behaviors.

Canonical Forms of Language

Spoken language systematically relates pairs of sounds and meanings. Accordingly, we organize our investigation of language development around the mastery of *syllables* and *sentences,* the canonical forms for the expression of sounds and meanings. In the following, I present case studies of apparent regressions in the acquisition of these forms, a brief survey of the infant's vocal development, and a detailed examination of the emergence of sentence comprehension. In each case, I argue that the "regression" in a manifest behavior is itself a function of maturationally progressive analytic processes.

The Emergence of the Phone in Infant Vocalization. The syllable is the ordinary minimal unit of speech sound that can be spoken in isolation. It has a straightforward acoustic definition—a sustainable speech sound that is bounded by nonsustained sounds. Under this description, possible "syllables" range from a single sustained continuant consonant (e.g., "s"), to a long diphthong surrounded by consonant clusters (e.g., "tfstroisplts"). Inasmuch as all vowels are continuant and have much more sustained speech power than other continuants, the typical center of a syllable is a vowel; the typical syllable boundary is a consonant. Accordingly, the canonical syllable has the form CV(C).

Each language has its own canonical syllabic structure, which the child ultimately masters. We can study the early stages of this process by examining the vocal output of the infant during the first year of life. A classic study of the phonetic development of the child's repetoire is that of Irwin and his colleagues (1946). Although their methods depended on phonetic transcription, they are adequate for the purpose of exploring such features as the development of syllables and consonants.

The data reveal two periods of expansion in the infant's phonetic repetoire, from 1 to 3 months and from 4 to 9 months. (An exhaustive analysis of Irwin's data is presented in Bever, 1961.) During the first period the typical vocalization is a vowel surrounded by two glottal stops or glottal continuants. The main differentiation during this period is in the variety of vowel sounds. During the fourth month, the child's vocal output stops increasing and differentiating. This regression reverses in the next month, when the consonant sounds differentiate—now the child characteristically produces strings with different consonants and the same vowel, as well as consonants in isolation. In light of the tripartite developmental schema outlined above, we can interpret this as a shift from the production and differentiation of complete syllables to the elaboration of component parts of syllables.

Recent work on the perceptual differentiation of speechlike sounds by infants is consistent with this interpretation. For example, Mehler and Bertoncini (1978) report that newborns respond differentially to distinct syllables (e.g., *pat* versus *tap*) better than to nonsyllabic consonant sequences that differ in the same way (e.g., *pst* versus *tsp*). Similarly, a variety of studies have shown that infants discriminate consonant transitions when they are placed in the context of a syllable but do not discriminate the same transitions out of context (see Juczsyk [1980], for a recent review).

Concomitant Behavioral Developments.   I have isolated two periods of expansion of the phonetic repetoire, interrupted by a period of relative vocal quiescence around age 3 months. Our interpretation suggests that the first period corresonds to a "syncretic." syllabic stage, whereas the second period corresponds to a more analytic, phone, stage. Other behavioral changes during the same period illuminate the related neurological developments associated with this shift. For example, Lewis (1954) delineated two phases of vocal "imitation" by the infant, with an intervening period with no imitation. At 1 to 3 months, the infant produces approximate imitations of adult vocalizations; at 4 months the infant stops imitating entirely and then starts to produce more refined imitations at 8 to 9 months.

Numerous other behaviors show a similar regression in their development around age 3 months. For example, the grasping response, the tonic neck reflex, the Moro response, and the plantar/dorsal response ratio all decrease sharply at that age, with certain replacement behaviors emerging at age 5 to 9 months, where relevant. (See Bever, 1961; Maratos, this volume; Prechtl, this volume).

All these behavioral regressions can be interpreted as reflecting an increase in the extent to which behavior is organized at the cortical level. In this view the period of "developmental quiescence" at the end of the third month reflects cortical inhibition of the lower brain systems, without developed structures with which to replace those systems. (McGraw, 1946). Accordingly, the shift in vocal development could be interpreted as "caused" by the shift from reflex to cortical organization of behavior. However, the matter is undoubtedly more complex (see Lecours, this volume). One could also argue that analytic phonetic differentiation is the developmental stage that must follow the syncretic syllabic stage, rendering cortical activity relatively more important.

The Perception of Canonical Sentences.   A characteristic function of language is to represent propositions. The sentence is the minimal independen linguistic unit that expresses a proposition.

The notion of a "sentence" is similar to that of a syllable, in the sense that it is the proposition-bearing structure that can be uttered in isolation; many phrases exist that unambiguously express a complete set of propositional relations (e.g., deverbal noun phrases in English, "the mooing of the cow" . . .). But these sequences cannot stand alone as separate utterances. Only a specific subset of proposition-bearing sequences can stand alone—the sentences. In fact, we must *define* the sentence as the unit that can be uttered alone and that native speakers perceive as presenting phrases that have basic propositional relations to each other (*actor, action, object, modifier*) (Wundt, 1914).

Each language has its own "canonical" sentence form (Greenberg, 1961). In English it is "actor, action (object)." with an explicitly tensed verb. It would be easy to think that such an order reflects and is caused by the "natural" order of thoughts (Bruner, 1974; McNiell, 1979; Osgood, 1977). Many languages (e.g., Turkish) have different canonical sentence orders, so this cannot be an overriding universal principle. However, the proposal that there is a psychologically natural order of linguistic elements partly defines the problem I focus on in this section. I suggest that the young child acquires a set schema that represents his or her interpretation of the canonical sentence in his or her language. As he or she matures, this schema is analysed interally, and distinct subparts are differentiated, both clauses and phrases within clauses. As these components become differentiated, the natural behavioral order constraints can take effect; accordingly, older children are more sensitive to such natural-order constraints than are younger children.

Early Canonical Sentence Comprehension

Certain evidence indicates that children develop a canonical sentence schema at an early age. The basic technique we have used to investigate this is an "acting-out" sentence comprehension paradigm, developed by Bever,

Mehler, and Valian (Bever, 1970a). Children characteristically are presented first with a number of intransitive sentences, such as "the pig is sleeping," "the rabbit is hopping," etc. In each case, the child is to pick the corresponding toy animal and make it "act out" the sentence. After this common training on how to act out intransitive sentences, the experimenter shifts to the more complex sentence forms of interest.

In our first studies we focused on the child's comprehension of reversible and nonreversible active, passive, and cleft sentences. "Reversibility" refers to the semantic possibility of having either the object or the subject of the sentence be the actor (e.g., "the cow kisses the pig"). Irreversible sentences of two types occur, semantically normal ("the policeman eats the candy") and semantically absurd ("the candy eats the policeman"). Table 8.1 presents the percentage of 2-year-olds who correctly acted out each sentence type.[1] Two-year-olds perform randomly on passives and subject-initial cleft sentences, regardless of semantic constraints. However, it is remarkable that children as young as 2.0 perform correctly on active sentences and on object-initial cleft sentences. Two-year-olds, however do not correctly comprehend passive and subject-first cleft sentences. In fact they perform at a chance level, both on the passive and on the subject-first cleft sentence.

It is appropriate to conclude that the 2-year-old child uses a fixed template for sentence processing:

$NP-V-(NP) = actor-action-(object)$

Only sentences with this superficial form can be processed at all. Because the passive and subject-first cleft sentences do not conform to this template, the child performs randomly on them. The hypothesis that the child uses a canonical template is further supported by the fact that performance on object-first cleft sentences is *better* than chance during the second year. This is explained by the fact that the child can treat such sequences as "it's *NP* that *NP-V*," by ignoring everything but the last *NP-V* subsequence: That part of the sentence conforms to one of the two versions of the canonical sentence, allowing the child to comprehend the *actor-action* relation and act on the other animal as the object by a process of elimination.

These results have been replicated in various ways, (e.g., de Villiers & de Villiers, 1978; Maratsos, 1977). It is important to note that differences in methodology can increase or decrease the child's apparent overall linguistic

---

[1]Characteristically we accepted any approximately correct action as "correct"; For example, young children often interpret the verb "lick" as though it were actually, "bump hard with the nose." Our main focus was to determine which noun was chosen as the actor and which as the object. For further methodological details, see Bever (1970a) or Slobin (1978a).

TABLE 8.1
Proportion of Reversible Sentences Acted Out Correctly
by Children 2.0 to 5.8

| | | Simple[a] | | | | | Cleft[b] | | |
	N	Subject First	Object First	Δ	N	Subject First	Object First	Δ
2.0–2.7	25	66	58	8	30	87	73	14
2.8–3.3	34	70	34	36	21	81	65	16
3.4–3.7	32	73	39	34	28	89	69	17
3.8–3.11	34	80	63	16	32	96	55	41
4.0–4.3	35	87	56	31	34	96	76	20
4.4–4.7	25	90	62	28	21	93	82	11
4.8–5.7	43	97	92	5	30	86	86	−1

(Taken from Bever, 1970, Figures 6 & 7)

[a]Sample simple sentences—Subject first: the cow pushes the zebra
Object first: the zebra is pushed by the cow

[b]Sample cleft sentences—Subject first: it's the cow that pushes the gorilla
Object first: it's the zebra that the cow pushes

After 6 warm-up trials with making single, small toy animals act out intransitive sentences, children acted out three subject- and three object-first simple sentences or cleft sentences, presented in a pseudorandom experimental order. The simple-sentence and cleft-sentence experiments involved different children. Only actual responses are taken into account in this table.

capacity. For example, young children perform less well on all sentences if they are forced to choose between two pictures rather than act out the sentence (Turner & Rommetveit, 1967). We were primarily concerned with the child's pattern of the perception of grammatical relations and consequently accepted many approximate actions that other researchers might score as incorrect. Finally, our pretraining technique, in which children learned how to play the "acting-out" game with simple intransitive sentences, filtered out some potential subjects before they even came to the main experiment with transitive verbs. In fact, we were unable to use 12% of the 2-year-old subjects because they did not succeed at the intransitive-verb task. Nevertheless, even these children may have been able to understand the sentences in general, but not in our laboratory: The experimental setting upset some of the children, some should have been taking a nap, were hungry, sick, etc. In brief, the preceding results should be interpreted as bearing on the child's pattern of discriminating the actor from the object of a sentence, *not* an assessment of the child's absolute linguistic capacity.

Our results showed that the 2-year-old child has a remarkable capacity for the actor/object discrimination. I have interpreted the child's early capacity to distinguish the actor from the object as the result of the *NP–V–(NP)* canonical template that reflects the dominant surface word-order pattern of English (Bever, 1971). As I mentioned previously, this cannot be proposed as a structural *linguistic* universal, because some languages may have common forms in which the object precedes the subject. However, the notion that the subject precedes the object because that order corresponds to the way we think about the world has a certain intuitive appeal. In this view, the child builds up a structural *NP–V–NP* expectation, based on the order in which he or she thinks of the corresponding concepts. Several researchers have argued that the *actor ... object* order is behaviorally natural because of the fact that actors are characteristically animate and therefore character-istically have an intention to act *before* they do so. (See, especially, Bruner, 1974) In this view, the speaking child starts out thinking about the actor's intention—this makes it most natural to express the actor as the first noun in the sentence. Although such a description cannot account for *all* sentences (e.g., those depicting unintended acts), the claim is that such sentences are relatively rare. Osgood and Bock (1977) have embedded the natural-order hypothesis within more technical models of speech processing, with much the same theoretical result. They furthermore examined a number of languages and concluded that the natural *actor ... object* order is followed in the majority of cases. This is strong presumptive evidence for the existence of such a behaviorally natural order.

My later analyses depend on the assumption that the child's first stage of canonical sentence comprehension relies on a *structural* template, rather than on such a behaviorally based predisposition. It is necessary to consider the inadequacies of the "natural-order" hypothesis as applied to the child's comprehension of simple sentences. First, this position cannot explain the young child's relative success with the object-first cleft sentences, inasmuch as they specifically violate the natural order. Second, we would expect the child's performance on subject-initial cleft sentences to be as good as on simple actives, rather than at chance level. Third, performance on passives should be systematically reversed, as opposed to being at chance level. Finally, we would expect the young child's performance to be influenced strongly by the relative semantic probabilities: On the naturalness hypo-thesis, it is the overall semantic organization that is the ultimate cause of the standard word order. Nevertheless, the young children are relatively un-affected by the semantic constraints as we manipulated them.

In sum, the pattern of comprehension in the young child is inconsistent with the natural-order hypothesis. We can also utilize a direct behavioral experiment involving sentence processing to demonstrate the structural basis of the canonical sequence. We presented young children with reversible sentences containing a subject or object relative clause, as shown in Table 8.2 (Townsend, Ottaviano, & Bever, 1979). These sentences have a superficial *NVN* sequence initially (in subject relatives) and finally (in object relatives). One second after each sentence, the child was presented with a probe word (a verb) and asked if it had occurred in the sentence. The results showed that the youngest children responded relatively quickly to verbs located in the surface sequence that conformed to the canonical-sentence structure. Clearly, this result does not depend on the semantic sense of the sentences, but on the extent to which they exhibit *apparent* canonical sequences. (We return later to the performance of older children and adults on this task).

A different way to demonstrate that the canonical sentence is defined structurally rather than in terms of semantics or word order is to use non-English sentences that preserve potential semantic patterns and relative order of the subject and object. This can be achieved by presenting children with *NP–NP–V* and *V–NP–NP* sequences. We did this on the same kind of acting-out task as described previously, and found that children perform randomly throughout ages 2 to 4 (Table 8.3). (The basic pattern is replicated in Slobin & Bever, 1981.)

TABLE 8.2
Reaction Time (Seconds) to Recognize Probed Verbs in Complex
Sentences With and Initial and Final *NVN* Sequence
(Taken from Townsend et al., 1979, Table 1; 12 3-year-old Subjects)

	Initial V	Final V
V in *NVN* sequence	$2.29\text{–}SR^a$	$2.18\text{–}OR^b$
V not in *NVN* sequence	$3.29\text{–}OR^b$	$2.67\text{–}SR^a$

[a]Subject Relative (*SR*): *The owl scratched the fox* that touched the monkey.

[b]Object Relative (*OR*): The owl that scratched *the fox touched the monkey*.
(The superficial *NVN* sequence is underlined.)
　Subjects heard each sentence, followed by a probe word. They responded "yes" or "no" to indicate whether the probe word was, or was not, in the sentence. The critical positive probes were the first-clause or second-clause verb ("scratched" or "touched") above.

TABLE 8.3
Percentage of Initial Nouns Taken as Actor in Acting-Out Task

Age	N	NNV[a]	VNN[b]
2	18	51	46
3	21	43	42
4	12	43	49

[a]NNV–"the cow the horse pushes"

[b]VNN–"pushes the cow the horse"

The procedure was similar to that described in Table 8.1.

Random performance on these nonsentential sequences, even at the oldest age (4), is startling, inasmuch as each sequence does correspond to a possible within-sentence arrangement. *NP–NP–V,* appears in relative clauses ("the horse the cow licks . . . "), whereas *V–NP–NP* appears in indirect object constructions ("give your dog a bone") and in questions with "be", and "have" ("has the dog a bone?"). Apparently, even a 4-year-old child cannot generalize from these constructions to interpret the test sequences systematically. In our interpretation this is because the test sequences violate one or another canonical sentence feature. The relative-clause sequence can never appear as an isolated sentence. The imperative indirect-object sequence does not present an uninterrupted *V–NP = Action–Object* sequence; the transitive *"have + NP + NP"* questions are limited to just "have" and "be".

We also can consider sentence comprehension in other languages, which have different kinds of canonical sentences. For example, Sinclair and Bronkhart (1972) found that French children perform randomly on acting-out sentences that did not have articles and inflections on the verb. (e.g., *"garcon pousser fille"*). Because French word order is like that of English, in this case the natural-order hypothesis has the same difficulty in accounting for the result: Even though the word order represents the canonical "actor–action–object" sequence, the sentence fails to have a criterial property of a French sentence—determiners and inflectional endings. Accordingly, young children cannot perform at all systematically on such sequences.

Certain languages allow us to show that the canonical-sentence form acquired by children does not necessarily depend on fixed word order. For example, in Turkish all six orders of *actor, action,* and *object* are linguistically acceptable, so long as the object inflection is attached to the object noun (in definite noun phrases). This is reflected in the fact that 2-year-old

Turkish children respond correctly to all word orders with an object inflection; at the same time, they perform randomly on all sequence orders when the inflections are deleted, despite the fact that there is a favorite grammatical order, *VNN*. (Slobin & Bever, 1981; Slobin, 1980). This result further disproves the natural-order hypothesis for the priority of actors before objects. Remarkably young Turkish children ignore word order and focus on the criterial clue—object inflection. In our interpretation, the Turkish child constructs an unordered canonical sentence scheme:

> *Ninf* = Object
> *V* = Action
> *N* = Actor

It is the general thesis of this chapter that the 3 to 4-year-old differentiates the internal structure of the canonical sentence forms. During this phase we might expect the appearance of such mentally "natural" strategies as "the first noun is the actor." This strategy can appear only *after* the child has analyzed the internal structure of the canonical-sentence form. During the early period of its use, the canonical sentence is a syncretic whole, and does not afford the child any internal structure over which natural generalizations can be applied.

Several experimental results confirm this expectation. By about age 3½, children perform systematically *worse* on the passive and object-first cleft sentences (Table 8.1). The performance decrease in the passives has been replicated by several different investigators. The decrease in passive comprehension can be taken as an example of a "developmental regression." Although a regression, we now interpret it as a function of the *progressive* internal differentiation of the constituent phrases of a canonical sentence. Once the child develops an internal differentiation of the parts of the sentence, then the natural word-order constraint can have its effect. In other words, we can accept the naturalness hypothesis as a true fact about sentence processing, so long as we do not invoke it to account for the child's first sentential schemata. Once the child segregates the initial noun phrase, the naturalness hypothesis can apply, decreasing comprehension on passives and other object-first sentences and increasing it on subject-first sentences.

A developmental increase in the tendency to interpret the first noun as an actor also occurs in other languages. For example, children speaking German (Mills, 1979) and Hebrew (Frankel et al, in press; Frankel & Arbel, in press) show a tendency to take the first noun as the actor, except when

there is an explicit object inflection on the initial noun. We found a similar
result in Serbo-Croatian (Bever & Slobin, 1981; Slobin, 1981). Serbo-
Croatian is particularly interesting because all sequence orders are grammatical. Furthermore, some noun-inflection systems do not differentiate subject and object, and some do. This makes it possible to test the separate effects
of work order, subject inflection and object inflection. The basic findings are
consistent with our interpretation of the English data. The 2-year-old Serbo–
Croatian children respond systematically only to the sequence in the *NVN*
form.

As shown in Table 8.4, children 2.0 to 2.7 respond randomly if the
inflected noun phrase is initial (regardless of whether it is inflected to be
subject or object), and they choose the first noun as the actor if the first noun
is uninflected, regardless of whether the final noun is inflected and in which
way. The conclusion from this is that the child starts out with a canonical-
sentence form:

$$N \text{ (not infl)} -V-N = Actor-Action-Object$$

Sentences departing from that form are acted out in random order. The *NVN*
sequence is the dominant order in adult speech, which may explain why it is

TABLE 8.4
Percentage of Initial Nouns Chosen as Actors in Acting-Out Task
in Serbo–Croatian
(From Slobin and Bever, 1980)

| Age | N | Final Inflections | | Initial Inflections | | No Inflection |
		NVO	NVS	SVN	OVN	NVN
2/0–2/7	16	72	67	50	47	67
2/8–3/3	16	78	44	82	13	74

NVO   Dete HRANI PSA   "The CHILD feeds the dog"
NVS   PAČEL jubi devojčica   "The girl kisses the duckling"
OVN   Čoveka grebe Pile   "The chicken scratches the man"
SVN   Lovac juri jagnje   "The hunter chases the lamb"
N = noun without an explicit suffix
S = noun with explicit subject-marking suffix
O = noun with explicit object-marking suffix
Same procedure as described in Table 8.1, with native speakers of Serbo–Croatian in
Yugoslavia.

salient for the child. Furthermore, the fact that the child must master many different inflections and also accept sentences with no inflections may explain why there is an early dependence on word order.

It remains to be seen why the Serbo–Croatian child responds systematically to sentences with no initial inflections. One possibility is that the confusing and ambiguous nature of inflectional endings in Serbo–Croatian makes sentence processing impossible if the initial noun phrase presents an ambiguous inflection. A fixed word-order schema would render irrelevant any inflection on the final noun phrase. This restriction demonstrates that the 2.0 to 2.7-year-old is *not* using the natural-order strategy, inasmuch as that would apply to all sentence types (especially those with initial subject-inflected nouns).

This interpretation is supported by the later developments in the child's comprehension patterns (Table 8.4). The natural word-order strategy becomes extremely strong by age 2.8 to 3.3, *except* in the case of inflected object-initial sentences. That is, as in German and Hebrew, the initial-object inflection becomes particularly important and has much more effect in blocking the natural-order strategy than does a final-subject inflection. In Serbo–Croatian, this may be because a final-subject inflection cannot block the left–right application of the natural-order strategy until the very end of the sequence, after the strategy has *already* applied.

Turkish sentences (of the sort we were studying) always present an object inflection. Is there any evidence of the order strategy appearing at the ages corresponding to its appearance in other languages? A weak effect exists, but only for the uninflected (i.e., ungrammatical) *NNV* sequences. This suggests that when the Turkish child differentiates an interal analysis of the canonical-sentence form, the unambiguous clarity of the omnipresent object inflection blocks the natural word-order strategy (see Slobin & Bever, 1980).

In brief, the natural-order strategy can be interpreted as available to the child only after he or she has analyzed the internal structure of the canonical sentence into phrases, and only if the structure of the language allows some ambiguity of propositional relations.

One of the most startling results was the fact that the young children often indicated that they were aware of the oddness of semantically irreversible sentences. For example, one 2-year-old responded to "the candy eats the policeman" by picking up the candy and bouncing it all over the policeman. When asked what happened, she reported, "it ate him," and announced, laughing, "the policeman's inside the candy's tummy. That's silly."

Differentiation of the phrases internal to a sentence makes it possible for the 3-year-old child to respond with sensitivity to the semantic implications of the opposite word order. For example, the child can now consider as separate phrases "policeman," "candy," and "eat," comparing the relative likelihood of either noun phrase as the actor. This differentiation underlies the increased sensitivity to semantic constraints as the child gets older. This too, can be characterised as a regression in the child's ability to process semantically unlikely sentences. (Table 8.5). However, we see that it is a natural consequence of the internal differentiation of the parts of the sentence, making it possible to consider alternate propositions made up of the same phrases. Such an interpretation resolves a puzzle implicit to the anecdote about the young child who noticed that it was funny that the candy would eat the policeman, even as she was correctly acting it out. In an earlier discussion of the young child's insensitivity to semantic constraints, I argued that young children simply do not know enough about the world to apply such constraints and that only by age 3½ have they accumulated sufficient worldly experience (Bever, 1970a). This unlikely hypothesis has been questioned by some (Macnamara, 1972) on the reasonable grounds that even young children know a great deal about the world, especially the part of the world we were testing. It is reasonable to claim that a young child knows that candy usually is eaten, and does not do the eating. Our own subject indicated this by her humor at the reverse situation. The present explanation for the emergence of semantic strategies in comprehension is that the young child cannot make use of his or her knowledge in sentence comprehension because the sentence is treated as an impenetrable object that does not allow the child to consider

TABLE 8.5

Percentage Correct on Probable and Improbable Active Sentences
(From Bever, 1970)

Age	N	Probable[a]	Improbable[b]	Probable–Improbable
2	83	80	68	12
3	79	88	49	39
4	77	90	57	33
5	24	100	75	25

[a]Probable–the policeman eats the candy

[b]Improbable–the candy eats the policeman

Same procedure as described in Table 8.1.

any alternative interpretations to the one specified by the canonical structure. The older child has available an analysis of the separate phrases, can consider alternative interpretations, and responds according to the more natural constraints.

The differentiation of Interclause Relations. The previous investigations focused on the isolation of semantic relations within clauses. Given that recursion is an essential feature of language, it is important to investigate the child's comprehension of the relationship between clauses. Here too, we can anticipate the possibility that the child starts out with a canonical-structural schema governing the relationship between clauses. As he or she analyzes the internal structure of the schema, so that the clauses are assigned separate representations, natural-order strategies can come into play.

Temporally related clauses with the conjunctions "before" and "after" offer a distinction similar to that between structural organization and natural order in the interpretation of within-clause grammatical relations. In structural terms, the meanings of the conjunctions specify exactly the order of the events mentioned in the clauses and also specify which clause is main and which subordinate. In behavioral terms, there is a principle of natural temporal order that has been suggested (Clark & Clark, (1968); Townsend & Bever, (1978). On this principle the order of the clauses most naturally corresponds to the order of the events described. Indeed, Clark and Clark (1968) have argued that the basic strategy that children use to interpret temporal sentences is the temporal-order strategy. We can formulate it as the following:

First clause = first event

The temporal-order strategy involving relations between clauses is *prima facie* similar to the word-order strategy within clauses. Accordingly, we would expect that 3 to 5-year-old children would be particularily susceptible to it, whereas younger children would not. We found that the temporal-naturalness strategy does characterize the comprehension of complex sentences at age 3. Children acted out two-clause intransitive sentences like those in Table 8.6. The results are also summarized in Table 8.6. We found that the sentences that conform to the naturalness constraint are consistently responded to better by age 3. (In these experiments we counted only those responses in which both actions were acted out, because we were primarily concerned with order comprehension. As before, we also accepted under-

TABLE 8.6
Percentage Correct Action Orders in Two-Clause Sentences (Only Case Where Both Clauses Were Acted Out)

Age	N	After S_1, S_2[a]	S_2 After S_1[b]	Before S_2, S_1[c]	S_1 Before S_2[d]	$\bar{E}$ After	$\bar{E}$ Before	$\bar{E}$ in Natural Order		$\bar{E}$ not in Natural Order	
2	16	53	50	66	65	52	66	14	59	58	1
3	18	68	34	53	71	51	62	11	70	44	26
4	22	95	43	61	95	69	78	9	95	52	43

[a]After S_1, S_2 (Natural order)—after the cow jumped the pig ran

[b]S_2 after S_1—the pig ran after the cow jumped

[c]Before S_2, S_1—before the pig ran the cow jumped

[d]S_1 before S_2 (Natural order)—the cow jumped before the pig ran
Similar to the procedure described in Table 8.1.

standable variants on the actual actions performed by the child. Finally, we acted out the two choices for the child, if he refused to act them out himself—the order of presented choices was randomized).

Two-year-old children, however, show no effect of temporal order—rather they appear to find sentences with "before" easier than those with "after," independent of surface order. We argued that this reflects a canonicial complex-sentence form;

> *Main clause = Main event*
> *Subordinate clause = subordinate event*

which, in the case of temporally ordered events appears as *Event 1–Event 2.* That is, the 2-year-old recognizes that there are separate events in a main and subordinate clause, but does not attend to their relative position in the surface order. Rather, he or she is using an unordered canonical complex-sentence strategy which is appropriated for sentences with "before":

> *NP V (NP) = main event = first event*
> *CONJ + NP V (NP) = subordinate event = later event*

Feagens (1980) found that young children also perform well on sentences with "until," which is temporally similar to "before." As the older child analyzes the internal structure of the complex sentence into two sequential separate clauses, then the natural-order hypothesis can apply, leading him or her to understand the order of events according to the order of mention. This development leads to a *decrease* in the developing child's capacity to act out sentences that do not conform to the temporal-order strategy. However, this regression is appropriately interpreted as the result of a progressive differentiation of the internal structure of complex sentences into separate clauses. Once clauses are segregated as separate parts of a sentence, the effects of order of mention can follow "naturally" and determine the child's performance. (The shift to a temporal strategy in older children is also reported by Feagens.)

We also kept careful track of the number of refusals on each sentence type and the number of instances in which only one of the two actions was acted out. The 2-year-old children acted out both clauses in "before" and "after"-sentences with the same overall frequency (39%). However, the distribution of the incomplete responses further supports the canonical complex-template interpretation. The main clause is acted out alone three times as often as is the subordinate clause.

The temporal-order strategy has an intuitively clear basis in speech behavior—we tend to think of events in the order in which they are presented to us. Furthermore, order of events is one of the most basic ways in which propositions are related in discourses. Another central interpropositional relation is *cause–effect.* (Townsend & Bever, 1978) We have not studied this experimentally ourselves. However, Piaget (1950) reports that children go through a phase of saying sentences like "we're in a tunnel because it's dark in here" or "I'm in the water because I'm wet." In these cases the child maintains a cause–effect order of propositions despite the fact that the conjunction structurally requires the reverse interpretation. That is, the child appears to use a natural causal-order strategy:

First clause = cause

This strategy is reflected in relative comprehension difficulty among adults of sentences that fail to conform to it. (Townsend & Bever (1978). My own observation is that the overriding effect of the clause-order strategy in the speech of children occurs during the third to fourth year. Younger children seem to grasp the correct causal relation of those cause–effect sentences they can deal with at all. This is consistent with the proposal that only by the fourth year do children clearly differentiate and focus on the first clause as part of a complex sentence. Two-year-olds seem, in contrast, to give greater relative weight to the most recent clause. For example, in the temporally ordered two-clause sentences, the second clause was acted out alone three times as often as the first clause (Table 8.7).

The emergence of focus on the first clause at age 4 is also born out by a version of the verb-probe test described in the foregoing. Subjects were presented with verbs following coordinate constructions; the verb was either from the first or second clause. Three-year-olds showed a clear recency effect—the most recent verb was the most quickly identified. Four-year-olds, however, strongly reversed this pattern. This overall developmental shift to relatively fast latency to initial verbs was found with several other two-clause constructions (Table 8.8). (Townsend et al., 1979).

Inter–Intraclause Relations: Pronouns. Whole clauses can be related by subordinating conjunctions such as "before" and "after." There are other kinds of connections between clauses; for example, pronoun relations that link a phrase in one clause to a phrase in another. The examples in Table 8.8 demonstrate pronominal constructions that we presented to children to

TABLE 8.7
Percentage of Types of Response to Temporal Sentences Produced
by 2-Year-Old Children

	After S_1, S_2	S_2 After S_1	Before S_2, S_1	S_1 Before S_2
Both clauses	41	37	35	43
Only first clause	5	8	0	4
Only second clause	22	12	21	2
Refused totally	33	43	43	51

From the same experiment as in Table 8.6.

TABLE 8.8
Recognition Latencies (Seconds) to Verbs in Initial and Final Clauses
(From Townsend et al., 1979, Table 1)

Age	N	Coordinate[a]		Comparative[b]		Temporal[c]		Main–Relative[d]	
		First V	Second V	First V	Second V	First V	Second V	First V	Second V
3	12	3.5	2.7	2.2	2.4	2.6	2.6	2.8	2.4
4	12	2.0	2.9	1.3	3.0	1.9	2.0	1.8	2.0
5	12	1.6	1.4	1.6	1.8	1.2	1.2	1.3	1.0

[a]Coordinate–the owl scratched the fox and he touched the monkey
[b]Comparative–the owl scratched the fox faster than he touched the monkey
[c]Temporal–after (before) the owl scratched the fox he touched the monkey
[d]Main–Relative–the owl (that) scratched the fox (that) touched the monkey
From the same experiment as presented in Table 8.2.

act out with toys. The child had two different toy animals in front of him or her at each trial. In each case, the question was, did the child choose one or two animals to perform the actions? For adults there is only one circumstance in which the choice of two animals is required—when the noun in an initial main clause precedes the pronoun in the following subordinate clause. All the other cases allow the pronoun to be interpreted as the same or different

TABLE 8.9
Percentage of Times in Which the Same Actor Was Chosen to ACt Out
Both Clauses of Sentences with Pronouns

Age		2	3	4
Main Clause	Subordinate Clause			
(a) Noun	Pronoun	54	66	45
Pronoun	Noun	36	46	34
Difference		18	20	11
1st Clause	2nd Clause			
(b) Noun	Pronoun	46	80	56
Pronoun	Noun	44	34	21
Difference		2	46	35

After (before) the cow jumped, he slept
After (before) he jumped, the cow slept
The cow slept after (before) he jumped
He slept after (before) the cow jumped
Same paradigm as in Table 8.6. Each subject was presented with each of eight possible pronoun–noun combinations with *Before* and *After*. Only sentences in which the clauses were acted out in the correct order are included.

animal. Table 8.9 presents the frequency with which, at each age, the child chose the same noun to carry out both actions.

We restrict our discussion to the cases in which the child acted out the clauses in the correct temporal order, inasmuch as the interaction between acting-out order, structure, and in correct order could be quite complicated.

Two aspects of the main/subordinate clause relation appear to determine the child's choice in those cases where adults would have a choice. At all ages the child shows some relative tendency to match the noun and pronoun when the noun is in the main clause and the pronoun is in the subordinate clause (Table 8.9a). Furthermore, an order strategy emerges, by the third year, of matching the noun and pronoun relatively more often when the noun precedes the pronoun (Table 8.9b). This also reflects the child's shift from relating clauses by sensitivity to a subordinate marker to relating them in terms of their serial order.

The Differentiation of the Sentence Constituent. I have suggested that several apparent regressions in the child's ability to comprehend sentences are in fact due to a progressive development of an internal analysis of the canonical-sentence form. The internal differentiation of *parts* of sentences make the sentences vulnerable to the overriding effect of natural order and semantic constraints, which in turn can lead to decreased performance on those constructions that do not conform to the natural order or likely meaning. If the child is developing an internal differentiation of sentences, we should be able to observe changing patterns in how he or she processes sentences for purposes other than comprehension. In particular, we should find systematic patterns in the way he or she organizes linguistic material in immediate memory.

We tested this prediction in several ways. First, we studied the ability of children from ages 3 to 6 years to repeat simple three-word sequences. We used four kinds of sequences, as shown in Table 8.10, all of which drew on the same set of words, arranged in one of four ways: sentences, backward sentences, word-class paradigms, and "random." The "forward" sentences were of the form "adj-noun-verb." This form was not the simplest canonical-sentence structure. We used it, however, because the normal three-word canonical sentence (e.g., "boys like girls") is also well formed when uttered backward. Our purpose in including the backward sequences was to isolate the effect of syntax, as opposed to an effect of words that are related in a semantic field. The paradigm and the random sequences were included to isolate the effect of word class itself. Finally, we isolated the effect of the semantic field by comparing the performance on those sequences that are unified in such a field (the forward and backward sentences) with those sequences that are not united in such a field (the random and paradigm sequences).

TABLE 8.10

Percentage of Words Recalled for Each Type of Word Sequence

Age	N	Sentence (S)[a]	Backward (B)[b]	Paradigm (P)[c]	Random (R)[d]	Effect of "Word Order" S–B	Effect of "Word Class" P–R	Effect of "Semantics" $\dfrac{(S+B)-(P+R)}{2}$
3	23	32	33	18	15	–1	3	11
4	24	40	23	23	22	17	1	11
5	19	38	33	27	28	5	–1	8
6	17	44	38	33	25	6	8	12

[a]Sentence: nice boys laugh small cows eat green leaves grow
[b]Backward: laugh boys nice eat cows small grow leaves green
[c]Paradigm: laugh eat grow boys cows leaves nice small green
[d]Random: laugh boys small green grow cows leaves nice eat
Subjects were presented for immediate recall with nine-word sequences, one from each of the types exemplified, in a random order across subjects.

Each child was presented with three sequences of each type at once, with a pause after each triplet (for a total of nine words in each stimulus). The sequence types and the sequences within each type were presented in varying orders, counterbalanced across age and sex.

The results show that children reached a ceiling of about one sentence correctly recalled by age 4 (Table 8.13). Their performance on the other sequence types developed much more slowly. In fact, performance on backward sentences was *worse* at age 4 than at age 3, and performance on random sequence was worse at age 6 than at age 5. We also examined the separate effect of word order, semantic field, and word class. Semantic-field effect is greatest at age 3, word order at age 4, and word class at age 6. This relative order of structural properties is consistent with our findings in the sentence-comprehension tasks reviewed previously. The absolute age, however, is about a year older than for the effects we found in those experiments. This might be because sentence repetition is a less natural task than sentence comprehension or because the grammatical sentence form we used was not the simplest canonical one.

These results indicate the following: At age 3 the child treats the repetition task primarily as a problem in isolated word recall, making use of the semantic connectedness among the words. At age 4, word order is dominant when it corresponds to a possible sentence. *Ex hypothesi,* this reflects the emerging isolation of the separate words as distinct parts of each sentence, in distinct locations. By age 5, semantic effects do obtain, even when the sequence is not an actual sentence (as in the backward sequences). Finally, at age 6, the child is able to make use of word-class information as an aid to recall: The developing internal analysis of parts of the sentence has progressed to the point where the internal structure of different words is being learned.

The emergence of a focus on the word, as opposed to the complete sentence, can be tested in another way. We adapted a technique of Savin and Bever (1970) to extract information about the relative ease of thinking of the beginning of a sequence in terms of the first word, or in terms of the first word of a particular sentence. The technique is to present subjects with sets of three-word sentences, such as those in Table 8.11a and b. The listener's task is to press a key as soon as he hears a target sentence—he or she is informed of the target either as "the story, 'boys kiss girls'," or as "the story that begins with the word 'boys'." All the sentences are three-word "subject–verb–object" sentences, so the structure of the target sentence is always predictable. Furthermore, the subject is told that the target is the *only* sequence that begins with the word "boys." That is, the two kinds of instruction are logically *identical* in these materials, and the listeners know this. Table 8.11a presents the reaction times for the two instructions presented to college undergraduates. Despite their knowledge that the instructions are functionally

TABLE 8.11a

Latencies (msed) for Responses to Sentences, Given Initial Word or
Whole Sentence as Targets (Eight Subjects)

Word Latency[a]	Sentence Latency[b]	Word–Sentence Difference	Percentage of Subjects Having Positive Difference
290	251	39	100

[a]Initial word target: "boys"

[b]Whole sentence target: "boys like girls"

Subjects hear a series of three-word sentences, listening for a particular target sentence. When the target is heard the subject purshed a button. The given targets were either the entire sentence ("setence latency") or only the first word ("word latency").

TABLE 8.11b

Latencies (msec) for Responses to Sentences, Given Initial Word or
Whole Sentence Targets, for Subjects of Different Ages

Age	N	Word Latency	Sentence Latency	Word-Sentence Difference	Percentage of Subjects Showing Positive Difference
4	17	1255	993	+262	71
5	22	795	892	−97	46
6 + 7	26	541	609	−168	39
8 + 9	19	409	441	−32	47
10 + 11	35	329	322	+7	63

Same procedure as described for Table 8.11a.

identical, adults respond faster with sentence instructions than with word instructions. This is particularly striking because their response time characteristically is faster than the time it takes to complete the word "boys." That is, *thinking* about the initial word as the first sounds of the anticipated sentence leads to faster response times than thinking of it as the initial word of *some NVN* sentence, even before the word is over. Another way of putting this is to say that in these experimental conditions (McNiell & Lindig, 1973) the sentence is a more accessible level of linguistic processing than the word.

We adapted this technique for use with children between the ages of 4 and 12. We built an electrically triggered jack-in-the-box, which jumped out when the child hit a button at the right time. This maintained the younger childrens' interest in the reaction-time task. Each younger child was told that the jack-in-the-box liked to hear certain stories and that the subject should hit the button as soon as the right story started, so that the jack-in-the-box could hear it too. The experimenter told the child before each trial what the next target story would be—sometimes presenting it in terms of the initial word, "boys," sometimes presenting the entire sentence. Table 8.11b displays the mean reaction times on these tasks across age. Older children are increasingly fast on both tasks. Like the adults, the 4-year-olds are significantly faster with sentence instructions than with word instructions. Six-to seven-year-old children, however are reliably faster with word instructions. This is consistent with our claim that these children are going through a period of analyzing the internal structure of each sentence and of each word in the sentence—relatively speaking, children at this age tend to process sentences literally as sequences of words. Accordingly, the level of the word is more easily accessed than the level of the sentence.

Regressions in Cognitive Performance

The preceding discussion reviews a variety of developmental phenomena in language comprehension that are best understood as due to the 2- to 5-year-old child's increasing differentiation of the constituent parts of sentences. This phenomenon is not limited to linguistic development; rather it is characteristic of all aspects of cognitive development during this age period. (See also the chapters by Mehler and by Strauss, in this volume.) In each aspect, we find the same stages as in the development of sentence processing—an initial stage of fixed capacity, followed by a stage at which internal differentiation of the structure allows contingent generalizations to dominate behavior, leading to temporary regressions in manifest capacity.

Conservation of Inequalities. The acquisition of the ability to make relative numerosity judgments has been studied a great deal because of its centrality to the emergence of the concept of number itself. In this discussion I do not address the latter question, just as the preceding sections do not explore the child's acquisition of the concept of a structurally well-formed sentence. Consider the child's ability to maintain his or her perception of numerical inequality despite perceptually confusing transformations of stimuli. For example, if a child of 5 is presented with an array like that on the left in the following, he or she will volunteer that the top row has more and will maintain this even if the array is transformed so that it looks like the array on the right.

    0 0 0 0 0 0   000000

    0   0   0   0   0   0   0   0

A 3- to 4-year-old child does not respond in this way. After volunteering that the upper row on the left has more, the child characteristically concludes that the lower row on the right has more, even though he or she has just observed its transformation from the row on the left. (Bever, Mehler, & Epstein, 1968; Mehler & Bever, 1967). Furthermore, the 2-year-old child performs like the 5-year-old on this task. Here we have an instance of a clear regression—the 3-year-old "loses" a capacity, and performs systematically worse than before.[2]

Our original interpretation of this phenomenon was that the 2-year-old was using a basic capacity that had specific limits on its domain of application. The 3-year-old was postulated to develop a perceptual generalization, "things that look bigger have more." Further research has suggested that the 2-year-old's capacity for relative numerosity judgments is sensitive to many minor stimulus and methodological variables. In my present interpretation the 2-year-old has available set schemata for assessing quantities; by age 3, the child's concept of quantity includes a differentiation of the internal constituents of quantified material. With such a differentiation, contingently true generalizations can be recognized (e.g., that larger things tend to have more constituents). Again, in our present reinterpretation, the 3-year-old child has differentiated the internal structure of a problem, allowing true generalizations over that structure to take effect. That is, the 2-year-old child is, by hypothesis, just as capable of learning such generalizations, but he or she cannot apply them to those objects and behaviors that are not yet internally differentiated.

---

[2]Notice that this task can be interpreted as "conservation of an inequality relation," which might seem to have great implications for Piagetian interpretations of conservation experiments in general. I now think that the entire matter is muddled; in any case, it is not directly germane to the present discussion. The many replications of our original findings yield results that differ in a variety of ways, usually interpretable as due to differences in methodology or scoring technique. In particular, we were not concerned to use the standard test of conservation in which the child is presented with an "equal" array, and must maintain the report of equality under transformation. Our reluctance to use the equality relation is because the terms for expressing it ("the same") tend to be ambiguous; "same" might refer to physical identity or to numerical identity or to identity of constituent material. Use of terms like "same amount" may not resolve the ambiguity for a 2-year-old who does not understand "amount." Furthermore, the child must choose between three alternatives (the arrays are "the same" or "this one has more" or "that one has more"). It is no surprise that a 2-year-old cannot handle this level of complexity, just as he or she cannot comprehend subject-initial cleft sentences.

Second, we include in our studies only children who recognize the original relationship correctly—other researchers report results from *all* children they study, including those who may not have correctly perceived the relative amount in the first array. Obviously, this procedure deflates success at all ages, although it is not motivated by an understanding of conservation. Conservation requires that a child demonstrate that he maintains a relationship under transformation—if the child does not understand the original relationship between two arrays, how can he or she be expected to conserve it?

It is important to note, however, that other research does usually report a decrease in the child's performance from age 2 to 3, even if the 2-year-olds do not perform better than chance on the particular task.

Regressions in Learning Capacity

The research on the onset of nonconservation during the third year of life has a parallel form of argumentation to the research on the onset of perceptual strategies in sentence comprehension. In each case an internal analysis of the stimulus situation makes possible the effect of contingent generalizations, which are false in crucial cases, and which underly temporary regressions in overt capacity. In each case, I have attempted to show the inadequacy of our earlier hypothesis that it is the child's "discovery" of these generalizations that causes the regressions; in each case, I appeal to the internal different-iation of a set capacity as a precursor to the application of independently recognizable contingent generalizations.

We can test the child's proclivity to analyze the internal structure of situations in which there is no relevant contingent generalization. If the 3-year-old child exhibits an analytic predisposition in such situations, that will confirm our claim that this can underly the different behavior patterns of 2- and 3- to 4-year-old children. "Place learning" offers such a situation. The child is presented with two inverted cups on each trial; one cup has a reward under it, the other does not. The child is invited to pick up the cup he or she wishes on each trial.

This experimental version of "which hand has the candy?" can be deployed in a variety of ways. We first extended downward in age a series of experiments by Weir (1964), showing that older children tend less than younger children to "maximize" in a probability learning paradigm. In this paradigm one of the cups (e.g., the one on the left) has the reward more often than the one on the right, on a random schedule. The most rational strategy in this situation is to maximize (i.e., *always* to choose the more frequent cup).

TABLE 8.12
Performance on 5:3 Two-Choice Probability Place Learning

Age	N	Trials to Maximize	Percentage of Subjects Who Maximize	Percentage of Subjects Who Minimize	Percentage Individual Maximizing Choices on Last 10 Trials	Percentage of Alternations
2	16	17	63	18	75	20
3	30	—	47	0	68	43
4	6	—	17	0	57	66

On each of 40 trials subjects chose one of two inverted cups with different toy animals on them (e.g., a lion on the left and a zebra on the right). The maximizing cup covered an M & M candy 5/8 times, the minimizing cup the other 3/8 times, on a random schedule. Criterion for "maximizing" or "minimizing" was six choices in a row of the appropriate cup.

Children, however (as well as rats and many adult humans), often do not do this. Rather, they choose both stimuli to some extent. We used this paradigm with children aged 2 to 4, as a way of probing the child's internal representation of choice sequences. In our first study, we used a reinforcement ratio of 5:3 between the cups. Children were run through 40 trials, after the game had been explained to them. We found that the frequency of choosing the more probable cup was significantly higher in the 2-year-olds. (Table 8.12) Furthermore, significantly more 2-year-old subjects developed a maximizing strategy. (We defined *maximizing* as choosing the more probable cup six times in a row and *minimizing* as choosing the less probable cup six times in a row.)

We replicated this experiment, using a 5:4 ratio, to see how sensitive the young child's performance is to small differences in reward probability. The results are similar to the first experiment, with decreasing numbers of maximizers among the older children (Table 8.13).

The number of "minimizers" also decreases with age in both studies, although it is consistently less than the number of maximizers at age 2. We can reconstruct the child's behavior in the following way: the 2-year-old chooses one cup and sticks with it for a few trials. This reflects the fact that in the first experiment more than 80% of the 2-year-olds were either maximizers or minimizers. If the cup continues to pay off more than the other cup, the child stays with it. This is reflected in the fact that the ratio of maximizers to minimizers is lower for the 5:4 experiment than the 5:3 one— it makes less difference. In sum, the 2-year-old uses two rules:

1. Pick the same cup as the preceding trial.
2. If it is the losing cup more often than not (in the last few trials) shift to the other cup and continue to apply Rule 1.

TABLE 8.13
Performance on 5/4 Two-Choice Probability Place Learning

Age	N	Trials to Maximize	Percentage of Subjects Who Maximize	Percentage of Subjects Who Minimize	Percentage Maximizing Choices on Last 10 Trials	Percentage of Alternations
2	20	27	52	16	40	16
3	25	27	40	12	59	51
4	17		6	0	39	68

Same procedure as described in Table 8.12 with 5/9 trials reinforced on the maximizing cup, and 4/9 on the minimizing cup.

The older child appears to be attempting to turn the same kind of formulations into a more comprehensive rule that will cover *all* the cases. Although the individual algorithms may differ, the overall net effect will be to increase the number of alternations, following both positive and negative reinforcment. This is reflected in the increase with age in the number of alternation trials in both experiments. (The individual formulations used by the older subjects appear to differ greatly, which is why I do not present an analysis here). Both younger and older children can be viewed as applying rules. But only the older child insists that the domain of the rules be each part of the situation—the younger child is content with a more global treatment (and a more rewarding one). Again, we do not have to postulate that the basic mechanisms for solving the problem differ between younger and older children. Rather, the older children develop an internal trial-by-trial representation of the situation, which then presents them with the (impossible) task of attempting to predict each trial specifically.

Probability learning can bring out a subject's desire to impose a complete structure, but the problem does not have any trial-by-trial structure itself and therefore cannot reveal systematic differences in the subject's analytic sensitivity (as opposed to his or her zeal to make complete predictions). Discrimination learning, however, offers such a possibility because we can vary the number of dimensions that a given task offers.

We used a version of the "which cup has the candy?" task in a way that allowed us to vary the number of discriminable dimensions. In the basic paradigm the child was presented with the two cups—each now having the same small toy animal mounted on it (e.g., a lion). The child's task was simply to learn that the reinforcement was always on the left (or right). Children were run through 40 trials after the game was explained to them. The results (Table 8.14) showed that 2-year-olds are capable of mastering this discrimination with a very small number of trials. (Our criterion was six correct choices in a row.) Three-year-olds also do so, but with somewhat

TABLE 8.14
No. of Trials to Criterion (Six Correct in a Row) in a Left–Right
Place-Learning Experiment

Age	N	Same Animals	N	Different Animals
2	24	1.9	22	1.8
3	26	3.6	23	5.3
4	22	2.9	18	2.9

Subjects chose on each of 40 trials one of two inverted cups. The same cup (right or left) always covered an M & M candy. In the same-animals condition, each cup had the same toy animal mounted on it. In the different-animals condition, each cup had a different toy animal mounted on it.

more difficulty (nonsignificant in our studies). Why should this be so? Why should there be *any* tendency for simple place learning to be more difficult for 3-year-olds than for 2-year-olds? In our general theory, the 3-year-old is more aware of potentially different aspects of the situation. In the case of our studies, the cups could vary slightly in their position, the animals might have had some individual differences, and so on. If the 3-year-old is more aware of the possible features to discriminate, then he or she is more likely to try out false hypotheses.

We achieved control over this possibility by making the cups easier to differentiate—we placed *different* animals on each one (e.g., a lion on the left, an elephant on the right). This roughly *doubles* the discriminative cues available for a subject—the subject could learn either Rule 1 or Rule 2:

1. Pick the one on the left (or right).
2. Pick the lion.

This increase in discriminability is reflected in a slightly improved performance by the 2-year-old children. The 3-year-olds, however, now do significantly worse, both compared with the 2-year-olds in the different-animal condition and compared with 3-year-olds in the same-animal condition. This developmental regression can be interpreted as due to the 3-year-old's increased sensitivity to the potential internal dimensions of a situation, and his or her prediliction for mastering all discriminable dimensions. Thus, by hypothesis, the 3-year-old attempts to learn both Rule 1 *and* Rule 2 separately, which leads to increased learning time for the task. It is not the case that the 3-year-old is simply less effective than the 2-year-old—rather, he or she is aware of more dimensions and unable as yet to integrate them into a single solution.

This interpretation is further supported by the behavior of children when the above situations include uncued reversal of the reinforcement (i.e., the reward is suddenly consistently placed under the previously unrewarded cup.) In this paradigm, subjects were reversed either: (1) 10 trials after they reached criterion on the initial learning; or else (2) after 40 initial learning trials were completed Table 8.15).

Two-year-olds tolerate reversal fairly well, learning the reversed situation in three times as many trials as the original discrimination, both in the same-animal and different-animal condition. Older children also learn it almost as readily as original learning, when the animals are the same. When the animals are different, however, the performance of the older children is considerably worse than on the original learning. This follows from the view that the 3-year-old has learned both rules as separate entities and so has twice as much to unlearn as the 2-year-old.

Ordinarily one would not turn to such behaviorist paradigms for support of a cognitive theory. However, these studies elicit regressions in effective

TABLE 8.15

Age	N	Reversal Learning Same Animals	N	Different Animals
2	24	6.1	22	6.8
3	26	5.4	23	14.2
4	22	2.0	18	2.6

Continuation of the experiment described in Table 8.14. The reinforced cup is reversed (after up to 40 trials initial learning) without any indication to the subject.

performance, independent of any worldly contingent probabilities. Accordingly, they demonstrate our general thesis in domains independent of language and explicit concept development—3-year-olds differentiate the internal structure of situations more deeply than 2-year-olds but are often unable to integrate the dimensions they diffentiate. Hence, they can perform *less* well than 2-year-olds on certain tasks.

A Correlation With the Emergence of Cerebral Asymmetries for Words. There is no obvious neurological change at age 3 that accounts for these developments. However, we have found a relation between the extent of right-earedness for word perception and the extent to which a 3- to 5-year-old child uses the natural-order strategy in sentence comprehension (Bever, 1971). It would be tempting to conclude that the emergence of cerebral asymmetry causes the emergence of the strategy by making possible internal analysis of sentence structure. Such a causative relation, however, is not necessary. In our present interpretation, the left hemisphere is dominant for all analytic activity, at any age. That is, the fact that the 3- to 5-year-old is analyzing the lexical structure of sentences could underly both the emergence of the natural word-order strategy *and* the emergence of cerebral asymmetry for the word level of language behavior (Bever, 1980).

Comprehension Regressions in Second-Language Learning. We have outlined the fact that a large number of different developmental phenomena occur at the time when the child is integrating the internal structure of the canonical sentence. It appears that he or she is developing an internal dimensional analysis in a variety of situations, not just language processing. That is, we can conclude that such strategies as *"NP 1 = the subject"* develop because of a general maturation by the child which results in an increased analysis of the internal structure of *all* activities. Our general hypothesis, however, leaves open the possibility that this strategy can emerge during language learning even at an older age. On our account the strategy emerges as a by-product of the child's attempt to provide an internal analysis of the sentence into component parts. If that occurs at ages other than 3 to 4 in special populations, then we might expect the natural-order strategy to emerge in those populations.

Children learning English as a second language comprise such a population. We found that as their overall ability in English increases, they go through a period of relative dependence on the natural-order strategy. We tested this in 30 Spanish-speaking children ages 6 to 7 (Table 8.16). We first recorded a conversation with each child in English. The child was encouraged to tell his or her favorite story, or to say what happened on the way to school, etc. Six independent judges listened to the interviews with each child and rated the child along a number of dimensions, including overall mastery of English. We also analyzed the utterances for mean length of utterance (MLU). This yielded three ways of ordering the children by age, by MLU, or by assessed mastery of English.

Each child participated in an acting-out task, using both active/passive and subject-first/object-first cleft sentences. (The methodology is presented in Bever & Denton [1980]—it is basically similar to the acting-out procedure outlined previously. However, we gave extra attention to making sure that the children knew the English names of each animal, sometimes discussing it in Spanish with them). There is no pattern as a function of age or by MLU group. However when subjects are ranked by assessed mastery of English, they show a marked decrease in performance on object-first constructions. (Subjective mastery of English was assessed by a panel of native speakers, who listened to recorded sentences of free speech by each child).

We interpret this result in the following way. As the Spanish-speaking child first deals with English, he or she sets up a canonical sentence; then, as his or her mastery of English improves overall, he or she analyzes the internal structure of the canonical sentence, which allows for the application of the natural word-order strategy. This indicates that the appearance of the strategy is not necessarily a function of biological maturation, although it may be in the natural course of first-language acquisition. Its independence of

TABLE 8.16
Percentage Correct in English Sentence Paradigms With 6-7-Year-Old Spanish-Speaking Children

Mean-Rated English English Ability (on 7-pt. scale)	N	Subject First	Object First	
3	8	75	52	23
4	8	92	47	45
5	8	92	42	50
6	6	92	70	22

Children acted out sentences in the same kinds of paradigm described in Table 8.1. They are grouped according to increasing mastery of conversational English.

maturation is further support for our view that the regressions occur as a function of a standard pattern of learning rather than as a function of maturational dynamics alone.

Performance Regressions in Difficult Conservation Tasks

We can also demonstrate that regressions in conservation tasks can occur at different ages. To show this we used a version of weight conservation with children ages 3 to 12. We found that children go through at least two periods of performance regression, apparently due to different analyses of the internal structure of what effects how much something weighs.

Each child was presented with two large transparent plastic boxes. (The boxes about 1 foot long x 8 inches deep x 8 inches high; they also had handles on the top). The child observed the experimenter pour a cup of Puffed Wheat (a lightweight commercial cereal) into each box. The experimenter then closed each box and discussed with the child whether one of the boxes would be harder to pick up (heavier than the other) or whether they would be the same. After the child agreed that they would be the "same" (virtually all children did so agree, even at age 3), the experimenter turned on a fan inside one of the boxes. (The other box contained an identical fan that was left off.) The child again reported on which box would be harder to pick up. Then the fan was turned off, with the child again reporting on relative weight. Then the fan on the other box was turned on, with a weight report from the child. Finally, both fans were turned off and the child reported for the last time on the relative weight of the boxes.

The results are presented in Table 8.17. Like most tests of conservation in the concrete-operational child, reliable conservation does not occur until age 7. However, conservation of the blowing phase was not reached reliably even at age 12. Furthermore, there are *two* performance regressions, points at which older children perform worse than younger children. Such results highlight the extent to which the measure of conservation depends on the emergence of a physical theory that allows the child to rationalize his answer—whereas the child does have such a theory for the weight of objects at rest, he does not have an integrated theory about the weight of objects moving in a closed system. Thus, it is not that these children do not have conservation, they lack the compensating physical knowledge that would make conservation behavior possible in this situation.

The performance regressions are interpretable as the result of internal analysis of the physical structure of the problem. Basically there are three phases of this analysis—younger children seem to assume that the blowing (or most recently blowing) box is the heavier of the two (if they report a difference at all). This would seem to relate to the strategy that "if it looks

TABLE 8.17
Percentage of Answers as to Which of the Two Boxes is Heavier

Age	N	Same	Stage $1^a + 3^b$		Same	Stage $2^c + 4^d$	
			Blowing More	Static More		Just Blown More	Static More
3–4	64	44	38	19	59	30	13
5–6	45	35	39	23	44	30	27
7–8	38	66	17	16	89	10	4
9–10	48	45	21	37	85	8	9
11–12	35	58	31	12	91	6	2

Children were presented with two large transparent plastic covered boxes. Each box had a cup's worth of puffed rice (a commercial cereal) in a small pile. The children first agreen that each box would have "the same" difficulty of being lifted, or the same weight. Then the conditions were run in order; in each condition the child was asked, "are they the same weight (difficulty of lifting) or does one have more (is one harder to lift)?"

[a] Stage one—A fan inside the first box is on, creating a "snowstorm in a box."

[b] Stage 2—The fan is off—the cereal is spread out evenly on the bottom.

[c] Stage 3—A fan inside the other box is on.

[d] Stage 4—Both fans again off.

bigger, it must have more." Because the blowing box looks like a box with a cereal "snowstorm" in it, it looks like it has more in it. At a later age the child seems to base his or her decision on a theory of how weight works—namely, the box that has more cereal lying on the bottom weighs more. Accordingly, at this later stage, the box that is blowing is reported as weighing *less* than the other. (By this age, we were able to get many verbal reports confirming this interpretation). Finally, at ages 11 and 12, those children who still do not conserve tend to report that the (recently) blowing box weighs more. At this age, they have many elaborate theories as to why this is true, always bearing on a theory of how weight expresses itself. Some argue that the puffed wheat striking the bottom does so harder than that striking the top, because of gravity; some argue that it is because of a conversion of the fan's energy to mass (!); some argue that the increased motion creates increased inertia (!); etc.

This conservation experiment demonstrates that children's performance on such tasks depends on their internal analysis of the nature of the phenomenon and how to measure it. As the child's theories about these matters change, so does his or her performance. In brief, just as in sentence perception, regressions are not limited to age 4 to 5. They occur also in other domains as a function of the child's attempts to analyze the internal structure of a problem.

Conclusion—the Integration of Knowledge and Behavior

I have demonstrated that many apparent regressions in behavior can be interpreted as the result of an increasing capacity to process the internal structure of a domain of behavior. This increase may be understood as the result of internal neurological developments, as during the first year; it may be viewed as the result of normal maturational processes, perhaps more dependent on environmental stimulation, at later ages. Finally, as in the case of second-language learning or physical conservation, it may occur under the impact of special efforts to acquire a new skill or scientific knowledge.

Such interpretations remove some of the mystery surrounding apparent developmental regressions. Although we do not understand exactly how the child goes about analyzing the internal structure of his or her world we must accept that he or she does so. The demonstration that apparent regressions can be interpreted as the direct result of such analysis removes their status as paradoxical phenomena.

A central problem of developmental psychology is to isolate what is the result of a quantitative change and what is the result of a qualitative change. I have discussed three developmental phases—the canonical, the analytic, and the structurally integrated. I have not explained how the first and third of these are discovered by the child, nor do I think that there are any satisfactory theories available that attempt to explain how such structures are learned. In each case the child arrives at a rich internal structure with very little specific environmental shaping. Accordingly, these structures appear to result from the environmental selection of internally generated structures. In that sense, the emergence of the initial structures, and their final integration, rests on innate qualitative developments.

The internal differentiation process that underlies the apparent regressions during the analytic phase is directly interpretable as due to a *quantitative* increase in general intelligence. If we define intelligence as the ability to maintain different variables in mind at the same time, then we can interpret the changes in the analytic phases of development as the result of cumulative increase in such capacity. In this view developmental regressions are important because they isolate periods of quantitative consolidation in mental growth.

REFERENCES

Bever, T. G., & Denton, N. P. The perception system of speech may be learned separately for each language. *The Bilingual Review,* In press.

Bever, T. G., Mehler, J., & Epstein, J. What children do in spite of what they know. *Science,* 1968, 162, 979–998.

Bever, T. G. The cognitive basis for linguistic structures. In *Cognition and Language Development,* New York: Wiley, 1970.

Bever, T. G. The comprehension and memory of sentences with temporal relations in the child and adult. In *Advances in Psycholinguistics,* Amsterdam: North Holland, 1970.

Bever, T. G. The dominant hemisphere is the locus of perceptual learning in speech behavior. In *Mechanisms of Language Development,* New York: Academic Press, 1971.

Bever, T. G. Broca & Lashley were right: Cerebral dominance is an accident of growth. In *Biology and Language,* Cambridge, Mass.: M.I.T. Press, 1980.

Bever, T. G. *Development from vocal to verbal behavior in children.* Undergrad Dissertative Harvard, 1961.

Bruner, J. From communication to language; a psychological perspective. *Cognition,* 1974, 3, 255–287.

Bullowa, M., Jones, L., & Bever, T. G. The development of vocalization in infants. In *The acquisition of language "SSRC conference on first language learning; 1961,"* Child Development Monographs, 1964.

Clark, H., & Clark, E. Semantic distinctions and memory for complex sentences. *Quarterly Journal of Experimental Psychology,* 1968, 20, 129–138.

deViliers, J., deVilliers, P. A. A cross-sectional study of the acquisition of grammatical morphemes in child speech. *Journal of Psycholinquistic Research,* 1973, 2(3), 267–278.

Ervin-Trip, S. Imitation in childrens language. In *E. M. Lerneberg,* Cambridge. Mass.: M.I.T. Press, 1964.

Ervin-Tripp, S. Discourse agreement; how children answer questions. In *Cognition and Language Development,* New York: Wiley, 1970.

Feagens, L. Childrens understanding of some temporal terms denoting order duration and simultaneity. *Journal of Psycholinquistic Research,* 1980, 9(1), 41–57.

Frankel, D. G., & Arbel, T. *Probabilistic assignments of sentence relations on the basis of differentially–weighted interpretive cues.* In preparation, 1980.

Frankel, D. G., Amir, M., Frenkel, I., & Arbel, T. A developmental study of the role of word order in comprehending Hebrew. *Journal of Experimental Child Psychology,* 1980, in press.

Greenberg, J. M. Some universals of grammar with particular reference to order of meaningful elements. In *Universals of Language,* Cambridge, Mass.: M.I.T. Press, 61.

Irwin, O. C., & Chen, H. P. A. A reliability study of speech sounds observed in the crying of newborn infants. *Child Development,* 1941, 12, 351–368.

Irwin, O. C. Reliability of infant speech data. *Journal of Speech Disorders,* 1945, 10, 227–235.

Irwin, O. C. Infant speech; the problems of variability and the problem of diagnosis. *Journal of Speech Disorders,* 1947, 12, 287–289.

Irwin, O. C. Infant speech: the effect of systematic reading of stories. *Journal of Speech and Hearing Research,* 1960, 3, 187–190.

Johnston, J. R., & Slobin, D. I. The development of locutive expressions in English, Italian, Serbo–Croation and Turkish. *Journal of Child Language,* 1979, 6(3), 529–545.

Juczsyk, P. Infant speech perception: a critical approach. In *Perspectives on the study of speech,* Hillsdale, N.J.: Lawrence Erlbaum Associates, 1980.

Lewis, M. M. *Infant speech: a study of the beginnings of language.* London: Routledge Kegan 1936.

MacNamara, J. Cognitive basis of language learning in infants. *Psycholinguistic Research,* 1972, 79(1), 1–13.

Maratsos, M. Children who get worse at understanding the passive: A replication of Bever. *Journal of Psycholinguistic Research,* 1974, 3, 65–74.

McGraw, M. B. Maturation of behavior. In *Manual of Child Psychology,* New York: Wiley, 1946.

McNeil, D. *The conceptual basis of language.* Hillsdale, N.J.: Lawrence Erlbaum Associates, 1979.

McNeill, D., & Lindig, K. The perceptual reality of phonemes syllables words and sentences. *Journal of Verbal Learning and Verbal Behavior,* 1973, 12, 419–430.

Mehler, J., & Bertoncini, J. Infants and perception of speech and other acoustic stimuli. In *Psycholinguistics Series II,* The Hague: ELLK Science Books, 1978.

Mehler, J., & Bever, T. G. A cognitive capacity of young children. *Science,* 1967, Oct. 6th, 141–150.

Osgood, C., & Bock, J. Salience and sentencing: some production principles. In *Sentence production: Developments in Research and theory,* Hillsdale, N.J.: Lawrence Erlbaum Associates, 177

Piaget, J. *The psychology of intelligence.* London: Routledge & Kegan 1950.

Savin, H., & Bever, T. G. The nonperceptual reality of phoneme. *Journal of Verbal Learning and Verbal Behavior,* 1970, 9, 295–302.

Sinclair, H., & Bronckart, J. P. SVO a linguistic universal? A study in developmental psycholinguistics. *Journal of Experimental Child Psychology,* 1972, 14, 329–348.

Slobin, D. I., & Bever, T. G. *Children use canonical sentence schemata.* (In preparation) 1980.

Tighe, L., & Tighe, T. J. Discrimination Learning: two views in historical perspective. *Psychological Bulletin,* 1966, 66(5), 353–370.

Townsend, D. J., & Bever, T. G. Interclause relations and clausal processing. *Journal of Verbal Learning and Verbal Behavior,* 1978, 17, 509–521.

Townsend, D. J., Ottaviano, D., & Bever, T. G. Immediate memory for words from main and subordinate clauses at different levels. *Journal of Psycholinguistic Research,* 1979, 8(1), 83–101.

Turner, E. A., & Rommetveit, R. The acquisition of sentence voice and reversability. *Child Development,* 1967, 38, 649–660.

Turner, E. A., & Rommetveit, R. Experimental manipulation of the production of active and passive voice in children. *Language and Speech,* 1967, 10, 169–180.

Turner, E. A., & Rommetveit, R. Focus of attention in recall of active and passive sentences. *Journal of Verbal Learning and Verbal Behaviour,* 1968, 7, 543–548.

Weir, M Developmental changes in problem-solving strategies. *Psychological Review,* 1964, 71(6), 473–490.

Werner, H. The concept of development from a comparative and organismic point of view. In *Concept of Development,* Minneapolis: University of Minneapolis Press, 1957.

Wundt, W. *Volkerpsychologie & Erster Band: Die Sprache.* Leipzig: Verlag von Wilhelm Engelman 1911.

III MIDDLE CHILDHOOD

9 Ancestral and Descendant Behaviors: The Case of U-Shaped Behavioral Growth

Sidney Strauss
Tel-Aviv University

Recently Bower (1974b, 1979) expanded on a previously presented argument (Bower, 1974a; Bower & Paterson, 1972) about the developmental relations between various behaviors. One of the essential points of the argument was that the notion of continuous, additive, incremental change may be an unsatisfactory model of behavioral development in human ontogenesis. He further claimed that competences characterizing developmental functioning may be discontinuous and cyclical in nature. The notion of cyclicity or developmental repetition is not a particularly new idea (Piaget, 1970; Werner, 1948). However, Bower has offered some interesting examples of this phenomenon and, furthermore, he has suggested at least one research paradigm that can exploit it in studies of human development so that we can empirically establish the existence of connections between various behaviors.

Part of the evidence brought forth to support this claim comes from what I call U-shaped behavioral growth, which is comprised of three phases: (1) a behavior appears at a point in time in the child's development; (2) it disappears at a later point; and (3) it reappears at a still later age. Part of the problem of U-shaped behavior growth is to determine the nature of the developmental relations between the three phases and elaborating this point comprises a large part of this chapter.

There are three points I would like to make at the outset so that there will be no misunderstanding about my opinions. The first point is that there is a multitude of examples of U-shaped behavioral growth and they have been documented elsewhere (Strauss, in press; Strauss & Stavy, in press). This phenomenon has been found in language acquisition (morphological systems, syntactic structures, semantic relations, phonological rules), artistic expression, conservations, social cognition, face and voice representation, motor skills, and other areas. To my mind, there is no doubt that the phenomenon exists. Whether we will be able to learn something interesting by studying the phenomenon seems to me to be the important question.

The second point is that the Phase 2 drop in performance is not a case of regression. As I show later on, the drop in performance either reflects a reorganization of the mental apparatus underlying the performance, thereby signifying cognitive advance, or it occurs as a result of one mental system interfering with another. The interpretation of the Phase 2 drop in perform- ance as a progressive reorganization or an interference depends, in part, on how we view the relation between Phases 1 and 3.

The third point is that U-shaped behavioral growth is not necessarily an artifact of experimental situations. In some cases it might, indeed, be an artifact of a circumstantial intersect between a particular task and the development of rules for problem solving. For example, Siegler (1976, 1978, 1981) has developed a technique in which he predicts drops in perform- ance and subsequent recovery, and his cases suggest that these performance curves are circumstantial. On the other hand, it has been argued elsewhere (Strauss & Stavy, in press) that there are cases where the three phases represent a deeper developmental phenomenon.

The structure of the argument of the present chapter rests on the claim that the significance of the phenomenon of U-shaped behavioral growth increases as a function of the degree of connectedness between Phases 1 and 3. If the Phase 1 and 3 behaviors or organizations underlying the behaviors are different and are not developmentally related then it seems to me that there is nothing unique about U-shaped behavioral growth. On the other hand, if we can demonstrate that Phases 1 and 3 are developmentally related and are not mere happenstance, we may be in a position to make some interesting claims about sequences in developmental psychology.

I discuss three types of relations that can exist between Phase 1 and 3 behaviors or organizations underlying the behaviors and point out what these relations mean for U-shaped behavioral growth and vice versa. These relations are that Phases 1 and 3 are: (1) identical; (2) not identical but developmentally connected; and (3) analogous.

Each of these relations brings various problems in its wake and my discussion of them leads me to consider the many possibilities of appearances of behaviors, their disappearances, and nonappearances as well as the information their combinations can produce that would enable us to better understand the genetic course of development and the links that exist between behaviors. The attempt here is to place Bower's arguments into a larger framework that will allow various ways of examining relations between behaviors.

Fig. 9.1 provides us with five basic types of sequences of behaviors over time that serve as the basis for much of the discussion in this presentation. The first line in Fig. 9.1 is the representation of incremental, continuous growth of a particular behavior or functional system. The second line is the schematization of the notion of repetition. To borrow an example of repetition from Bower (1974 a, 1974 b), primary walking appears somewhere during the first month (A_1), and disappears around the third month (D_3), and secondary walking appears around age 11 months (A'_1). The disappearance can be natural, as in the example just provided, or due to some pathology, such as the normal development of language, subsequent brain insult that leads to aphasia, and the following reappearance of language functioning. The third line represents the appearance of a behavior and its disappearance at, say, age 11 months. This can be a natural occurrence, as in the case of infant babbling, or it can be the result of some pathology such as deafness or blindness. The fourth line constitutes pathological development such that a behavioral system that normally functions from birth (e.g., vision) does not appear (N_0). Finally, the fifth line indicates that a behavioral system that should appear at birth does not, (N_0), but it does appear at, say, 6 years of age (A_6). This type of development can be illustrated by von Senden's (1960) work, in which he reported behaviors of individuals who were blind from birth due to congenital cataracts and underwent an operation that restored their vision.

Identical Behaviors

The claim here is that the same behavior occurs at two noncontinuous points in ontogenesis and I call this the strong form of the connectedness argument. In this category we have two primary goals. The first is to determine whether or not the Phase 1 and 3 behaviors are, indeed, isomorphic. If they are not, the behaviors in question do not belong to this category. If they are isomorphic, the analysis shifts to the second goal, to determine the nature of Phase 2. The main point of this section is to show the sort of arguments that seem necessary to make the strong form of the connectedness argument. To illustrate this category I cite two examples of U-shaped behavioral growth that have been claimed to be from this category: the development of: (1) walking; and (2) the concept of temperature—an intensive physical quantity.

1. Walking

An illustration of the relation between primary and secondary walking was provided in the foregoing and I now elaborate slightly on it. Primary walking is that "walking" exhibited by neonates when they are supported. According to Bower (1974b), this behavior disappears somewhere around the third

Time (can be read as weeks, months, years)

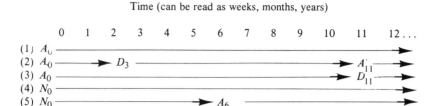

FIG. 9.1. Five Types of Developmental Sequences.

month and secondary walking appears at approximately age 11 months.

Given our above analysis, the first thing one would want to know is whether or not primary and secondary walking are isomorphic. That they are similar is undeniable because both involve a serial motor behavior of leg movements. That they are isomorphic is questionable because primary walking uses an adductor pattern (a scissorlike movement in which the neonate's foot that is moving forward moves inward and "gets caught" on the stationary foot, whereas secondary walking has an eductor pattern (the moving foot moves outward and then inward in a semicircular pattern, returning to the center line). Thus, these patterns of walking are quite different in their content. In addition, they are different in form. That is, the context into which the behaviors are set is different. For example, secondary walking has the additional elements of posture and balance whereas primary walking does not.

A related point pertains to the Phase 2 disappearance of primary walking. It is true that the walking itself cannot be evoked after around the third month; however, the serial leg movement does not disappear because infants between 3 to 8 months, when supine, kick in a bike-pedaling movement that is similar to the walking movement. In addition, infants from around 8 months until secondary walking onset can walk with support. Thus, there seems to be no waning of the serial leg movement itself. Rather, its performance can be found in different contexts. The more general question of whether behaviors disappear and, if they do, what their fate is, is discussed later.

Until this point, we have questioned Bower's thesis that primary and secondary walking are isomorphic and that the disappearance of the former is a real disappearance. This strong position is obviously not correct. Let us now turn to the next example, which is somewhat harder to handle.

2. Development of Temperature Concepts

For the past 5 years, a research group under my direction at Tel-Aviv University has been studying the development of physical and mathematical concepts. We have found U-shaped behavioral growth in the development of understanding of physical concepts or, more specifically, what is called intensive physical quantity. This sort of quantity remains unchanged despite changes in its amount, or what is called extensive physical quantity (Carnap, 1966). I illustrate these two terms with an example from temperature. Suppose we have three cups (A, B, and C) each filled with cold water of the same temperature. Now let us pour the water from cups A and B into a fourth, empty cup (D) and compare the temperature of the mixed water in cup D with the untouched water in cup C. In this example, the temperature, being an intensive physical quantity, remains constant even though the water increases in its extensive quantity (i.e., its amount). Other examples of intensive physical quantity are sugar-water concentrations, viscosity, and hardness. The growth curves of how children solve tasks measuring children's understandings of these intensive quantities have all been U-shaped. In this section I describe the U-shaped behavioral growth curve for temperature because it provides us with a good example of the sorts of problems one encounters when trying to make the strong form of the connectedness argument. Due to space limitations I cannot present the temperature experiment and its results in their entirety and I refer the reader to Strauss, Stavy, and Orpaz (1977) and Strauss and Stavy (in press) for a fuller account of this study.

In addition to temperature being an intensive physical quantity, its changes can also be considered a ratio, the mathematical concept described in the foregoing. We can alter the temperature of water by changing the amount of heat (by heating or cooling) such that the change in temperature will be proportional to the amount of heat added and inversely related to the amount of water. A ratio is one quantity divided by another and, to use the tasks in the Strauss et al. (1977) study as an example, we considered the ratio: number of candles under a cup of water/amount of water. If we ask children to compare the temperatures of water in two cups, each of which has a certain number of candles under it, we are asking children to compare two ratios.

An analysis of how ratios can be manipulated indicated three principal ways. The first is the direct function. Using our task as an example, an increase in the numerator (number of candles) increases the temperature. The second way is the inverse function, where the cups have the same number of candles under them and where one cup has more water than the other. The cup with less water will be hotter; hence, the inverse function. Finally, the third way is proportion, where both the number of candles and amount of water vary proportionally. The intensive physical quantity task and the three ratio tasks are illustrated in Fig. 9.2.

On the basis of previous research (Stavy, Strauss, Orpaz, & Carmi, in press) conducted on sugar-water concentrations (also an intensive quantity and a ratio of amount of sugar/amount of water) we predicted a U-shaped behavioral growth curve on intensiveness tasks for temperature. We

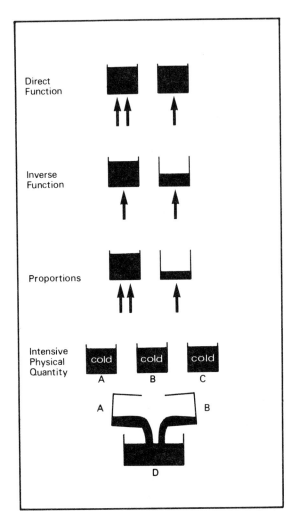

FIG. 9.2   Temperature tasks measuring direct function, inverse function, proportions, and intensiveness

tested 200 middle-class children from ages 3½ to 13½, with 10 age groups and 20 children per age group.

The percentage of correct judgments per task across age is found in Table 9.1. As can be seen: (1) the direct function was solved by practically all of the children; (2) the inverse function's developmental path showed few children correctly solving the task until age 9, at which time the percentage of children producing correct judgments increased significantly; (3) the proportions task

TABLE 9.1
Percentage of Children Producing Correct Judgments on Various Tasks
for the Temperature Concept

Age	Direct Function	Inverse Function	Proportion	Intensive Quantity
4	90	0	0	65
5	100	5	5	35
6	100	0	0	15
7	100	5	5	50
8	100	25	15	30
9	100	60	65	55
10	100	50	50	55
11	100	60	70	85
12	95	90	—	85
13	100	100	—	80

was solved quite similarly to the inverse function task; and (4) the intensiveness tasks' solutions showed the predicted U-shaped curve.

In order to interpret the U-shaped curve finding we looked at the sorts of justifications children provided for their judgments. We found three developmental periods that gave rise to the three phases in the U-shaped curve. In the first phase, which gave rise to the correct judgments on the left side of the curve, children justified these judgments with identity reasoning ("It is the same water you had before") or with reference to the act of pouring ("You only poured it"). The second phase was characterized by incorrect judgments that were accompanied by justifications referring to the amounts of water. For example, children argued that the cup with more water was colder (or hotter, depending on the task) than the untouched cup that had less water. Every child who produced incorrect judgments on these tasks justified them with arguments of this type. Finally, in the third phase, correct judgments were accompanied by identity justifications that could not be distinguished from the Phase 1 justifications. Some children mentioned that the amounts of water are not relevant when judging these tasks (i.e., they argued that the variable they took into account in the previous phase was not relevant), whereas a few children referred to physical law explanations ("Water at the same temperature doesn't change its temperature all of a sudden when you mix it").

Given these data, we must now pose the same questions we asked when criticizing Bower's work; that is, are Phase 1 and 3 behaviors isomorphic and what is the nature of the Phase 2 drop in performance?

2.1. Are Phase 1 and 3 Behaviors Isomorphic? The answer to this question has two general parts. The first part pertains to the *content of the judgments* themselves. The judgments are clearly identical because in Phases

1 and 3 the children produce correct judgments. This fact may not be particularly enlightening because there are only two choices here: Either children say that the temperatures are the same (i.e., produce the correct judgment) or that the temperatures are not the same (i.e., produce the incorrect judgment). Nevertheless, a positive answer is necessary to the analysis of whether or not the content of the judgments is identical in order to proceed to the more interesting, second part of the question.

Here the analysis centers on the *content of the justification.* As previously noted, most Phase 1 and Phase 3 justifications were identical in that the children referred to the act of pouring or produced identity justifications. In contrast, however, some older children spontaneously produced the argument that the amount of water is irrelevant to the final temperature if the water was originally the same temperature. These are the data available to us at present. With the exception of some of the older children, who referred to the irrelevance of the amount of water, one cannot distinguish between the Phase 1 and Phase 3 justifications.

I would now like to take the foregoing and carry it a few steps further to see how far we can push the argument and what conclusions can be reached about isomorphic behaviors. First, let us make the assumption that were we to probe older children who did not spontaneously produce the argument about the irrelevance of the amount of water we would find that they, too, would produce that justification. This assumption invites the obvious comparison to younger children. That is, would they produce that justification if probed? Perhaps their mental organization does not even take into account the amount of water as a potentially relevant variable. This would be seen in contrast to the older children, who once mistakenly understood that that variable was relevant but now reject that reasoning.

Inasmuch as this study has not yet been conducted let us speculate further about the alternatives at hand. The first possibility is that, indeed, younger children will not produce this justification when probed. There is some evidence to support this alternative but it comes from different content (sugar-water solutions). There it was found that Phase 1 and Phase 3 identity justifications for intensiveness tasks had different significance (Stavy et al., in press; Strauss & Stavy, in press), but because the sugar-water intensiveness tasks contain two variables (amounts of sugar and water) and the temperature intensiveness tasks contain only one variable (amount of water), a direct analogy between them is impossible. If this possibility were to be confirmed we would be forced to drop the claim that the Phase 1 and 3 behaviors are isomorphic.

The second possibility is that, when probed, younger children will produce the same reasoning as the older children. At this point we could understand this finding in two ways. First, we could argue tht the issue of the amount of water being relevant or irrelevant is not the issue that distinguishes between the younger and older children, and we must search for other areas where one can differentiate between these children. This view suggests that there must be differences between the Phase 1 and 3 judgments and justifications and we must persevere in finding them.

The second way to understand this finding is to conclude that the Phase 1 and 3 behaviors are isomorphic. The naysayers could argue that the intensiveness task for temperature is so simple (there is only one variable to attend to) and limited (the range of correct justifications is very restricted) that the younger and older children representing Phases 1 and 3 could in fact produce identical judgments and justifications. This sort of task, being so simple and limited, might be unrepresentative of general developmental trends and, as a consequence, uninteresting. To take this stance means to accept the evidence as being a case of the strong form of the connectedness claim and shifts the argument to the representativeness of the task.

For the sake of the argument let us assume that Phase 1 and 3 judgments and justifications are isomorphic and may even be representative of a class of developmental sequences. This will allow us to consider the question posed earlier.

2.2. What is the Nature of Phase 2? If it is the case that Phase 1 and 3 behaviors are isomorphic we should want to know what happens in the Phase 2 drop in performance. A claim put forth elsewhere (Strauss & Stavy, in press) is that Phase 2 is a product of an interaction between two representational systems, one that pertains to physical matter and its properties (intensiveness) and another that pertains to functions (direct function, inverse function, and proportions).

For the intensiveness tasks we found that the youngest children's Phase 1 correct judgments with identity reasoning were replaced by reasoning that took into account the different amounts of water. Here children argued that the cup with more water was, say, colder. The Phase 2 reasoning that more water is colder is direct function reasoning, which, when applied to intensive physical quantities such as temperature, produces an incorrect judgment. This reasoning is replaced by correct judgments and identity justifications among the oldest children that are identical to the Phase 1 behaviors.

If one accepts this account of the Phase 2 drop in performance in the framework of Phases 1 and 3 being isomorphic behaviors, then we would have to argue that the Phase 2 representational system of functions interferes with and suppresses the correct early identity reasoning, which is then reinstated among the older children. A description of the nature of that suppression and the subsequent reinstatement of former reasoning should be the goal of those interested in treading these uncertain waters.

2.3 Summary and Conclusions. The point of the foregoing was not to show whether or not isomorphic behaviors appear at noncontinuous points in ontogenesis. As was seen, the issues were too knotty and the data too weak to make such a strong claim. Instead, the attempt was to show the kinds of data, argumentation, and reasoning that strike me as those that should be brought to bear on deciding how we can know whether two behaviors are identical. The informed reader will have recognized that we have been taking a brief visit to the site of old battlefields in the history of psychology.

The assumptions underlying my analysis were that there are two main areas that need to be examined in order to set the stage for the claim that two behaviors are isomorphic. First, the content of the behaviors in Phases 1 and 3 has to be identical. For primary and secondary walking we saw that this was not the case (the former has an adductor pattern and the latter has an eductor pattern), whereas for temperature we found identical judgments and justifications, although the case for justifications was not altogether clear.

Second, the form or context of the behaviors in question has to be identical. This is generally a difficult nut to crack. In the case of walking, the context of the serial leg movement is different in primary and secondary walking. Primary walking occurs when the infant is supported, whereas secondary walking is embedded in the context of balance and posture. Hence, the significance of the serial leg movements is different for the two types of walking.

For temperature, our problems are much more difficult and the following analysis of the difficulty should indicate the nature of the problems. The general question here is: How do we know which behaviors comprise the context or form of the behaviors that we want to claim are isomorphic? Let us take the case of sugar-water solutions, which parallels temperature in that it can be viewed both as a ratio comprising the direct function, inverse function, and proportions and as an intensive physical quantity. We have argued (Stavy et al., in press) that the functions set a context for the under-standing of the Phase 1 and 3 behaviors (i.e., the patterns of solutions for the functions can serve as the framework for understanding Phases 1 and 3 in the U-shaped behavioral curve for intensiveness). There are two main reasons that allow us to make such a claim. First, the tasks for the functions and intensive physical quantity were similar in that they all contained two variables (sugar and water) and their manipulations. One can demonstrate and it was found that one can use proportional reasoning (as well as identity reasoning) to solve intensive physical quantity tasks. In addition, propor-tional reasoning includes the direct function and the inverse function. As a consequence of the internal relations between the direct function, inverse function, and proportions and the relations between proportional reasoning and intensiveness, we were able to use the development of reasoning about functions as the context for understanding the development of reasoning about intensiveness. In the case of sugar-water solutions this context allowed us to show that the identity reasoning in Phases 1 and 3 was different and that the strong form of the connectedness argument does not apply for these solutions.

The problem we face when analyzing Phases 1 and 3 for temperature is that we do not have a situation parallel to that of sugar-water solutions. At first glance it appears that there is a parallel both because we have the direct function, inverse function, proportions, and intensiveness for temperature and sweetness and because we found U-shaped behavioral growth curves for intensiveness for both sweetness and temperature. It turns out that there is a parallel between sugar-water solutions and temperature for the two functions and proportions because for both contents there are two variables (amounts of sugar and water; number of candles and amount of water). However, in contrast to sugar-water solutions, intensiveness tasks for temperature have only one variable to which the children can attend—the amount of water. Children cannot use proportional reasoning to solve intensiveness tasks for temperature, so it and the functions it includes cannot provide a context or the form into which the Phase 1 and 3 behaviors could fit and could gain meaning.

I do not have a solution to this problem but I have raised it because it strikes me as one that gets to the heart of the issue of how we can determine whether or not two behaviors are identical. This is about as far as my thinking about these issues has carried me and, having made the points I wanted, we can now turn to the second category of relations between Phases 1 and 3.

Developmentally Connected Behaviors

This category is a weaker form of connectedness between Phases 1 and 3 because the claim is not that the identical behavior occurs at two noncontinuous points in ontogenesis but, rather, that two nonidentical behaviors occur at these points. There is an endless number of nonidentical behaviors at various points in ontogenesis, so if we are going to say something interesting we will have to find a developmental relation between some of them.

Flavell (1972) offered a taxonomy of developmental sequences that could exist between two items that are thought to be functionally related. I am interested in asking the following question: How can we know if two behaviors are functionally related? There are two principal ways to establish such a link. The first way is to analyze the tasks and the knowledge and mental organizations needed to solve them. If one were to find an inclusion relation between the two behaviors (let us say the behaviors found in Phases 1 and 3) it could be argued that they are functionally related. The problems besetting inclusion relations are very difficult and I will not enter into them here (see Strauss, in preparation).

The second way to establish the existence of a functional relation between two behaviors is through experimental manipulation. Exploring how one can do this is what occupies much of this section. In so doing, I take the logic of experimentation found among embryologists and try to expand on it to show how it can apply to experiments in developmental psychology. The purpose of some embryological research is to find relations between ancestral cells and their descendants and the parallel in developmental psychology research would be to find functional relations between two behaviors. Bower (1974b, 1979) has written about this parallel and, to my mind, it could be instructive only if we view it as a metaphor. Strictly speaking, there are variables governing relations between ancestral and descendant cells in embryology that have no obvious counterpart in developmental psychology (e.g., sometimes the cell itself is less important than its spatial location in the embryo [Wolpert, 1978]). This lack of a psychological counterpart suggests that we should keep our discussion to the level of metaphors.

An example of the logic of experimentation found among embryologists can be taken from Jacogson (1980), who traced the embryonic formation of frogs' brains and spinal cords, which are formed by seven compartments separated by boundaries that are not crossed by cells during development. The purpose of the experiment was to determine the point in development when these boundaries were established.

The technique used for following lineages of different types of neurones from ancestral cells was to mark cells in the early embryo and trace their descendants. The method of experimentation was to inject a tracer substance into a single cell in a series of embryos at successively later stages of development. It was found that the ancestry of all cells in each compartment was traced back to seven groups of founder cells in the 512-cell blastula.

Jacobson (1980) asked whether or not there was a causal relation between individual ancestral cells in the blastula and specific types of neurones. His answer was negative, because there was no constant relation between individual ancestral cells in the blastula and specific types of neurones. In the 512-cell blastula, at the time of the origin of each compartment, there are 20 founder cells whose descendants mingle in later development before the individual types of neurones and glial cells become differentiated.

Jacobson (1980) concluded that although it is the case that "certain types of neurones and assemblies of different types of neurones always develop in certain compartments, such associations do not prove causal relationships (p. 5)." He suggested, however, that there are two ways of determining such a relation. The first is to find mutations that alter compartmentation and then to observe the effects on cell differentiation. The second is to look for evidence of compartment-specific properties that enable cells belonging to the same compartment to cohere and thus prevent cell mingling between compartments.

Now then, what could all of this mean for developmental psychology? We certainly do not have the ability to locate psychological equivalents of individual cells nor do we have markers to trace lineage from ancestral to descendant behavior. The most we can do is to hope to learn from the logic of experimentation employed by embryologists. The first type suggested by Jacobson is to look for a mutation. Space considerations do not allow me to discuss different types of mutations and their relations to developmental psychology. One result of a mutation is that it can lead to a different, non-adjusted course of development. In the case of developmental psychology we should look for a pathology that disrupts one system to see how it influences that system and allied systems' development. If we were to find that a pathology in one system is accompanied by the absence of development or even nonnormative development of another system we could claim that the first system is necessary for the normal development of the second system.

The second type of evidence offered by Jacbson for determining causal relations between ancestral cells and descendant neurones was to find a mechanism that prevents cell mingling between compartments. For developmental psychology the metaphor could be to find cases where there is a dedifferentiation of a system whose normal development is towards differentiation and to determine its effects on the development of allied systems. If we were to find that dedifferentiation in one system leads to a disruption in the normal development of an allied system we could reasonably claim that the first system is a prerequisite for the second system.

A third type of evidence, which was not offered by Jacobson, is to attempt to accelerate the ancestral cells 'development and to observe its effects on hypothesized descendant cells. The parallel for developmental psychology would be to accelerate the Phase 1 behavior and observe whether that influences the disappearance of Phase 2 and the appearance of Phase 3.

In a more general sense, the route suggested by research strategies in embryology when trying to determine whether or not two behaviors are functionally related is to demonstrate that a change in the timing and/or form of the ancestral behavior is followed by a change in the timing and/or form of the descendant behavior. If we can find instances of this phenomenon we can, under certain circumstances, claim that the two behaviors are developmentally connected.

Taking a lead from the embryologists we can argue that changes in the timing and/or form of the onset of the ancestral behaviors can be: (1) achieved by accelerating the appearance of the ancestral behavior; (2) determined by monitoring pathologies in the onset or in the developmental course of the ancestral behavior and (3) observed in cases where instability in one area blocks the acquisition in another area.

1. Acceleration Studies

I borrow the case of primary and secondary walking cited earlier in order to illustrate how one can determine whether or not two behaviors are developmentally connected via acceleration studies. It is true that in the previous section I brought forth arguments as to why I thought that primary and secondary walking were not identical behaviors, the strong form of the connectedness argument. It might be thought that to use the same behaviors to illustrate the weak form of the connectedness argument is to take a fall back position; however, Bower (1974b) also seems to have taken the position that primary walking is an ancestor to secondary walking. To use his words: "If practice of the first phase of a repetitive sequence [primary walking] accelerates the appearance of the second phase [secondary walking], with all other variables held constant, then, I think we can reasonably conclude that the two phases of development stand in some kind of causal relationship to one another [p.315, material in brackets added]."

Bower (1974b) cited the work of André–Thomas and St. A. Dargassies (1952) as a case in point. They exercised the primary walking behavior of young infants and observed that: (*1*) the primary walking disappeared at a later age than infants who did not have this behavior exercised and (*2*) those who had primary walking exercised began secondary walking at a significantly earlier age. Bower (1974a), then observed that: "Since the early training produced effects on the later behavior, the study demonstrated that primary walking is indeed the ancestor of secondary walking [p.143]."

The above research paradigm, then, would look something like that found in Fig. 9.3. Here the top line represents the control group or the normal ontogenetic course of primary and secondary walking, whereas the second line is the experimental group that received some sort of training or exercise. If the appearance of A' in the experimental group appears significantly before A' of the control, the claim is that A and A' are developmentally connected.

What seems to me to be missing in this argument is what is found in the bottom line: the influence of actually restricting primary walking, as occurs when infants are swaddled. Although Bower (1974a) had mentioned swaddling, it was not used as evidence in the foregoing paradigm. What we find, of course, is that restriction of primary walking leads to neither a loss nor a retardation of the appearance of secondary walking. As a result, the picture is now somewhat more complicated than before. Had we seen that the restriction of A was followed by the significantly late arrival or nonarrival of A' (which it was not) and the exercise of A led to the significantly early arrival of A' (which it did), we could be fairly confident that a connection exists between A and A'. However, given the aforementioned additional information about the restriction of A, one could argue that what is being evidenced in the preceding paradigm is an interaction between training and behavior (secondary walking) and not between two behaviors (primary and secondary walking), as Bower would have it. Now with this I do not want to say that there is no connection between primary and secondary walking. Rather, I am arguing that the evidence from the paradigm as presented by Bower and the additional evidence I offered cannot establish that such a connection exists.

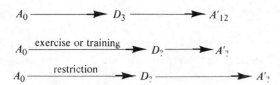

FIG. 9.3. Acceleration Paradigm and Results Evidencing Developmental Connectedness Between A and A'.

The final question is: Even if a connection could be established in the example of primary and secondary walking, might it not prove to be an example that applies to motor behaviors alone? That is, its generality may be limited because one would be hard pressed to find a case in, say, higher mental activities where the restriction of exercise or practice of a particular function A would be followed by a *non*retarded onset of function A' that is dependent on A.

2. Pathologies

In this section I discuss two clinical situations that allow the test of developmental relations between systems that give rise to different behaviors: (1) the appearance of a normally functioning system and its subsequent pathological disappearance; and (2) the nonappearance of a normally appearing system and its later appearance. In both kinds of clinical situations the general issue raised is about sensitive periods and the necessity of normal development of the earlier system for the normal development of the later system.

2.1 Disappearances of Behaviors. The situation described here is that a behavioral system appears and subsequently disappears and does not reappear. The research comparisons generally relate to the effects of early experience of one system on the behavioral development in allied systems. The clinical paradigm allowing the test of these effects is found in Fig. 9.4.

The first line represents the normal appearance and development of a functional system such as vision. The second line indicates the disappearance of vision at age 2 years, whereas the third line shows that blindness

FIG 9.4. Developmental Courses Whose Comparison Yields Information About the Role of Early Experience on Subsequent Behavioral Development.

occurred at age 6 years. The bottom line represents the nonappearance of vision from birth.

Bower (1974b) cited Drever's (1955) work as an example of this paradigm for the notion of functional relations in development. Drever had shown that for certain spatial tasks, adolescents who had been blind from approximately ages 5 or 6 (line 3) solved spatial problems with error scores quite similar to blindfolded sighted subjects (line 1). It was also found that those who had become blind earlier than 4 years of age (line 2) made significantly more errors on these same tasks. A functional relationship was understood here such that: "the first phase of a skill or concept may be a *necessary* acquisition if the second phase is to appear at all [Bower, 1974 b, p. 316]." The first phase Bower referred to is the phase up to age 6, and the second phase was adolescence. The basic idea here is that the timing of the loss of vision during the first phase was different (early or late blindness), and this affected the second phase differentially. The type of relatedness here is, of course, the weak form of relatedness. Incidentally, it should be noted that Drever grouped congenitally blind (line 4) with those whose blindness onset was from age 4 (line 2). This distinction should generally be made in the experimental design.

My understanding of Drever's work was quite different. First, he showed that vision and tactile–kinesthetic cues are ultimately bound and, although he did not mention it, one would imagine that imagery and linguistic codes also influence solutions to spatial tasks. Second, the data show that the second phase existed for those who had a more limited visual experience. These individuals solved the spatial problems also; however, they made more errors in their solutions.

In order for a developmental connection to be established between the two phases, in the event that Phase 1 ancestral behavior appears at different ages, we should see at least one of two conditions in the Phase 2 descendant behavior: a difference in its timing or form. The existence of more errors or less errors in Phase 2 when comparing children represented by the first three lines in Fig. 9.4 does not meet this condition and, as a consequence, it seems to me that the evidence from the example provided in Drever's work does not allow us to confirm Bower's claim that the first phase must be acquired if the second is to appear at all.

It also seems to me that Bower's (1974b) report of his study on auditorally guided reaching of sighted infants in a dark room as compared to Fraiberg's (1968; Fraiberg & Freedman, 1964; Fraiberg, Siegel, & Gibson, 1966) studies of the same behavior with blind infants could fall within the same general category as the foregoing example.

2.2 Nonappearances and Subsequent Late Appearances of Behaviour. The cases discussed here are those in which a normally appearing system or behavior fails to appear *from birth* and then appears at a later time. These situations generally are studied with an eye toward obtaining data about the effects of deprivations of various durations where experimentation is conducted to investigate the direct effects of this deprivation on the system or the behavior itself and its indirect effects on other systems. This is to be contrasted with the aforementioned category, where one measures the effects of the duration of exercised systems or behaviors that disappear. In other words, in the present category, one measures the effect of limited deprivations of experience, whereas in the previous category one measures the effects of limited experiences. Both categories allow one to determine the existence of developmental relations between various behaviors.

An example of this category comes from animal experiments, which have often proved to be quite useful as models of normal and abnormal functioning and development of psychological systems and processes in humans. For instance, the study of human visual defects has been enhanced by models of the development of visual perception in animals. The types of animal studies I have in mind are those reported in this volume by Marc Jeannrod (Chapter 13) where, after monkeys and cats have been reared in visually deprived surroundings from birth, they are exposed to a normal visual environment at varying points in their ontogenesis. The results of these experiments have repeatedly shown that early visual deprivation has cellular, neurophysiological, and behavioral consequences. This deprivation results in the degeneration of cells in the lateral geniculate, abnormal patterns of firing, and amblyopia (a profound loss of visual acuity due to nonoptic factors).

A parallel condition in humans for determining whether or not there is a critical period in the development of amblyopia is the clinical condition of congenital cataracts. In the optimal case for this determination, a cataract of fixed opacity develops before or shortly after birth and prevents normal pattern vision until it is surgically removed. At that point, given correct refraction, one would expect the visual acuity to rise quickly to normal. Thus, by plotting visual acuity as a function of the age of surgery we can accurately determine the sensitive period for amblyopia. We would expect that the later the surgery the poorer the vision and that only early surgery should completely prevent amblyopia.

Results of the animal experiments (von Noorden, Dowling & Ferguson, 1970) and human clinical studies (Ackroyd, Humphrey, & Warrington, 1974; Gregory, 1974; Hebb, 1949; von Senden, 1960) have led to the following predominant, contemporary model of vision neurophysiology. Roughly, it is that the organism has an innate visual organization that, if "validated" by environmental information, becomes consolidated. Once consolidated it is difficult to disorganize it. However, there seems to be a critical period in which this system needs "validation" and, if the visual organization does not receive the vital information within this period, the structure becomes disorganized and loses the potential to be organized as in the consolidated system.

The representation of the research paradigm to test the above is found in Fig. 9.5. Recent research on the development of visual acuity in normal and congenital bilateral cataract infants has been conducted using this paradigm (Goldblatt & Strauss, 1980; Goldblatt, Strauss & Hess, 1980). In our sample of cataract infants, after a period of time in this condition (depending on the degree of blindness and social factors such as the responsibility of the parents) these children undergo an operation in which the cataracts are removed, after which these infants cannot exhibit visual accommodation (i.e., focus on near or far objects).

In the aforementioned paradigm, lines 2 and 3 represent the infants who are born with severe corneal opacity and whose visual recoveries occur at say, ages 6 and 12 months. Line 1 is, of course, a representation of those infants born with normal vision, whereas line 4 shows those infants born blind who have not had their cataracts removed up to the first year of life.

Within the paradigm found in Fig. 9.5, two logics of experimentation can be found. The first type of experiment pertains to the visual system itself as it relates to perceptual development (e.g., the development of visual acuity). In this type of study we would examine children from lines 1, 2, and 3. Infants who have normal vision from birth (line 1) would serve as a normative base line of comparison for the other two groups. In the cases of infants who have recovered from blindness at ages 6 and 12 months, we would obtain data about their perceptual organization immediately after the operation. The comparisons of the children's visual acuity immediately after the operation would show us the degree to which visual acuity is experience dependent. Subsequent postsurgery testing of these same children would show us both the rate and extent to which the visual acuity can return to normative acuity. The data obtained from experiments that have the aforementioned logic underlying them can serve as a basis for the second logic of experimentation within this category of connectedness between behaviors.

The second logic of experimentation pertains directly to the topic of developmental connectedness between behaviors or systems. Following the example of visual deprivation just provided, the sort of issue one would be

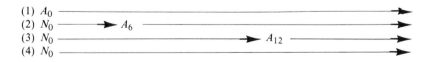

FIG. 9.5. Developmental Courses Whose Comparison Yields Information About the Role of Experience Deprivation on Subsequent Behavioral Development.

looking at here is, for example, how a system allied to vision that should be affected by blindness (e.g., auditorally guided reaching) develops under conditions of varying amounts of visual deprivation. Briefly, the auditorally guided reaching behavior is measured by presenting blind infants with an object that makes noise and observing whether or not they reach for it.

In research of this type, infants representing all four lines in Fig. 9.5 have to be included. In the first line we have a normal, sighted infant and in this case we would present the object that makes noise to such infants when they are in a dark room (Bower, 1974b). In the second and third lines we can present the object before and after cataract surgery and can test the postsurgery reaching at various times to observe its development. In the fourth line we have blind infants whose development can also be measured at different times (Fraiberg, 1968).

I now provide a brief scenario of a possible finding that could shed light on the developmental connectedness between vision and auditorally guided reaching. The possible finding is that infants who were born sighted (line 1) have a particular development sequence that serves as a base line comparison. Blind infants who have not regained sight (line 4) develop differently than do the normal, sighted infants and they, too, serve as a base line for comparison. Infants who were blind at birth due to congenital cataracts and who had the cataracts removed at an early age (line 2) eventually behave like normal sighted infants, whereas those who were operated on at a later age (line 3) continue to behave as if they were blind. The conclusion to be reached from this type of data is that there is a developmental connectedness between vision onset and the development of auditorally guided reaching.

3. Instability in One Area Blocking Acquisition in Another Area

I would now like to describe briefly a fortuitous finding in a study (Strauss & Rimalt, 1974) that bears on a specific aspect of the general paradigm of the disappearance of behaviors.

It touches on the area of how the disappearance of a behavior affects allied behaviors. From this we shall be able to draw conclusions about relations between behaviors within a structural framework.

The research was conducted in an attempt to test the organizational disequilibrium model (Strauss, 1972, 1975; Strauss & Ilan, 1975), which has sometimes been termed oblique interactions (Cellerier, 1972). The main purpose of the Strauss and Rimalt (1974) study was to measure the results of a training procedure that took advantage of structural mix. Structural mix, or transitional reasoning, is the natural condition in which the child has constructed at least two functional structures, say, the preoperational and concrete operational structures. The training procedure required the children

in our study to alternate successively judgments about a task, these judgments being products of the two cognitive structures.

The principle concepts in question were conservation of discontinuous
quantity and area. We had determined in a pilot study that two other
concepts, length and continuous quantity conservation, were constructed
between the acquisition of discontinous quantity, which is acquired first, and
area, which is acquired last. The training was administered so that the
discontinuous quantity and area concepts (and presumably the structures
underlying them) were successively alternated.

Four operational levels were compared (Table 9.2). As can be seen, the
pretest operational levels of the subjects increased from a to d in terms of the
extent to which the concrete operations structure was applied to the various
concepts. In all cases, the subjects were preoperational for area conservation:
the to-be-trained-for concept.

Our expectations for the effects of the training procedure were that few
Level a children would conserve for area conservation because they were
preoperational for all of the concepts and there was no structural mix to be
manipulated. In the cases of Levels b, c, and d, we hypothesized that there
would be rather substantial percentages of subjects who would acquire the
area conservation concept and that the percentages would increase from b to
c to d.

TABLE 9.2

Frequency of Experimental Subjects' Pretest Operational Levels for
Various Conservation Concepts

Operational Level	Discontinuous Quantity	Length	Continuous Quantity	Area
a				
Preoperational	12	12	12	12
Transitional	0	0	0	0
Operational	0	0	0	0
b				
Preoperational	0	13	13	13
Transitional	2	0	0	0
Operational	11	0	0	0
c				
Preoperational	0	2	10	12
Transitional	0	10	2	0
Operational	12	0	0	0
d				
Preoperational	0	0	0	23
Transitional	0	9	5	0
Operational	23	14	18	0

The findings were that the following percentages of subjects conserved for area conservation two weeks after training: Level a—25%; Level b—46%; Level c—8%; Level d—74%. The obviously unexpected finding was the case of Level c, and it is the dynamics of what happened here that bears on the topic of this section.

The reader may have noticed that none of the pretest Level c subjects were operational for length and 10/12 were transitional. It turns out that 50% of these subjects were *posttested* as preoperational for length (i.e., they reverted to a lower level of reasoning on length conservation and they remained at the *preoperational level for area*). An analysis of Levels b and d subjects with the same posttest profile for discontinuous quantity, length, and continuous quantity were *operational for area*. The difference between the Level c and Level b and d children was that the Level c children reverted to a lower level of reasoning on length conservation whereas Levels b and d children did not. Those who reverted for length were preoperational for area whereas those who did not revert to a lower level for length became operational for area.

What happened here was that we wanted to determine the mechanisms of structural elaboration by accelerating the acquisition of a particular concept (area) and we found that structural disruption interfered with the acquisition of area conservation. That is to say, our findings indicated that subjects do not acquire an ontogenetically later concept if there is some sort of instability or oscillation in the application of the structure to ontogenetically prior concepts. Thus, we can argue that there is a developmental connection between these conceptual areas.

In sum, we have looked at three types of experiments in which the ancestral behavior is manipulated and the effects of that manipulation are measured on what is thought to be the descendant behavior. The argument in each type of experimentation was that a change in the timing or form of the descendant behavior would indicate a functional relation between it and the ancestral behavior.

In the case of acceleration studies, I pointed out a methodological problem in Bower's work and suggested that the conclusions he reached for primary and secondary walking might be restricted to motor behaviors. Studies on pathological development was the second type of experiment and here I dealt with cases of limited deprivation and limited experience and their implication for determining relations between behaviors or systems. Finally, the third type of experiment presented dealt with dedifferentiation or instability in one area blocking acquisition in another area as a test for developmental relations between behaviors. The foregoing indicated that the logic of experimentation in embryology can be useful as a heuristic for research in developmental psychology.

Analogous Behaviors

This category of relations, that can exist between Phase 1 and 3 behaviors, has two variants. What is common to these variants is that the Phase 1 and 3 behaviors are evoked by different experimental procedures. In the first type the behaviors are different but are thought to be analogous due to an analysis of the behaviors. In the second type the behaviors are similar but because they are evoked by different procedures they are thought to be analogous. I present briefly one example of each type of analogous behavior and then point out problems associated with this category. The examples that illustrate the two types of analogous behaviors are: (1) object tracking and object permanence; and (2) judgments of nonconservation of weight.

1. Object Tracking and Object Permanence

In this category, analogous behaviors, as determined by a formal description of the behaviors, appears at two noncontinuous points in ontogenesis. An example provided by Bower includes relations between object tracking and object permanence (Bower, Broughton, & Moore, 1971; Bower & Paterson, 1972). One can present infants between the ages 12 and 20 weeks a stationary object in the center of a track; this object will then move to the right, stop, and then move back to the center of the track. This can be repeated several times and one observes that infants at this age can track the object without difficulty. If, however, after this procedure the object were to move to the left, these infants will look to the right, thereby ignoring the visual displacement of the object and looking for it where it was previously seen. Infants stop making these errors at age 20 months.

The analogous behavior comes from errors on object permanence tasks made by Stage 4 infants. The task involves showing an infant a toy that is hidden under one of two cloths. Infants at this stage will retrieve the toy without difficulty. If this procedure is repeated for the same cloth several times the infant will respond correctly in all cases. However, if after this procedure the toy is placed under the other cloth, the infant will look for it under the cloth where it had appeared earlier. Here we see an analogous strategy between types of errors produced by younger and older infants.

2. Judgments of Weight Nonconservation

As mentioned earlier, in this category the behaviors are similar and are evoked in response to different testing procedures. The case I have chosen to examine is that of judgments of nonconservation of weight. The development of weight conservation (Piaget, 1970) is tested in the following manner: Two clay balls are presented to a child who is asked whether or not they are the same weight. After confirming their equal weight the shape of one ball is changed into, say, a pancake and the child is then asked to judge whether or not they are the same weight and to explain why.

Dasen has reported in this volume (Chapter 10) and elsewhere (Dasen & Christie, 1972) that in some studies the percentage of children producing correct judgments on the conservation task rises through age 9 or 10 (this is the usual case) and at approximately age 10 or 11 there is a significant drop in the percentage of children solving this task correctly. This sort of example does not meet the criterion for analogous behavior as presented in this section because the procedure for assessing weight conservation was the same at all ages.

In contrast, I present evidence from a considerable and growing literature that after children have developmentally produced nonconservation and then conservation judgments they can abandon this conservation concept for nonconservation in the face of empirical evidence to the contrary. Because in this latter case the procedure for assessing weight conservation is different from the traditional assessment procedure, this is a case of analogous behavior as defined in the foregoing.

The subject was first brought up by Smedslund (1961) in a study where conserving children were shown empirical evidence of weight nonconservation when the experimenter surreptitiously removed some clay while changing the shape of one of the balls. It was found that 6 of 13 children successfully resisted this evidence by claiming that some clay must have fallen off, the scale was broken, etc. This resistance was seen by Smedslund to be a confirmation of Piaget's notion of logical necessity but the question must remain open because 7 of 13 children accepted this phenomenon. Subsequent research of a similar nature indicated that an even larger percentage of children who conserved did not resist (Brison, 1966; Hall & Kingsley, 1968; Hall & Simpson, 1968; Halpern, 1965; Kingsley & Hall, 1967; Smith, 1968).

Further evidence for nonconservation in similar experimental situations was found among college students. Kingsley and Hall (1968) indicated that college students are likely to accept empirical evidence of weight nonconservation. In contrast, Miller, Schwartz, and Stewart (1973), Strauss, Danziger, and Ramati (1974), and Towler and Wheatley (1971) showed that few college students accept this experience, whereas Chiseri (1975) provided data suggesting that college students' acceptance of this phenomenon can be manipulated. Again, despite the contradictory findings, all the foregoing reported that acceptance of empirical evidence of weight nonconservation was accompanied by sophisticated explanations.

One other interesting set of findings should be noted here because it adds to the general picture presented so far. Strauss and Liberman (1974) found that *fewer* older children ($\bar{x}$ age = 12.0) than younger children ($\bar{x}$ age = 8.7) spontaneously rejected weight nonconservation experiences. Similarly, Miller and Lipps (1973) reported that 53% of their older and 60% of their younger children rejected similar experiences. In both experiments it was noted that the older children produced sophisticated justifications when explaining the nonconservation of weight phenomenon whereas the younger children did not.

This type of evidence, gathered from different procedures, suggests that, when tested by the traditional Piagetian technique, children at first do not conserve and then do conserve. At a later age, when children are administered tasks providing empirical evidence of nonconservation, children sometimes produce judgments of nonconservation again. These latter judgments are accompanied by sophisticated justifications that are not produced by younger, preoperational children.

Taking a look at this sort of evidence it is possible to argue (as I did in Strauss, 1972, 1975) that another way to interpret these studies is to consider them as instances of -1 studies such as those of Kuhn (1972) and Turiel (1966). In these studies, children were presented information in argument or empirical form that was characteristic of judgments from a lower, former level (-1). To use the Smedslund (1961) study as an example of what this means, we can think of it as an instance where concrete operational children were being provided with empirical evidence of nonconservation for which these very same children had argued in their prior (-1) preoperational stage. When presented with information characteristic of a former level of reasoning most children rejected it. The Kuhn and Turiel studies, as well as those of Rest (1969; Rest, Turiel & Kohlberg, 1969), indicated that children comprehended -1 reasoning yet they rejected it as inadequate and nonpreferred.

Given the foregoing argument that there is a similarity between the nonconservation studies and Turiel and Kuhn's studies, we then are faced with the discrepancy that some investigators found fairly ubiquitous acceptance of -1 information whereas Kuhn, Turiel, and Rest's studies indicated considerable resistance to -1 experiences. In an attempt to delineate the reasons for this discrepancy, I developed several arguments that may explain some of the difference (Strauss, 1972).

The first explanation pertained to types of diagnosis, inasmuch as some experimenters probed Ss' reasoning and others did not. That probing can show a much different picture of Ss' understanding of the -1 problem than nonprobing was shown by Strauss and Liberman (1974). A second explanation related to the medium of -1 judgments: Turiel (1966) presented the -1 structure in argument form, Kuhn (1972) presented arguments and classification of materials, whereas Smedslund (1961), Hall and Kingsley (1968), and others presented -1 empirical outcomes of physical deformations. One would intuitively imagine that the violation of an expected empirical law has a different status than a violation of an argument or a classification of material that one had previously used predominantly. A third explanation of the discrepant results pertained to the content of the −1 information: Turiel's work was about moral judgments, Kuhn's (1972) and Miller and Lipps' (1973) dealt with logical concepts, and the other studies' content was physical concepts.

Given these remarks, which point out the methodological problems in this area, there are two principal explanations for evidence of nonconservation judgment repetitions: (1) structural reversion; and (2) content reversion. Before outlining these points, I first present a distinction that imposes constraints on and, hopefully, clarifies the general discussion. The distinction is between reversion and regression. Reversion is defined as a temporary, local production of judgments or justifications that have similarities to productions from a prior stage. Regression, on the other hand, is defined as a long-term, general production of reasoning that has similarities to reasoning from an earlier stage. The discussion here focuses on reversion. Let us now begin our discussion of the three explanations mentioned.

2.1. Structural Reversion.   This explanation has been offered by Dasen and Christie (1972). Their claim was that there is a reversion in some concrete operational children's cognitive functioning to the preoperational weight nonconservation structure and evidence for this is found in these children's judgments. This reversion was thought to occur around the time of the appearance of the formal operations structure. Evidence of the emergence of formal operations reasoning comes from the sophisticated, formal concepts used to justify nonconservation. Thus, these children apply partially understood concepts that interfere with the solution of formerly correctly solved weight conservation concepts. This situation of a juxtaposition of two distant stages has also been described by Kohlberg and Kramer (1969) and Cambon and Sinclair (1973) as a condition that can lead to progressive structural development.

Implicit in this type of explanation is the understanding that prior stages remain in potential even though they have been "passed through." This, of course, is one of the fundamental notions in Werner's (1948; Werner & Kaplan, 1963) orthogenetic principle. An explicit statement of this idea was made by Werner and Kaplan (1963):

> A further issue . . . concerns the "fate" of the genetically earlier modes of functioning when higher functions and forms have emerged. At least with regard to humans it must be maintained that with the attainment of higher levels, lower levels of functioning are not lost . . . one often finds a partial return to more primitive modes of functioning before progressing towards more full-fledged higher operations; we may refer to this tendency as a manifestation of the genetic principle of spirality [p. 8]."

This principle has at least three parts: (1) lower levels of cognitive functioning are not lost; (2) they support the higher levels; and (3) they can be returned to in the service of progressive functional development. This return to a lower level before progressive development occurs has sometimes been described as structural oscillation (Inhelder, 1941; Langer 1969 a, 1969 b; Strauss, 1972; Turiel & Rothman, 1972).

The main problem with this approach arises in an analysis of the nature of the return to the former level of reasoning. In cases such as those presented in the foregoing, we observe a child producing a judgment of nonconservation. Such a judgment need not indicate a return to a lower level of reasoning (i.e., a former structure). If the justification is part of the criterion of the structure that produces the judgment, we cannot claim that the Dasen and Christie (1972) evidence constitutes a case of structural reversion. What their data and the Miller *et al.* (1973) and Strauss and Liberman (1974) data described previously may be indicating is that older children are using a different set of strategies, which appear on the surface to be producing lower level judgments.

In sum, it has been suggested that the evidence for structural reversion revolves, in part, around methodological considerations. It was further noted that if one includes both judgments and justifications as criteria for stage assessment the evidence for structural reversion becomes seriously weakened.

2.2 Content Reversion.   The second type of explanation for the evidence presented earlier has been proposed by Turiel (1966, 1973, 1974). His main argument is that structuralist theory is, in its essence, transformational. Each stage represents a transformation of the prior one, and the prior one, having been transformed, does not exist in potential. What does remain is the content of the prior stages so that what appears to be regressions to former organizations or forms of reasoning is really a reuse of former content. Or as Turiel (1974) expressed it: "Earlier stages appear to remain because earlier structure is present in later stages as content [p. 18]." The empirical evidence presented for this position was that children are found to comprehend but to reject −1 information and prefer +1 arguments to −1 arguments despite the fact that they had previously constructed the −1 structure and had not yet come to reason at the +1 level.

In sum, I have shown two examples of analogous behaviors. In each of the cases (weight nonconservation and object tracking permanence), the behaviors, which we think may be developmentally related, are evoked by different testing procedures. In other words, we have different behaviors within different contexts. The only reason to justify calling them analogous would be if we could demonstrate that the behaviors have the same function within the different contexts. And herein lies the rub, because the tools at our disposal for analyzing the context, let alone the function of a behavior within the context, are so dull that the exercise would seem rather fruitless. Similarly, the picture for empirically testing the developmental relations between the two behaviors seems rather bleak. Finally, the fate of the Phase 2 behavior (the drop in performance) was discussed.

Summary

The systematic study of the phenomenon of U-shaped behavioral growth, which is only in its infancy (Strauss, in press; Strauss & Stavy, in press), served as the springboard for this chapter. The intent underlying the foregoing was to map out how we can establish experimentally the existence of developmental links between two behaviors or systems. The reason this strikes me as important is that a determination of the nature of the developmental connection between Phases 1 and 3 is critical for understanding all three phases of the U-shaped behavioral growth phenomenon.

In this chapter I elucidated three types of developmental relations that can exist between two behaviors that appear at noncontinuous points in ontogenesis and the experimental design needed to make claims about these relations. The *first* type, identity relations, was fraught with problems of theory and method and I presented only the nature of data and argumentation needed to establish whether or not two behaviors are identical. In the *second* type, nonidentical but developmentally connected behaviors, there were three conditions by which we could determine if the behaviors or systems are developmentally connected, these three being inspired by the logic of experimentation in embryology. The first experimental approach was acceleration studies, which may turn out to be the only ethical way to determine experimentally the existence of a link between Phases 1 and 3. The second approach was to look at clinical cases (pathologies) to determine how the pathologically late appearance or disappearance of one system affects other systems that are claimed to be developmentally related. The third approach was to examine cases where there is instability or oscillation in one system and to observe its effects on another system. The *third* type of developmental relation, analogous behaviors, had as its main problem the issue of how we can analyze what is analogous and what is not. In addition, the question was raised as to whether or not we can manipulate the analogous behaviors experimentally.

If the foregoing was inspired by the phenomenon of U-shaped behavioral growth, it can certainly be asked what it can mean for U-shaped behavioral growth. The main implication of this chapter for the phenomenon is that the analysis provided here can be used to: (1) establish the type of relation that exists between Phases 1 and 3; (2) suggest how one can test experimentally the nature of the relation; and (3) help in speculating about the nature and role of Phase 2 in the U-shaped behavioral growth curve.

ACKNOWLEDGMENT

This chapter is Working Paper Number 2 of the Tel-Aviv University Study Group on Human Development. I would like to thank members of the study group, David Feldman, Lynn Goldsmith, Jerome Kagan, and Carol Smith for their insights and comments on an earlier version of the chapter. The research reported on the development of temperature concepts was supported by a grant awarded by the Chief Scientist's Office of the Israeli Ministry of Education.

REFERENCES

Ackroyd, C., Humphrey, N. K., & Warrington, E. K. Lasting effects of early blindness: A case study. *Quarterly Journal of Experimental Psychology*, 1974, *26*, 114–124.

André -Thomas & Dargassies, St. A. Cited in Bower, T. G. R. *Development in infancy*. San Francisco: Freeman, 1974. *Etudes neurologiques sur le nouveau-ne et le jeune nourrison*. Paris: Masson, 1952.

Bower, T. G. R. *Development in infancy*. San Francisco: Freeman, 1974. (a)

Bower, T. G. R. Repetition in human development. *Merrill–Palmer Quarterly*, 1974, *20*, 303–318. (b)

Bower, T. G. R. *Human development*. San Francisco: Freeman, 1979.

Bower, T.G.R., Broughton, J. M., & Moore, M. K. The development of the object concept as manifested by changes in the tracking behavior of infants between 7 and 20 weeks of age. *Journal of Experimental Child Psychology*, 1971, *11*, 182–193.

Bower, T. G. R. & Paterson, J. T. Stages in the development of the object concept. *Cognition*, 1972, *1*, 47–55.

Brison, D. W. Acceleration of conservation of substance. *Journal of Genetic Psychology*, 1966, *109*, 311–322.

Cambon, J. & Sinclair, H. *Relations between syntax and semantics: Are they "easy to see?"* Unpublished manuscript, University of Geneva, 1973.

Carnap, R. *Philosophical foundations of physics*. New York: Basic Books, 1966.

Cellerier, G. Information processing tendencies in recent experiments in cognitive learning— theoretical implications. In S. Farnham-Diggory (Ed.), *Information processing in children*. New York: Academic Press, 1972.

Chiseri, M. J. Amenability to incorrect hypotheses in the extinction of conservation of weight in college students. *Merrill-Palmer Quarterly*, 1975, *21*, 139–143.

Dasen, P. R. & Christie, R. D. A regression phenomenon in the conservation of weight. *Archives de Psychologie*, 1972, *41*, 145–152.

Drever, J. Early learning and the perception of space. *American Journal of Psychology*, 1955, *68*, 605–614.

Flavell, J. An analysis of cognitive–developmental sequences. *Genetic Psychology Monographs*, 1972, *86*, 279–350.

Fraiberg, S. Parallel and divergent pattern in blind and sighted infants. *Psychoanalytic study of the child*. (Vol. 23), 1968.

Fraiberg, S. & Freedman, D. A. Studies in the ego development of the congenitally blind infant. *Psychoanalytic study of the child*. (Vol. 19), 1964.

Fraiberg, S., Siegel, B. L., & Gibson, R. The role of sound in the search behavior in a blind infant. *Psychoanalytic study of the child*. (Vol. 21), 1966.

Goldblatt, A., & Strauss, S. *A retrospective study on the effects of congenital cataract operations on visual acuity development: Evidence for a sensitive period?* Unpublished manuscript, Tel-Aviv University, 1980.

Goldblatt, A., Strauss, S. & Hess, P. A replication and extension of findings about the development of visual acuity in infants. *Infant Behavior and Development*, 1980, *3*, 179–182.

Gregory, R. L. *Concepts and mechanisms of perception.* London: Duckworth, 1974.

Hall, V. C., & Kingsley, R. Conservation and equilibration theory. *Journal of Genetic Psychology*, 1968, *113*, 195–213.

Hall, V. C., and Simpson, G. J. Factors influencing extinction of weight conservation. *Merrill–Palmer Quarterly*, 1968, *17*, 319–334.

Halpern, E. The effects of incompatibility between perception and logic in Piaget's stages of concrete operations. *Child Development*, 1965, *36*, 491–497.

Hebb, D. O. *The organization of behavior.* New York: Wiley, 1949.

Inhelder, B. *The diagnosis of reasoning in the mentally retarded.* New York: John Day, 1941.

Jacobson, M. Clones and compartments in the vertebrate central nervous system. *Trends in Neurosciences*, 1980, *3*, 3–5.

Kingsley, R., & Hall, V. C. Training conservation through the use of learning sets. *Child Development*, 1967, *38*, 1111–1126.

Kohlberg, L., & Kramer, R. B. Continuities and discontinuities in childhood and adult moral development. *Human Development*, 1969, *12*, 93–120.

Kuhn, D. Mechanisms of change in the development of cognitive structures. *Child Development*, 1972, *43*, 833–844.

Langer, J. Disequilibrium as a source of development. In P. H. Mussen, J. Langer, & M. Covington (Eds.), *Trends and issues in developmental psychology.* New York: Holt, Rinehart, & Winston, 1969. (a)

Langer, J. *Theories of development.* New York: Holt, Rinehart, & Winston, 1969. (b)

Miller, S. A., & Lipps, L. Extinction of conservation and transitivity of weight. *Journal of Experimental Child Psychology*, 1973, *16*, 388–402.

Miller, S. A., Schwartz, L. C. & Stewart, C. An attempt to extinguish conservation of weight in college students. *Developmental Psychology*, 1973, *8*, 316.

Piaget, J. Piaget's theory. In P. H. Mussen (Ed.), *Carmichael's manual of child psychology.* New York: John Wiley, 1970.

Rest, J. *Hierarchies of comprehension and preference in a developmental stage model of moral thinking.* Unpublished doctoral dissertation, University of Chicago, 1969.

Rest, J., Turiel, E., & Kohlberg, L. Level of moral development as a determinant of preference and comprehension of moral judgments made by others. *Journal of Personality*, 1969, *37*, 225–252.

Senden, M. von. *Space and sight.* London: Methuen, 1960.

Siegler, R. S. Three aspects of cognitive development. *Cognitive Psychology*, 1976, *8*, 481–520.

Siegler, R. S. The origins of scientific reasoning. In R. S. Siegler (Ed.), *Children's thinking: What develops?* Hillsdale, N.J.: Lawrence Erlbaum Associates, 1978.

Siegler, R. S. Developmental sequences within and between concepts. *Monographs of the Society for Research in Child Development,* 1981, *46*, 1–74.

Smedslund, J. The acquisition of conservation of substance and weight in children. III. Extinction of conservation of weight acquired "normally" and by means of empirical controls on a balance scale. *Scandanavian Journal of Psychology*, 1961, *2*, 85–87.

Smith, I. D. The effects of training procedures on the acquisition of conservation of weight. *Child Development*, 1968, *39*, 515–526.

Stavy, R., Strauss, S., Orpaz, N., & Carmi, G. U-shaped behavioral growth in ratio comparisons. In S. Strauss (Ed.) *U-shaped behavioral growth,* in press.

Strauss, S. Inducing cognitive development and learning: A review of short-term training experiments. I. The organismic–developmental approach. *Cognition*, 1972, *1*, 329–357.

Strauss, S. A reply to Brainerd. *Cognition*, 1975, *3*, 155–185.

Strauss, S. (Ed.). *U-shaped behavioral growth*. New York: Academic Press. In press.

Strauss, S., *On inclusion and developmental sequences*. In preparation.

Strauss, S., & Ilan, J. Length conservation and the speed concepts: Organizational disequilibrium training between concepts. *Journal of Educational Psychology*, 1975, *67*, 470–477.

Strauss, S., & Liberman, D. The empirical violation of conservation laws and its relation to structural change. *Journal of Experimental Child Psychology*, 1974, *18*, 464–479.

Strauss, S., & Rimalt, I. Effects of organizational disequilibrium training on structural elaboration. *Developmental Psychology*, 1974, *10*, 526–533.

Strauss, S., & Stavy, R. U-shaped behavioral growth: Implications for theories of development. In W. W. Hartup (Ed.), *Review of child development research. (Vol. 6)*. Chicago: University of Chicago Press, in press.

Strauss, S., Stavy, R., & Orpaz, N. *The child's development of the concept of temperature*. Unpublished manuscript, Tel-Aviv University, 1977.

Towler, J. O., & Wheatley, G. Conservation concepts in college students: A replication and critique. *Journal of Genetic Psychology*, 1971, *118*, 265–270.

Turiel, E. An experimental test of the sequentiality of developmental stages in the child's moral development. *Journal of Personality and Social Psychology*, 1966, *3*, 611–618.

Turiel, E. Stage transition in moral development. In R. M. W. Travers (Ed.), *Second Handbook of research on teaching*. Chicago: Rand McNally, 1973.

Turiel, E. Conflict and transition in adolescent moral development. *Child Development*, 1974, *45*, 14–29.

Turiel, E., & Rothman, G. R. The influence of reasoning on behavioral choices at different stages of moral development. *Child Development*, 1972, *43*, 741–756.

Werner, H. *Comparative psychology of mental development.* New York: International Universities Press, 1948.

Werner, H., & Kaplan, B. *Symbol formation*. New York: Wiley, 1963.

Wolpert, L. Pattern formation in biological development. *Scientific American*, 1978, *239*, 124–137.

10 Cross-Cultural Data on Operational Development: Asymptotic Development Curves

Pierre R. Dasen
*Faculté de Psychologie et
des Sciences de l'Education
Université de Genève*

The object of this chapter is to review some developmental data obtained in cross-cultural studies of Piaget's concrete operations and to discuss some aspects that can be related to "dips" or discontinuities in cognitive development. I restrict my discussion to the developmental curves representing the speed or rate of acquisition of concrete operations in a population, leaving aside the more important question of the qualitative aspects (structures, stages) of Piaget's theory. Generally speaking, these qualitative aspects have been found to be quite universal, whereas cultural factors seem to influence the rate at which children move from one stage to the next (Dasen, 1972, 1973, 1975a, 1977a).

The "rate" of attainment of concrete-operational concepts in a given population may be represented by plotting the frequency of concrete-operational behavior over age; the developmental curves thus obtained tend to approximate a normal ogive (Dasen, 1972; Kamara & Easley, 1977). An example of such curves gleaned from the cross-cultural literature and collected on the same graph was presented by Dasen (1973, Fig. 1, p. 157; 1977a, p. 170) for the conservation of quantity (liquids). Although the various curves are not strictly speaking comparable because of the heterogeneity of experimenters, techniques, and situations, such a graph shows clearly that there is an extremely large range of variation in the rates of development of conservation of quantity, and similar graphs would be obtained with other concrete-operational concepts. Considering general trends only, one may distinguish at least two different types of curves.

A first type of curve indicates a steady increase of conservation behavior over age, all or most subjects eventually reaching Stage 3. Compared to curves obtained with Western children, these curves either overlap completely, or there may appear a time lag that reflects relatively unimportant cultural or experimental factors.

A second type of curve, namely those reaching an asymptote below 100% is more puzzling. They indicate that a more or less large proportion of the population does not seem to reach Stage 3 (the fully concrete-operational substage on any one concept). I devote a large part of my discussion to the interpretation of these asymptotic curves, which represent a phenomenon related to "dips" in development curves. In particular, I attempt to demonstrate that the level these asymptotes reach in a particular population is partly determined by eco-cultural variables (to be subsumed in a simplified fashion under the general heading: "cultural relevance" of a particular concept). I also suggest that in some cases, these asymptotic curves may represent a "performance" rather than a "competence" measure. Most of this cross-cultural material is almost anecdotic, and hardly sufficient to generate new theoretical models. However the cross-cultural situation presents some advantages over more conventional methods; in particular, a careful selection of the populations compared may enable us to find extremes on variables that are too homogeneous to be studied within Western culture. Hopefully, cross-cultural studies will suggest some hypotheses that later may be integrated usefully in more general developmental models.

One variable open to cross-cultural investigation is the "cultural relevance" of a particular concept or conceptual domain. It has been argued by Berry (1976) that ecological demands placed on a group of people, plus their cultural adaptation to this ecology, will lead to the preferential development of certain cognitive skills. For example, populations relying on hunting and gathering as a livelihood, and that tend to be nomadic, are expected to develop high spatial skills and concepts. In other words, spatial concepts are ecologically and culturally relevant to a nomadic, hunting society, whereas they may be less relevant to a sedentary population.

In order to test Berry's functional model (much simplified for the purpose of this chapter) within Piagetian developmental psychology, I have selected three populations that can be placed on Berry's eco-cultural dimension: (1) Eskimos (Cape Dorset) at one extreme (nomadic, hunting, low food-accumulating, low population density); (2) African agriculturalists (Adio-podoumé) at the other extreme (sedentary, high food-accumulating, high population density); and (3) Australian Aborigines (Hermannsburg) in an intermediate position but definitely on the nomadic side. Three Piagetian tasks were used to assess the development of topological, projective, and Euclidean spatial concepts: (1) linear, reverse, and circular orders; (2) rotation of landscape models; (3) horizontality (level of liquid in a tilted bottle). The details of the argument, sample characteristics, and procedures have been presented elsewhere (Dasen, 1975a, 1977a). The results are presented in Figs. 10.1, 10.2, and 10.3.

ORDERS

Percentage of subjects at stage 3

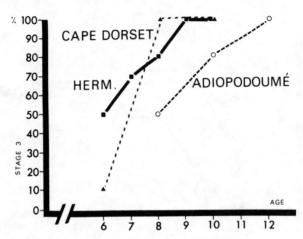

FIG. 10.1.   Orders: Percentage of subjects at Stage 3.

FIG. 10.2.   Rotation: Percentage of subjects at Stage 3.

ROTATION

Percentage of subjects at stage 3

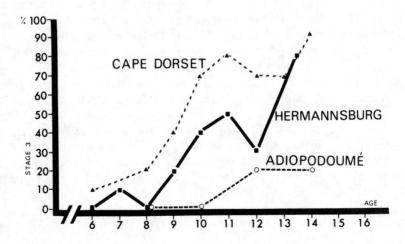

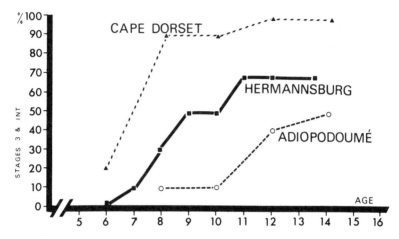

FIG. 10.3.   Horizontality: Part 1: Percentage of subjects at Stages 3 and intermediate.

The hypothesis is clearly supported; the ordering of the developmental curves follows the ordering of the samples on the eco-cultural scale. The statistical significance of the differences in the proportions of children in each age group reaching the concrete-operational stage was computed according to a scheme proposed by Kamara and Easley (1977). The developmental curves are significantly different beyond the .05 level in each comparison (except between the Hermannsburg and Cape Dorset samples on orders).

Some of the developmental curves are asymptotic, particularly those of the Adiopodoumé sample on rotation and horizontality. It is my contention that the level of these asymptotes is, at least partially, determined by the cultural relevance (or rather, irrelevance) of the concepts involved. It would certainly be wrong to conclude from these results that "cognitive development" (or any such generic term such as "intellectual capacity") is faster (respectively, higher) in Eskimos than in Ebrié Africans. What the results do mean to me is that there are more Eskimo than Ebrié African children reaching the concrete-operational stage in the area of spatial conceptualization, because spatial concepts are relevant (indeed selectively indispensable) in Eskimo culture, whereas they are less relevant in the African context.[1]

On the other hand, some concepts may be more relevant in an African than in an Eskimo culture. For example, the concepts of number, or of quantity,

---

[1]"African" is used here in the context of Berry's model as a handy contraction and does not apply to all African cultures, whose diversity I would not wish to ignore.

weight, and volume, seem to be important in a population that produces food on a seasonal basis, has to store it between harvests, and exchanges it on markets. In traditional Eskimo and Australian Aboriginal cultures, however, these concepts are rather irrelevant. Number concepts, for example, are rudimentary in both cultures. Game is caught and eaten by the family group whenever available; the distribution of the meat follows qualitative rules (specified pieces are distributed according to kinship or social relations). There is no mercantile, quantitative exchange of food. Thus we may expect that the members of the African group will attain concepts of conservation of quantity, weight, and volume more rapidly (or in larger numbers) than do Eskimos and Australian Aborigines. There is little reason, however, to expect a difference between the latter two populations. The results concerning this second hypothesis are presented in Figs. 10.4, 10.5, and 10.6.

The second hypothesis receives partial support from the data. If the age range of 12 to 14 years is considered alone, the order of the developmental curves follows the ordering on the eco-cultural scale: The proportion of children reaching the concrete-operational stage (over age) is significantly larger ($p = .05$) in the Adiopodoumé sample than in the two other samples on all three tasks. The differences are not statistically significant between the Hermannsburg and Cape Dorset samples.

If the complete age range is considered, the differences are statistically significant in two cases only: between Adiopodoumé and Cape Dorset on conservation of quantity and between Adiopodoumé and Hermannsburg on

FIG. 10.4.   Conservation of quantity: Percentage of subjects at Stage 3.

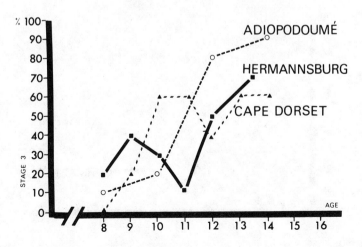

CONSERVATION OF **QUANTITY**

Percentage of subjects at   stage 3

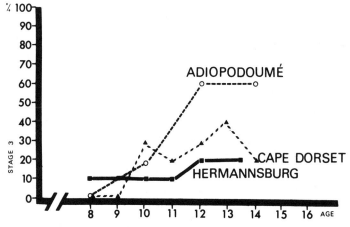

FIG. 10.5.   Conservation of weight: Percentage of subjects at Stage 3.

FIG. 10.6.   Conservation of volume: Percentage of subjects at Stage 3

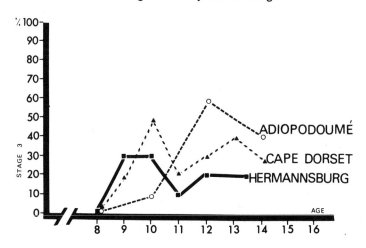

conservation of weight. A lengthy discussion would be needed to consider all the conjectures likely to explain the details of these results. For example we could ask to what extent "pseudoconservation" is involved (I come back to this point later in this chapter), we could consider the age at which children are usually drawn into the economic activities (such as selling foodstuffs on markets) that are likely to be related to the concepts of conservation, or we could question the appropriateness of the Adiopodoumé sample, which included some children whose fathers did not in fact practice full-time agriculture, but were fishermen or were engaged in wage employment. I would not like to engage in a lengthy digression on this subject, but it should be mentioned that more recently, I have administered the tasks of horizontality and conservation of quantity to another sample of West African children (Baoulé, Ivory Coast) as well as a sample of East African children (Kikuyu, Kenya). Both these samples would have been situated more at the extreme sedentary/agriculturalist end of Berry's eco-cultural scale than the Adiopodoumé sample, In both cases, the results on horizontality were exactly as those obtained in Adiopodoumé, whereas the developmental curve for conservation of quantity (Stage 3—full conservation) rose steeply from age 7 to reach 100% conservation at age 10, and there was no overlap at all with the Cape Dorset and Hermannsburg curves. If these Baoulé or Kikuyu samples had been used in the original comparison, the second hypothesis would have been supported over the whole age range.

As a conclusion to this first part, I wish to retain the suggestion that the rate of cognitive development may be determined in part by eco-cultural factors. In short, Piaget's concrete operations are not completely "universal," but some concepts are more culturally relevant than others and are thus developed more rapidly.

I have suggested elsewhere (Dasen, 1977a, 1981) that the first of Piaget's major stages, that of sensorimotor intelligence, is "strongly" universal, whereas the second major stage, that of concrete operations, is only "weakly" universal. This summary statement, based on a literature survey as well as on my own data, follows a distinction put forward by Flavell and Wohlwill (1969) between "strong" and "weak" sequential invariance:

A sequence is strongly invariant if it is both universally present and universally fixed in the childhoods of undamaged human beings. For instance, we imagine that all intact human infants achieve primary and tertiary circular reactions, and achieve them in that order only. A sequence is weakly invariant if, when present, it is universally fixed. One may be able to find children who do not attain A, or B, or both; but for all children who do attain both, the order of attainment is the same [p. 84, fn].

The strong sequential invariance and universality of the sensorimotor stage was demonstrated in a recent longitudinal study reported by Dasen, Inhelder,

Lavallée and Retschitzki (1978). The weak universality of concrete operations (at least at the performance level—we come back to this point shortly) is attested by the "asymptotes" in the development curves, such as those presented in this chapter. In attaining concrete-operational concepts, all children follow the same sequence of substages, but not all children reach the last substage. These asymptotes are not actual "dips" in development curves, insofar as they do not indicate a regression in any one individual, but they do indicate a discontinuity—and therefore attract our attention.

There are some indications that the asymptotic curves that we have discussed do not always reflect the cognitive "competence," or underlying structure, but rather a "performance" or spontaneous use of a concept. Such a distinction has been elaborated by Flavell and Wohlwill (1969) within Piagetian theory and suggested in cross-cultural work by Heron and Dowel (1974) and Bovet (1974), before being further expanded by Dasen (1977b).

A small training experiment with the Eskimo sample, reported by Dasen (1975b, 1977a), suggests that 12 to 14-year-old nonconservers could acquire the concept of conservation of quantity (liquids) very easily. Of seven subjects of this age, four moved from Stage 1 (complete nonconservation) to Stage 3 (complete conservation) only through the exposure, over 12 days in the average, to other concrete-operational tasks; a further three subjects moved from Stage 1 to Stage 2 (transitional), but reached Stage 3 after only a few training sessions (using a technique devised by Lefèbvre & Pinard, 1972). My contention is that these subjects did in fact have the competence for conservation but, for some reason (e.g., its lack of relevance in the traditional culture), did not display it on the initial testing. On the other hand, four subjects aged 10 and 11 made no progress between the first and second pretests and then moved only to the transitional stage during the conservation training. It is my contention that these subjects did not initially have the necessary concrete-operational structure for conservation, but that they would have been able to acquire it.

Subsequent training studies were carried out by Dasen, Lavallée, and Retschitzki (1979), Dasen, Ngini, and Lavallée (1979) and Lavallée and Dasen (1980) with both West African (Baoulé) and East African (Kikuyu) children, the concepts studied being the conservation of quantity (liquids), the quantification of class inclusion, and horizontality. In all cases a statistically significant training effect was obtained, the training proved to be stable over time, and a statistically significant generalization to other concrete-operational concepts indicated that a truly operational restructuring had occurred. In most cases, the training was sufficient to reduce or bridge the time lag observed between non-Western and Western results. Very rapid learning, an indicator for "actualization" of underlying competence, occurred most strikingly in 12- to 14-year-old Kikuyu children for the quantification of class inclusion, and for the concept of horizontality in 36% of Baoulé children (aged 13 to 14 years) but in only 5% of Kikuyu children of approximately the same age. No actualization was evident in younger children on any of the concepts trained.

These results suggest that the competence/performance distinction may be relevant to some but possibly not all of the asymptotic development curves. This is a partial limitation to our conclusion that concrete operations are only "weakly" universal. In fact, in most cases, the underlying competence for concrete-operational concepts may well be "strongly" universal, although the rate of development of this competence may also be affected by ecocultural factors. Asymptotic curves or discontinuities may occur because this competence cannot always be applied immediately to a specific situation, especially if the latter deals with a culturally irrelevant content. In other words, according to Cole and Scribner (1974): "we are unlikely to find cultural differences in basic component cognitive processes" but we may find them in the way these basic operations are "organized into functional cognitive systems" to produce a total performance [pp. 193–194]. The asymptotic curves that we have described are thus not structural but functional "dips"—a case quite different from the "repetition hypothesis" discussed by Strauss and others in this volume.

Another example of what appears to be a culturally determined "regression" is presented in Fig. 10.7. The percentage of conservation answers is much lower in the sample of adults (n = 10) than in the 15- to 16-year-old children. One interpretation is that the adolescents had more or a better schooling than the adults, who, at the same age, would not have displayed more conservation behaviour than as adults. The second hypothesis is that they have "regressed" (i.e., they may have used conservation concepts while in the Western-type school situation, where the concepts are relevant, but no longer make use of them when they return to a more traditional life as adults). In the absence of a longitudinal follow-up study it is impossible to decide which hypothesis is correct; I believe it is the second one, because, on a concept that is culturally more relevant (horizontality), this "regression" in adults does not occur (Fig. 10.8).

If we return to the data reported in Fig. 10.7, we notice another apparent "dip" on conservation of quantity and volume at age 11, and similar discontinuities were found by de Lemos (1969) on the same population tested 5 years previously. In this case it is quite possible that the early rise in conservation answers is due to what Bovet (1974) has called "pseudo-conservation," but at the time of collecting these data, I was not aware of this phenomenon and therefore could not take the necessary steps to check it. No other cross-cultural study has reported similar results. If the "pseudo-conservation" hypothesis were confirmed, we would have here another example of a dip that is not an actual regression, but the expression of an earlier stage, which does not occur, or at least has not been reported, in European children (although similar pseudoconservation phenomena seem to occur for other concepts).

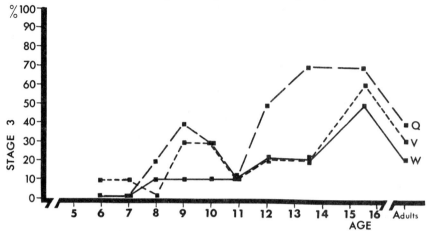

FIG. 10.7   Hermannsburg: Percentage of subjects conserving quantity, weight, and volume.

FIG. 10.8.   Horizontality: Percentage of subjects at Stage 3 (a & b)

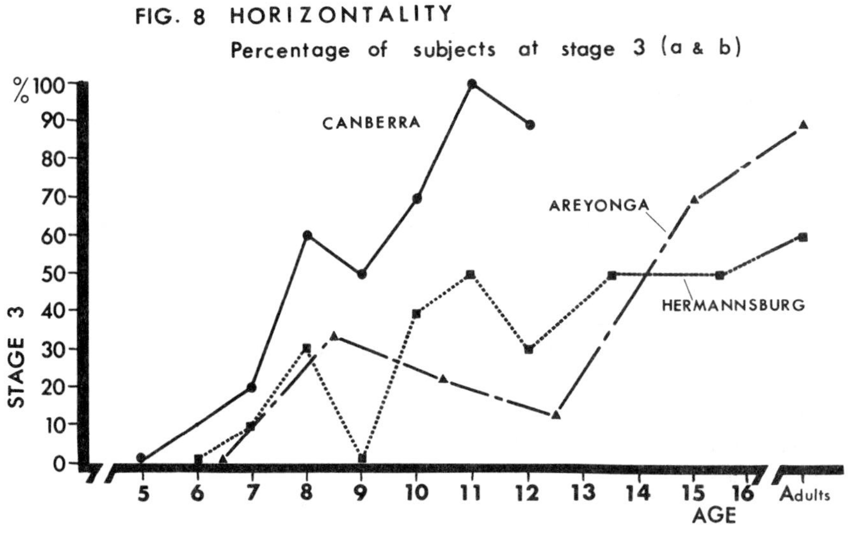

A similar case of a "pseudodip" has been reported by Dasen and Christie (1972) for conservation of weight in Western children and has been discussed at length by Strauss in his contribution to this volume. In this case again, the apparent regression is not a return to a lower form of behavior, but reflects an intermediate step on the road to a higher form of behavior. It is a "dip" only if we look at actual performance instead of searching for the underlying competence.

In each of these examples, a "dip" occurred at the performance level. If we had left it at that, we may have concluded erroneously that a regression had occurred in the course of development. When questioning the child further, or using additional techniques such as training methods—in other words, when attempting to reach the underlying competence—it became evident that the "dip" in performance was functional, or reflected the normal course of development. This is not to say that dips in performance may not be interesting or of practical importance in their own right, but the examples we have produced should serve as a "caveat" for the interpretation of such discontinuities. Generally speaking a "dip" seems to be an indicator, a road sign drawing attention to a possibly interesting phenomenon that needs to be studied through other means.

ACKNOWLEDGMENTS

This research was supported in part by a postgraduate research scholarship at the Australian National University, a postdoctoral research fellowship from the Canada Council, the Groupe de Recherches Nordiques de l'Université de Montréal, and by the Fonds National Suisse de la Recherche Scientifique (Grants Nos. 1.133.69, 1.7640.72, and 1.5550.74 to Professor Bärbel Inhelder).

REFERENCES

Berry, J. W. *Human ecology and cognitive style*. New York: Sage/Halsted/Wiley, 1976.

Bovet, M. C. Cognitive processes among illiterate children and adults. In J. W. Berry and P. R. Dasen (Eds.), *Culture and cognition*. London: Methuen, 1974.

Cole, M., & Scribner, S. *Culture and thought: A psychological introduction*. New York: Wiley, 1974.

Dasen, P. R. Cross-cultural Piagetian research: A summary. *Journal of Cross-Cultural Psychology*, 1972, *3*, 23–39.

Dasen, P. R. Biologie ou culture? La psychologie interethnique d'un point de vue Piagétien. *Psychologie Canadienne*, 1973, *14*, 149–166.

Dasen, P. R. Concrete operational development in three cultures. *Journal of Cross-Cultural Psychology*, 1975, *6*, (2); 156–172. (a)

Dasen, P. R. Le developpment des opérations concrètes chez les Esquimaux Canadiens. *Journal International de Psychologie*, 1975, *10*, (3); 165–180. (b)

Dasen, P. R. Are cognitive processes universal? A contribution to cross-cultural Piagetian psychology. In N. Warren (Ed.), *Studies in cross-cultural psychology*, (Vol. 1). London: Academic Press, 1977. (a)

Dasen, P. R. Cross-cultural cognitive development: The cultural aspects of Piaget's theory. *Annals of the New York Academy of Sciences*, 1977, *285*, 332–337. (b)

Dasen, P. R. "Strong" and "weak" universals: Concrete operations and sensorimotor intelligence. In B. Lloyd and J. Gay (Eds.), *Universals of human thought: Some African evidence*. Cambridge University Press, 1981.

Dasen, P. R., & Christie, R. A regression phenomenon in the conservation of weight. *Archives de Psychologie*, 1972, *41*, 145–152.

Dasen, P. R., Inhelder, B., Lavallée, M., & Retschitzki, J. *Naissance de l'intelligence chez l'enfant Baoulé de Côte d'Ivoire*. Berne: Hans Huber, 1978.

Dasen, P. R., Lavallée, M., & Retschitzki, J. Training conservation of quantity (liquids) in West African (Baoulé) children. *International Journal of Psychology*, 1979, *14*, 57–68.

Dasen, P. R., Ngini, L., & Lavallée, M. Cross-cultural training studies of concrete operations. In L. Eckensberger, Y. Poortinga, & W. Lonner (Eds.), *Cross-cultural contributions to psychology*. Amsterdam: Swets & Zeitlinger, 1979.

de Lemos, M. M. The development of conservation in Aboriginal children. *International Journal of Psychology*, 1969, *4*, (4); 255–269.

Flavell, J. H., & Wohlwill, J. F. Formal and functional aspects of cognitive development. In D. Elkind and J. H. Flavell (Eds.), *Studies in cognitive development*. New York: Oxford University Press, 1969.

Heron, A., & Dowel, W. The questionable unity of the concrete operations stage. *International Journal of Psychology*, 1974, *9*, (1); 1–9.

Kamara, A. I., & Easley, J. A., Jr. Is the rate of cognitive development uniform across cultures?—A methodological critique with new evidence from Themne children. In P. R. Dasen (Ed.), *Piagetian psychology: Cross-cultural contributions*. New York: Gardner/Halsted/Wiley, 1977.

Lavallée, M., & Dasen, P. R. L'apprentissage de la notion d'inclusion de classes chez de jeunes enfants Baoulés (Côte d'Ivoire). *Journal International de Psychologie*, 1980, *15*, (1); 27–41.

Lefébvre, M., & Pinard, A. Apprentissage de la conservation des quantités par une méthode de conflit cognitif. *Revue Canadienne des Sciences du Comportement*, 1972, *4*; 1–12.

11 Dialectics of Development

Jonas Langer
University of California, Berkeley

Change in cognitive development is a dialectical process of synthesizing the equilibrium and disequilibrium conditions of each progenitor stage. Thus, cognitive development consists of a sequence of stages in progress. There are five criteria for determining developmental progress (Langer, 1969, pp. 178–180). Determination of developmental progress from a weaker progenitor stage to a more powerful successor stage requires findings of:

1. Change in the form, not the content, of the subject's transformational interactions.
2. Conservation and stability of the change over the long term.
3. Quantitative increase in the subject's means of adaptation.
4. Qualitative advance in functioning, marked by a relative shift in dominance from the environment to the subject, such that the subject takes an increasingly active role in his or her adaptive interactions with the environment.
5. Decrease in the role of chance in determining the subject's behavior (i.e., the subject increasingly acts to construct efficient means of regulating his or her interactive adaptation and self-organization).

Reciprocally, developmental regress from a more powerful to a weaker stage requires findings of long-term: (1) change in the form of interactions that is; (2) stable; and (3) decreases adaptiveness; such that (4) the functional dominance shifts (relatively) to the environment; and (5) increases the role of chance in subject–object interactions and in the organization of the subject's behavior.

Each stage is the necessary potential progenitor of a successor stage. The

233

functional structures of progenitor stages are inherently weak and disequil-ibrated. Associated with developmental progress, then, is enrichment of functional structures. This very enrichment increases the probability that at each stage: (1) the subject will spontaneously generate anomalous or incomplete cognitions; (2) the subject may be provoked into producing perturbative cognitions; and (3) the subject will comprehend and appreciate contradictory cognitions presented by others. These possibilities are the necessary conditions of each predecessor stage for continuous developmental increase in the disequilibrium in and transformation of its functional struc-tures, and the formation of its successor stage.

Thus, developmental increase in the probability of disequilibrium is the antithesis of the increase in the probability of equilibration, which also marks progressive change. Equilibrium conditions are sources of integrity, coher-ence, and virtuosity. Disequilibrium conditions are sources of potential, criticalness, and creativity. Their synthesis constitutes the continuous dia-lectic of cognitive development at each stage.

This dialectical formulation encompasses the previously proposed longi-tudinal model of cognitive development, namely, an inverted pyramidal model of sequential stages (Langer, 1969b, pp. 172–177). On the one hand, the functional structures of each succeeding stage are transformations of the functional structures of their predecessor stage. On the other hand, the functional structures of predecessor stages do not dissolve into those of their successors. Nor do they atrophy. Rather, they continue to evolve under the influence of the functional structures of the sequence of successor stages. For instance, sensorimotor representative activities by adults, who have devel-oped formal operational cognition, are patently more advanced than those produced by 18-month-olds, who have not progressed beyond the sensori-motor stage.

The present proposal, then, does not attribute a role to regression in the process of progressive development. Rather, it finds the source of cognitive developmental change in progressive self-generative disequilibrium within the functional structures of each stage (Langer, 1969a, 1971).

Mental organization consists of an intricate network or open grid system of sets of different functional structures. These functional structures are at different developmental stages. They are also of varying centrality to the organization of cognition. The gridwork radiates outward and is open on the outside so as to interact with the physical and social environment.

The dynamics of the gridwork, then, insure constant internal and external interaction. Thus, the permanent possibility for: (1) integrative disequil-ibrium within parts of the gridwork; (2) coordinative disequilibrium between different parts of the gridwork; and (3) transactional disequilibrium be-tween some part(s) of the gridwork and some part(s) of the environment. And, thus the permanent conditions for developmental change.

Because each subsequent mental organization is more powerful than its progenitor, it is irreducible to its weaker predecessor. In order to account for how weaker and incomplete functional structures generate more powerful and complete functional structures, a fundamental assumption is made. No level of organization, including the original primitive and the most mature, can adequately provide its own internal coherence or enrichment. The structural developmental tendency at all stages must therefore always be toward a potentially more advanced form of organization in order to provide progressive coherence and enrichment. This can be achieved only through the process of transformational interaction (Langer & Sugarman, 1978).

There are three forms of transformational interaction, that is, interactions that vary as a function of the subject's developmental stage. Integrative relations internal to a single system of functional structures comprise the first. Coordination between the different systems of functional structures that comprise the subject's mental organization is the second. Transaction between the subject's mental organization and the physical and social environment constitutes the third form of transformational interaction.

Our research on processes of development investigates primarily the two forms of intrasubject transformational interaction. Findings on coordination between systems (operative and figurative) have been reported elsewhere (Langer, 1974). Therefore, the present remarks about coordination are limited to summary conclusions.

Coordinative transformational interaction consists of implicatory relations between functional structures. These implicatory relations include conceptual, factual and symbolic feedback and feedforward. Three factors condition coordination. First, as is the case for all three forms of transformational interaction, coordination varies as a function of developmental status. Coordination increases with developmental progress. Second, coordination varies as a function of whether the functional structures are in phase (equilibrium) or out of phase (disequilibrium) with each other, as measured by their respective structural development. Third, coordination requires cognitively constructing possible relations between previously parallel forms of thought so that they may interpenetrate. The integrative disequilibrium conditions of the functional structure that is in the process of changing determines the probability of interpenetration. Interpenetration includes seeking, selecting, and applying one form of cognizing to the resolution of disequilibrium in another. To illustrate, the probability that children will coordinate their figurative cognition of appearance and reality with their operative conception of conservation increases when: (1) these two forms of knowledge are out of phase (disequilibrium) such that the figurative "outstrips" the operative; and (2) the operative is marked by stage mixture (a symptom of integrative disequilibrium). The result is some progressive change in the conception of conservation (Langer & Strauss, 1972).

The analyses presented here focus on our current findings on integrative relations within a single system, that of operative functional structures. Two complementary strategies are used to analyze integrative transformational interaction. The first consists of detailed comprehensive analyses of the components making up the reasoning produced by subjects about a given problem. The aim is twofold. The first is to discover internal disequilibrium, as well as equilibrium, between these components. The second is to determine whether there are any conceptual transformative consequences of such self-generated discordance. The second, complementary research strategy consists of experimental simulation of internal integration of possible transformations in order to determine whether they produce conceptual progress in subjects.

Transformational Integration

In ongoing longitudinal and intergenerational research on the development of logical, experimental, and moral reasoning, 100 subjects between 10 and 55 years of age have been tested. There are six results from the first testing (Haan, Langer, & Kohlberg, 1976; Kuhn, Langer, Kohlberg, & Haan, 1977) that are relevant to the present discussion:

1. All subjects develop concrete operational reasoning[1] about both experimental and logical problems no later than early adolescence.
2. Progress in operational cognition continues during the late teens and, often, into the twenties.
3. Many adults (almost half) do not evidence even the rudimentary

---

[1] As is well known, the basic initial research on the structure and development of operational cognition was performed by Piaget and his colleagues, using what Piaget called the clinical method of research (Inhelder & Piaget, 1958, 1964). The development of operational cognition was divided by Piaget into two major stages, concrete and formal operational reasoning. Concrete operations of negation and reciprocity develop from middle to late childhood. They are referred to as concrete operations because their application is limited to elementary transformations of concrete phenomena. Children do not reversibly coordinate their concrete operational transformations of negation and reciprocity with each other. This is the basis for the theory that, at most, children's cognitive structures constitute groupings or semigroups of unintegrated logical operations. Adolescents begin to coordinate operations with each other by reversible transformations. This means that they cognitively operate on or transform possible or hypothetical phenomena, that is, that they engage in hypotheticodeductive reasoning. This formal composition of operations by operations is the reason for: (1) labeling them formal operations; (2) the general theory that their structural organizations constitute groups of operations; and (3) the specific hypothesis that they are integrated with each other to form the logical group of four transformations INRC (Beth & Piaget, 1966).

beginnings of formal operational reasoning (i.e., nonsystematic hypothetical–deductive reasoning).[2]

4. Most adults do not evidence comprehensive, fully formed formal
   operational reasoning (i.e., systematic hypothetical–deductive reasoning.

5. On the whole, operational reasoning by 50-year-old male and female
   parents is comparable to that of their 21- to 30-year-old male and
   female offspring. But, the comparability is not due to intrafamilial
   duplication.

6. There are substantial indications of finer grained, sequential steps in the
   development through the stages of concrete and formal operational
   reasoning than that previously reported.[3]

Our initial testing, like previous research on the development of formal
operational reasoning, was limited to subjects' spontaneously produced
cognitions when presented with a problem. The current longitudinal testing
has been greatly expanded. It includes elaborate probing designed to provoke
subjects to reason as extensively and as intensively as they can about a given
problem. The aim of this research, which is relevant to the present discussion,
is to discover self-generated possibilities and discordances that we have

---

[2] Comparatively few studies have followed up the hypothesis that formal reasoning develops
during adolescence. Our findings and those of other investigators have been less than clear-cut
as to: (1) whether formal operations is acquired by all adolescents or even by all adults (Elkind,
1961, 1962; Higgins-Trenk & Gaite, 1971; Jackson, 1963; Leskow & Smock, 1970; Lovell,
1961; Neimark, 1970; Ross, 1973; Smedslund, 1963; Towler & Wheatley, 1971; Wason &
Johnson-Laird, 1972); and (2) whether producing formal operational reasoning is preserved
throughout mature adulthood (Keasey, 1970, 1972). With a couple of tangential exceptions
(Dennis & Mallinger, 1949; Sanders, Laurandeau, & Bergson, 1966) there has been no
attention to cognitive developmental progression or regression during old age. Moreover, little
research of any kind has been done on the mechanisms of progress from concrete to formal and
within formal operational reasoning (Black, 1976; Smock & Harris, 1969; Youniss & Furth,
1967).

[3] According to Inhelder and Piaget (1958), each major stage is decomposable into two
sequential substages, a rudimentary and a consolidated phase. It may be that (and it is part of the
purpose of the follow-up longitudinal research to determine whether) our finding of more
developmental steps than two per stage may be due to the wider age span we have been sampling
and the finer grained analyses of the data that we have been making. Together they have made it
possible for us to detect more of: (1) the functional structures of advanced reasoning; and (2) the
developmental transformations in these forms. It should be noted that Inhelder and Piaget
(1958) only reported fragments from the protocols of subjects up to the age of 16 years.

hypothesized as characterizing the functional structures of developing cognition.

The results presented are limited to experimental reasoning about only one of the tasks we are using. It consists of a much elaborated version of the pendulum problem used by Inhelder and Piaget (1958). In our version, the subject is presented with a simple apparatus consisting of a weight suspended from a string. The length of string is adjustable, and a set of six different weights is provided. Consequently, there are, at least, four possible independent variables: (1) the length of the string; (2) the heaviness of the suspended weight; (3) the angle or height from which the pendulum is set in motion; and (4) the force of the push used to set the pendulum in motion. The overall task for the subject is to determine experimentally the cause of two dependent variables, the oscillatory: (1) rate; and (2) speed. This requires isolating variables and keeping all variables constant while varying one, so as to determine which variables to exclude and which to include.

The dialectical thesis we pursue here is that the functional structures of each stage are progressively disequilibrated yet more powerful than the forms of reasoning out of which they are generated. Predecessor forms appear more consistent precisely because they are relatively impoverished cognitions. Closer structural and longitudinal examination reveals their inherent incoherence.

Examination of only three stages of experimental reasoning is sufficient to establish general hypotheses derived from the dialectical thesis. These hypotheses include that in the course of this three-stage sequence there is increase in: (1) the production of possibilities, that is, more and new independent and dependent variables; (2) the construction of more and new logical (necessary) and physical (contingent) relations within and between independent and dependent variables; and (3) the difficulties in structuring these possible and impossible relations, particularly their implications for operations of inclusion, exclusion, and separation of variables. More specific derivative hypotheses are considered throughout the description of the three stages of experimental thought that develop from late childhood to middle adolescence.

Stage 1. First-Order Experimental Reasoning by 10- to 11-Year-Olds.
The earliest stage analyzed here for its progenitor functional structures is that often diagnosed as consolidated concrete operational reasoning. A composite sketch of this first stage can be obtained from the data on six *S*'s between the ages of 10 and 11 years.

First-order experimental reasoning appears relatively straightforward and limited. Usually, the *S*'s do not consider spontaneously all the possible independent variables. 1A10's[4] experimentation was most impoverished in this regard. The only variable spontaneously produced by 1A10 was weight. She tested three weights and globally indicated that they had differential effects. The heaviest weight "makes it go the fastest." If other variables had not been suggested to her, 1A10 would have been finished. The other 10-and 11-year-old S's spontaneously considered two or three, but not all, independent variables. They both: (1) overtly seriated weights; and (2) globally indicated their differential effects. Coseriation was most differentiated in the conclusion drawn about length. Thus, 1A10 found that "shorter (string length) makes it go faster."

Verification activity is not considered necessary at this stage. Consequently, experimentation is not absolutely necessary in determining causal relations. Sometimes experimentation is used and sometimes it is not. For instance, 1A10 performed experiments with weight and length but not with starting position height and not with force of push. For height and push she was satisfied with making assertions such as it goes faster "because you're pushing it", as if the causal relation is self-evident or, perhaps, even tautological and therefore does not require empirical verification.

Inductive reasoning is not based on binary operations of implication. Invariably, the S's affirmed each independent variable that they spontaneously predicted. They never excluded a variable as ineffective. They affirmed each variable whether or not they had experimentally tested it. Moreover, they affirmed each variable regardless of the objective results of their experimentation.

Whether or not variables are held constant during experimentation is not a matter of concern, let alone deductive logic. Sometimes S's vary only one variable at a time and sometimes two or more. For instance, in one experiment 1D11 confounded two independent variables, weight and height, in an attempt to affirm one, weight. He predicted that the "heavier, the slower; lighter, the faster." Then he tried swinging (1) the heaviest weight from a high starting position (about 70°), followed by (2) the lightest weight from a medium starting position (about 45°). At this stage S's see nothing wrong with their experimental procedures. Interestingly, confounding independent variables was more frequent in the 11 than the 10-year-old S's. We shall return to this.

---

[4] S labeling is as follows: The first digit indicates the testing session; 1 for the initial testing and 2 for the longitudinal follow-up 5 or 6 years later. The uppercase letter that follows identifies the subject. The last two digit gives the S's age at the time of testing. For instance, 1A10 is subejct A when first tested at age 10 years and 2A16 is the same subject when retested in the longitudinal follow-up at age 16 years.

Further analysis confirms the comparative paucity of the preadolescent's experimental cognition. It also reveals that the thought processes are inherently unstable and weak.

Overall, no attention was paid by the 10-to 11-year-old S's to relating within and between the conditions of independent and dependent variables. There was one exception in 10-to 11-year-olds' spontaneous reasoning. It represents the initial development beyond direct functional and intuitive relating of variables. It takes the form of structuring conditional relations. As already noted, S's additively coseriate one independent variable with one (global) dependent variable, in which speed and rate are fused. For instance, S's determine that Weight A > Weight B > Weight $C \rightarrow$ Speed/Rate A > Speed/Rate B > Speed/Rate C. These conditional relations remain ordinal, even though the measuring instruments necessary for cardinal quantification are readily available for S's' use in the testing session.

By the end of this stage, the S's generalize this first-order conditional relation to most of the independent variables. For instance, 1C10 successively coseriated the independent variables weight, push, length, and height with a fused dependent variable, speed/rate. This is followed, rapidly, by symptoms of the inherent weakness of and internal contradictions within the S's initial conditional structure of additive coseriation.

Contradictory symptoms are found in the S's' provoked experimental reasoning. As the S's get older, even within this 10-to 11-year period, it is easier to provoke them into both: (1) producing empirical contradictions; and (2) reflecting upon empirical contradictions:

(Does weight have anything to do with it?)
Could I try?
(Sure. Why are you putting on that one?)
Because it's light.
(OK. You put on E.)
I think it will go faster because it has less weight and it will go faster.
(OK. Could you show me by doing the ticking?)
You want me to . . . then do that one?
(Um-hum. Well do whatever you want to do. Just make sure you prove to me that weight)
OK.
—ticks—
—ticks—
Well it looks to me like they're going the same, now. I wonder why?
(OK. So do you think the weight has anything to do with it?)
Yeah, I think so, but . . .
(But what did you find?)
Just a little I guess.
(You think the weight has just a little bit to do with it.)

Well if I didn't put any on it. It goes faster.
(Tick out loud.)
—ticks—
What's this?
(I guess it's a blank one.)
—ticks—
Yeah, I think weight has something to do with it.
(What do you think weight has to do with it?)
Well if you put more weight on it would slow it down. And no weight at all it goes fast.
(OK. Could you show me with the heavy weight?)
Again?
(Which would be the heaviest weight?)
Could I try this?
(Sure.)
(uses the balance to find a heavy weight)
I think it would be N.
(OK.)
—ticks—
—ticks—
It goes faster. I think it goes faster.
(Without anything on it.)
Yeah. I'll try this one.
—ticks—
It goes faster with no weight on. Than with any weight.
(OK. It goes faster with no weight on.)
Yeah.

Such contradictions in provoked experimental reasoning are the necessary precursors for binary operations of inductive implication. Yet, as the protocol reveals, even this subject, who is almost 12 years old, still has recourse to subjective measurement. This is 1E11's only way of resolving the contradiction. Even when experimenting with variables she has not predicted herself, she cannot exclude them. Her experimentation, albeit contradictory, remains for the while an inclusive structure limited to unary additive operations.

Subject 1C10 was the only S who ever produced an experimental disconfirmation of an independent variable that she had spontaneously predicted.

Let me try something here.
(OK. You're putting on G. Oh, you're going to put on two at the same time.)
Yeah.
(You put on G and E together.)
OK tick tick tick . . . no.
(Now you just put on G.)

It seems like it goes pretty much the same speed with one and two on. Cause E doesn't weigh that much.

This is, then, the first indication of a spontaneous tendency to construct experimental disconfirmation. It is necessary to the formation of second order, binary operations of inductive implications about inclusion and exclusion of variables. So far, however, 1C10 resorts to his inclusive structures for resolving the spontaneous contradiction, just as 1E11 had in her provoked experimental reasoning. At most, 1C10 was empirically limiting his previously established conditional correspondence relation between weight and speed/rate, but without any understanding. More likely, 1C10 was simply contradicting it.

Subjects' construction of experimental tests and the measurement of results, during this stage, were quasi-subjective and quasi-objective. Observation and recording of results predominantly subserved subjective anticipations. Their experiments were more subjective demonstrations than objective tests. As demonstrations, they resulted in affirmation of S's predictions even when the observable data were clearly disconfirmatory. Consequently, the structure of S's reasoning necessarily resulted in inconsistent measurement operations. When the predictions were true, the measurements were necessarily objective; they corresponded to the physical effect. When the predictions were false, the measurements were necessarily subjective; they did not correspond to the physical effect.

A related structural weakness in experimental reasoning is also beginning to develop during the first stage. The 11-year-old S's, as compared with the 10-year-old S's, tend to anticipate spontaneously more independent variables. They are also more likely to engage in quasi-experiments with variables, whether they spontaneously produce them or whether they are suggested by E. Consequently, it is increasingly necessary to structure the independent variables in second-order relations to each other. But, this is precisely what these 11-year-old S's cannot do. Sometimes, they confound independent variables with each other and sometimes they do not. Even when they do not, 11-year-olds give no indication that this is deliberate. Rather, they give every indication that it is fortuitous. The structural potential for spontaneously producing directly contradictory results is cleary evolving.

Through appropriate probing it is possible to provoke S's to begin to consider additive compensations between independent variables:

(If weight increases, what happens to the ticking?)
We increase it?
(Yeah.)
It would go faster.
(Is that always so?)
What?

(Is that always so? Would that always happen? If we increase the weight, would it always go faster?)
Depends upon the string length and everything.
(Could you explain what you mean? Like how does it depend upon the string length? Say we increased the weight.)
OK. Here it goes pretty fast and then we'll put the string . . .
(You just put the string up one?)
It goes a little slower.
(Oh, you took it down one.)
Yeah.
(OK. Good. So let's say we increased the weight, we put a bigger weight on. We first did it and then we put a bigger weight on. And so what I want to know is, is there any way the pendulum wouldn't go faster if we put a bigger weight on? How could we make it still go the same rate? Could we do something to the string length?)
Yeah, we could bring it down a notch, probably.
(Uh-huh. And what would that do?)
It would make it go . . . well, the string length would have a farther ways to go and so it goes pretty fast this way, so it would probably go the same speed with a heavier weight.

The fragility of compensatory structures at this stage is revealed by a further probe. It results in 1C10 contradicting himself:

(If weight and string length increase, what happens to the rate?)
It would probably go slower, a little slower.
(Why would it go slower?)
The length of the string and the weight would just . . . you know, it would go shhhhh, it would come way up here, cause there's so long a string and it'd take a longer time to get where it's going.
(Uh-huh. That's how the string length would make it take longer.)
Yeah.
(OK. Cause it had a longer distance to travel.)
And the weight would give it more push to it when you dropped it, it'd go . . . give it more push.
(OK. So those are two reasons why it would go slower?)
Um-hum.
(Good. Would it go a lot slower if you did both of them than if you only did one of them? Or would it go just as slow if you did both of them?)
It'd probably go just as slow if you did both of them.

On the one hand, weight and length are additive when both are increasing. On the other hand, weight and length are construed by 1C10 to be either: (1) nonadditive; or (2) differentially effective. If the latter is the proper interpretation, then 1C10 may be in transition to multiplicative compensations. In either case, the structure of compensation is internally contradictory.

Finally, during this stage, symptoms of internal contradiction may be found in another facet of propositional reasoning about variables. For instance, after he had finished his spontaneous experimenting, 1C10 was asked what you have to do to make sure not to change the rate. His answer was that you should keep the "same weight ... and the same amount of push" on the pendulum. His reference to weight is both: (1) consistent with his initial additive coseriation; and (2) inconsistent with his subsequent disconfirmation of the conditional for light weights. The formal weakness of this conditional was further revealed in his answer to the folow-up probe: "Do you have to do all these things not to change the rate?" He did not assert that they were necessary. Rather, he thought that they were "probably" necessary.

Stage 2. Second-Order Experimental Reasoning by 14- to 15-Year-Olds. The experimental reasoning that subjects began to generate during their late childhood is first elaborated during early adolescence. The dialectical thesis implies that Stage 2 functional structures should be both more equilibrated and disequilibrated than Stage 1. This is confirmed by the data from seven 14- to 15-year-old S's.

The functional structures of experimental thought become richer and more powerful. More independent variables are predicted spontaneously. All spontaneously generated and provoked independent variables are tested experimentally. This has become a necessary component of the logic of experimentation. Hypostheses are no longer tautologous. Experiments are used as a means of disconfirming as well as of confirming independent variables. Efforts are made to test one variable at a time while keeping others constant. But, as we shall see, this scheme is still not fully necessary at Stage 2. So, S's are neither systematic nor successful in keeping variables constant. Efforts are also made to measure results objectively. Experiments are no longer merely demonstrations of tautologous hypotheses. At times they are used to provide the empirical content, the data, for the second-order, binary operations of inductive implications about the inclusion and exclusion of independent variables.

At the same time, the internal disequilibrium within the functional structures of Stage 2 experimental reasoning become more frequent and more encompassing. When 1H14 was first tested, at 14 years of age, the procedures used were less elaborate than those devised for our longitudinal follow-up. The data are therefore less comprehensive. Nevertheless, 1H14's data are consistent with the dialectical hypothesis. For instance, 1H14 begins by an objective experimental test of weight and concludes by excluding it as an independent variable determining a global dependent variable, speed/rate. However, she immediatelly follows it up with an experiment in which she confounds weight and height of starting position.

This leads her falsely to include weight. These results contradict her previous findings. Moreover, because she is confounding variables, 1H14 is led to internally contradictory, nonseriated findings on the effects of different weights:

> The higher it is in the air and the heaviest, the faster it goes. But now I see smaller (lighter) one goes fastest.

Indeed the frequency of confounding independent variables increases during this stage. There are at least two reasons for this. First, S's are considering more variables. Second, S's are developing second-order experimental operations. They are trying: (1) to structurally relate independent variables to each other by additive and multiplicative combination; and then (2) to relate their combined value to a global dependent variable, speed/rate.

The weakness in S's' second-order experimental structures is not limited to confounding independent variables. It extends to uncertainties about additive and multiplicative calculations. For instance, 1J14 began by systematically: (1) excluding starting position angle, weight, and force of push; and (2) including length of string. However, he was not sure of the combined effect of variables he had excluded. This led him to simultaneously vary weight and push in order to determine whether together they would affect the rate:

> (Why did you change weights there?)
> Cause I wasn't sure.
> (You weren't sure about what?)
> I wasn't sure that if it was heavier if you pushed it hard . . . cause I don't know. Like the pendulum in the planetarium, I was wondering if you pushed that if it would go faster, but it wouldn't I don't think.

Subject 1J14 hypothesized that combining excluded variables might create a new, effective variable. Experimentation is therefore necessary for disconfirmation. Propositional operations are not sufficient. When negative results are generated, S accepts them, though with apparent lack of conviction.

Subjects' concern with difficulties in combining independent variables are not limited to those they have previously disconfirmed. More often they are trying to calculate the intersective effects of independent variables they have previously confirmed. Subject 1K14 has just affirmed weight; predicts that length is an effective variable; and tries to determine their compensatory relation:

> And the longer the string, the longer it's going to take, too.
> (Now you unrolled the string two winds.)
> Yeah.
> (And what weight are you putting on?)
> E.

(How come you're putting on E? Any particular reason for putting on E?)
It seems the lightest and W seems . . . I don't know if it's the heaviest, but it's a lot heavier. N is probably the heaviest.
It took 7, 7-something seconds last time. It took 6½ that time. I think the longer the swing, the less time it takes.
(Can you do another experiment to find out? How would you do a good experiment to find out?)
I'll try W.
Yeah, same. It took 6 last time so it should take 5½.
(It took 6 last time so it should take 5½ this time?)
I don't understand this.
(What did you get?)
6.
(6 seconds)
A little more, but . . .
(Why did you think that it would take 5½ this time?)
If the other one went ½, this one should go more than ½ a second less.
Let's see if I can do it with this thing.
(What do you think about the string length?)
On one of them, on E, it went slower, took less time to go 5 seconds, with longer string. But when I did it with the W, it took more time. So . . . I don't know. I'll do this one more time, just to make sure it's right.
(You're going to do W again.)
Yeah. 6½ seconds.
(6½ seconds)
That's what the other one was. Maybe it's the weight and the length of the string combined.
(Um-hum. How would that work?)
The heavier the weight, the longer the string, the more force you're going to have pulling down on it. Like this has more pulling down than the E weight would.

Here too, S's remain fundamentally uncertain. This uncertainty is the result of two factors. One is logical. They are beginning to combine variables multiplicatively. The other is physical. They are beginning to invent hidden causal variables that are the multiplicative result of observable variables. It is 1K14's expectation that the composition of weight and length forms force. This expectation is the source of his internally contradictory attempts to find compensatory relations. Subject 1K14's experimental observations are subordinated to his logical assumptions. This is the more usual result at Stage 2. Like its reciprocal, subordination of logical thought (just illustrated by a fragment of 1J14's protocol), it is a central disequilibrating condition.

A complementary structural defect, only barely beginning to develop at Stage 2, lies in the treatment of dependent variables. Rate and speed are fused in the subjects' cognitions. Thus 1I14, who was almost 15 years old, concluded on the basis of his observations that the rate decreases as the pendulum is "slowing down." He does not take into account the compensations between distance and time. This defect leads the subjects to fluctuate between rate and speed in their experimental observations, measurements, and generalizations. They do not keep the experimental variable constant in their experiments. Physically, rate and speed are partially dependent and partially independent. The intersect of subjective lability and physical partial independence between dependent variables provide further structural conditions for internal contradictions in experimental reasoning that come to fruition in the next stage.

Stage 3. Third-Order Experimental Reasoning by 16- to 18-Year-Olds. Experimental reasoning continues to develop during this period. As compared to the second stage, experimental functional structures become progressively rich and equilibrated during Stage 3. As expected, they also become progressively contradictory and disequilibrated. The data base for our analysis of Stage 3 is seven 16- to 18-year-old *S*'s.

Because experimental reasoning becomes very elaborate during Stage 3, recounting it requires lengthy description. Consequently detailed illustration of this transitional stage is limited to the representative performance of two longitudinal subjects, 2A16 and 2L16. Both subjects produced far more complex and more disorganized experimental reasoning than they had 5 to 6 years earlier. What follows is still but a small sample of their experimentation.

Subjects spontaneously attempted experimental tests of all their hypotheses. They experimented with single independent variables while keeping others constant. They experimented with the relations between independent variables. They combined variables to determine compensations. Independent variables were now also combined in semisystematic attempts to discover mediating hidden variables, whether spatiotemporal or causal, which might cause observed results. Subjects also began, although in only minor ways, to experiment with the dependent variable. Here most of their reasoning was limited, at best, to keeping the dependent variable of their focus constant, without having conbinatorial control over the other dependent variable. Provocation by examiner elicited rudimentary consideration of the relations between: (1) the two dependent variables, rate and speed; and (2) the various independent variables and the two dependent variables. This latter form of experimental combinatorial did not, however, elicit any mediating, third-order causal variables, which are otherwise a main development in experimental thought during this stage.

These advances in the equilibrium conditions of experimental reasoning are complemented by increases in the disequilibrium conditions. For instance, 2L16, who was almost 17 years, systematically: (1) predicted, disconfirmed, and excluded weight, angle of starting position, and force of push; and (2) predicted, confirmed, and included string length. Also, he determined the effect for the same dependent variable throughout, namely, rate. He does this by careful objective measurement and continuous recording, using the stopwatch, ruler, paper, and pencil that are made available to all subjects. Only now, then, can the subjects be said to be generating true empirical data.

Throughout, 2L16 accepted his negative findings as well as his positive findings. But he always accepted disconfirming data with a measure of uncertainty never evidenced when he found affirming data. Thus, as soon as he discovered an effective variable, the length, 2L16 set out to combine it with the variables he had previously found ineffective:

> I don't think weight'll matter at this length either.
> (You're going to check weight again though?)
> Yeah.
> Times 10 swings/11.2 sec.—Rechecks G against "X" on weight scale—
> Times 10 swings/11.6 sec.—
> I made it go faster but it's probably . . . just a mistake.
> Unwinds string to full length.
> Times 10/15.1 sec.—checks length with ruler—21½ inches—
> I'm still trying to see if . . . (Weight?) Weight will . . .
> Times 10/14.9 seconds.
> Can I give it a push or something?
> (Mm, hm.)
> Tries giving it a push—watches it swing two times, then stops it.

Although his results are negative, 2L16 continues to check combinations of variables he has previously found ineffective.

In his experiments, 2L16, like the other subjects at Stage 3, is: (1) forming compensatory relations between independent variables; and (2) searching for hidden variables that are the resolution of combinatorial relations between independent variables. These are main sources of the disequilibrium conditions that increase during this stage:

> (What do you have to do if you want to make sure not to change the rate?)
> Oh, as the previous time before? I'd get the angle, try and get it exact, and the length. I'd contradict myself, if I say to get the weight the same.
> (Would you have to do anything else besides the angle and the length then?)
> Yeah, I would say—just from what I would think from common sense that the weight would have to be the same.
> (Anything else?)
> In fact, I'd say you wouldn't have to push it, neither. I'd try and keep the push the same.

(Do you have to do all those things—not change angle, weight, push, and length?)
According to what I got you wouldn't have to keep the . . . um . . . I'll say you wouldn't have to keep the weight the same. I think the push affects it some.
(So you'd keep the angle, length, and push the same?)
Yeah.
(And why would you keep the weight the same, just to play it safe?)
Yeah.

They are also sources of 2A16's constant confounding of independent variables. It should be recalled that 2A16 did not confound any independent variables when she was 10 years old. An illustrative fragment from her protocol relates to an experiment in which 2A16: (1) started by pushing the pendulum bob hard from a 20° starting position and then pushing it softly from 5°; and (2) ended by pushing hard from 90° and then pushing softly from 20°:

If you want the ticking to go fast, you push it lightly.
(Could you show me?)
(You should tick out loud.)
Can I try it for a second?
(Go ahead.)
You want me to tick? (If you like.) —S varies both force and angle— Tick, tick . . . It goes the same. (What did you just do?) I pushed it harder expecting it to tick slower, because the farther it went out here it wouldn't . . . give it less . . . like it would take longer to get to the pole so it wouldn't tick as often, but like if I just pushed it here, it wouldn't take as much time to pass the pole.
(Did you push it with the same strength out here as you did here or did you push it harder?)
I think I pushed it harder out here because if I pushed it hard here then it would go farther again.
(You took it way out, you took it out there and pushed it hard, and then close again and you pushed it soft. What did you conclude from that?) It does the same thing.
(Is there anything else that might make a difference?)
Um, it just seems to be going the same.
(What did you just do?) I took it out farther and pushed it harder. (Did you let it go?) I didn't just let it go, I kind of pushed it.—S varies both force and angle—
(What are you doing now?)
I just took it out a little ways and let it go.
When I just took it out again a little ways it's faster. When I take it out a little ways and let it go, it goes faster.

Subject 2A16 also confounded the dependent variables of speed and rate throughout her experimentation. This was often compounded, by apparently

confounded independent variables. In one such experiment, 2A16 had just
concluded that the angular degree of starting position affects the rate. Then
she proceded to vary both the length and the angle:

(Do you think the length of the string has anything to do with it? Why don't you
try it?)
It does make it go faster. (With what weight?) F.
(What are you finding out?) I'm trying to see if . . . I expected W to go faster
than F with the long string and I'm not sure if it did or not. So I'm trying to
see if it does with a short string.
I don't know, I think they're the same.
I was thinking if I gave it a little time to swing, I could see how it ticked. (O.K.
So you're going out farther?) Yeah.
I think they're the same. (So what determines the rate?)
The shorter, the faster.

2A16's initial response to direct probing about the relations between rate and
speed was that they constitute a single dependent variable:

Isn't the speed the same as the rate?
(Why do you say that?) 'Cause I don't know the difference. (Think of speed as
how quick it goes through the air. Would that make it be the same as the rate?)
Well, you said the rate was when it passed this. (How often?) It seems the same
to me.

The probing returned to this issue, later in the interview, after 2A16 had
continued to confound rate and speed in her experimentation. Consistent
with her previous inability to separate the dependent variables, 2A16
continued in this vein:

(Like if speed changes, does rate have to change?)
Rate is like the rhythm of the speed. So if the speed gets faster, then the rate will
get faster, the rate at which it moves.
(Can you show me that?)
I'm afraid I'll be wrong though. OK . . . I want it to go faster so I'm making this
shorter. Making it longer to see if the rate will go slower. The rate is slower.
(So what did you just do?)
I made the string longer and the speed is slower and rate is slower than when I
made the string shorter.
(If the rate of swinging increases, what happens to the speed at which it is
swinging?)
The speed increases with the rate.
(Is that what you just showed me?)
Yes.
(Is that always so?)
Yes.

(Can the speed not change?)
No.
(Can you show me that?)
We're saying that if the rate doesn't change the speed won't change.
(Mm, hm.)
I don't know how . . . I can't change anything so it has to stay the same. I mean if I don't change the rate . . . then I can't change the speed 'cause I'm not moving it . . . doing anything.

A counterexample was provided by E in which the height but not the length was varied so that the speed but not the rate changed. This led 2A16 to a conceptual reversal. To begin with she adopted a hypothesis of total independence between the two dependent variables:

I knew you could prove me wrong! The rate can stay the same as speed changes. The speed does go slower.
(So what's the relation between rate and speed?)
I don't know how to . . . should I define both of them; or well, what's similar in them?
(Yeah.)
It's different because you can change the speed and the rate will stay the same and it's . . . . They don't have any relation. The relation between the rate and the speed—there isn't any.
(Why do you think there isn't?)
Because I can't see any similarities, in the experiments, the rate and the speed change.

Further probing revealed that 2A16's hypothesis was, at best, inconsistent:

(If the rate of swinging does not change, what happens to the speed at which it is swinging?)
It can go faster or slower.
(If the speed of swinging increases, what happens to the rate at which it is swinging?)
It stays the same.
(Is that always so?)
Is it okay if I experiment? When the speed increases the rate increases and when the speed decreases, the rate decreases.
(So would you say there's a relation, isn't there?)
Yeah.

Thus, 2A16 concluded that: (1) speed is independent of rate, at the same time as;(2) rate is dependent on speed.
This provoked inconsistency in experimental reasoning about dependent variables was preceded by spontaneous contradictions in 2A16's determina-

tions of independent variables. Contradictory reasoning about the independent variables was usually compounded by simultaneous confounding of the dependent variables. In one set of experiments, 2A16 began by affirming the height of the starting position on three separate occasions. One instance will suffice:

> (What are you doing now?)
> I just took it out a little ways and let it go. When I just took it out again a little ways it's faster. When I take it out a little ways and let it go, it goes faster.

Several experiments later, 2A16 found contradictory results. Interestingly, the contradictory findings were accompanied by a deformation in 2A16's memory about her previous affirmative conclusions:

> (Did you say something else before that affected the rate?) How far you drop it out. (Do you think that's the case?) I can't remember. (Why don't you try it?) With the same weight? (Do whatever you want.)
> (Do you remember what it was you said?) I said that it went the same but I expected it to go faster when I didn't push it, when I didn't hold it out far. (So what are you going to test now?)
> If I hold it out farther it will go faster.
> Tick . . . (What weight is that?) F.
> It still seems the same.
> No, I just had F on.

2A16 replicated the exclusion of height as an independent variable in a subsequent experiment. She concluded that if you increase "the height from which you drop it, nothing happens." However, because she confounded dependent variables, 2A16 reverted to affirming height two experiments later:

> (So what makes it go faster or slower?)
> I think the height at which you drop it.
> (What are you doing now, just dropping it from different heights?) Yeah. (And were you changing anything else?) No.

A compounding source of internal contradictions was lability of experimental method. Sometimes, 2A16 did not confound or combine independent variables in her experimental test of height, as in the preceding fragment. Sometimes, 2A16 did, as in her next experiment where she concluded that "both weights when I drop them from high they go faster than when I drop them from low." This followed previous affirmations of weight as an independent variable.

Simulated Transformational Integration

In a continuing series of simulation experiments we have been investigating the integrative transformational interaction between segregated or contradictory cognitions (Langer 1969a; Ruff, 1975; Schwartz, 1970). For paradigmatic purposes these studies have focused on transformational processes in developing quantitative classificatory predication. Classification is a particularly appropriate concept for these purposes because it is central to the development of logical thought during childhood and to the formation of concrete-operational structures (Inhelder & Piaget, 1964).

Several results, previously reported, constitute the empirical context for the findings reported here:

1. Conditions designed to induce successive integration of previously segregated cognitive considerations about class inclusion have a progressive effect. This progressive effect is greatest for the oldest children tested, 10-year-olds, who already have developed relatively powerful class structures.
2. Conditions designed to induce successive disintegration (i.e., enhancing the segregation of cognitive considerations) have an apparently disorganizing effect. This disorganizing effect is greatest for the youngest children tested, 5-year-olds, who still have relatively weak class structures.
3. Conditions designed to induce conflict without integration between cognitive considerations have an apparently disorganizing effect.

In sum, the evidence supports the hypothesis that conditions designed to simulate integration between consistent cognitions about class inclusion concepts may lead to progress. Both conditions designed to simulate disintegration and conditions designed to simulate conflict between cognitions may lead to temporary disorganization. Our recent experimental focus therefore turned to testing conditions that would simulate the possible integration of conflicting or impossible cognitions about classification.

Two main conditions of simulating integration between contradictory cognitive actions have been explored so far. One condition was designed to induce integrating contradictory relations between predicating properties of the whole and of the major part. The second condition was designed to induce integrating contradictory relations between predicating different properties of the whole. Both conditions were provoked by presenting children with impossible classification tasks. The objects for classification consisted of round beads. Most were red round beads; some were blue round beads. The children were instructed, for instance, to place the round beads (the whole) on one side of the table and the red beads (the major part) on the other. Because of the impossible classification demand being made this condition has the potential for simulating cognitive conflict of the type described in the previous section. In order to measure the validity of the simulation condition, the behavior of the children was also scored with the elaborated Brind stages of criticalness used in our previous research (see Langer, 1969a, for a fuller description). It consists of a seven-stage sequence: (1) naive credulity; (2) uncertainty or diffuse distress; (3) stereotyped rejection or global negativism; (4) specific rejection; (5) positive correction; (6) constructive interpretation; (7) amusement or disgust.

Both part/part and part/whole simulation conditions consisted of three phases. The first phase of both conditions was designed to provoke children into transforming impossible into possible classification tasks. Children were presented with forms that could be cut with scissors and could be colored with markers. Together with the experimenter, children cut the forms into different shapes and used the markers to change the color of the forms.

In the part/whole condition, this transformational activity was followed by presenting children with eight yellow square and four yellow triangular pieces of paper. As in the impossible task condition, children were asked to put the yellow pieces (the whole) in one box and the square pieces (the major part) in another box. Children's criticalness of this request was measured using the elaborated Brind seven-stage model. Children's initial sorting behavior was recorded. If a child did not recognize the conflicting demands, E guided him by questions such as "Aren't these squares you put in the square-box also yellow?" If a child did not change the forms by cutting or coloring in order to transform the impossible into a possible part/whole classification task, E reminded him of his earlier cutting and coloring of the forms. If necessary, he was also asked questions about whether it would help to change the shape and the color.

The same procedure was used in the whole/whole condition except that the focus was on predicating two different properties of the whole. For instance, presented with forms that were all square and all yellow, the impossible demand was made to put the square ones in one box and the yellow ones in another box.

The second phase was designed to be a nontransformable impossible task in both the part/whole and the whole/whole conditions. This was achieved by using Masonite objects that the children could not transform. Children's criticalness and sorting behavior was recorded. The procedure then reverted to that of the first phase. When necessary the children were guided into recognizing the dilemma. Then its resolution in principle was discussed. For example, tools that could cut Masonite were discussed by E and S but were not presented to S.

The third phase of both the part/whole and whole/whole conditions was the same as the first phase, with two exceptions. The first part, in which E and the children cut and colored forms,was omitted, and the shapes and colors used were changed. Otherwise this phase, like the first, consisted of actually transforming the objects so that the conflicting predicates could be successively integrated into a ready resolution.

Twenty kindergarten and first-grade children received the part/whole provoked condition. Eighteen kindergarten and first-grade children received the whole/whole condition. Prior to this, all S's were extensively pretested on two problems about class inclusion and the quantification of predicates. One problem used geometric objects and the other flowers. On the basis of their performance on these pretests two comparable groups were constituted for each of the two simulation conditions. Those children whose reasoning about the two pretests' problems was entirely preoperational constituted one group, the intuitive group. The other, the mixed group consisted of children whose reasoning about the two pretest problems was partially preoperational and partially concrete operational. The two pretest problems were repeated on the posttest. They were followed by a third, generalization problem involving fruit.

With rare exceptions neither the part/whole nor the whole/whole intuitive groups changed in their criticalness across the three phases of the two provoked conditions. Invariably they were measured at Stage 1 (naive credulity) during the first transformational phase and remained that way through the second impossible phase and the third transformational phase.

Half the mixed part/whole group were scored at Stage 2 (uncertainty or distress) or above in their criticalness during the first and second phase of this provoked condition. This increased to about four-fifths of the S's during the third phase. A quarter of the mixed whole/whole group were scored at Stage 2 or above during the first phase. This increased to three-quarters of the S's by the second phase and remained stable during the third phase.

Overall, then, the mixed conceptual groups were more advanced in their criticalness to begin with than the intuitive groups, and the mixed conceptual groups progressed in their criticalness during the provoked conditions whereas the intuitive groups did not.

The criticalness results indicate that the external experimentally constructed conflict between classificatory considerations remained just that for the intuitive groups. Consequently, no conceptual change was expected to occur in either intuitive group. This was confirmed by the data. Neither the part/whole nor the whole/whole intuitive group evidenced any progressive change from pre- to posttest. If anything, an occasional S in each group evidenced some conceptual slippage from pretest to posttest. That is, aspects of their predicative attribution became more disorganized during the posttest.

The criticalness results indicate that at least by the end of the simulation condition, most of the S's in both mixed groups were cognizant of the conflict between the classificatory considerations. It was therefore expected that these groups would change from pre- to posttest. The findings were that both groups evidenced some progressive elaboration in their conception of class inclusion and its quantification. Moreover, this conceptual progress was evidenced on the generalization problem on the posttest, as well as the two repeat problems.

Finally, the criticalness results indicate that the mixed group in the part/whole provoked condition began with and sustained a somewhat more advanced critical cognition than the whole/whole transitional group. It was therefore expected that the part/whole transitional group should evidence more conceptual advance. The difference found was in the predicted direction but did not quite achieve statistical significance.

These results on the process of developmental change warrant two conclusions. First, children at the intuitive stage did not cognize the potential conflict within the impossible task. Consequently, experimental attempts to relate it to integration between impossible aspects of the problem did not yield progressive change. If any change was produced it was of a minor disorganizing nature. Second, children at the mixed stages between the intuitive and the concrete operational became increasingly cognizant of the impossibility and related it to integrating their contradictory considerations of the phenomenon. The consequence was some progressive elaboration of their already partially structured concept of class inclusion and its quantification.

"Dark Ages"

Part of the *Encyclopedia Britannica* (1962) entry on DARK AGES reads:

> With the progress of medieval studies in the 19th century it became impossible for historians to dismiss one of the great constructive periods in human activity with an epithet implying contempt for its achievements, and the phrase became obsolete. It remains, nevertheless, the fact that the six centuries following the collapse of the Roman empire are in a special sense dark through the insufficiency of historical evidence. Even so, it is necessary to remember that intellectual work of the highest quality was done by exceptional individuals in ages when life was insecure and its environment discouraging to thought. The ages which form the prelude to medieval history are dark when compared with the time which followed, but the foundations of medieval civilization were laid in these obscure centuries. (Volume 7, page 61)

The dialectical thesis about the stage sequence comprising cognitive development subsumes the structural law of temporal displacement or vertical decalage (Piaget, 1954), the functional law of analogy (Werner, 1948), and their combination in the concept of spirality (Gesell, 1946).

Together, these laws assert that development *within* each stage always consists of progress from relatively disorganized functional structures to relatively organized functional structures. Development *between* successive stages always consists of reconstructing relatively primitive and weak forms of acting into more advanced and powerful forms of acting. Entailed in this model is the hypothesis that when a new stage develops it always progresses through the sequence stipulated for within-stage development. The illustration often used is the development from the sensorimotor to the conceptual stages. The claim is that is consists of reconstructing presentational actions into representational operations. Development within the stages of conception progresses from transductive preoperations, which are relatively prelogical and egocentric, to formal operations, which are both logical and objective.

An implication of these developmental laws, drawn by Werner and Kaplan (1963), by Piaget and Inhelder (1969), and by Gesell (1946), is that temporary regress accompanies and is necessary for progress. Usually, both the progress and the regress have been attributed to the new stage that is beginning to develop. Thus, on the one hand, transductive preoperations are claimed to constitute a cognitive step forward as compared with sensorimotor activity. On the other hand, transductive preoperations are hypothesized to be a step backward into egocentric subjectivity as compared with the most advanced sensorimotor stage, that of representative activity.

These structural developmental laws, then, have long been invoked to account for apparent repetitions between levels of behavior in the course of ontogenetic progress. The early literature on apparent repetitions during ontogenesis, such as in the walking reflex, was reviewed by Valentine (1946). More recent research has focused on apparent developmental repetitions from visual to motoric modes of object permanence (Bower, 1974), from sensorimotor identity to permanence judgments (Moore, 1974, 1975), from sensorimotor anticipations to concrete operational conceptions of weight conservation (Mounoud & Bower, 1974), and from conventional to principled levels of moral judgment (Kohlberg & Kramer, 1969). Sometimes the results of these studies are also used as evidence for the hypothesis that an intervening period of decline, dissolution, or regression is necessary for the transition between phases of apparent repetitions. For instance, McGraw (1943) applied the hypothesis to motor development and Turiel (1974) critically evaluated its applications to moral development.[5]

---

[5] Psychoanalytic claims of dissolution have been made about the hypothesized psychosexual stage sequence. Old stages must be permanently dissolved in order that new, more advanced psychosexual stages may develop, with their remnants incorporated into the new stages. But these are claims about: (1) affective, not cognitive, development; and (2) the necessity of permanent dissolutions and incorporations, not temporary regressions, for the development of more advanced stages.

The grounds for positing that ontogenetic "dark ages" are necessary accompaniments to progress have not been compelling, at least in structural developmental theory. They are not compelling regardless of whether regression is attributed to behaviors of new, more advanced stages or to behaviors of intervening periods between apparently repetitive phases. Like the hypothesis of historical "dark ages," its ontogenetic analogues are based on insufficient evidence. The data cited are certainly not sufficient to fulfill the criteria for determining regression, listed at the outset of this chapter. However, the insufficiencies in the developmental analyses are not primarily due to lack of historical data. Rather, they are usually due to inadequacies in the structural developmental data, both in their type and in their content. The type of the data base is not adequately longitudinal, structural, or both. Invariably, the content of the data base does not include the disequilibrated conditions for potential novel cognitions of the progenitor and successor stages' functional structures. And, invariably, it does not include the equilibrated conditions of the transitional stage's functional structures.

Rather than appeal to regression, it seems more likely that the disequilibrium conditions of progenitor stages are sources for generating potential cognitions that prefigure aspects of successor stages. The history of science is replete with early conceptions that foreshadow in rudimentary forms, and often internally contradictory ways, advanced contemporary scientific conceptions. For instance, Aristotle's concept of antiperistasis as an explanation of motion seems to anticipate, in rudimentary form, an aspect of classical theory of thermodynamics (Bochner, 1966). Similarly, in ontogenesis the flashes of precocity exhibited by children are symptomatic of the construction of rudimentary but novel conceptions that anticipate later and more powerful thought. One instance should suffice to make the point. S was 3 years 4 months when she was being taken to a restaurant. She wanted to take her security blanket with her. She was told that one is not allowed into restaurants with a blanket. S argued her case with two counterexamples. First, she recalled that she had her blanket with her in an "airplane restaurant." S was referring to a flight on which she both had her blanket with her and was served dinner. Second, S observed that babies have their blankets with them when they are in restaurants. Thus, presented with the argument $p \cdot \bar{q}$ (blanket is incompatible with restaurant going) she countered with empirical evidence of $p \cdot q$ (blanket is compatible with restaurant going). By this transductive negation S was potentially anticipating the possibility of a binary operation (but without compensation and therefore preoperational) that is not actualized until late childhood or early adolescence.

Consider the aforementioned illustrative claim that progress from sensorimotor representation to transductive preoperations is necessarily coupled with regressive steps backward into darkening egocentricity. One implication of the present analysis is that this claim misses the disequilibrium conditions of the advanced functional structures of sensorimotor activity. Our data on early cognitive development bear out this implication. As part of an ongoing investigation of the origins and early development of logical cognition, 6- to 60-month-old S's are presented with quasi-continuous malleable objects made of PlayDoh (Langer, 1980; Langer, in preparation). The first test phase of one condition consists of presenting three small PlayDoh balls. The S's are allowed to transact with them as they wish in free play for a minimum of 2½ minutes. During the second test phase, all three balls are removed. The E combines two balls under the table so that the S's cannot observe the transformation. The E does nothing to the third ball. The S's are presented with the resultant, one bigger ball and one small ball. Again, S's are allowed to transact with them as they wish in free play. Children under 18 months continue to transact with the transformed set as if nothing changed in the number and magnitude of objects (Langer, 1980). Some 18-month-old S's begin not to (Langer, in preparation):

Phase II: Invisible composition, underneath the table
(E removes balls 2 and 3 and composes them into a large ball)
1. Right hand picks up the remaining ball 1.
2. RH sets ball 1 down in front of self.
3. RH begins to point (closed palm, extended index finger) toward E, who has taken the other two balls.
   (E places the large composed ball on the table.)
4. *RH* immediately picks up large ball.
5. *RH* places large ball near self and ball 1.
6. *RH* again begins to point (requesting) to E . . . finally vocally, "eh, eh" (high pitch).
   (E extends her empty hands to show that she has nothing that she is hiding.)
7. Looks around the room (suspiciously).
8. Looks at large ball.
9. *RH* picks up large ball.
10. *RH* holds large ball.
11. Looks at large ball held by RH near eyes. (*18ML*, pages 29 and 30)

The behavior is symptomatic of advanced preverbal cognition of quantity. The number transformation from three to two objects was not visible to subject 18ML. Nevertheless, he searches for the third object when E gives him back only two objects. This reflects his equilibrated structure of numerical permanence.

Number permanence is yet to be compensated by logical composition of quasi-continuous quantity. When one malleable object is added quasi-continuously to another, two complementary results are produced. First, the number of objects does not increase, it decreases. One quasi-continuous object added quasi-continuously to another equals one quasi-continuous object, not two. Second, the magnitude of the resultant is larger than each of the objects added together. Subject 18ML does not infer these two complementary transformations. Searching for a third object, then, reflects both: (1) an equilibrated structure of number permanence; and (2) a disequilibrated structure of logical composition.

This kind of structural developmental data is prerequisite to determining both the equilibrium and disequilibrium conditions of advanced functional structures of sensorimotor prelinguistic cognition. Clearly, there can be no appeal to regressive egocentricity in order to explain the simultaneous construction by 18-month-olds of numerical permanence coupled with nonadditive composition.

A second implication of this analysis is that the regression claim confounds the disequilibrium conditions of transductive preoperations with regress to predecessor forms (Langer, 1977). The proposed dialectical thesis, then, obviates the theoretically encumbering assumption that it is necessary to appeal to regression in order to account for developmental progress. Moreover, the assumption of regression in the service of progression is not a necessary ingredient of structural developmental theory. In fact, it has its theoretical roots in romantic philosophy (Abrams, 1953) from whence it passed into psychoanalytic theory (Kris, 1952). At the same time, the proposed dialectical thesis points to the type and content of data that need to be generated in order to determine more adequately the structural development of both sensorimotor representations and transductive preoperations.

It is this type (structural and longitudinal) and content (equilibrium and disequilibrium conditions of predecessor and successor stages) that has characterized the data used throughout this analysis of the dialectics of development. It constitutes the data base for our analysis of progressive equilibrium and disequilibrium. The thesis is that they constitute the conditions of integrative transformational interactions within functional structures. As such they constitute one of the three mechanisms of cognitive development.

This dialectical analysis of integrative transformational interaction is the basis for the experimental conditions designed to simulate integrative disequilibrium. These conditions result in some, but limited, progressive cognitive elaboration (second section). But progressive elaboration was restricted to S's whose functional structures were already a mixture of the predecessor and the successor stages. Otherwise, no progress was found. These results are consistent with previous findings on both integration within a single system (Langer, 1969a) and coordination between two systems (Langer, 1974).

These simulation results, and the findings of other studies on cognitive (Strauss, 1973) and moral (Turiel, 1969) development, permit two empirical generalizations. If the subject's functional structures are mixed, then a variety of training intervention is likely to produce some limited progress. If the subject's functional structures are not mixed, then training is less likely to produce even limited progress. These empirical generalizations conform to the structural developmental hypothesis that the predecessor stage of the subject is the predominant determiner of subsequent progress (Langer, 1969b).

Nevertheless, the generalization that mixed but not unmixed stages are susceptible to induced progress seems paradoxical on two grounds. The first applies to structural developmental theory in general. If unmixed stages are highly resistant to change, then the probability of development is minimal whenever a child's functional structures are not mixed. There would then be relatively little opportunity for a child at an unmixed stage to develop to the mixed stage when the probability of induced progress becomes maximal. The second concerns the dialectical thesis on change. If each stage is an organization of partially equilibrated and partially disequilibrated functional structures, then both mixed and unmixed stages should be partially equilibrated and disequilibrated. But then, unmixed stages could be expected to be equally susceptible to progressive change as mixed stages.

Total resolution of the paradox is beyond the scope of the present chapter. The general lines of solution are suggested, however. The findings on self-generated internal integration (first section) prove that the disequilibrating conditions for change exist at every stage. Their probability should actually increase with each progressive stage, although the degree is indeterminate at this point. Thus, the dialectical thesis predicts continuous evolution of cognitive functional structures. Ours is hardly the final stage.

Indeed, the dialectical thesis predicts that unmixed stages are as susceptible to progressive change as mixed stages. This is exactly what is found when we analyze self-generated integrative transformational interaction. The probability of change at unmixed stages has been found to be minimal only in experiments that attempt to simulate transformational interaction. But no experimental conditions can properly simulate the integrative form. By their very nature they must operate via another form of transformational interaction, particularly, transactions between subjects and the environment. This account implies that the main cause of development when a child is at an unmixed stage is integrative, not transactional, transformational interactions.

Another, perhaps complementary, resolution of the paradox is that most inducement studies have devised training methods that are relevant to the disequilibrium conditions of mixed stages. They may do this wittingly or unwittingly. Therefore, the training methods may not be appropriate to the disequilibrium conditions of unmixed stages. The necessary results are negative for unmixed and positive for mixed stages. This account implies that training methods based on the disequilibrium conditions of unmixed stages would increase the probability of induced progress during those stages.

Indirect partial support can be found in some training studies (Inhelder, Sinclair, & Bovet, 1974). More direct support has just been found in an intensive training experiment (Black, 1976). But adequate direct tests of this hypothesis will be made only when the experimental conditions simulate the disequilibrium conditions of unmixed stages. Prerequisite to such experimental tests is analysis of self-generated integrative transformational interaction at each stage of cognitive development, whether mixed or unmixed.

Structural developmental analysis of cognitive disequilibrium involves two prerequisite determinations. The first is comprehensive diagnosis of the subject's developmental status, in the case of ontogenesis, or of historical status, in the case of scientific progress. The second is experimental and can be applied only to ontogenesis. It includes two complementary components: (1) follow-up probes to explore the extent of the subject's reasoning; and (2) counterconditions designed to test the subject's conception. Both of these methods were used in the present analyses of contradictions in the cognitive development of adolescents. When these prerequisite determinations can not be fully realized, as is often the case in the history of ideas, then the analyses may remain equivocal. A case in point is Aristotle's physical theory of place (*topos*). It is both: (1) the outermost kinetic boundary of that which contains; and (2) the innermost motionless boundary of the container. These two conceptions of space have led to three different analyses. They have been analyzed as totally contradictory (Duhem, 1913), partially contradictory (Bochner, 1966), or noncontradictory (Kusnezow, 1960).

The dialectical thesis proposed here is not contingent on subjects being consciously aware of the structural weakness(es) in their reasoning, at any stage of development. To illustrate, subject 1A10 (whose reasoning was discussed in the first section) gave no overt indication of any confusion, distress, or difficulty. Six years later, this same subject 2A16 gave only occasional overt indications of having conceptual difficulty. Historical parallels readily come to mind. For instance, two different conceptions of heat were formulated simultaneously in the initial research (1780 to 1840) on thermodynamics by Lavoisier, Laplace, Carnot, and Clapeyron (Bochner, 1966). Heat was operationally defined as both molecular motion and coloric fluid. At the time, however, the inconsistency between these two conceptions was only partially cognized. At other times and about other phenomena, such as quantum electrodynamics, internal contradictions may be more overtly appreciated. According to Wigner (1964):

> Equally remarkable is the present application of invariance principles in quantum electrodynamics. This is not a consistent theory—in fact, not a theory in the proper sense because its equations are in contradiction to each other. However, these contradictions can be resolved with reasonable uniqueness by postulating that the conclusions conform to the theory of relativity [p. 997].

Thus, the dialectics between disequilibrium and equilibrium are not contingent on subjective awareness. Rather, their objective antithetical conditions and synthesis, whether conscious or not, are consistent with the structural developmental principle of directionality (Langer, 1969b). Structural development is a synthetic process that interweaves two antithetical organismic tendencies. These are to maintain continuity in order to conserve organismic integrity (survival and organizational coherence) and to elaborate discontinuity in order to develop.

In the present view, progressive disequilibrium is as inevitable as progressive equilibrium in development. Moreover, there is nothing particularly disturbing or darkening in the hypothesis that advanced cognition is marked by disequilibrium as well as equilibrium. Consideration of some parallel conditions of disequilibrium in contemporary physics may be illuminating. We have already encountered it in the aforementioned theory of quantum electrodynamics. Physical theories of space are at least as contradictory. The current situation has been summarized by Bochner (1966):

> (i) in the *ordinary* physics of our planetary system, space continues to be Newtonian; (ii) in the theory of single electrons or similar particles (that is, in the so-called quantum field theory), it is the space of special relativity; (iii) in the physics of our galaxy and beyond it becomes the space of general relativity; and (iv) the "statistical" space of quantum mechanics may be viewed as being different from, and thus inconsistent with, any "non-statistical" space, Newtonian or relativistic [p. 155].

Advanced structural integration of hypotheticodeductive contradictions includes logical compensations between direct and inverse operations. On this there is agreement (Piaget, 1974). But, in the present view, no structural developmental priority is attributed to direct operations over negation, notwithstanding the apparent ontogenetic precedence of affirmation over disconfirmation in advanced experimental reasoning (see first section). Moreover, the present findings are that hypotheticodeductive contradictions, including those between affirmation and disconfirmation, are only beginning to develop during early adolescence, whereas Piaget (1974) reports that this ontogenetic period marks their developmental resolution.

The origins of direct (affirmation) and inverse (negation) operations are contemporaneous developmentally. The apparent ontogenetic precedence of one over the other is an intersective function of the conceptual phenomenon and developmental stage being investigated. Thus, experimental affirmation appears to precede experimental disconfirmation in adolescent hypotheticodeductive thinking.

The results are different when investigating the origins and early development of logical reasoning. As mentioned previously, in an ongoing investigation of logical cognition, subjects ages 6 to 60 months are presented with quasi-continuous malleable objects made of PlayDoh. The combinativity transformations generated by 6- to 12-month-old babies support three hypotheses (Langer, 1980). First, decomposition precedes composition. Babies (1) bite and pull apart objects into more and smaller objects before (2) they press and push objects together into fewer and bigger objects. Second, decomposition and deformation have contemporaneous origins. Babies press on and push into objects, so as to deform them, at least as readily as they decompose them. Third, deformation precedes composition. Deformation can be considered as a control for composition. The reason is that the sensorimotor abilities required to deform objects are sufficient for composing PlayDoh objects, such as by pushing and pressing one into another.

These three hypotheses imply that the origins of logical negation precede affirmation when the combinativity transformations involve decomposing and composing quasi-continuous malleable objects. On the other hand, affirmation (composing) dominates negation (decomposing) when 6- to 12-month-olds apply combinativity transformations to discrete nonmalleable objects such as blocks (Langer, 1980). The structural developmental model that emerges is that of original symmetry in the infant's universe (Langer, 1980, Chapter 16).

Whether found in early (weak) or advanced (powerful) stages of scientific thought or of individual cognition, progressive disequilibrium is a necessary condition for further development. Progressive disequilibrium, then, is as much a mark of cognitive development, including mature cognitive development, as is progressive equilibrium.

ACKNOWLEDGMENTS

This is an expanded version of a paper presented at an OECD conference on "Developmental and Learning Curves", St. Paul de Vence, April 1974.

The research reported in this chapter was supported in part by USPHS Grant HD 03617 on The Intergenerational Studies in Development and Aging at the Institute of Human Development, University of California, Berkeley; it was conducted with the assistance of Mimi Lou and Geoffrey Saxe.

REFERENCES

Abrams, M. H. *The mirror and the lamp.* Oxford: Oxford University Press, 1953.

Beth, E. W., & Piaget, J. *Mathematical epistemology and psychology.* Dordrecht: D. Reidel, 1966.

Black, A. E. *The coordination of logical and moral reasoning during adolescence.* Unpublished doctoral dissertation, University of California, Berkeley, 1976.

Bochner, S. *The role of mathematics in the rise of science.* Princeton, N.J: Princeton University Press, 1966.

Bower, T. G. R. *Development in infancy.* San Francisco: Freeman, 1974.

Dennis, W., & Malinger, B. Animism and related tendencies in senescence. *Journal of Gerontology,* 1949, *4,* 218–221.

Duhem, P. *Le systeme du monde.*(Vol. 1). Paris, 1913.

Elkind, D. Quality conceptions in junior and senior high-school students. *Child Development,* 1961, *32,* 551–560.

Elkind, D. Quality conceptions in college students. *Journal of Social Psychology,* 1962, *57,* 459–465.

Gesell, A. The ontogenesis of infant behavior. In L. Carmichael (Ed.), *Manual of Child Psychology,* New York: Wiley, 1946.

Haan, N., Langer, J., & Kohlberg, L. Family patterns of moral reasoning. *Child Development,* 1976, *47,* 1204–1206.

Higgens-Trenk, A., & Gaite, A. J. *Elusiveness of formal operational thought in adolescents.* Paper presented at the meeting of the American Psychological Association, Washington, D. C., September 1971.

Inhelder, B., & Piaget, J. *The growth of logical thinking from childhood to adolescence.* New York: Basic Books, 1958.

Inhelder, B., & Piaget, J. *The early growth of logic in the child.* New York: Harper & Row, 1964.

Inhelder, B., Sinclair, H. & Bovet, M. *Learning and the development of cognition.* Cambridge, Mass: Harvard University Press, 1974.

Keasey, C. *The nature of formal operations in preadolescence, adolescence and middle age.* Unpublished doctoral dissertation, University of California, Berkeley, 1970.

Keasey, C. Formal operations in females from eleven to fifty-four years of age. *Developmental Psychology,* 1972, *6,* 364.

Kohlberg L., & Kramer, R.B. Continuities and discontinuities in childhood and adult moral development. *Human Development,* 1969, *12,* 93–120.

Kris, E. *Psychoanalytic explorations in art.* New York: International Universities Press, 1952.

Kuhn, D., Langer, J., Kohlberg, L., & Haan, N. The development of formal operations in logical and moral judgment. *Genetic Psychology Monographs,* 1977, *95,* 97–188.

Kusnezow, B. G. Die lehre des Aristoteles von der relativen und absoluten bewegung im lichte der modernen physik. In G. Harig (Ed.), *Sovietische beitrage zur geschichte der naturwissenschaften.* Berlin: Deutscher Verlag der Wissenschaften, 1960.

Langer, J. Disequilibrium as a source of development. In P. H. Mussen, J. Langer, & M. Covington (Eds.), *Trends and issues in developmental psychology.* New York: Holt, Rinehart & Winston, 1969(a).

Langer, J. *Theories of development.* New York: Holt, Rinehart & Winston, 1969(b).

Langer, J. Mental regeneration. In M. Wolins & M. Gottesman (Eds.), *Group care.* New York: Gordon & Breach, 1971.

Langer, J. Interactional aspects of cognitive organization. *Cognition,* 1974, *3,* 9–28.

Langer, J. Cognitive development during and after the preconceptual period. In M. H. Appel & L. S. Goldberg (Eds.), *Topics in Cognitive Development.* New York: Plenum. 1977.

Langer, J. *The origins of logic: 6 to 12 months.* Academic Press, 1980.

Langer, J. *The origins of logic: 1 to 2 years.* In preparation.

Langer, J., & Strauss, S. Appearance, reality and identity. *Cognition,* 1972, *1,* 105–128.

Langer, J., & Sugarman Bell, S. The developmental theories of Werner and Piaget. In G. Steiner (Ed.), *The psychology of the 20th century.* Zurich: Kindler, 1978.

Leskow, S., & Smock, C. D. Developmental changes in problem-solving strategies: Permutation. *Developmental Psychology,* 1970, *2,* 412–422.

Lovell, K. A follow-up study of Inhelder and Piaget's "The growth of logical thinking." *British Jounal of Psychology,* 1961, *52,* 143–153.

McGraw, M.B. *The neuromuscular maturation of the human infant.* New York: Columbia University Press, 1943.

Moore, M.K. *The genesis of object permanence.* Unpublished doctoral dissertation, Harvard University, 1974.

Moore, M. K. *Object permanence and object identity*. Paper presented at the meetings of the Society for Research in Child Development, Denver 1975.

Mounoud, P., & Bower, T. G. R. Conservation of weight in infants. *Cognition*, 1974, *3*, 29–40.

Neimark, E. A preliminary search for formal operation structures. *Journal of Genetic Psychology*, 1970, *116*, 223–232.

Piaget, J. *The construction of reality in the child*. New York: Basic Books, 1954

Piaget, J. Recherches sur la contradiction. *Etudes d'epistemologie genetique* (Vol. 32). Paris: Presses Univeritaires de France, 1974.

Piaget, J., & Inhelder, B. *The psychology of the child*. New York: Basic Books, 1969.

Ross, R. J. Some empirical parameters of formal thinking. *Journal of Youth & Adolescence*, 1973, *2*, 167–177.

Ruff, F. K. *Aspects of developmental transition*. Unpublished BA dissertation, University of California, Berkeley, 1975.

Sanders, S., Laurandeau, M., & Bergeron, J. Aging and the concept of space: The conservation of surfaces. *Journal of Gerontology*, 1966, *21*, 281–286.

Schwartz, C. R. *Developmental aspects of class inclusion*. Unpublished doctoral dissertation, University of California, Berkeley, 1970.

Smedslund, J. The concept of correlation in adults. *Scandinavian Journal of Psychology*, 1963, *4*, 165–173.

Smock, C. D., & Harris, J. S. *Developmental changes in problem solving strategies: Effects of practice on solution to permutation problems*. Unpublished manuscript, University of Georgia, 1969.

Strauss, S. Inducing cognitive development and learning. *Cognition*, 1973, *1*, 329–357.

Towler, J. O., & Wheatley, G. Conservation concepts in college students: A replication and critique. *Journal of Genetic Psychology*, 1971, *118*, 265–270.

Turiel, E. Developmental processes in the child's moral thinking. In P. H. Mussen, J. Langer, & M. Covington (Eds.), *Trends and issues in developmental psychology*. New York: Holt, Rinehart & Winston, 1969.

Turiel, E. Conflict and transition in adolescent moral development. *Child Development*, 1974, *45*, 14–29.

Valentine, C. W. *The psychology of early childhood*. London: Metheun, 1946.

Wason, P. C., & Johnson-Laird, P. N. *Psychology of reasoning*. Cambridge, Mass: Harvard University Press, 1972.

Werner, H. *Comparative psychology of mental development*. New York: International Universities Press, 1948.

Werner, H., & Kaplan, B. *Symbol formation*. New York: Wiley, 1963.

Wigner, E. P. Events, laws of nature, and invariance principles. *Science*. 1964, *145*, 995–999.

Youniss, J., & Furth, H. G. The role of language and experience on the use of logical symbols. *British Journal of Psychology*, 1967, *58*, 435–443.

IV NEUROLOGICAL MODELS

12 Correlates of Developmental Behavior in Brain Maturation

André Roch Lecours
Centre de Recherches en Sciences Neurologiques
Université de Montréal
Centre de Rééducation du Langage et
de Recherche Neuropsychologique
Hôtel-Dieu de Montréal

The conception of maturation [refers to the] process of the progressive organization of functions and of their morphological substrata which go on through the life span of the individual and tend to infinity, albeit the exponential curve of maturation is constantly bent by the stresses and strains of life experiences into a parabolic curve.[1]

The process of brain maturation, which in man does not reach its term before at least 15 and conceivably many more years of life have elapsed, is reflected in biological changes of several orders (chemical, electrical, anatomical, etc.). Contemporary knowledge of these changes is indeed scarce and fragmentary; understanding of their signification is still more so. The best known of them—this does not need to be a truism—are (some of) those easily accessible to observation, that is, (some of) those accessible to observation by simple means. Such are, on the whole, the few morphological changes I intend to discuss. Among these morphological changes, I lay particular weight on the *myelinogenetic cycles* of brain maturation. There are two main reasons to this choice: On the one hand, known facts about the tempo of myelinization in different parts of the human being's central nervous system, although incomplete and established using rather crude techniques, are comparatively numerous and precise; on the other hand, myelinogenisis is the only parameter of biological maturation of which I have some

[1] From Yakovelev, P.I. Morphological criteria and maturation of the nervous system in man. In *Research Publications of the A.R.N.M.D. (39): Mental Retardation*, 3-46, The Association for Research in Nervous and Mental Disease, New York, 1962.

knowledge through personal research . Bearing on more than 250 normal human cerebra—fetal, infantile, and adult—prepared in whole-brain gapless serial sections[2], this research was conducted nearly 15 years ago, in collaboration with Paul Ivan Yakovlev (Yakovlev & Lecours, 1967). I do hope that my dependence on Yakovlev's works, thought, and teachings will be obvious throughout my argument (Yakovlev 1948, 1960, 1962, 1963, 1968, 1970, 1972).

The study of some of the morphological parameters of brain maturation, for instance encephalometric measurements (head circumference, brain weight, etc.), yields only global data and, therefore, can hardly be put in parallel with the development of specific behavioral patterns (and still less with particular aspects of specific behavioral patterns). Other parameters are defined in relation to anatomically restricted systems or regions of the brain. Such are, for instance, myelinogenesis and corticogenesis. The study of parameters of the latter type has shown that morphological maturation of the brain follows—at least in certain aspects—species-specific time schedules; it has also shown that these time schedules vary widely in different systems or regions of the brain, each thus displaying a more or less characteristic cycle of maturation. It seems reasonable to assume that these cycles of formal maturation reflect the functional maturation of the brain and, therefore, that they can be related to the emergence and gradual differentiation (in humans) of specific behavioral patterns such as locomotion, manipulation, and expression (through articulated speech and language or otherwise) (Yakovlev & Lecours, 1967; Lecours, 1976). It is of course not possible to demonstrate, beyond doubt, the validity of this assumption; besides apparent common sense, however, reported cases of retarded or arrested behavioral development, concomitant to well-documented retarded or arrested morphological maturation of the brain (Kemper et. al., 1973), render it highly probable. It remains an altogether different question to ask whether or not current knowledge concerning morphological maturation of the brain is precise enough to lead to plausible correlations with any of the (heterogeneous and more or less precisely defined classes of) behavioral events known as *dips in learning curves*: Although it seems reasonable to raise this question, one might predict that the Saint-Paul-de-Vence meeting will leave it unsettled.

ENCEPHALOMETRICS

In the course of its first 20 to 24 months of existence, that is, from early gestation to about the end of the first postnatal year, the human brain increases in size and weight at a stupendous—and, as far as I know, regular— rate (Altman & Dittmar, 1962). From≈50 grams (g) at mid-gestation, brain

---

[2] Thickness: 35μ. Coloration: Weigert's hematoxylin.

weight increases to $\simeq$200g around the 30th gestational week, to $\simeq$400g at birth (if at term) and to $\simeq$1000g when the child is 1 year old (Yakovlev, 1962; Altman & Dittmar, 1962). From then on, the increase in brain weight progresses at a much slower pace till puberty when it reaches $\simeq$1250g in girls and $\simeq$1375g in boys (Yakovlev, 1962; Epstein, 1974a); it is believed that, as a rule, brain weight remains stable for a good while thereafter. A similar course of events is observed with regard to head circumference: it increases from $\simeq$34 centimeter (cm) at birth (if at term) to $\simeq$46cm a year later ($\simeq$one cm per month), and to $\simeq$54cm around puberty and thereafter ($\simeq$half a cm per year from age 2 to 10).

Had they been interested, Marshall La Palice's[3] soldiers might have proposed the following assertion:

1. The period of increase in encephalometric values is also a most critical period as to behavioral development and active learning.
2. There is no evidence that the moment of stabilization in encephalometric values does or should coincide with the end of brain maturation and/or with attainment of maximal learning capacities (nor, eventually, with the beginning of decline in learning capacities).
3. There exists no obvious behavioral correlate, even global, to the biphasicity of encephalometric maturation (very rapid from early gestation to the end of the first postnatal year, and thereafter very slow till the end of the cycle at about the time of puberty. Figs. 1 and 2A).
4. If absolute encephalometric values bear any direct relationship at all to the learning capacities of normal individuals, the clinical expression of this relationship can be and often is reversed, accentuated, masked, modified by other factors—usually social factors—of much greater importance.
5. Pathologically impaired learning capacities have been observed to coexist with both normal and abnormal encephalometric values.
6. Only grossly abnormal encephalometric values can be safely correlated with pathologically impaired learning capacities.

One might heretofore consider it reasonable to disregard encephalometrics as a likely morphological correlate of particular developmental behaviors, *dips* included (obviously). Well, this is not Epstein's idea of *phrenoblysis* (Epstein, 1974a; Epstein, 1974b); he describes, on the one hand, *dips* in the developmental curve representing the brain-weight/body-weight ratio, that is, periods during which brain is relatively ahead and periods during which

---

[3] *Un quart d'heure avant sa mort, il etait encore en vie.*

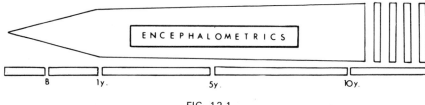

FIG. 12.1.

body is relatively ahead (Fig. 12.2B); and he describes, on the other hand, *dips* in a curve globally representing behavioral acquisitions related to "various mind functions" (Fig. 12.2C). Epstein's contention apparently is that times when body grows relatively faster than brain might be somewhat inauspicious to psychometrics. He could be right.

SURFACE CONFIGURATION OF THE BRAIN

Yakovlev's Telencephalon Impar, Semipar, and Totopar (Yakovlev, 1968). In the ≃4-week embryo, the endbrain is a median holosphere—this holosphere is the *anlage* of the rhinic structures of the adult brain. In the ≃8-week embryo, paired paramedian vesicles are developing lateral to the median holosphere—these paramedian vesicles are the *anlage* of the limbic structures of the adult brain. In the ≃12-wek embryo, further dorsolateral evaginations begin to appear bilaterally—these further evaginations are the *anlage* of the supralimbic structures of the adult brain. It is on the basis of these developmental events in brain morphology that Yakovlev has grounded his division of the cerebral "hemispheres" into (Fig. 12.3):

1. A *telencephalon impar*[5], or rhinic lobe, having to deal[6] with endo-kinesis, or visceration (the *visceral sphere of motility-expression*, e.g., heartbeat, peristalsis); a median structure is thus related to the motility of ablateral organs.
2. A *telencephalon semipar*, or limbic lobes, having to deal[6] with *ereismo-kinesis*, or emotion (*e(x)motion* or the *expressive-emotional sphere of motility-expression*, e.g., emotional vocalization and mimicry—*body-bound movements*).
3. A *telencephalon totopar*, or supralimbic lobes, having to deal[6] with *telokinesis*, or effectuation (the *effective-transational sphere of motil-*

---

[5] Yakovlev's terminology in italics.
[6] Specifically but not exclusively.

ity-expression, e.g., manipulation of tools, language production—*object-bound movements*). Yakovlev'e telencephalon totopar includes, in the term of more classical neuroanatomy, (the greatest part of) the frontal, temporal, parietal, and occipital lobes.

The behavioral events pertaining to the theme of this volume belong mostly with object-bound motility. Although all three of Yakovlev's telencephalons no doubt participate in the genesis of these events, their more specific neuroanatomical substratum thus lies within the supralimbic compartment of the cerebral hemispheres. The morphological maturation of this compartment, as far as surface configuration of the brain is concerned, can be summarized in the following terms: (1) Its *anlage* is the last to appear during embryogenesis (end of the third gestational month); (2) once its development begins, it rapidly becomes of paramount quantitative importance, the supralimbic surfaces crowding the limbic and rhinic surfaces toward the midline and the limbus of the hemispheres; (3) it is the one with the longest maturational cycle, that is, it is the last to acquire its definitive surface characteristics (cf. infra); (4) according to Yakovlev, it is the *last to yield to the involutionary changes* of normal senium (Yakovlev, 1962).

Sulcation in the Supralimbic Lobes. According to Larroche (1967), the parieto-occipital and calcarine fissures begin to be seen near the end of the fifth gestational month (that is, 4 to 6 weeks after the hippocampal fissure). The sylvian and rolandic fissures are observed to appear and deepen at the end of the sixth and during the seventh month. These are said to be *primary fissures*. The earliest *secondary fissures* to be seen are the first temporal, characteristically present at the end of the seventh month, and, early during the eighth month, the superior frontal, the precentral, the postcentral, the second temporal, and the cingulate. From then till birth, that is, during the ninth and tenth gestational months, and particularly during the last 6 weeks, secondary sulcation proceeds at a rapid rate (Yakovlev, 1962). Still open at birth, the rostral part of the sylvian fissure is closed—that is, opercularization of the insula is complete— at the end of the first month of postnatal life (Yakovlev, 1962). Primary and secondary fissures keep deepening for at least 6 months after birth (Yakovlev, 1962) and probably much longer. Very few *tertiary fissures* are visible during early postnatal life (Yakovlev, 1962). According to Yakovlev, tertiary sulcation begins to be preeminent toward the end of the second year and goes on till and maybe through adulthood; it is markedly asymmetrical and becomes as characteristic for each person as are facial features and fingerprints (Yakovlev, 1962). In the human adult, about two-thirds of the cortical mantle are ploughed in the depth of fissures of different orders.

Asymmetry in Surface Configuration. The existence of asymmetries in the superficial configuration of the cerebral hemispheres has long been known: Eberstaller (1884) observed that the left sylvian fissure is often longer than the right; von Economo and Horn (1930), then Pfeiffer (1936), reported that doubling of Heschl's gyrus is more common in the right than in the left hemisphere; Kakeshita (1925) was probably the first to notice that the surface of the *planum temporale* is often greater in the left than in the right temporal lobe, a fact that has been further documented in recent years (Gerschwind & Levitsky, 1968; Teszner, 1972; Wada et al, 1973; and Rubens et al, 1976); other configurational asymmetries of this type have been described (von Bonin, 1967). According to Broca (1865), who attributed the discovery to Gratiolet (1854), such asymmetries in the surface configuration of the supralimbic lobes are there to be seen during fetal life. This was recently confirmed by Wada et al. (1973) who showed that

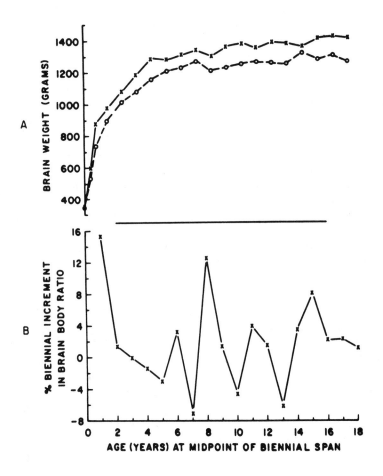

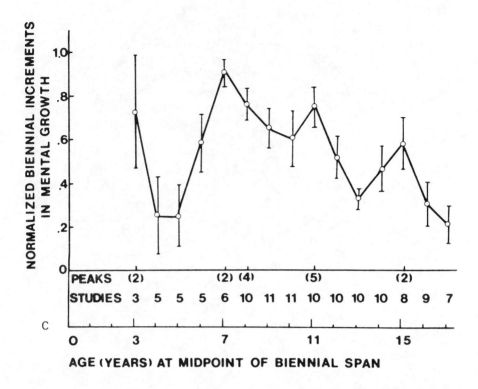

FIG. 12.2. A: Average brain weight at different ages [Boyd, E. (1962). In P. Altman and D. Dittmar (Eds.), *Growth*, p. 346, Federation of American Societies of Experiemntal Biology, Washington, D.C.]. B: Biennial increments in brain/body ratio [Dullemeijer, P. (1971) in R. E. Myers and W. M. Krogman (Eds.), *Cranio-Facial Growth*, pp. 45–76, Pergamon, New York]. C: Biennial increments in "various mind functions." [A and B from Epstein, H. T. "phrenoblysis: special brain and mind growth periods. I. Human brain and skull development." *Developmental Psychobiology*, 7(*3*), 207–216 1974. C from Epstein, H. T. "Phrenoblysis: special brain and mind growth periods. II. Human mental development." *Developmental Psychobiology*, 7(*3*), 217–224, 1974.]

morphological asymmetries can be observed in the frontal (operculum) and temporal (planum) lobes as early as the 29th gestational week. I remember that Yakovlev also used to point to such asymmetries (particularly in relation to Ecker's central lobule) when, several years ago, he undertook the study of his "normative collection" of fetal brains. I am not so sure that he considered them to represent a systematic and constant phenomenon.

Surface Configuration of the Brain Versus Developmental Behavior. Somehow, the study of the surface morphology during brain maturation is interesting in itself. This is fortunate because the parallel one can attempt to

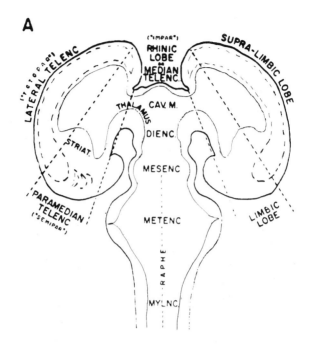

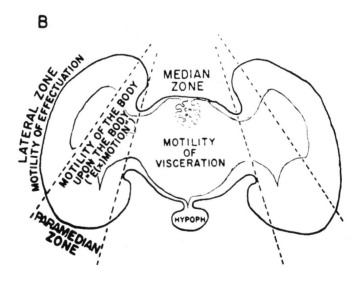

FIG. 12.3. From Yakovlev, P. I. "telencephalon 'impar', 'semipar' and 'totopar': morphogenetic, tectogenetic and architectonic definitions." *International Journal of Neurology, 6,* 245–265, 1968.

draw between surface morphology and developmental behavior does not lead to very specific considerations. In summary:

1. The period during which gross changes occur in surface configuration of the brain is also a most critical period as to behavioral development and active learning.
2. Pathologically impaired learning capacities have been observed to coexist with both normal and abnormal brain surface configuration.
3. The relative mushrooming of supralimbic surfaces, maximal in humans among all mammals, apparently correlates with maximal increase in learning capacities related to complex behaviors.
4. The well-documented phenomenon of functional lateralization in relation to certain forms of behavior (among Yakovlev's *effective-transactional* sphere of motility-expression) is probably subtended by morphological asymmetries in supralimbic structures; if so, these asymmetries precede behavioral development.[7]
5. The study of the surface confirguration of the brain at different maturational stages does not yield much by way of a biological interpretation of *dips in learning curves*.

---

[7]Enfin, notre regretté collègue Gratiolet a signalé un fait qui a été rappelé il y a quelques mois par M. Bertillon, et tout récemment par M. Baillarger dans son discours à l'Académie: c'est quo dans le développement du cerveau, les circonvolutions de l'hémisphère gauche sont en avance sur celles de l'hémisphère droit. Les premières sont déjà dessinées à un moment ou les autres ne sont pas encore apparentes. L'hémisphère gauche, qui tient sous sa dépendance le mouvement des membres droits, est donc plus précoce dans son développement que l'hémisphère opposé. On comprend anisi pourquoi, dés les premiers temps de la vie, le jeune enfant se sert de préférence des membres dont l'innervation est alors la plus parfaite, pourquori en d'autres termes il devient droitier. Le membre supérieur droit, ètant dés l'origine plus fort et plus adroit que le gauche, est appelé, par cela même, à fonctionner plus souvent; et il acquiert dés lors une supériorité de force et d'adresse qui ne fait que s'accroître avec l'age . . . C'est cette chose complexe et difficile (*articulated language*) que l'enfant doit apprendre à l'âge le plus tendre, et il y parvient à la suite de longs tâtonnements et d'un travail cèrèbral de l'ordre le plus compliqué. Eh bien! ce travail cérébral, on le lui impose a une époque très rapprochée de ces périodes embryonnaires ou le développement de l'hémisphère gauche est en avance sur celui de l'hémisphère droit. Dès lors, il ne nous répugne pas d'admettre que l'hémisphère cérébral le plus développé et le plus précoce soit, plus tô que l'autre, en état de diriger l'exécution et la coordination des actes a la fois intellectuels et musculaires qui constituent le langage articulé. Ainsi naît l'habitude de parler avec l'hémisphère gauche, et cette habitude finit par faire si bien partie de notre nature, que lorsque nous sommes privés des fonctions de cet hémisphère, nous perdons la faculté de nous faire comprendre par la parole (From Broca, P. Sur le siége de la Faculté du langage articulé. *Bulletin de la Sociètè d'Anthropologie,* 1865, 6, 337–393.)

CALLOSOGENESIS

Rakič and Yakovlev have studied the morphological development, among other nervous structures, of the cerebral commissures (Rakič & Yakovlev, 1968). Some of their data concerning corpus callosum are of interest in relation to what has just been said about maturation of the supralimbic cortical surfaces:

1. As one would expect, given the chronology in the apparition of the primordia of rhinic, limbic, and supralimbic structures (cf. infra), fibers of the anterior commissure begin to cross the midline before ($\approx$10-week human embryo) those of the corpus callosum ($\approx$13-week embryo).
2. The enormous quantitative predominance gradually acquired by corpus callosum over other commissural systems obviously reflects that acquired by supralimbic over other cortices.
3. For some reason, the genu of corpus callosum grows at a faster rate than its splenium and body during gestation whereas, after birth, the relative growth rate of the splenium is greater than that of the genu and body (Fig. 12.4). (Should this be considered the mechanical effect of a mere formal rearrangement? Or could it be that passage from an always obscure to an often luminous environment is accompanied by a postnatal maturational spurt in interhemispheric collateral fibers to and from visual associative cortices?)
4. The sagital surface section of the corpus callosum increases rapidly from the end of the fourth gestational month ($\approx$23mm^2) to birth ($\approx$67 mm^2) and to the end of the second year of postnatal life ($\approx$148 mm^2); it keeps increasing thereafter, although at a slower rate, till adulthood ($\approx$325 mm^2). I have noted a discrepancy between these figures and global encephalometrics (cf. infra): Whereas brain weight increases by $\approx$35% between the end of the second postnatal year and adulthood, the callosal surface in sagital section increases by $\approx$115% between the second year and adulthood (in humans). Both cycles are thus biphasic but very differently so from a quantitative point of view. Because a very large proportion of the increase in brain weight should be accounted for by the maturation of supralimbic structures, this discrepancy is indeed most intriguing.

Now, if I turn back to morphology–behavior correlations, it is quite obvious that I am due for another lapalissade. Let us be brave: Phylogenetically and ontogenetically, increment in callosal bulk, like increment in supralimbic cortical surfaces, is contemporary with increment in learning capacities related to complex behaviors (a not-so-unexpected co-occurrence in view of the fact that a large majority of callosal axons originate from supralimbic cortical cells).

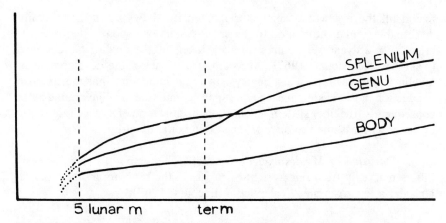

FIG. 12.4.   Relative growth rate of callosal genu, body and splenium. From Rakič, P. and Yakovlev, P. I. "Development of the corpus callosum and cavum septi in man." *The Journal of Comparative Neurology, 132,* 45–72, 1968.

But then, farfetched speculation being the lot of anyone who agrees to write more than a half page under the title of this chapter, an occasion perhaps arises at this point. Let us be audacious: One of the several possible explanations of the discrepancy between brain weight and callosal surface in sagital section(cf. supra) might be that new interhemispheric association fibers from supralimbic cortices keep crossing the midline for many years after birth. If so, the same might hold true with regard to intrahemispheric association bundles. In such circumstances, it is conceivable that behavioral phenomena such as *dips in learning* might somehow reflect a temporarily unfilled need for new anatomical associations in given areas of the cortical mantle. This might in turn belong with an hitherto undefined but possibly rather tight time schedule in morphological maturation. Because the human being's central nervous system contains at least 10 and possibly 100 billion neurons, and because each of them establishes at least 10 and perhaps up to 300,000 synaptic contacts with its congeners (cf. infra), some might wish to consider the foregoing speculation as belonging with science fiction (which, when "good," as everyone knows, may show a tendency to acquire varying degrees of reality).

MYELINOGENESIS

Yakovlev's Definition of "Myelogenetic Cycle". Yakovlev has empirically defined the myelogenetic cycle (or myelinogenetic cycle) of a given system or region of the nervous system as the period extending from the time of the first appearance of stainable myelin sheaths (Loyez' method) in that system or region till the age when the tinctorial intensity shows no further visually discernable gain as compared to the same system or region in the (normal) brain of a 28-year-old adult arbitrarily taken as a standard of reference (Yakovlev & Lecours, 1967). According to Yakovlev, the development of myelin in the sheaths of a fiber system is an indication that the impulse conduction in this system has become space committed in an invariable path; consequently, the fiber system that has reached the term of its myelinogenetic cycle may be assumed to have reached functional maturity.

The Duration of Myelinogenetic Cycles. The tempo of myelinogenesis differs markedly from one system or region of the brain to another. Let us consider a few examples (Yakovlev & Lecours, 1967):

1. In the vestibulo–cerebellar (or inner) division of the inferior cerebellar peduncle, the cycle begins early during the sixth fetal month and finishes around the end of the eighth; it is thus very brief and entirely prenatal.
2. In the optic radiations of the thalmus, the cycle begins a little before birth at term and is completed early during the fifth postnatal month; again, the cycle is brief but, this time, it is mostly postnatal (Figs. 12.5, 12.6, 12.12B, 12.13, and 12.14).
3. In the somesthetic radiations of the thalmus, the cycle begins during the ninth or tenth gestational month and finishes at the end of the first postnatal year or early in the second; again, the cycle is mostly postnatal but, this time, its duration is of intermediate length (Figs. 12.6 and 12.14).
4. In the acoustic radiations of the thalamus, the cycle begins at or very soon after birth at term and is not completed before the child is at least 3 years of age; the cycle is thus entirely postnatal and nearly thrice as long as that of the somesthetic radiations (Figs. 12.6, 12.8, 12.9, 12.12B, 12.13, 12.14, and 12.16).
5. Still longer is the cycle of the nonspecific thalamic radiations, which begins at about 3 postnatal months and does not reach its term before the middle of the first decade of life if not later. The temporal difference in the myelinogenetic cycles of the specific and nonspecific thalamic radiations is particularly well seen, at 3 years, in a section through the occipital horn of the lateral ventricle, showing the stratum sagittale externum (optic radiations from the lateral geniculate body, cycle completed) and internum (nonspecific radiations from the pulvinar, cycle still in progress) (Figs. 12.5, 12.6).
6. The most protracted myelinogenetic cycle of them all is that of the short tangential fibers of the intracortical neuropil in nonspecific association areas of the supralimbic cortex. As shown by Kaes' studies (1907), it

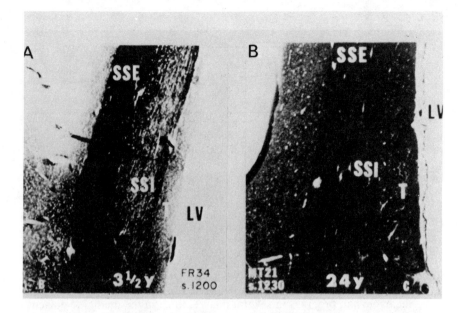

FIG. 12.5.   The stratum sagittale internum, the stratum sagittale externum and the tapetum (A) at three years and (B) in the adult. From Yakovlev, P. I. and Lecours, A. R. "The myelogenetic cycles of regional maturation of the brain." In, A. Minkowski, ed., *Regional Development of the Brain in Early Life*, pp. 3–70, Blackwell, Oxford and Edinburgh, 1967.

begins more than a year after birth and its term, possibly with important individual variations, is not reached before several decades of life have passed (Figs. 12.14 to 12.16)

Graphic Representation of Myelinogenetic Cycles. Depending on how (anatomically and functionally) homogeneous and well defined is a con-

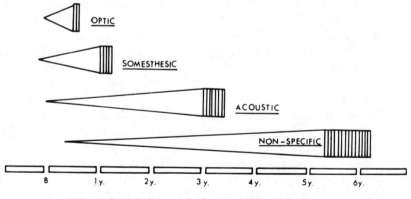

FIG. 12.6.   Myelinogenetic Cycles of Thalmic Radiations.

279

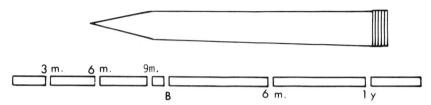

FIG. 12.7.   Myelinogenetic Cycle of the Medial Lemniscus

sidered system or region, different graphic representations of myelinogenetic cycles can be used:

1. In the case of (relatively) well–individuallized homogeneous fiber systems an elongated isoceles triangle adequately conveys the message. The different cycles of thalamic radiations (cf. supra), for instance, are easily summarized in that manner (Fig. 12.6).

2. In the case of a single tract of heterogeneous origin and composition, the cycle can progress in several phases: thus, in the medial lemniscus, myelinogenesis progresses rapidly from the 6th to the 9th foetal month and, thereafter, much slowlier till the end of the first postnatal year. An elongated pentagon provides an acceptable graphic representation of this particular type of myelinogenetic evolution (Fig. 12. 7). In both the triangular and the pentagonal representations, the width and length of graphs indicate progression in the intensity of staining and density of myelinated fibers; the vertical stripes indicate the approximate term of the cycle (Yakovlev & Lecours, 1967).

3. The multiple phases in myelinogenesis of successive constituents of a same system can be represented in successively interpenetrating isoceles. Myelinogenesis of the acoustic fibers, from semicircular canals (Klossovskii, 1963) to Heschl's cortex, is an interesting example; it can be presented either in detail (myelinogenesis of the acoustic nerve, of the trapezoid body and lateral lemniscus, of the brachium of the inferior colliculus, of the geniculo–temporal—or acoustic—radiations (Fig. 12.8) or more globally (myelinogenesis of the prethalamic as opposed to that of the postthalamic component of the central acoustic pathway (Fig. 12.9)

4. An elongated quadrilateral graph is useful, finally, as a composite representation of the sequence of events in myelinogenesis of several fiber systems belonging with a same family. For instance, known or presumed data about myelinogenesis in the association bundles of the cerebral hemispheres can be represented in that manner. The slope in the two short sides of the graph indicate different tempos in the beginning and term of the cycles of different long association bundles (Fig. 12.10); before the age of 4 to 8 postnatal weeks, the only

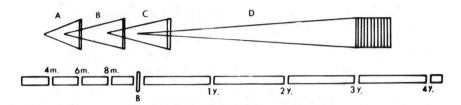

A: ACOUSTIC NERVE
B TRAPEZOID BODY AND LATERAL LEMNISCUS
C: BRACHIUM OF TI INFERIOR COLLICULUS
D: ACOUSTIC RADIAIIONS

FIG. 12.8. Myelinogenesis of the Acoustic Pathway

supralimbic association systems showing hematoxylin stainable myelin sheaths are short U-fibers, most of them between *primary* cortices and their immediately adjacent *secondary* cortices; long axonal fibers linking specific association areas (*secondary* cortices) to one another, for instance the long axons of the fasciculus arcuatus (Geschwind, 1965) (Fig. 12.11), begin and terminate their myelinogenetic cycles sooner than long fibers to and from nonspecific association areas (*tertiary* cortices), for instance, long axons to and from the inferior parietal lobule.[8]

Global Profile of Telencephalic Myelinogenesis. Among Yakovlev's telencephalons (Fig. 12.3), the supralimbic one (telencephalon totopar) is the last to initiate and, probably by several years, the last to complete (if ever) its myelinogenetic maturation. Within the supralimbic lobes (on the whole), fibers systems related to primary cortices initiate and complete their cycles sooner than those related to secondary cortices, and the latter initiate and complete their cycles sooner than fiber systems related to tertiary cortices (Figs. 12.17, 12. 18).[8]

Myelinogenetic Cycles and Behavior. I have already acknowledged personal preconceptions that led me to assume (cf. *supra*) that cycles of formal brain maturation are somehow related to the emergence and gradual differentiation of behavioral patterns. One of Yakovlev's favorite arguments,

[8]In Flechsig's maps, the central lobule of Ecker, the calcarine area and Heschl's gyri are classified as *primoridal myelinogenetic fields*; the candal thirds of the third and second frontal convolutions, the posterior half of the first temporal convolution, and the occipital surfaces immediately concentric with the calcarine area are classified as *intermediate myelinogenetic fields*; the inferior parietal lobule and part of the prefrontal convexity are classified as *terminal myelinogenetic fields*. Among long axons, the axial fibers in the gyri of the latter are the very latest to intiate and complete their myelinogenetic maturation; thier cycle is probably not complete before at least 7 years of life (Figs. 12.10, 12.17).

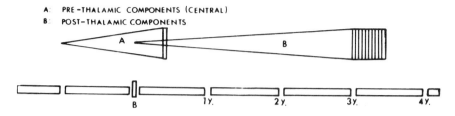

FIG. 12.9.   Myelinogenesis of the Acoustic Pathway

in candid discussions of this topic, consists of an opposition between optic versus acoustic myelinogenetic and behavioral maturation. I shall now try to summarize his argument (by way of an illustration of my own):

As I said a moment ago, myelinogenesis of the central acoustic pathway is short and largely prenatal in the prethalamic component (fifth gestational month to fourth postnatal month) whereas it is long and entirely postnatal in the postthalamic component (birth to end of third postnatal year); in striking contrast, both components of the central optic pathway, the prethalamic and the postthalamic, have short meyelinogenetic cycles, contemporarily completed in one rapid spurt between the eighth fetal and the fifth postnatal month (Figs. 12.12, 12.13). Thus: On the one hand, the myelinogenetic cycle of the acoustic pathway is biphasic, short, and mostly gestational in the helicogeniculate component and much longer—that is, lasting through at least the first 3 years of infancy—in the geniculotemporal component. On the other hand; the myelinogenetic cycle of the central optic pathway is monophasic, short, and perinatal in both the retinogeniculate and the geniculocalcarine components. One might consider the following parallel between this sequence of events in morphological brain maturation and the timetable followed by different modalities of sensory informations as they successively become factors of behavioral development in the human fetus and infant:

1. Early in and through gestational life, the fetus is submitted to gravitational (vestibular) and acoustic (cochlear) stimuli: movements of its own body, external sounds, and sounds of maternal life (cardiac beats, respiratory and intestinal noises, etc.) transmitted through the amniotic

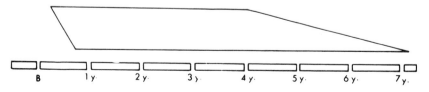

FIG. 12.10.   Myelinogenesis of Long Association Bundles

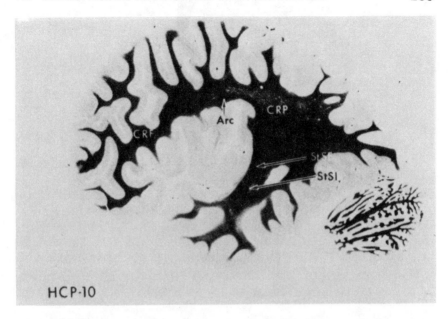

FIG. 12.11.   The fasciculus arcuatus (Arc) in a case of retarded behavioral and myelinogenetic maturation. From Kemper, T. L., Lecours, A. R., Gates, M. J. and Yakovlev, P. I. "Retardation of the myelo- and cytorchitectonic maturation of the brain in the congenital rubella syndrome." In *Research Publications of the A.R.N.M.D. (Vol. II): Early Development*, pp. 23–62, The Association for Research in Nervous and Mental Disease, New York, 1973.

sac and the maternal body wall, that are impermeable to photic stimuli. One could suggest—an assumption that is substantiated by the precocity and brevity of myelinogenesis in the prethalamic acoustic pathway (Fig. 12.12A)—that the central apparatus for the integration of such acoustic (and vestibular) stimuli is laid down in the brainstem tegmentum (During this phase of ontogenesis).

2. Birth is the moment of an abrupt change as to the types of inputs that besiege one's central nervous system: On the one hand, visual inputs enter into play as a paramount factor of behavioral development. If the short perinatal myelinogenetic cycle of both the prethalamic and the postthalamic components of the optic pathway is to be taken as a reliable indication, visual inputs rapidly assume a role of which certain aspects will remain physiologically unchanged from infancy to adulthood. On the other hand, the relative importance of positional and auditory stimuli decreases dramatically, and the latter assume a radically different role, soon to be largely oriented toward the acquisition of articulated speech and language. The existence of a chronological correlation between the long period during which this apprenticeship takes place and the protracted myelinogenetic cycle of the postthalamic component of the acoustic pathway might thus be taken into consider-

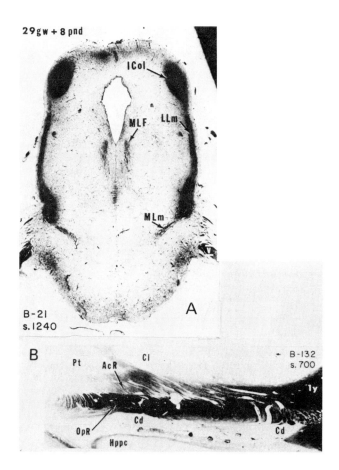

FIG. 12.12. A: Coronal section. Prethalamic acoustic fibers after 29 weeks of gestation and one week of postnatal life (LLm: lateral lemniscus; ICol: inferior colliculus). The myelinogenetic cycle of the lateral lemniscus has nearly reached its term. B: Sagital section through the sublenticular part of the internal capsule. Post-thalamic acoustic and optic fibers [radiations] after one year of postnatal life. Myelinogenetic cycle has reached term in optic radiations, is still progressing in acoustic radiations. Both figures from Yakovlev, P. I. and Lecours, A. R. "The myelinogenetic cycles of regional maturation of the brain." In, A. Minkowski, ed., *Regional Development of the Brain in Early Life*, pp. 3–70, Blackwell, Oxford and Edinburgh, 1967.

ation. In this respect, the length of myelinogenesis in subcortical and intracortical associative axons is also of potential interest.

It should be apparent, from the foregoing considerations, that Yakovlev's conception of *myelinogenetic cycles* is an essentailly dynamic one. It differs, in this respect, from Flechsig's (1907, 1920, 1927) rather static schedules, which disregarded the importance of the differential myelinogenetic tempos in the different components of man's central nervous system. Although more elaborate in that sense, Yakovlev's position is closer to Langworthy's (1933).

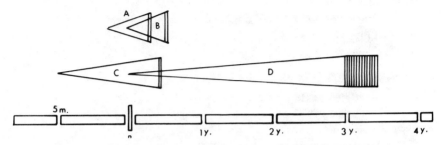

A: PRE-THALAMIC OPTIC (RETINOGENICULATE)
B: POST-THALAMIC OPTIC (GENICULOTEMPOP/.L)
C: PRE-THALAMIC ACOUSTIC (HELICOGENICULATE)
D: POST-THALAMIC ACOUSTIC (GENICULOCALCARINE)

FIG. 12.13.   Myelinogenesis of the Central Optic and Acoustic Pathways

Myelinogenetic Correlates of the Development of Speech and Language. In a recent (neurophilosophical) essay (Lecours, 1976), I attempted to correlate known facts concerning the tempos of myelinogenetic maturation in humans to a classical fragmentation of the behavioral events that take place during acquisition of articulated speech and language. I shall now briefly summarize this essay (Fig. 12.14):

1. *Babbling behavior* (Fig. 12.14, Graph A) is the production of un-specific acoustic responses to unspecific stimuli, visceral and somatic as well as visual and acoustic. A certain role might be attributed to unspecific feedbacks in babbling production but, whatever the stimuli triggering or maintaining it, it seems to be essentially a motor game aiming at an initiation to the use of buccal, lingual, pharyngeal, and laryngeal muscles as tools for sound production. If one is to rely on the state of myelinogenesis at the time when babbling behavior begins to occur (advanced myelinization in roots of cranial nerves, in prethalamic pathways for all sensory modalities, and in other brainstem structures, in optic radiations (Fig. 12.14, Graphs 1, 3, 4, 5, & 8).), one is led to the following conclusion: Either babbling is entirely or partially governed from cortical levels and this is done through very immature connections between cortical and subcortical levels; or else, babbling is governed mostly from subcortical levels where an advanced degree of anatomical maturation has already been achieved.

2. *Echolalic behavior* (Fig. 12.14, Graph B) is the production of sounds as specific imitative responses to specific acoustic stimuli. Sounds are heard then mimicked in the activities of the infant's buccophonatory apparatus; these activities generate, in turn, specific proprioceptive and auditory feedbacks. Consequently, echolalia requires the presence of an already functional—if not necessarily fully mature—sensorimotor anatomo–physiological substratum. At the time when echolalia becomes a

285

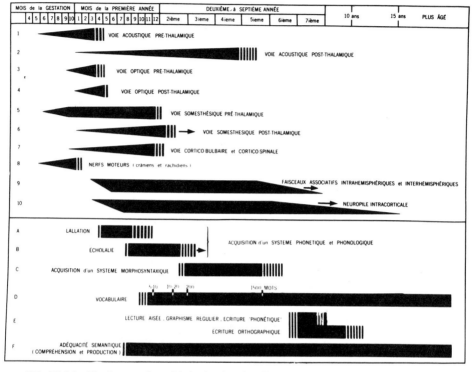

FIG. 12.14 Myelinogenetic and behavioral cycles. From Lecouns, A. R., et al., *L'Aphasie*, Flammarion, Paris, 1979.

dominant form of the child's speech activities[9], that is, during the second year of life, the pathways presumably involved in its production (cranial nerves[10], prethalamic acoustic and proprioceptive pathways, postthalamic acoustic and proprioceptive pathways, corticobulbar pathways, U-fibers, and arcuate fasciculus) have all reached a certain degree of myelinogenetic maturation although not all of them have reached the term of their cycle (Fig. 12.14, Graphs 1, 2, and 5 to 9). If these structures indeed constitute the circuit subserving echolalic behavior in the young child, this type of linguistic activity thus begins when maturation of its anatomical substratum is not quite complete and the imitation of speech sounds gets closer and closer to targets as anatomical maturation progresses toward its term.

3. Progressive mastery of a community–accepted morphosyntactic convention takes place, grossly, between 18 to 24 months and 4 to 6 years

---

[9] Behavioral data (Fig. 12.12) have been abstracted from different sources (Ey et al., 1963; Gesell & Amatruda, 1964; Osterrieth, 1966; Lenneberg, 1967; and Berry, 1969).

[10] V, VII, VIII, IX, X, XII.

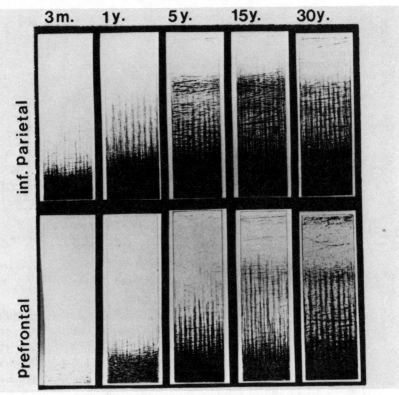

FIG. 12.15. Myelinogenesis of the intracortical neuropil in nonspecific associative cortices. From Kaes, Th. *Die Grosshirnrinde des Menschen in ihrem Massen und in ihrem Fasergehalt*, Gustav Fischer, Jena, 1907.

of age (Fig. 12.14, Graph C); apprenticeship more largely related to semantic adequacy, both in language production and in language comprehension, begins earlier and does not reach a peak for at least 15 and probably many more years (Fig. 12.14, Graph F) (its complete cessation might indeed be a definite sign of disease or senility). The neuroanatomical apparatus governing the comprehension and production of meaningful language is not precisely known. Mostly from pathological evidence (Geschwind, 1965; Wernicke, 1874; Nielsen, 1965; Lhermitte & Gautier, 1965; Lhermitte, 1968; Lecours et al., 1979), one may nevertheless assume that specific association cortices, nonspecific association cortices, and their axonal connexions to and from one another (particularly those to and from the left inferior parietal lobule) (Geschwind et al., 1968) play a primordial role. If so, learning, stocking, and using linguistic segments in production and comprehension of meaningful words and sentences might depend primarily on the gradual constitution of a complex net of associations whose

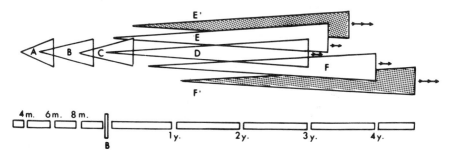

A ACOUSTIC NERVE
B TRAPEZOID BODY AND LATERAL LEMNISCUS
C BRACHIUM OF THE INFERIOR COLLICULUS
D ACOUSTIC RADIATIONS
E SHORT ASSOCIATION FIBERS FROM PRIMARY AND SECONDARY ACOUSTIC CORTICES
E′ LONG ASSOCIATION FIBERS FROM SECONDARY ACOUSTIC CORTICES
F INTRACORTICAL NEUROPIL IN PRIMARY ACOUSTIC CORTICES
F′ INTRACORTICAL NEUROPIL IN SECONDARY ACOUSTIC CORTICES

FIG. 12.16.   Myelinogenesis of the Acoustic Pathway

anatomical substratum is apparently laid down in these supralimbic cortical areas. It is probably significant, therefore, that the long period during which semantics and syntax are progressively and concurrently acquired is grossly contemporal with the protracted myelinogenetic cycles not only of the postthalamic component of the acoustic pathway (Fig. 12.14, Graph 2), but also of the intrahemispheric and interhemispheric association bundles (Fig. 12.14, Graph 9), and of the still longer cycles observed in the intracortical neuropil (Fig. 12.14, Graph 10), especially in nonspecific association cortices (Rubens et al., 1976). The contemporaneity of semantic maturity, that is, the capacity to understand and produce abstract language, and myelinogenetic maturity in the neuropil of the inferior parietal lobules and prefrontal convexities is particularly striking (Fig. 12.15).

4. If learning to read mostly meant establishing associations between the objective visual world—seen objects, qualities of seen objects, relations between seen objects and actions—and seen visual signs, as would be the case if the visual rather than the acoustic linguistic code were first acquired, it is likely that this apprenticeship could begin quite early during the first year of life. Indeed, because U-fibers myelinate earlier than longer association fibers, one might suggest that the constitution of associations between seen objects and seen signs could begin to take place somewhat earlier than the constitution of associations between seen objects and heard signs. As a rule, however, learning to read (and write) means establishing a secondary net of associations, that is, linking a new set of visual signs to a learned set of auditory signs, them-

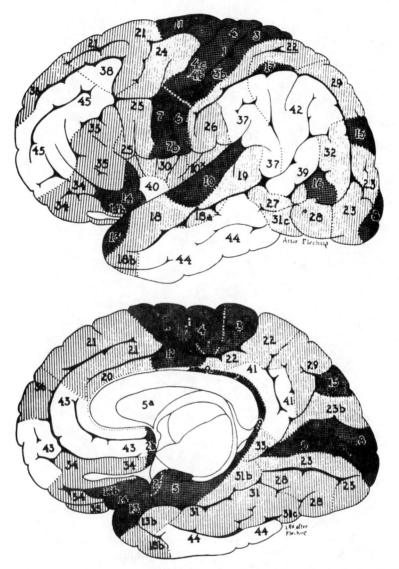

FIG. 12.17.   Flechsig's myelinogenetic fields. From Bailey, P. and von Bonin, G. *The isocortex of Man*, University of Illinois Press, Urbana, 1951.

selves already associated to objects and events of which they have become symbols (Brain & Walton, 1969). This difference between the two apprenticeships might explain, at least in part, why the optimal period for learning to read and write apparently occurs after 5 years of age (Fig. 12.14, Graph E): It is probable—and this is substantiated by

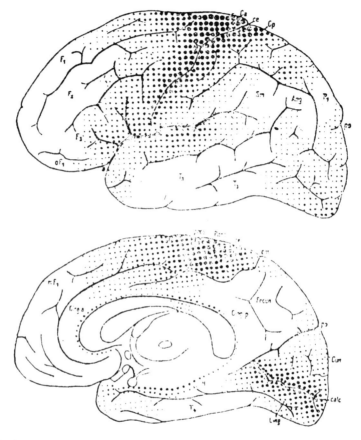

FIG. 12.18.   Myelination of the cerebral cortex in a 19-day old child; after C. Vogt and O. Vogt; from Bailey, P. and von Bonin, G. *The Isocortex of Man*, University of Illinois Press, Urbana, 1951.

the great variety of focal brain lesions resulting in disorganization of the written code (Hécaen, 1972)—that several association bundles as well as the intracortical plexuses of several cortical areas, which characteristically have protracted myelinogenetic cycles (Fig. 12.14, Graphs 9, 10, and Fig. 12.15), are of the utmost importance in the acquisition of a symbolic code used to represent another symbolic code.

It would be difficult for me to go further with this type of speculation but I have left out an obvious question with regard to myelinogenetic maturation and language acquisition: Are there differences in the myelinogenetic tempos of symmetrical structures in the left versus the right cerebral hemisphere? I do not know. If such differences do exist, Yakovlev and I have not noted them when studying Yakovlev's Warren Museum collection; but then, we were not looking for them. Moreover, one would not expect such differences to be gross and long lasting; therefore, they might have shown only in a few specimens if at all, or else, thick (35μ) whole brain hematoxylin preparations (Bertrand, 1930) just might not be adequate in this respect.

Myelinogenesis Versus Dips and Drops in Learning. Till now, I have cautiously avoided tackling the problem of myelinogenetic cycles in relation to the main topic of this volume. I will now attempt to come back to *dips and drops* in two main steps and several intricate substeps:

1. In the foregoing discussion of echolalia, I opposed it to babbling, almost as if the two were without any relationship to one another. This served my purpose (which was to oppose the short cycle of prethalamic to the long cycle of postthalamic acoustic fibers) but might be valid only to a certain extent; indeed, one might gain better insight on speech acquisition by also considering the possibility of a babbling–echolalia developmental continuum. In any event, echolalia *per se* can be regarded as a developmental continuum (prosodic mimicry first, then articulated imitation getting progressively closer to target with quantitative and qualitative *dips* here and there). I have already described and graphically illustrated (Fig. 12.8, 12.9) the multiphasicity in the myelinogenetic cycle of the acoustic pathway. I might have proposed a more hypothetical (and more complex) but probably valid—on the whole—multiphasic graphic representation, taking into account (besides prethalamic and postthalamic acoustic fibers), for instance, myelinogenesis in short association fibers between primary and secondary acoustic cortices, in long association fibers out of acoustic cortices, and in the neuropil of acoustic cortices (all of which are among the structures presumably involved in echolalic behavior). Let us now consider such an (approximate) representation (Fig. 12.16). Similar representations could be proposed in relation to the proprioceptive and the motor (both pyramidal and extrapyramidal) pathways presumably involved in echolalic behavior. Thus, the obvious question: If any, what could be the effect, on the echolalia (or babbling-echolalia) developmental curve, of the composite multiphasicity in morphological maturation of the neuroanatomical structures presumably involved in echolalic behavior? More generally, could not multiphasicity in morphological maturation be somehow related to multiphasicity in behavioral maturation? In other words, could behavioral *dips*, or, at least, certain behavioral *dips*, somehow reflect relatively small, even minute (and, as yet, temporally ill-defined) differential tempos in morphological (therefore physiological, chemical) brain maturation? Perhaps. If so, certain behavioral *dips* might conceivably correspond to periods during which the brain would,

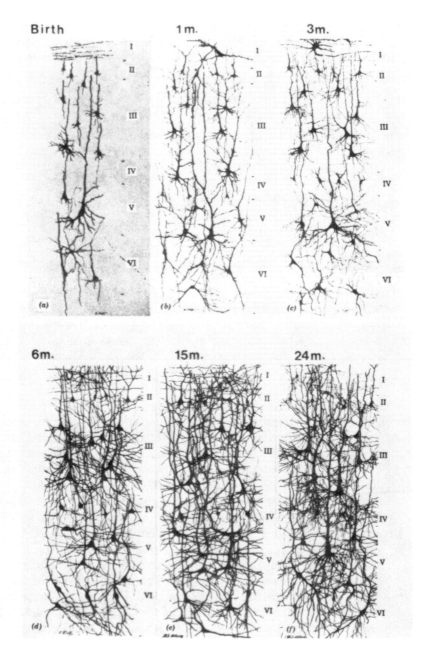

FIG. 12.19. Cytoarchitectonic maturation in frontal and parietal neocortex. From Conel, J. *The Postnatal Development of the Human Cerebral Cortex (Vols I-VI)*, Harvard University Press, Cambridge, 1939–1960.

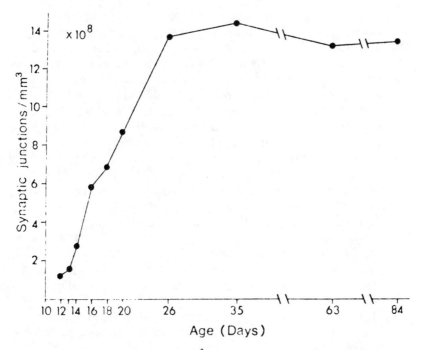

FIG. 12.20 Number of synapses per mm^3 in parietal cortex molecular layer of rat (postnatal). From Aghajanian, G. K. and Bloom, F. E., *Brain Research, 6,* 716–727, 1967.

as it were, be waiting for further morphological maturation—in parts of given fiber contingents or cortical areas—in order to carry on with further (quantitative and/or qualitative) progressive acquisitions related to a given behavior.

2. Let us call *vertical* multiphasicity this sequential myelinogenetic maturation in (centripetal or centrifugal) fibers of a same functional system (Fig. 12.16). As a direct consequence of this terminological choice, we are now bound to ask ourselves if the notion of *horizontal* multiphasicity might eventually be helpful. Indeed, the metaphor would not apply badly to interaction between stages of myelinogenetic maturation at given "levels" of different functional systems (e.g., optic, somethetic, acoustic, thalamic radiations (Fig. 12.6)). With regard to our actual preoccupation, the most relevant levels are probably those of subcortical (intrahemispheric and interhemispheric) association fibers and, even more so, those of intracortical association plexuses (intracortical neuropil). I will leave graphic illustration to your collective imagination. Just keep in mind:

a) That myelination of short (U) precedes that of long subcortical association fibers and is of briefer duration.

b) That differential myelinogenetic tempos of a smaller order have been observed to occur within a same level, for instance, long subcortical association fibers. (Flechsig (1901, 1920, 1927) numbered his *myelinogenetic fields* in the order of their progressive myelination: 1 to 10, *primordial fields*, (e.g., lips of the calcarine fissure); 11 to 20, *early intermediate fields* (Yakovlev, 1962), (e.g., rostral half of the first temporal); 21 to 35, *late intermediate fields* (Yakovlev, 1962) (e.g., foot of the third frontal convolution); 36 to 45, *terminal fields* (e.g., inferior parietal lobule) (Fig. 12.17).)

c) That myelination of the intracortical neuropil is very late beginning and very long lasting (Kaes, 1907) (Fig. 12.13), with primary preceding specific associative, and specific associative preceding nonspecific associative cortices (Kaes, 1907; Vogt, 1900; Vogt C. & Vogt, O., 1902, 1904) (Fig. 12.15, 12.18).

d) That additional zest in combining and computing differential tempos of myelinogenetic maturation could be legitimately provided by taking into account the protracted myelinogenetic cycle of nonspecific thalamic radiations (Yakovlev & Lecours, 1967) (Fig. 12.6).

e) That the existence of individual variations is not excluded, particularly in relation to the intracortical neuropil of nonspecific associative cortices.

Given these considerations, the notion of *horizontal* multiphasicity, if at all pertinent, might be considered in relation to *dips in learning and development* curves observed to occur: (1) relatively late in behavioral development; and/or (2) in behavioral acquisitions based on complex sensorimotor interactions.[11]

---

[11]Not everybody agrees as to the pertinency of correlating myelinogenesis to the emergence and gradual differentiation of specific behavioral events. Marcus Jacobson, for instance, does not appear to be particularly impressed by this notion. In his own words (1970): "The emphasis on myelination as an indication of functional maturation of the brain was once popular, but should now be regarded as an oversimplification. Although it is obvious that the behavioral capacities of newborn animals increase during the period of myelination, there is no reason to regard the former as a direct consequence of the latter" (p. 179). As far as I know, nobody ever suggested that there exists a cause–effect relationship between myelinogenetic and behavioral maturation; obviously, myelin sheaths do not govern behavior all by themselves; neither do synapses, fibers of the intracortical neuropil, and so forth. This does not mean, however, that more or less systematic temporal relationships are not there to be observed between certain events in normal myelinogenetic (or cytogenetic, or synaptogenetic, etc.) maturation and certain events in normal behavioral maturation. Unless I missed the point, the existence and signification of such temporal relationships is all that has been discussed by Paul Broca, Theodore Kaes, Paul Flechsig, Cecile Vogt, Orthello Langworthy, Paul Yakovlev, and others. In other words, I fail to perceive the pertinency of Jacobson's oversimplification statement.

CORTICAL NEURONOGENESIS

As shown by the studies of Brodmann (1925), of Bailey and von Bonin (1951), of Conel (1939-1960), and others, tectogenesis of the human cortex also follows a protracted prenatal and postnatal time schedule (Fig. 12.19). According to Yakovlev (1962), cytoarchitectonic and myeloarchitectonic maturation are concomitant with regard to Flechsig's *primordial* and *terminal fields*; temporal correlation is less consistent in the case of some of Flechsig's *intermediate fields* (Fig. 12.17). Also according to Yakovlev (1962), the: "eulaminate homotypical isocortical zones of the frontal and temporoparietal subdivisions of the supralimbic lobe appear to maintain to a highest degree through the human life-span the quasi–embryonal plasticity of their dendritic and axonal plexus as compared to the dendritic and axonal plexus of the limbic lobe where it apparently congeals early in life into a relatively fixed pattern" (pp. 24–25).

I suspect that one who would know much more than I do about cytoarchitectonic maturation of the cerebral cortex could define regional maturation cycles (with differential tempos and all sorts of multiphasicities) that might be considered plausible candidates as morphological correlates of *dips and drops in learning*.

SYNAPTOGENESIS

Fragmentary data have been obtained, during the past 15 years or so, on synaptic maturation in cats, rabbits, chicks, and so forth; it has been shown that, as a rule, the development of axodendritic synapses precedes that of axosomatic synapses; it has also been shown that the number of synapses keeps increasing over periods of various lengths in different brain structures of different animals (Jacobson, 1970; Purpura et al., 1964; and Gruner & Zahnd, 1967) (Fig. 12.20).

A large team of pathologically patient morphologists might someday undertake a study of regional synaptogenesis in the human brain. Because the estimated number of synaptic contacts in the adult human brain is somewhere between 100 billion and 30 trillion, such a study might lead to the definition of rather intricate cycles of synaptogenetic maturation. These, in turn, could prove an incentive to one finding interest in seeking plausible morphological correlates of *dips and drops in learning*.

Had we a clear integrated view of brain maturation, causal relationships might be sought between its different moments and different aspects of behavioral maturation. For the time being, we are light years away from such a view, especially in the case of the human brain. Therefore, we are bound: either to proclaim that brain and behavior are somehow related (perhaps even that brain maturation and behavioral maturation are somehow related) and thereafter forget about the whole problem; or else to rely on fragmentary (and sometimes uncertain) data and surmise, conjecture, speculate, and hypothesize. If one believes the latter approach appropriate and is interested in man's brain and behavior, some of the morphological parameters I have discussed are probably of interest. Although known only in a gross manner, myelinogenesis has long been and, in my opinion, remains the only one of these parameters on which we have both a global and a detailed view. One might thus be inclined, *faute de mieux*, to consider certain (specific) myelinogenetic events as gross (specific) indicators of progressively more "mature" behavioral capacities in normal subjects.

This notwithstanding, I would surely be the king of oversimplifiers if I maintained that multiphasicity in myelinogensis is the cause of *dips and drops in learning*. Indeed, all I am ready to maintain, here and now, is the remote possibility of a concomitancy relationship between the two.

Altman, P., & Dittmar, D. *Growth*, Federation of American Societies of Experimental Biology, Washington D. C., 1962.

Bailey, P., & von Bonin, G. *The Isocortex of man*, University of Illinois Press, Urbana, 1951.

Berry, M. F. Language Disorders of Children: *the Bases and Diagnoses*, Appleton-Century Crofts, New York, 1959.

Bertrand, I. *Techniques Histologiques de Neuropathologie*, Masson, Paris, 1930.

Brain, R., & Walton, J. N. *Brain's Diseases of the Nervous System*, Oxford University Press, London, 1969.

Broca, P. Sur le siège de la Faculté du langage articulé. *Bulletin de la Sociètè d'Anthropologie*, 1865, *6*, 377–393.

Brodmann, K. *Vergleichende Lokalisationslehre der Grosshirnrinde*, J. A. Barth, Leipzig, 1925.

Conel, J. *The Postnatal Development of the Human Cerebral Cortex* (Vols. I-VI), Harvard University Press, Cambridge (Mass.) 1939–1960.

Eberstaller, O. Zur Oberflächenanatomie der Grosshirnhemisphären. *Wein. Med. Blaetter*, 1884, *7*, 479–482, 542–582, 644–646.

Epstein, H. T. Phrenoblysis: special brain and mind growth periods. I. Human brain and skull development. *Developmental Psychobiology*, 1974, *7(3)*, 207–216. (a)

Epstien, H. T. Phrenoblysis: special brain and mind growth periods. II. Human mental development. *Developmental Psychobiology*, 1974, *7(3)*, 217–224. (b)

Ey, H., Bernard, P., & Brisset, Ch. *Manuel de Psychiatrie*, Masson, Paris, 1963.

Flechsig, P. Developmental (myelinogenetic) localisation of the cerebral cortex in the human subject. *Lancet*, 1901, *2*, 1027–1029.

Flechsig, P. *Anatomie des menschilichen Gehirms und Rückenmarks auf myelogenetischer Grundlage*, Georg Thieme, Leipzig, 1920.

Flechsig, P. *Meine myelogenetische Hirnlehre*, J. Springer, Berlin, 1927.

Geschwind, N. Disconnexion syndromes in animals and man. *Brain*, 1965, *88*, 237–294, 585–644.

Geschwind, N., & Levitsky, W. Left right asymmetries in temporal speech region. *Science*, 1968, *161*, 186–189.

Geschwind, N., Quadfasel, F. A., & Segarra, J. Isolation of the speech area. *Neuropsychologia*, 1968, *6*, 327–340.

Gesell, A., & Amatruda, C. S. *Developmental Diagnosis*, Harper & Row, New York, 1964.

Gratiolet, L. P. *Mémoire sur les plis cérèbraux de l'homme et des primates*, Bertrand, Paris, 1854.

Gruner, J. -E., & Zahnd, J. -P. Sur la maturation synaptique dans le cortex visuel du lapin. In, A. Minkowski, ed., *Regional Development of the Brain in Early Life*, pp. 125–133, Blackwell, Oxford and Edinburgh, 1967. (See Purpura's discussion.)

Hécaen, H. *Introduction a la Neuropsychologie*, Larousse, Paris, 1972.

Hécaen, H., & Dubois, J., eds., *La naissance de la neuropsychologie du langage*, 108–121, Flammarion, Paris, 1969.

Jacobson, M. *Developmental Neurobiology*, Holt, Rinehart & Winston, Inc., New York, 1970.

Kaes, T. *Die Grosshirnrinde des Menschen in ihrem Massen und in ihrem Fassergehalt*, Gustav Fischer, Jena, 1907.

Kakeshita, T. Zur Anatomies der operkularen temporal Region (Vergleichende Unter-Suchungen der rechten und linken Seite). Arbeit Neurologischen Institut Wein., 1925, *27*, 292.

Kemper, T. L., Lecours, A. R., Gates, M. J., & Yakovlev, P. I. Retardation of the myelo- and cytoarchitectonic maturation of the brain in the congenital rubella syndrome. In *Research Publications of the A.R.N.M.D. (51): Early Development*, 23–62, The Association for Research in Nervous and Mental Disease, New York, 1973.

Klossovskii, B. N. *The Development of the Brain* (Translated from the Russain and edited by Basil Haigh), Macmillan, New York, 1963.

Langworthy, O. Development of behavior patterns and myelination of the nervous system in the human foetus and infant. *Contributions to Ebriology*, 1933, *139*, 1–57.

Larroche, J.-C. Maturation morphologique du système nerveux central: ses rapports avec le développement pondéral du foetus et son âge gestationnel. In A. Minkowski (Ed.), *Regional Development of the Brain in Early Life*, 247–256, Blackwell, Oxford and Edinburgh, 1967.

Lecours, A. R. Myelinogenetic correlates of the development of speech and language. In E. H. Lenneberg and E. Lenneberg (Eds.), *Foundations of Language Development—A Multidisciplinary Approach*, (*1*), 121–135, Academic Press, New York, 1976.

Lecours, A. R., Lhermitte, F. et collaborateurs *L'Aphasie*, Flammarion, Paris, et P. U. M., Montreal, 1979.

Lenneberg, E. H. Biological Foundations of Language, John Wiley & Sons, New York, 1967.

Lhermitte, F. Bases physiologiques de la mémoire. *L'Evolution Psychiatrique*, 1968, *4*, 579–603.

Lhermitte, F., & Gautier, J. -C. Correlations anatomo-cliniques de l'aphasie. *La revue du praticien*, 1965, *15*, 2309–2323.

Myers, R. E., & Krogman, W. M. *Cranio-Facial Growth*, Pergamon, New York, 1971.

Nielsen, J. M. *Agnosia, Apraxia, Aphasia—Their Value in Cerebral Localization*, Hafner, New York, 1965.

Osterrieth, P. *Introduction a la psychologie de l'enfant*, Presses Universitaires de France, Paris, 1966.

Pfeiffer, F. A. Pathologie der Horstrahlung und der corticalen Horsphare. In O. Bumke & O. Foerster (Eds.), Handbuch der Neurologie (*6*), 533–626, Springer, Berlin, 1936.

Purpura, D. P., Shofer, R. J., Housepian, E. M., & Noback, C. R. Comparative ontogenesis of structure–function relations in cerebral and cerebellar cortex. *Progress in Brain Research*, 1964, *4*, 187–221.

Rakič, P., & Yakovlev, P. I. Development of the corpus callosum and cavum septi in man. *The Journal of Comparative Neurology*, 1968, *132*, 45–72.

Rubens, A. B., Mahowald, M. W., & Hutton, J. T. Assymetry of the lateral (sylvian) fissures in man. *Neurology*, 1976, *26*, 620.

Teszner, D. *Etude anatomique de l'asymétrie droite-gauche de planum temporale sur 100 cerveaux d'adultes*, These, Faculte de Medecine, Paris, 1972.

Vogt, C. *Etude sur la myélinisation des hémisphères cérèbaux*. Paris, 1900.

Vogt, C., & Vogt, O. Die Markreifung des Kindergehirns während der ers vier Lebensmonste und ihre methodologische Bedeutung. In O. Vogt (Ed.), *Neurobiologische Arbeiten* (Erster Serie, Erster Band), Gustav Fischer, 1902.

Vogt, C., & Vogt, O. Die Markreifung des Kindergehirns während der er vier Lebensmonste und ihre methodologische Bedeutung. In O. Vogt (Ed.), Neurobiologische Arbeiten (Erste Serie, Zweiter Band), Gustav Fischer, 1904.

von Bonin, G. Anatomical asymmetries of the cerebral hemispheres. In V. B. Mountcastle (Ed.), *Interhemispheric Relations and Cerebral Dominance*, 1–6, Johns Hopkins, Baltimore, 1967.

von Economo, C., & Horn, L. Ueber Windungsrelief, Masse und Rindenarchitektonic der Supratemporalfläche, ihre indivduellen und ihre Seitenunterschiede. *Zeitschrift Neurologischen Psychiatrie*, 1930, *130*, 678–757.

Wada, J. A., Clark, R., & Hamm, A. Asymmetry of temporal and frontal speech zones in 100 adult and 100 infant brains. Report read at the *Tenth International Congress of Neurology*, Barcelona, 1973.

Wernicke, C. *Der aphasische Symptomencomplex—Eine Psychologische Studie und anatomischer Basis*, Cohn & Weigert, Breslau, 1874.

Yakovlev, P. I. Motility, behavior and the brain: stereodynamic organization and neural coordinates of behavior. *The Journal of Nervous and Mental Disease*, 1948, *107*, 313–335.

Yakovlev, P. I. Anatomy of the human brain and the problem of mental retardation. In P. W. Bowman and H. V. Mautner (Eds.), *Mental Retardation*, 1–43, Grune & Stratton, New York, 1960.

Yakovlev, P. I. Morphological criteria of growth and maturation of the nervous system in man. In *Research* Publications of the A.R.N.M.D. (*39*): *Mental Retardation*, 3–46, The Association for Research in Nervous and Mental Disease, New York, 1962.

Yakovlev, P.I. Telokinesis and handedness: an empirical generalization. In J. Wortis (Ed.), *Recent Advances in Biological psychiatry*, 21–30, Plenum Press, New York, 1963.

Yakovlev, P. I. Telencephalon 'impar', 'semipar', and 'totopar': morphogenetic, tectogenetic and architectonic definitions. *International Journal of Neurology*, 1968, *6*, 245–265.

Yakovlev, P. I. The structural and functional 'trinity' of the body, brain and behavior. In H. T. Wycis (Ed.), *Current Research in Neurosciences* (*10*): Topical Problems in Psychiatry and Neurology, 197–208, Karger, Bassel and New York, 1970.

Yakovlev, P. I. A proposed definition of the limbic system In C. H. Hockman (Ed.), Limbic System Mechanisms and Autonomic Functions, 241–283, Thomas, Springfield, 1972.

Yakovlev, P. I. & Lecours, A.R. The myelogenetic cycles of regional maturation of the brain. In A. Minkowski (Ed.), *Regional Development of the Brain in Early Life*, 3–70, Blackwell, Oxford, and Edinburgh, 1967.

13 A Two-Step Model for Visuomotor Development

M. Jeannerod
Laboratoire de Neuropsychologie Expérimentale
INSERM, Bron, France

The role of visumotor mechanisms is to match the final position of a moving segment with a target located within extrapersonal space. This critical function involves additive components that can be classified tentatively under two main headings. Directional mechanisms would first determine the spatial pattern of the movement, by generating motor commands according to spatial coordinates of the target, as detected by visual "maps" in different brain areas. Gain-control mechanisms would account for the precision of the movement, by braking and stopping the trajectory at the proper location.

The two components may be thought of as relying on qualitatively different processes. The first would deliver a directional "pulse" and would operate "open-loop" once triggered. The other would work as an error-correcting mechanism through a continuous guidance of the trajectory or of part of the trajectory. Obviously, the two components must occur serially, because the processing of the error between the mobile segment and the target can be made only on the basis of some parameter of the movement. Determination of the critical parameter for the error-correcting mechanism will depend, in fact, on the hypothesis made about the nature of the directional mechanism. If the movement is thought to be coded in terms of the amplitude between an initial and a final position, then a parameter such as instantaneous velocity of the moving segment at a given time of the trajectory will be considered as relevant. In that case, a control of the gain during the movement itself (i.e., anticipating the final error) could be envisioned. If, on the other hand, the movement is thought to be coded in terms of the final position, then processing of the residual error at the end of the movement will have to occur. In that case, a logical inference is that the directional system would be imprecise "by design" and would generate movements with a gain systematically below unity; hence a fine-gain adjustment would be required to reach the target.

An example of a systematically hypometric ballistic movement can be found in ocular fixation saccades. In normal conditions, saccades toward an eccentric target usually fall short with respect to target location. Hence, they are completed within a short delay by a smaller "correction" saccade that brings the retinal fovea on the target. If the target is made to disappear before the initial saccade is completed (i.e., if the visual error feedback of the initial saccade is suppressed), the correction saccade does not occur (Prablanc & Jeannerod, 1975). A series of further experiments with suppression of the error feedback at various times before or during the initial saccade have shown that the information for the correction is picked up near the end of the initial saccade (Prablanc, Massé, & Echallier, 1978).

Ocular saccades might not be a typical example, however, because the correction is also made by a movement of a ballistic type. The oculomotor system thus seems to use a "microballistic" correction rather than a continuous control for the final adjustment of the trajectory. This might be due to intrinsic characteristics of eye movements where feedback signals necessary for continuous control are lacking. In fact, in visually guided limb movements gain control clearly seems to be exerted during the trajectory itself, as shown by the asymmetric shape of the velocity profile of the movement. Visual origin of at least part of this control is demonstrated a contrario when the visual "loop" is open (i.e., by preventing the view of the limb during the movement), which forces the movement to become imprecise and hypometric.

Developmental studies of visually goal-directed behavior seem to indicate a separate maturation of these two visuomotor mechanisms. In young infants, for instance, presentation of a graspable object will first elicit only a visual orienting response, tentative reach will occur at a later stage, and full precision will be the last acquisition (White & Held, 1967; Dodwell, Muir, & DiFranco, 1976). It seems that the corrective component is progressively added to the ballistic movement by using visual cues based on the relative position of the hand and of the object within the central visual field (Mc Donnell, 1975). This component will finally be incorporated into the trajectory, so that in the adult, continuous smooth visual braking will replace terminal correction.

Arguments for separate development of the "triggered" and of the "guided" components of visual reaching are also provided by experiemnts in animals reared under conditions of total or selective visual deprivation. For instance, in the Held and Bauer (1967) situation, baby monkeys can be reared with normal vision, but without any visual feedback from their limbs. Although only a few hours of experience are necessary after the view of the hands has been restored to observe arm movements clearly elicited by a visual stimulus, accurate visually guided reaching and grasping require several days of exposure under normal visual control to appear. In kittens also, a similar dissociation can be produced by deprivation procedures. After a 15-week total light deprivation from birth, inaccurate reaching movements of the forepaw can be observed almost immediately (within a few hours) after the animal has been placed in a lighted environment (Vital-Durand, Putkonen, & Jeannerod, 1974). Maturation of the guided component requires more complex and more prolonged visual exposure of the interaction between the moving limb and the environment. This is confirmed by experiments in kittens reared in normal conditions, except that they could not see their limbs, particularly when they were moving around. Testing revealed that the view of an obstacle was able to trigger an extension of the forepaws (placing reaction), although precise adjustment of the paw to the obstacle was lacking (Hein & Held, 1967). This temporal sequence in the appearance of the two components of visually guided reaching, artificially delayed by visual deprivation, is quite reminiscent of what has been observed in children born blind and having recovered vision in late childhood or in adulthood. In these subjects, inaccurate ballistic movements could be observed within a few days after recovery, although several weeks were necessary for the appearance of fine visually controlled prehension (Jeannerod, 1975).

Our aim in this chapter is to extend the same notion of a duality, both in normal functioning and in development, of visuomotor mechanisms. For this purpose we have used data on vestibulo-ocular responses and on optokinetic nystagmus, two easily recordable and quantifiable oculomotor reactions in the kitten.

Vestibulo-ocular Responses

Visual images remain stabilized on the retina during head rotation. This effect is achieved at least in part through the vestibulo-ocular responses (VOR), which compensate for head movements by rotating the eyeballs in the opposite direction. In the normal cat, the complete adultlike VOR appears late in life. Although ocular deviation in the direction opposite to induced head movements can be recorded at the age of 10 days, it is by far immature and incomplete.

In a recent study (Flandrin, Courjon, & Jeannerod, 1979) we used 17 kittens ranging in age from 10 to 63 days. Ag–AgCl electrodes were implanted to record binocular horizontal EOG. A head fixation device was sealed to the skull. During recording sessions, animals were secured to a rotating platform, with their head at the center of rotation. Vestibular stimulation in the horizontal plane was provided by a servo-controlled motor fed with velocity functions: 120–160°/sec. velocity steps and 0.03–0.5 Hz sinusoidal oscillation. Vestibular stimulation was made in the dark.

The earliest recordings were made at the age of 10 days (two kittens), which corresponds to the age of physiological eye opening. In the two animals, velocity steps constantly induced a steep deviation of the eyes in the compensatory direction (i.e., opposite to the head displacement). Tonic gaze deviation toward that direction was then maintained for about 5–25 sec and was followed by a slow return to the midline position. No nystagmic saccades could be seen on the records at this stage. The same picture was still observed at 18 days of age (two kittens) (Fig. 13.1, upper row). Sinusoidal rotation also evoked only slow compensatory displacements of the eyes.

The first nystagmic saccades in response to vestibular stimuli did not appear before approximately the 30th day. They could be observed in two kittens recorded respectively at 31 days and at 37 days. In a third kitten, where the recording sessions were started on the postnatal day 23, vestibular-induced saccades first appeared on day 35. At this stage, VOR was still very incomplete, with a few saccades of small amplitude superimposed to the slow component of the response. During response to sinusoidal oscillations, saccades were clustered in relation to the part of the stimulus with the highest velocity.

The normal, adultlike VOR pattern was not observed before approximately the 60th day. This fact was documented in seven kittens recorded between postnatal days 42 and 61. Up to about the 50th day, VOR did not differ substantially from what could be recorded earlier. From day 50, VOR improved rapidly up to its normal pattern on days 58, 59, and 61 respectively in three kittens. This rapid change can be seen in Fig. 13.1, where records from the same kitten on days 53 and 59 are presented. This evolution was also clearly seen with responses to sinusoidal oscillations.

Among the factors that might explain delayed maturation of VOR in the cat obviously are developmental constraints of the vestibular system itself. Another aspect to be considered, however, is the fact that the visual system also matures slowly in this species, which does not acquire its adult value of visual acuity before the third month (see the following). Hence, it can be suspected that the "need" for precise visual stabilization during head movements will not become apparent before acuity is optimal, and that VOR gain will increase rapidly when this condition is attained.

The respective contribution of vestibulo-ocular and visual factors in optimal development of VOR gain can be drawn from visual deprivation experiments. Kittens reared in the dark from birth and until the age of 4 months have been compared with a control group of kittens reared in normal conditions (Berthoz, Jeannerod, Vital-Durand, & Oliveras, 1975). Post-rotatory nystagmus, nystagmus during sinusoidal oscillations, visual suppression of vestibular nystagmus, and nystagmus following hemilabyrinthectomy have been used as indicators of the functional state of the vestibulo-ocular control system. The results show that most of the essential features of this

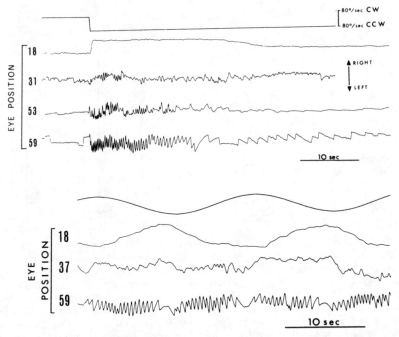

FIG. 13.1 Development of vestibulo-ocular responses in the kitten. Upper row: Evolution of responses to velocity steps as a function of postnatal age. Age of the animals (in days) is indicated on the left of the records. Lower row: Evolution of responses to a .05Hz sinsoidal oscillation of the animal. EOG records are from implanted, awake animals with the head rigidly fixed on a turntable. Note early development of a slow compensatory deviation of the eyes in response to passive head movements. Gain of the response increases later as shown by the appearance of a nystagmic pattern, where slow compensatory deviation of the eyes is interrupted rhythmically be return saccades. (From Flandrin et al., 1979).

control are present in dark-reared kittens. However, on closer examination an important difference with respect to normal behavior has been found in most of them. The number of nystagmic beats (or saccades) per unit of time, which is a good estimate of the gain of the response (the higher the gain of the slow phase, the higher the beat frequency), is about 35% smaller in dark-reared animals than in normals of the same age. This is exemplified in Fig. 13.2, which displays beat frequency and cumulative eye position during the slow phase in one normal and one dark-reared kitten during sinusiodal stimulation. These results have been confirmed by Collewijn (1977) in the rabbit.

Although the main features of the vestibulo-ocular reactions can be identified in dark-reared kittens, the precise tuning of the response to the head movement amplitude is lacking. The fact that this adaptive component relies on visual input is shown by the quick improvement of the response when the

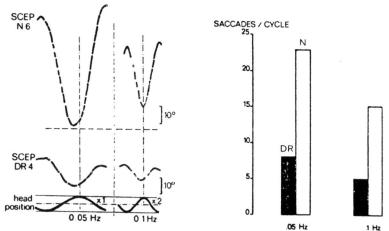

FIG. 13.2.   Influence of neonatal visual deprivation on VOR development in kittens. Left: Comparison of responses induced by head rotation in one normal (N6) and one dark-reared (DR4) kitten. In this diagram, the result is expressed as a plotting of the slow cumulative eye position (SCEP) obtained by adding up the slow phases of the nystagmus and deleting the nystagmic beats. Note a much higher gain in the normal animal as compared to the dark-reared one. Right: Plot of the number of nystagmic saccades per cycle of sinusoidal head rotation in the group of dark-reared (DR) animals as compared to the group of normals (N). The smaller number of saccades in DR animals is corroborative of the lower gain in their response to stimulation. In both parts of the figure, the values .05Hz and .1Hz refer to the frequency of sinusoidal oscillations. (Reconstructed from Berthoz et al., 1975).

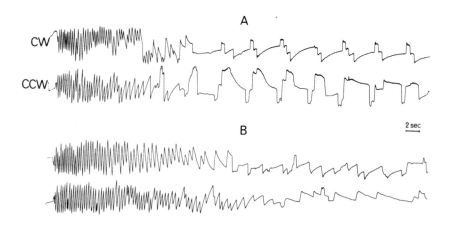

FIG. 13.3.   Recovery of normal vestibulo-ocular responses in dark reared kitten. A: VOR in response to a 160°/sec clockwise (CW) and counterclockwise (CCW) velocity step in one kitten reared in the dark for 4 months. B: Same animal after restoration of a normal visual environment for 24 hours. Note improvement of the gain, and disappearance of gaze instability.

normal visual conditions are restored. By comparing, in one animal reared in the dark for 4 months from birth, postrotatory VOR recorded in the dark at the end of the deprivation period (Fig. 13.3A) and after 24 hours of normal visual experience (Fig. 13.3B) substantial changes can be observed; namely, the gain of the responses (as tested by amplitude and duration of VOR) has improved by about 30%. In addition, the large oscillations that can be seen in the deprived animal (Fig. 13.3A) disappear when normal conditions are restored.

Optokinetic Nystagmus

Optokinetic nystagmus (OKN) is another typical visuomotor reaction aiming at maintaining moving objects stationary on the retina. It can be observed in most vertebrates when the whole visual field is displaced in front of the animal. In that case, the slow "pursuit" phase is oriented in the same direction as the moving field, and the fast "return" phase in the opposite direction. In our experiments we used a 1 meter in diameter striped drum (stripes at .1 cycles/degree), rotating horizontally around the stationary animal, at different velocities. The drum was illuminated from the inside. In the same way as for VOR, the gain of the response could be appreciated through the saccade frequency, or more directly by reconstructing cumulative eye position during the slow phase. Gain values were related to the velocity of the stimulus.

OKN was also found to maturate slowly in the kitten. Around day 25 a few saccades in the direction opposite to the rotating drum could be seen. This response was better observed with slow stimulus velocities, at the onset of rotation or when the direction of rotation was reversed. By postnatal day 50, OKN showed an adultlike pattern. At this stage, the gain was linearly related to velocity of the stimulus up to 30 degrees/sec (Flandrin et al., 1979). These results are in general agreement with those of Van Hof-Van Duin (1976). In normal adult cats, the frequency of beats increases with velocity up to about 50 degrees/sec and then remains at the same level if velocity is further increased (Honrubia, Scott, & Ward, 1967).

Since OKN is a purely visually induced reaction, neonatal visual deprivation might impair it to an even greater extent than it does for VOR. Seven kittens reared in the dark during the first 12 postnatal weeks were implanted for eye-movement recording. On the day of testing (i.e., when they were first exposed to a lighted enivronment), OKN was easily obtained in all seven kittens and persisted with no sign of habituation for testing periods of up to 20 min. The frequency of ocular saccades was correlated to the velocity of moving stripes in a range from 5 to about 15 degrees/sec. At higher velocities the nystagmus became disorganized, slowed down, and beat frequency became negatively correlated with drum velocity. In addition, OKN pattern was far from normal, and nystagmic beats were irregular in amplitude and somewhat erratically distributed in time (Fig. 13.4) (Vital-Durand & Jeannerod, 1974a). Finally, in two kittens, OKN was studied up to 3 weeks after the end of the "dark" period. No improvement was observed.

This effect of visual deprivation on OKN, as well as its slow maturation in the normal animal, might be due to a low visual "acuity." Warkentin and Smith (1937) for instance, have shown that normal kittens cannot resolve 3 cycles/degree moving visual gratings (as tested by OKN) before the 25th day. According to Mitchell, Griffin, Wilkinson, Anderson, and Smith, (1976), resolution of 5–6 cycles/degree stationary gratings cannot be obtained before the third month. Recent estimates in normal adult cats show that maximal resolution (stationary gratings) is 6 cycles/degree (Blake, Cook, & Crawford, 1974) or even 8–9 cycles/degree (Jacobson, Franklin, & McDonald, 1976). Early visual deprivation can produce losses in acuity. Ganz and Fitch (1968) showed that the inexperienced eye in monocularly deprived kittens is consistently poorer in resolving moving gratings. This effect was found to persist after a few weeks of binocular experience. Similarly, in monkeys reared in the dark for 3 to 6 months, the grating acuity can be decreased by a factor of two to six with respect to normals (Regal et al., 1976). However, it does not seem likely that a relatively low visual acuity could be the sole explanation for our results. First, the spatial frequency of our moving grating was extremely low. Second, and more convincing, results from another deprivation experiment seem to rule out this explanation.

Thirteen kittens were reared in the dark from birth. After the fourth week of age, kittens were exposed individually to unidirectional motion 1 hour per day, 6 days a week. They spent the rest of the time in the dark room. During exposure, the animal was placed on the bottom of a transparent cylindrical container (50cm in diameter), hanging in a vertical cylinder (1 meter high). Diameter of the cylinder was slightly larger than that of the container, so that the cylinder could rotate around the container. The cylinder was equipped with 10 cm wide vertical stripes, alternately black and white, and was diffusely illuminated from above. Rotation was at a constant speed (60°/sec or 20°/sec) and always in the same direction for a given animal. Total exposure time varied between 10 hours and 60 hours across different kittens. No difference in the results could be related to this variable.

When they were tested at the age of 18 weeks, animals that had been exposed to unidirectional motion readily exhibited OKN as they were stimulated with stripes moving in the direction that they had experienced. Frequency of nystagmic saccades increased as stripe velocity increased, and the relation held up to 50°/sec for most kittens, and even to 80°/sec for two of them (i.e., up to velocities higher than those presented during exposure sessions [60°/sec]). In addition, OKN persisted as long as stimulation was maintained. When the animals were presented with striped moving in the

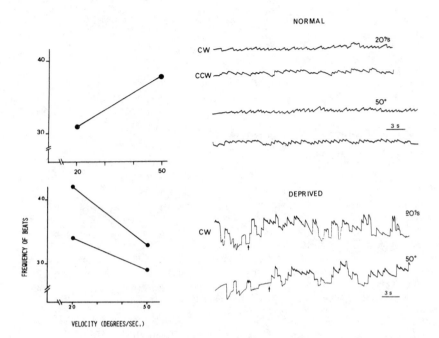

FIG. 13.4. Optokinetic nystagmus in one normal and one visually deprived kitten. In the normal animal (upper row) recorded at the age of 4 months, the OKN appears quite regular, and the frequency of saccades is clearly correlated to the velocity of the stimulus (indicated on the right of the records). In the deprived animal (lower row) recorded at the age of 4 months and reared in the dark up to the day of recording, note erratic distribution of saccades in time and in size. Frequency of saccades is no longer positively correlated to the velocity of the stimulus (Diagram at the lower left shows this negative correlatoni in 2 different animals.). CW: Moving stimulus directed clockwise; CCW: counterclockwise. In the lower records, only the CCW response is represented. Transition from CW to CCW stimulation is indicated by arrows.

direction opposite to the "experienced" direction, the initial saccades were erratic and oriented in all direction. After some time, the animals could display rhythmic saccades with normal orientation but only for low stripe velocities. When movement was shifted from the "experienced" direction to its opposite, OKN did not stop immediately; saccades with the same orientation and at a similar frequency usually persisted for several seconds (as if the animal had not "noticed" the shift in direction). By contrast, OKN of a correct orientation reappeared almost immediately, with a fast rise in saccade frequency, when the direction of the stripes was returned to the experienced direction (Fig. 13.5) (Vital-Durand & Jeannerod, 1974a, 1974b; Flandrin & Jeannerod, 1977).

Coexistence in the same kittens of a normal OKN in one direction and of an "immature" OKN (i.e., similar to that observed in dark-reared animals) in

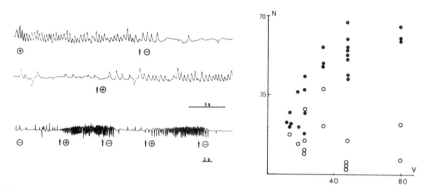

FIG. 13.5. Optokinetic nystagmus in two kittens submitted to unidirectional visual motion during early life. Records on the left, upper two rows: kitten exposed for 60 hours to CCW visual motion. Lower row: kitten exposed to CW visual motion for 25 hours. Arrows below the records indicate change in the direction of the stimulus from the direction "experienced" during exposure (+), to the "nonexperienced" (−). Diagram on the right : plot of frequency of nystagmic beats (N) versus velocity of the stimulus (V). Black circles: frequency of beats during stimulation in the "experienced" direction. Open circles: during stimulation in the "nonexperienced" direction. Compare these frequency/velocity diagrams with those obtained from normal and dark-reared kittens in Fig. 13.4. (From Vital-Durand & Jeannerod, 1974b).

the opposite direction calls for a specific effect of visual deprivation on OKN, rather than for a global effect on visual acuity.

Conclusion

The aforementioned results are in accordance with the general model of a two-step acquisition of visumotor behavior. Maturation of the two components seems to obey a rather precise timetable such that the guided part of the movement cannot be observed until the ballistic part is fully developed. Moreover, developmental constraints for these two components seem radically different. The ballistic component appears at a given postnatal time, independently from visual input. It might be related only to endogenous factors, including genetic coding of neural connections and postnatal maturation of structures and pathways necessary for its expression. VOR and OKN clearly follow this rule. They both involve gaze displacements in response to directional motion signals arising respectively from the labyrinth and from the retina. Visual deprivation prolonged for a postnatal time longer than the duration normally required for their expression probably gives a good idea of how far inbuilt mechanisms can go in specifying such open-loop visuomotor responses.

The guided component, on the other hand requires two conditoins: (1) that the ballistic component will be present; and (2) that feedback signals from visual environment will be available. Hence, detection of a residual error related to the execution of the ballistic component will trigger specific adjustment mechanisms. The fact that these errors are necessarily distributed asystematically requires that these mechanisms will develop under the control of external (visual) factors, and that they will remain modifiable enough to allow a wide range of adjustments. It could also be argued that this model bears a large adaptive value. In fact, the genetic constraints of visuomotor development, at least in higher mammals, must fulfill two essential conditions. One is that the system will be ready for use at the time when the young animal begins to interact with its visual world. The second is that this system will be *sufficiently inaccurate* so as to necessitate an improvement controlled by visual feedback. It seems to us much more economical functionally to add a limited but labile component in order to improve a rigid system, than to expect that the whole system will change. If this were the case, visuomotor coordination would become either totally rigid, as it is in inframammalian species, or totally unreliable, as it may become under pathological conditions.

ACKNOWLEDGMENTS

Collaboration of J. H. Courjon, J. M. Flandrin, and F. Vital-Durand in various steps of these stuides is gratefully acknowledged.

REFERENCES

Berthoz, A., Jeannerod, M., Vital-Durand, F., & Oliveras, L. L. Development of vestibulo-ocular responses in visually deprived kittens, *Experimental Brain Research*, 1975, *23*, 425–442.

Blake, R., Cook, S. J., & Crawford, M. L. J. Visual resolution in the cat. *Vision Research*, 1974, *14*, 1211–1217.

Collewijn, H. Optokinetic and vestibulo-ocular reflexes in dark-reared rabbits. *Experimental Brain Research*, 1977, *27*, 287–300.

Dodwell, P. C., Muir, D., & DiFranco, D. Responses of infants to visually presented objects. *Science*, 1976, *194*, 209–211.

Flandrin, J. M., Courjon, J. H., & Jeannerod, M. Development of vestibulo-ocular responses in the kitten. *Neuroscience Letters*, 1979, *12*, 295–299.

Flandrin, J. M., & Jeannerod, M. Developmental constraints of motion detection mechanisms in the kitten. *Perception*, 1977, *6*, 513–527.

Ganz, L., & Fitch, M. The effect of visual deprivation on perceptual behavior. *Experimental Neurology*, 1968, *22*, 638–660.

Hein, A., & Held, R. Dissociation of the visual placing response into elicited and guided components. *Science*, 1967, *158*, 390–392.

Held, R., & Bauer, J. Visually guided reaching in infant monkeys after restricted rearing. *Science*, 1967, *155*, 718–720.

Honrubia, V., Scott, B. J., & Ward, P. H. Experimental studies on optokinetic nystagmus. I. Normal cats. *Acta Oto-Laryngologica*, 1967, *64*, 388–402.

Jacobson, S. G., Franklin, K. B. J., & McDonald, W. I. Visual acuity of the cat. *Vision Research*, 1976, *16*, 1141–1144.

Jeannerod, M. Déficit visual persistant ches les aveugles-nés opérés.. Données cliniques et experiméntales. *Année Psychologique,* 1975, *75*, 169–196.

McDonnel, P. M. The development of visually guided reaching. *Perception and Psychophysics,* 1975, *18*, 181–185.

Mitchell, D. E., Griffen, F., Wilkinson, F., Anderson, R., & Smith, M. L. Visual resolution in young kittens. *Vision Research.*, 1978, *15*, 465–469.

Prablanc, C., & Jeannerod, M. Corrective saccades: Dependence on retinal reafferent signals. *Vision Research*, 1975, *15*, 465–469.

Prablanc, C., Masse, D., & Echallier, J. F. Corrective mechanisms in visually goal-directed large saccades. *Vision Research*, 1978, *18*, 557–560.

Regal, D. M., Boothe, R., Teller, D. Y., & Sackett, G. P. Visual acuity and visual responsiveness in dark-reared monkeys. *Vision Research*, 1976, *16*, 523–530.

Van Hof-Van Duin, J. Development of visuo-motor behavior in normal and dark-reared cats. *Brain Research*, 1976, *104*, 223–241.

Vital-Durand, F., & Jeannerod, M. Maturation of opto-kinetic response: genetic and environmental factors. *Brain Research*, 1976, *71*, 249–257.

Vital-Durand, F., & Jeannerod, M. Role of visual experience in the development of optokinetic responses in kittens. *Experimental Brain Research*, 1974, *20*, 297–302.

Vital-Durand, F., Putkonen, P. T. S., & Jeannerod, M. Motion detection and optokinetic responses in dark-reared kittens. *Vision Research*, 1974, *14*, 141–142.

Warkentin, J., & Smith, K. V. The development of visual acuity in the cat. *Journal of Genetic Psychology*,1937, *50*, 371–399.

White, B. L., & Held, R. Plasticity of sensorimotor development in the human infant. In J. Hellmuth, *The Exceptional Infant* (Vol. 1) Seattle: Special Child Publications, 1967.

Author Index

Subject Index